Eisenhower
&
Montgomery

Eisenhower

&

Montgomery

at the
Falaise Gap

William Weidner

Copyright © 2010 by William Weidner.

Library of Congress Control Number: 2009911880
ISBN: Hardcover   978-1-4415-9798-4
               Softcover   978-1-4415-9797-7

The 14 August 1944 letter from Bernard L. Montgomery to Omar N. Bradley is from the Omar Bradley Papers, Archives Section, U.S. Army Military History Institute, Carlisle Barracks, PA 17013-5021.

All twelve (12) copies of German radio messages, code named *ULTRA*, were copied from microfilm tape at the US Army Military History Institute at Carlisle Barracks, PA 17013-5021:

> XL 4405, XL 4425, XL 4913, XL 4991, XL 5715, XL 5728,
> XL 5835, XL 5845, XL 6128, XL 6136, XL 6330, and XL 6495.

All ten (10) photographs were taken by U.S. Army Signal Corps Photographers and are the property of the U.S. Army. The photograph of George S. Patton Jr. was obtained from the National Archives and Records Administration, 8601 Adelphi Road, College Park, Maryland 20740-6001. Photographs of Dwight D. Eisenhower and Bernard L. Montgomery at Montgomery's headquarters, of Eisenhower and Omar N. Bradley at Bradley's headquarters beside Eisenhower's car and the photograph taken of the same two generals on the steps of a stone building were obtained from the Dwight D. Eisenhower Presidential Library & Museum, 200 S.E. 4th Street, Abilene, KS 67410. Portrait type photographs of Generals Dwight D. Eisenhower, Courtney H. Hodges, William H. Simpson, and J. Lawton Collins, the photograph of Manton S. Eddy and Wade H. Haislip and the photograph of generals Eisenhower, Bradley, Leonard T. Gerow and J. Lawton Collins were all obtained from the U.S. Army Military History Institute, Collection Division, 950 Soldiers Drive, Carlisle Barracks, PA 17013-5021.

The Cover Design was enhanced by computer graphics at Adams' Quickprint, Inc., 2122 N. 12th Street, Grand Junction, CO 81501.

This book was printed in the United States of America.

To order additional copies of this book, contact:
Xlibris Corporation
1-888-795-4274
www.Xlibris.com
Orders@Xlibris.com
67325

Contents

In loving memory of
Edgar Carl Weidner and Nettie Rae Cooper-Weidner,
my parents

Preface

"I wrote this book in order to satisfy my historical curiosity . . ."[1]
British historian A.J.P. Taylor in *The Origins of the Second World War.*

It was 1983 or 1984; I was sitting at one of those long wooden tables in the Archives Room at the old US Army Military History Institute at Carlisle Barracks, Pennsylvania. I just finished reading several manuscripts when the assistant curator came to the table to ask if there was anything else I wanted to see. I told him no, but that I had a problem. I explained to him that my understanding of the events at the Falaise Gap in 1944 did not match the official [Bradley, Eisenhower] version of what had happened.

He looked at me for a second, and then walked to the opposite end of the table, and sat on the edge of the table next to the wall. He told me, as I recall, 'It was the alliance. Eisenhower was protecting the Anglo-American Alliance. The war against Germany would have been difficult, if not impossible to pursue without British cooperation. After the war, the Marshall Plan would have been hard to sell to the Europeans without British help. By 1949 or 1950 the United States was in a 'cold war' and later committed to NATO with the British leading the Europeans against our former ally, the Soviet Union. There was simply no good time for Eisenhower to antagonize the British without damaging our alliance over something that happened long ago.'

I expected an argument and was instead taken aback by his complete candor. My first emotion was one of utter disappointment. If he was so open with the 'grand secret,' how many other military historians must already know the truth? Then it hit me: of course, they knew, or at least most of them knew. Military history is not that complicated. All it took to uncover the 'Falaise Gap Secret' was an average intelligence and a little perseverance.

I have waited patiently for some enterprising writer to grasp the Falaise secret and straighten out the historical mess allied commanders made of their battles in Normandy. I have waited for nearly twenty-five years. That is long enough.

---

[1]   A.J.P. Taylor, *The Origins of the Second World War,* (New York: Fawcett Premier, 1961), 277.

Acknowledgments

The author wishes to thank Paul Johnson at the British National Archives in Kew, UK and Richard L. Baker at the United States Army Military History Institute in Carlisle Barracks, Pennsylvania for their kindly assistance.

I also wish to thank Colonel Roger C. Hagerty, United States Marine Corps [retired] and Lieutenant Colonel Donald K. Schneider, United States Air Force [retired], for reading initial drafts of the manuscript and offering excellent suggestions. I would like to thank Jay Gaas for reading through the last two drafts of the manuscript and performing the thankless job of copyediting. I also want to thank Tom Herzog for the wonderful maps he was able to produce on his computer, and thanks to Schuyler Daugherty of Adams' Quickprint, Inc. for his computer graphics work on the cover. Finally a thank you to Cousin James Weidner of the Weidner Publishing Group for an initial critique of the format and information about the publishing business which was extremely helpful.

The author acknowledges a special debt to Professor Dennis Showalter, past President of the Society for Military History and current professor of history at Colorado College. Professor Showalter's invaluable criticism enabled the author to create a more focused manuscript.

A father's thank you to daughters Jessica Ann Weidner and Meredith Jo Weidner for their love, understanding and patience, which somehow make it all worthwhile.

Introduction

"The real story of any great event is apt to be very different to what appears at the time. This is especially the case in war . . . The truth sometimes leaks out later; sometimes never."[2] Military historian B. H. Liddell Hart.

No hobby is at once as exciting and as frustrating as the study of military history. World War II remains the last "good" war. However, facts are often obscured by the so-called 'fog of battle' and viewed later through glasses, which romanticize but do not analyze the event. Glasses tinted by the Allied victory over fascism in Europe and by the inevitability history often confers on such momentous events have combined to grant senior Allied commanders an almost papal immunity from serious inquiry.

Historians must rely on accounts written by the generals who made the decisions, or the odd captain or colonel who kept a diary or wrote the unit's history. Equally important are the published and unpublished correspondence files and intelligence information. What did he know and when did he know it? Finally, there are accounts written after the event by biographers, journalists, and military historians.

A grateful public on both sides of the Atlantic has been willing to accept accounts written by senior generals that always seem to cast the author in a favorable light. Diaries, unit histories, and after action battle reports all seem to be written, or amended, to protect the reputation of the commanding officer.

Finally, biographers, journalists, and military historians often write more than one book. Eventually, the critical journalist and dedicated historian become part of the event they have written about. Historians often develop a personal attachment to their work, an emotional need to protect their own reputations by protecting the historical status quo. They have now become part of the story, defending the legacy they helped to create.

In the United States, Stephen E. Ambrose, a Louisiana State University history professor was lucky to be selected as the Associate Editor for *The Papers of Dwight David Eisenhower*. Ambrose used that opportunity as a springboard to create a small military history writing empire. It was an

---

2   B. H. Liddell Hart, *The Other Side of the Hill*, (London: Cassell, 1951), 139.

empire based on his access to Eisenhower's wartime papers. Ambrose can be forgiven if he is not overly critical of his benefactor.

In Britain, once the government-controlled press minted a new national hero from the victor of the Second Battle of El Alamein, access to Field Marshal Bernard L. Montgomery's papers became the huge prize. The task of carefully nurturing the reputation of Field Marshal Montgomery was given to Sir Denis Hamilton, who later passed it on to his son, Nigel Hamilton. The younger Mr. Hamilton has done a masterful job, skillfully negotiating the many minefields Montgomery had left behind for historians. To his great credit, Mr. Hamilton almost makes The Viscount Montgomery of Alamein a sympathetic historical figure. Montgomery comes across as a gallant, willful, headstrong, and thoroughly unlikable soldier. Nigel Hamilton has managed to create a large publishing enterprise based on the manuscripts left behind by the irascible, little British Field Marshal. Like Stephen E. Ambrose in the United States, Nigel Hamilton in Britain can be forgiven for not being too critical of his family's most lucrative benefactor.

Although Allied armies required less than four years from Pearl Harbor to the German surrender in May 1945, the amount of paperwork generated during that brief period is overwhelming. "US Army files alone weigh 17,120 tons and fill 188 miles of filing cases."[3] No single author could hope to master it in a lifetime. Therefore, historians have been granted considerable latitude in what they choose to write about and what they choose to ignore. Given the range of available information, much of it conflicting, it is possible to create more than one plausible scenario for any one incident. The key to understanding a general's personal account is to determine what he has left out. Contradictory information is often ignored or misplaced.

For twenty years Allied officers, their biographers and military historians have had the public forum pretty much to themselves. Then in the 1960s, Ladislas Farago's book, *Patton, Ordeal, and Triumph*, was published. A note on the back cover of Farago's book informs us, "The book survived an assault of lawsuits which sought to prevent its publication. That it was published is a testament to the courage and perseverance of the author and the original publisher."[4] An Oscar Award winning motion picture soon followed. General George S. Patton's reputation, which had been sullied by

---

[3]   Mark A. Stoler, *Allies in War Britain and America against the Axis Powers 1940-1945*, (New York: Oxford University Press, 2007), 250.

[4]   Ladislas Farago, *Patton, Ordeal and Triumph*, (New York: Astor-Honor, 1977), back cover.

war correspondents and comments from generals Dwight Eisenhower, W. Bedell Smith, and Omar Bradley, was well on its way to rehabilitation.

Our understanding of the war in Europe increased dramatically during the 1970s. The United States government released most of its remaining secret information through the 1974 Freedom of Information Act. In October 1977, the British began releasing information about their highly successful efforts to read secret German radio transmissions, code named *ULTRA*. It has become exceedingly difficult to support the existing historical record of the war in Europe.

Writing *Overlord* in 1984, Max Hastings observed, "Even 40 years after the battle, it is astonishing how many books have been published which merely reflect comfortable chauvinistic legends, and how few which seek frankly to examine the record."[5] Hastings' words are just as true now, 60 odd years after the event, as they were when he wrote them. A series of recently published books question the accepted view of the war in Europe. Yet the authors, for whatever reasons, seem to be repelled by the logic of their own arguments and fail to press home their points.

The names of famous generals such as Dwight David Eisenhower and Bernard Law Montgomery cast a very long shadow. Old wounds are still tender to the touch of historical scrutiny. Field Marshal Montgomery's accounts of the war in Europe have become a lightning rod for argument. Montgomery was the only senior commander to claim that his battles went exactly as he had planned them.

British politicians and military officers were sensitive about their declining status within the Anglo-American Alliance. This sensitivity influenced their behavior toward the Americans as Great Britain's reduced standing within the Alliance became more apparent in 1944 and 1945. General Montgomery and his mentor, Alan Brooke, never could adjust to the fact that American soldiers outnumbered British soldiers in Europe by a factor of four to one. They and their friends in the press on Fleet Street struggled to protect the reputation of the British Army.

Since the end of the war, British historians have made a valiant effort to nurture the Montgomery legend by omitting contradictory information and by blaming others for most of Montgomery's problems. The official British historian, Major L. F. Ellis, Australian journalist Chester Wilmot, Montgomery himself, and Montgomery's biographer Nigel Hamilton led this effort. A.J.P. Taylor wrote, "Historians often dislike what happened or

---

[5]   Max Hastings, *Overlord,* (New York: Simon & Schuster, 1984), 11.

wish it had happened differently. There is nothing they can do about it."[6]
Historians in Great Britain have been adjusting the historical record since
the end of the war with scant regard for what really happened.

Eisenhower and Bradley published their accounts of the war in 1948
and 1951 respectively. Military historian Dr. Forrest C. Pogue later wrote,
"Without any question, Eisenhower and Bradley [deliberately] weaken their
case against Montgomery."[7] This gave Montgomery's supporters some
latitude to embellish Montgomery's version of what had happened during
the war.

The Americans serving in Europe were never sure how their nascent
military and economic strength would affect their relationship with the
British. Despite repeated and perceptive encouragement from General
George C. Marshall in Washington, General Eisenhower refused to take
command of Allied Ground Forces in Europe. The Americans were new at
this game. The British had been playing it for nearly three hundred years. At
the highest level of the Allied command, Eisenhower was unsure if having
more American than British troops in Europe should influence the command
set-up at all. Eisenhower was a politically cautious; some would say naïve,
commander.

It would be easy to cast Anglo-American disagreement as a Montgomery/
Eisenhower or Brooke/Marshall conflict. That is too simple. Shortages
in manpower directly influenced British strategy and their approach to
military operations.[8] American generals in all other theaters throughout the
war shared the problem of getting the British to participate in offensive
operations. The problems General Eisenhower had with Montgomery in
northwest Europe were mirrored by disagreements US commanders had
with British commanders in Italy [Lieutenant General Mark W. Clark],[9] and
in the Far East [Lieutenant General Joseph W. Stilwell].[10]

The truth about the European campaign during World War II is so
unpleasant to discuss because it involves officers at the highest level of
the Allied command. Eisenhower, Montgomery, and Bradley were directly
involved. British historian B.H. Liddell Hart wrote, "The real story of any

---

[6]   A.J.P. Taylor, *The Origins*, 277.
[7]   Carlo D'Este, *Decision in Normandy*, (New York: Harper, 1994), 495. A letter
       from Dr. Forrest C. Pogue to Carlo D'Este dated 21 October 1980.
[8]   Carlo D'Este, *Decision*, 252-270. Also see Max Hastings, *Overlord*, 238.
[9]   Martin Blumenson, *Mark Clark*, (New York: Congdon & Weed, 1984), 210, 211.
[10]   Barbara W. Tuchman, *Stilwell and the American Experience in China, 1911-45*,
       (New York: MacMillan, 1971), 448, 467.

great event is apt to be very different to what appears at the time. This is especially the case in war . . . . The truth sometimes leaks out later; sometimes never."[11] This has been true about certain events during the Battle of the Falaise Gap.

The who, what, when, and where of the Second World War in Europe have been covered thousands of times in books and articles. The decisions made by commanders, the performance of units of every size and description, the quality of weapons employed and the results of battles large and small have all been documented time and again. It would seem to be worthwhile to consider the larger political issues and their influence, if any, on battlefield strategy. According to military theorist Carl von Clausewitz, ". . . war is not merely an act of policy but a true political instrument, a continuation of political intercourse, carried on with other means . . . The political object is the goal, war is the means of reaching it, and means can never be considered in isolation from their purpose."[12] Eisenhower was a student of Clausewitz; yet, for reasons that are difficult to understand, failed to apply his principles in Normandy.

Military historians have usually looked at the war in Europe as if it were an isolated tactical exercise. Unfortunately, sound tactics were not always the deciding factor. It would be difficult to overestimate the political significance of war in Europe to the government of Prime Minister Winston S. Churchill. Historians on both sides of the Atlantic have faithfully recorded the comings and goings of generals and their subordinates. British historians have been accurate in describing some of Dwight D. Eisenhower's decisions as politically motivated, but they have not been bold enough to apply the same level of scrutiny to their own countrymen.

Both Winston Churchill and Franklin Roosevelt were consummate politicians. Did efforts to retain political control of a fickle voting population have any effect on their military strategy as operations developed in France? President Franklin Roosevelt rarely interfered with General Marshall's decisions. However, as Minister of Defense and Prime Minister, Winston S. Churchill was in almost daily contact with his military chiefs concerning the events in Europe. He frequently questioned their actions and sought to influence their decisions. In his diary, Chief of the Imperial General Staff,

---

[11]   B.H.L. Hart, *The Other Side*, 139.
[12]   Carl Von Clausewitz *On War*, Edited and Translated by Michael Howard and Peter Paret, (New Jersey: Princeton University Press, 1989), 87.

Alan Brooke complained that the American, George Marshal, had the easier job. "He [Marshall] certainly had a much easier time of it working with Roosevelt; he informed me that he frequently did not see him for a month or six weeks. I was fortunate if I did not see Winston for 6 hours."[13]

The British and American systems of command were very different. For each military action, the Americans put one man in charge, on land it was usually the ranking Army officer. The British system of command was different; they had a committee system of command whereby three officers, one each from the Army, Navy, and Air Force shared the command.[14] For political reasons, the Allies employed a combination of both command systems with extremely poor results. The degree of cooperation and trust necessary to maintain a 'unified command' on the battlefield was simply lacking at the highest levels of the Anglo-American Alliance.

In 1939, the Germans displayed a new form of warfare in Poland. The press called it 'blitzkrieg', or lightning war. The centerpiece of the new German form of warfare was the concentration of armored divisions at the point of attack. When the same tactics were brilliantly successful in Western Europe in May-June 1940, the Americans were quick to adopt the methods and basic organization of the German armored division.

The British were unable to adapt. They could build tanks but the German blitzkrieg had little influence on the conservative World War I infantry/ artillery tactics embraced by senior British Army officers. The C.I.G.S., General Alan Brooke and his protégé, Bernard L. Montgomery, were the two most influential British Army officers during the war. Historian Raymond Callahan observed of General Brooke, "His ideas were shaped by his experiences as a gunner [in the First World War] on the Western Front . . . where British successes . . . were due in large part to the development of very sophisticated artillery techniques."[15] Callahan concludes that, "Brooke's [and Montgomery's] approach to battle . . . would remain heavily influenced by the experiences of World War I, especially of the victorious concluding months."[16]

---

[13]   Field Marshal Lord Alanbrooke, *War Diaries, 1940-1945*, edited by Alex Danchev and Daniel Todman. From Christopher Catherwood, *Winston Churchill*, (New York: Berkley Caliber, 2009), 133.

[14]   Sir Frederick Morgan, *Overture to Overlord*, (London: Hodder & Stoughton, May, 1950), 191.

[15]   Raymond Callahan, *Churchill and His Generals*, (Kansas, University of Kansas Press, 2007), 84.

[16]   Callahan, Churchill, and His Generals, 84.

Nor could the British Army break down the regimental command system around which so much glorious history had evolved. Because of the rigid control from the top demanded by World War I infantry/artillery operations and their beloved regimental system, the British were unable to develop the coordination between the combat arms so necessary for success on a World War II battlefield.

The British Army, like British society in general, remained committed to the traditional ways of doing things, with each branch of service jealously protecting its interests to the detriment of combined operations in the field. The British Army and British society were, and here one has to be careful by not inferring too much, both victims of a traditional system of behavior which had been instrumental in the creation the British Empire, but which was now contributing to Great Britain's overall economic and military decline.[17]

As British power declined, relative to the increasing military and economic might of the United States and the Soviet Union, British leaders struggled to retain strategic control of the powerful American force being deployed on their continent. *They fought bitterly to protect the grand illusion that Great Britain remained in the front ranks of the world's military powers.* They did not trust the Americans to get it right, either militarily or politically. The Americans caused C.I.G.S. Alan Brooke great distress. In late 1943 he wrote, "I despair of getting our American friends to have any strategic vision. Their drag on us has seriously affected our Mediterranean strategy and the whole conduct of the war."[18] Wartime Cabinet member, Harold Macmillan once remarked, "You will find the Americans much as the Greeks found the Romans—great, big, vulgar, bustling people . . . also more corrupt . . . We [British] must run AFHQ [Allied Headquarters] as the Greeks ran the operations of the Emperor Claudius."[19] Macmillan was undoubtedly pleased at Montgomery's ability to influence Allied strategy in Europe.

It is a central theme of this book that the British cabal of Prime Minister Winston Churchill, Chief of the Imperial General Staff, Alan Brooke, and the Allied Ground Forces Commander, General Bernard L. Montgomery

---

[17]   Correlli Barnett, *The Pride and the Fall: The Dream and Illusion of Britain as a Great Nation,* (New York: The Free Press, 1987), 100-106 and 119-124.

[18]   Arthur Bryant, *Triumph in the West, 1943-1946,* Based on the Diaries and Notes of Field Marshal, The Viscount Alanbrooke, (London: Collins, 1959), 74.

[19]   Charles Whiting, *The Field Marshal's Revenge, The Breakdown of a Special Relationship*, (Staplehurst: Spellmount, 2004), 77.

often played politics with military strategy, placing Allied soldiers at a great disadvantage. Greece, Singapore, Second El Alamein, Italy, the Falaise Gap, Arnhem, Antwerp, and Montgomery's magnificent Rhine crossing were a few examples of innocent British politics gone militarily wrong.

Churchill and Brooke believed the Americans could be hoodwinked into backing British strategy in Europe and the Mediterranean. They were wrong. After the Americans had joined the war in North Africa, ". . . the war moved into a new phase, one in which the issue for Churchill would be not whether the British army could win, but how to shape victory to support British interests."[20] The question of who was going to win the war was no longer in doubt. The question of Great Britain's political standing in the post-war world was, in the minds of many British soldiers and government officials, very much in doubt.

Winston Churchill was a grand master at the art of political intrigue. Callahan wrote, ". . . In the Prime Minister's view, British battlefield success was politically essential . . ."[21] Churchill saw a post-war world with the British colonies of Hong Kong and Singapore secure in Southeast Asia. He saw a continuation of the raj in India and a return to pre-war borders with a dominant political role for the old states of Western Europe. Churchill believed that post-war political success for England was tied directly to military success during the war. Sadly, despite Churchill's best efforts, the Europe of 1948 was going to be vastly different from the Europe of 1938 and the Empire—gone.

When Montgomery ordered the Americans to halt on the inter-Army Group boundary just south of Argentan on the evening of 12 August 1944, the Anglo-American military alliance was compromised. After the battle of the Falaise Gap, it became harder and harder for the Allied command to retain the illusion that tactical decisions were based on sound military doctrine. Instead, Montgomery's arguments that he command a single thrust aimed at Berlin continued unabated until the end of the war. Those arguments were based on little more than irrational egotism and a strong professional animosity toward the Americans. The Anglo-American military alliance was dead, and it required every ounce of General Eisenhower's considerable political skill to keep this secret from the public.

---

[20]   Callahan, *Churchill, and His Generals*, 146.
[21]   Callahan, *Churchill and His Generals*, 187.

Chapter 1

General Bradley in France

"Ike withheld comment then, but later . . . he confided to me his disappointment with Monty's progress. He felt that the British had sat down again, that Monty should have been more aggressive than he had been."[22] Bradley discussed a July 2 meeting with Eisenhower and Montgomery.

On 14 February 1943 the Germans attacked US held positions in Tunisia. Early reports from the battlefield were not good. The German attacks would lead to an embarrassing American defeat at the Kasserine Pass. The battlefield performance of several American commanders during the battle was unacceptable. US Army Chief of Staff, General George C Marshall decided to send one of his best generals to North Africa. Two days earlier, on his fiftieth birthday, General Omar N. Bradley had been given command of X Corps in Temple, Texas. But in light of the disaster unfolding at the Kasserine Pass, Marshall and his staff decided to send General Bradley to North Africa.

US General Dwight D. Eisenhower had been appointed Commander-in-Chief of Allied Forces in the Mediterranean Theater of Operations. One of the first things Bradley learned in Africa was, ". . . that Ike brooked no American criticism of the French or British—especially the British. Any American who criticized the British stood a very good chance of being busted and sent home. I came away with the opinions expressed back in Tom Handy's OPD: In his efforts to achieve harmonious 'coalition warfare, Ike has become excessively pro-British in his attitudes and thinking.'"[23] Generals George Patton, Tom Handy, and Albert Wedemeyer shared Bradley's opinion on Eisenhower's excessive pro-British behavior.[24]

---

[22]   Omar N. Bradley with Clay Blair, *A General's Life*, (New York: Simon and Schuster, 1983), 151.

[23]   Bradley, *A General's Life*, 133.

[24]   Martin Blumenson, *The Patton Papers, 1940-1945*, (Boston: Houghton Mifflin, 1974), 222. Also see: Albert C. Wedemeyer, *Wedemeyer Reports,* (New York: Henry Holt, 1958), 194.

Marshall told Eisenhower he must get along with his Allies. Marshall was strongly supported in this by President Roosevelt, who viewed the United States as 'the arsenal of democracy'. The policy dated from August/September, 1940, when the US traded fifty overage destroyers for ninety-nine-year leases on British military bases in the Caribbean. United States factories could produce the tanks, trucks, planes, and ships needed to gain the final victory, but it was up to the local US commander to insure that, whenever possible, local inhabitants did their share of the fighting. It saved thousands of American lives. Mark Clark in Italy was given the same instructions, as was Vinegar Joe Stilwell in China. General Clark bit down very hard on his lower lip. "Clark began to wonder whether the British were following a deliberate policy of self-aggrandizement . . . Gradually Clark came to believe in the existence of a [British] conspiracy . . . (But) Eisenhower absolutely insisted on unity, and Clark had to keep his feelings to himself."[25] General Stilwell was the only senior US officer relieved of his command because he could not get along with his Allies. Stilwell didn't get along with either the British or the Chinese under Chiang Kai-shek.[26] Many of the problems Stilwell experienced in China with the British were the same problems Eisenhower encountered in Europe and Mark Clark encountered in Italy. The British, short of men, were always slow to attack and quick to return to defensive warfare.

British officers could wink at each other over Eisenhower's title, knowing full well that they maintained operational control of all Allied forces in the air, on land, and on the sea. Put another way, British officers had operational control over all Allied forces in the Mediterranean. General Eisenhower had operational control of nothing.

Eisenhower's lack of command authority hardly mattered when the Allies were following British strategy in a theater, such as the Mediterranean, dominated by British forces. One year later, however, Eisenhower's unwillingness to assume command responsibilities in Europe would sometimes place Allied soldiers at a great disadvantage.

The British controlled Allied intelligence in the Mediterranean Theater and held all of the operational command positions. There was something for everyone in the command setup, everyone except American officers serving under Eisenhower. "I shared Patton's misgivings about Ike," Bradley wrote, ". . . Ike was too weak, much too prone to knuckle under to the British, often, as I have shown, at our expense. If I were to continue to serve as one of his battlefield lieutenants,

25   Blumenson, *Mark Clark*, 149, 150.
26   Tuchman, *Stilwell*, 448, 502.

it was clear that I must be much, much firmer in advancing American interests and strategy."[27] General Albert C. Wedemeyer, traveling around the world for his boss, George Marshall, also heard rumors about Eisenhower. General Wedemeyer wrote about a rumor he had, ". . . picked up in Algiers that General Eisenhower and . . . Bedell Smith could be counted on always to settle a dispute in favor of the British . . . . The gossip came to me from so many people that it was obvious it represented a widely held view. Even some of the men who were most loyal to Eisenhower nevertheless felt that Ike was leaning over too far in favoring the British."[28] Eisenhower's pro-British attitude would be reflected in decisions he made through the end of the war in Europe.

As a reward for his excellent performance in North Africa and Sicily, General Bradley was given a new assignment. He was ordered to meet with General Eisenhower on 3 September 1943 for a private conference. Eisenhower told Bradley, "I've got good news for you Brad. You've got a fancy new job."[29] Bradley's new job was the best assignment he could have hoped for. He was named the Commander of the new First United States Army for the much anticipated cross-channel invasion of Northwestern France.

The newly appointed First Army Commander left Sicily on the morning of September 8. After resting a week in England, General Bradley flew to the United States. He discussed his new position and the Sicilian campaign with Army Chief of Staff, George Marshall. In addition to his duties as First US Army Commander, Bradley would also serve as acting commander of First US Army Group. Bradley was asked to pick the key personnel for both headquarters.

President Franklin Roosevelt had delayed naming the Commander for *Overlord*, code name for the cross-channel invasion. He finally decided to name General Dwight D. Eisenhower as the commander in Cairo on December 6, 1943. George Marshall had been in line for the job and was disappointed at Eisenhower's appointment. But he bore his disappointment well, as Bradley later suggested. Roosevelt had decided that, ". . . he just could not sleep at night with Marshall out of the country."[30] He seemed to be waiting for Marshall to ask for the job, but Marshall, as much as he wanted it, never asked. Roosevelt thought that Marshall was just too important to the war effort to be given an overseas command.

---

27   Bradley, *A General's Life*, 151.
28   Wedemeyer, 194.
29   Bradley, *A General's Life,* 207.
30   Stephen E. Ambrose, *Eisenhower: Soldier, General of the Army, President Elect (1890-1952),* (New York: Simon and Schuster, 1983), 271.

Both Bradley and Eisenhower would have preferred to bring the entire Mediterranean command back to England for *Overlord*, but the British wanted to make some changes. British Admiral Bertram H. Ramsay had replaced Andrew B. Cunningham as Allied Naval Commander. Cunningham had been promoted to First Sea Lord on the death of Admiral Dudley Pound. British General Trafford Leigh-Mallory would be the Allied Tactical Air Commander. British General Bernard L. Montgomery would serve in two positions: Commander of all Allied Ground Forces and Commander of British 21st Army Group. General Miles C. Dempsey would Command British Second Army.

US General Dwight D. Eisenhower would again be the overall Commander; his title was Supreme Commander, Allied Expeditionary Force. Eisenhower's Deputy Supreme Commander would be British General Arthur Tedder, an airman. Eisenhower's Chief of Staff would be US General Bedell Smith.

It was assumed that, as the Allies gained ground in Normandy, additional Allied divisions would be committed within the beachhead. When enough Allied divisions had landed to create two British and two American armies, a change in the command structure had been agreed upon. Montgomery would give up his position as Allied Ground Forces Commander to General Eisenhower but he would retain Command of British 21st Army Group. Bradley would give up his post at First US Army and take Command of 12th US Army Group. General Courtney H. Hodges would move up to Command First US Army. Within 21st British Army Group, First Canadian Army would be activated under the command of Canadian General H.D.G. Crerar. At this point, it was anticipated that Bradley and Montgomery would be equals in the chain of command, each Army Group Commander reporting directly to Eisenhower, whose headquarters became known as SHAEF [Supreme Headquarters, Allied Expeditionary Force].

The position of Ground Forces Commander, as Eisenhower later explained, would be abolished. He wrote, ". . . in a theater so vast as ours each army group commander would be the ground commander in chief for his particular area; instead of one there would be three so-called commanders in chief for the ground and each would be supported by his own tactical air force."[31] Eisenhower did not insist on the implementation of his own plans for Allied ground operations until late March in 1945.

In the endless telling and re-telling of the invasion, the certainty of victory has washed away most of the doubts that must have plagued Allied commanders in the spring of 1944. There was, before the event, the very

---

[31]   Dwight D. Eisenhower, *Crusade in Europe*, (New York: Da Capo Press, 1977), 285.

real possibility that the invasion would fail, causing the deaths of tens of thousands of Allied soldiers and setting back the Allied war effort many months, if not years. The British had reservations about the invasion. Senior British officials, from the Prime Minister on down, would have preferred any assault on Hitler's fortress Europe except the one the Americans insisted upon, the cross channel invasion of western France. Winston Churchill related dreams he had, dreams of a tragic Allied defeat and the English Channel running red with the blood of Allied soldiers.[32]

The invasion of Europe was a risky affair. The sheer size of the operation beggars the imagination. To anyone who has witnessed a botched company exercise, the mere fact that senior officers in the United States and British Armies managed to get so many men, ships, and planes at the right place, at the right time was a glorious feat of arms.

The real possibility of failure created an atmosphere of intense Allied cooperation. Almost none of the problems Eisenhower had to deal with in the Mediterranean resurfaced during the spring of 1944. While the possibility of a German victory in Normandy remained, Allied cooperation continued to be strong. Generals Bradley and Montgomery developed a close, mutually supportive relationship through the planning stages of *Overlord,* through the invasion, the build-up in men and supplies, and the agonizing battles for expansion up to the month of August 1944. It was only after the German defeat became a certainty during the first half of August that problems within the Alliance resurfaced.

Allied plans for the invasion and the actual D-day invasion have been thoroughly documented elsewhere and will not be repeated here. However, several points should be mentioned. Allied planners were primarily concerned about getting a force of sufficient size ashore and keeping it ashore. It has been suggested that they did not pay sufficient attention to conducting offensive operations in *bocage* or hedgerow country. Getting troops over the invasion beaches required a reckless rush to the sea wall and a quick climb up the walls to silence the German defenders. Training troops for the *bocage* may have led to more caution during the critical invasion phase, when speed and dash were the order of the day.

---

[32]   Harry C. Butcher, *My Three Years with Eisenhower*, (New York: Simon and Schuster, 1946), 453. Also see Robert E. Sherwood, *Roosevelt and Hopkins, An Intimate History*, (New York: Harper & Brothers, 1948), 590, 591.

Allied logistical planners ignored Hindenburg's advice, ". . . in war, only the simple succeeds."[33] Given years to plan the invasion, they planned too well. They set-up three organizations (MOVCO, TURNCO, and EMBARCO) to control embarkation at ports in England, and established a strict order of priority for unloading supplies once they arrived in Normandy. It required only a few days for the system to collapse. Martin van Creveld wrote about success the Allies had unloading supplies directly over the beaches: "This . . . was achieved only by disregarding all the plans. The first breakthrough came on D+2 when it was decided to ignore the predetermined order of priorities and unload everything regardless."[34] Once the Navy decided that they could beach ships at low tide, unload supplies and pull their ships back off the beaches as the tide raised, a semblance of order returned to Allied logistics. The Navy had studiously resisted this idea prior to the invasion. "Thus, unloading proceeded not so much in accordance with the plans as without them," wrote van Creveld, "and in some cases against them, which was additional proof that the planning staffs had grossly overestimated the value of complex artificial arrangements and underestimated what determination, common sense and improvisation could achieve."[35]

Allied planners believed that if they were successful, the German defenders would be pushed back in a series of limited strategic withdraws. Each German withdrawal and Allied advance was drawn as a phase line on a map, timed in days from the date of the D-day invasion, which was June 6. The Allied planners based their logistical estimates on the assumption that ". . . the Allies hoped to reach the Seine by D+90 and the German border around D+360."[36] Logistical experts had warned all Allied commanders that there could be no major advance into Germany until the port of Antwerp was open and receiving Allied ships.[37]

Following their evacuation from Dunkirk in May-June 1940, British units were concentrated along the southeastern coastline, well positioned to fight off the anticipated German invasion. The Americans coming to England from the western Atlantic arrived on the western coastline and were usually stationed in northern or western England. This meant that, unless the British and American armies crossed paths, somewhere in England, prior to loading on ships, or crossed in ships mid-channel, loaded for the invasion, the British were going to land on the left flank and the Americans were going to land on the right.

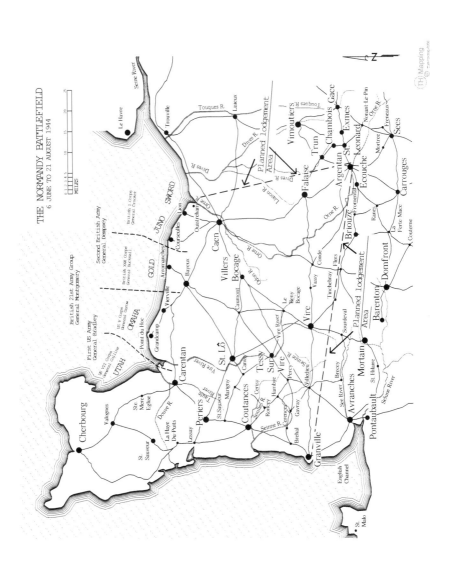

THE NORMANDY BATTLEFIELD
6 JUNE TO 21 AUGUST 1944

MILES

British 21st Army Group
General Montgomery

First US Army
General Bradley

Second British Army
General Dempsey

US V Corps
General Gerow

US VII Corps
General Collins

British I Corps
General Crocker

British XXX Corps
General Bucknall

Seine River

Le Havre

Trouville

Touques R.

Lisieux

Dives R.

Dives R.

Planned Lodgement Area

Vimoutiers

Touques R.

Chambois

Gace

Trun

Exmes

St. Leonard

Argentan

Nonant Le Pin

Orne R.

Freneaux

Sees

Mortree

Falaise

La Ferte Mace

Couterne

Ecouche

Cartrouges

Orne R.

Brioze

Rasnes

Fromentel

Conde

Flers

Condé

Vassy

Domfront

Barenton

Orne R.

SWORD

JUNO

GOLD

OMAHA

UTAH

Orne R.

Lion

Ouistreham

Courseulles

Caen

Arromanches

Bayeux

Vierville

Villers Bocage

Le Beny Bocage

Caumont

Orne R.

Vire River

Vire

Tracy Bocage

Souleuvre

Planned Lodgement Area

Mortain

St. Hilaire

Seline River

Grandcamp

Point du Hoc

Carentan

St. Lô

Tessy Sur Vire

Vire R.

Cerisy

Percy

Villedieu

Breecy

Avranches

Pontaubault

Taute River

Douve R.

Peritrs

St. Sauveur

Margny

Coutances

Soulles R.

Rostrey

Gavray

Brehal

Seinne R.

See River

Granville

English Channel

St. Malo

Cherbourg

Valognes

Ste. Mere Eglise

La Haye Du Puits

Lessay

St. Sauveur

Douve R.

N

BH Mapping

Pre-invasion planners asked Allied forces to get ashore quickly and move well inland. Montgomery explained, "We must blast our way on shore and get a good lodgement [area] before the enemy can bring sufficient reserves up to turn us out."[38] The planners envisioned a substantial lodgement area in Allied possession before any major attacks would be launched. The lodgement area Montgomery wanted included ". . . Granville-Vire-Argentan-Falaise-Caen . . ." Once the Allies captured these towns, Montgomery said, ". . . then we will have the lodgement area we want and can begin to expand."[39] Patton's Third Army would be sent into Brittany to open the vital ports for Allied use, while the other Allied Armies: Hodges US First Army, Crerar's Canadian First Army, and Dempsey's British Second Army would pivot northeast and attack toward the Seine and Paris.

The five invasion beaches, beginning from the east were: Sword, Juno, and Gold, the three British and Canadian beaches, and Omaha and Utah, the two American beaches. The invasion went well on all the beaches, except Omaha. The Americans on Omaha were a victim of rough seas, exposed beaches and the excellent German 352nd Infantry Division, which happened to be in the area on training maneuvers. Eisenhower had been warned to expect as many as 25,000 casualties on D-Day; the actual total was close to 10,000. No Allied division reached its D-Day objectives.

D-day operations produced a series of errors. There were widely scattered drops for the airborne troopers. Allied bombers were supposed to damage German beach defenses and instead killed hundreds of French milk cows. Shellfire from the big guns on Allied heavy cruisers and battleships was supposed to negate German costal artillery but was a big disappointment. Omaha beach had been a disaster for the Americans because of the excellent German 352nd Infantry Division, so the Americans improvised. General Bradley wrote, "Twelve destroyers moved in close to the beach, heedless of shallow water, mines, enemy fire, and other obstacles, to give us close support. The main batteries of these gallant ships became our sole artillery."[40] More than a few officers who survived D-day on Omaha were convinced they would not have made it off the beaches without supporting fire from those twelve destroyers. When Gee Gerow's

---

[38]   Nigel Hamilton, *Master of the Battlefield: Monty's War Years 1942-1944,* (New York: McGraw-Hill Book Company, 1983), 588.
[39]   Hamilton, *Master,* 588.
[40]   Bradley, *A General's Life,* 251.

V Corps headquarters finally got set up on shore, their first report began: "Thank God for the US Navy."[41]

While American offensives were constantly broken up by the rivers, swamps, and hedgerows in the Carentan, the British, operating in more open country should have enjoyed more success. At least this was how Montgomery's pre-invasion briefings sounded. Unfortunately, more open country also meant wider and deeper fields of fire for German artillery. It was on the British front near Caen that the Germans deployed the bulk of their armor and the finest artillery piece either side produced during the war, the dreaded German 88-mm. anti-aircraft gun. This weapon was also an excellent tank killer.

When the Americans occupied Cherbourg on June 27, Montgomery still had not taken Caen. The ground southeast of Caen was desperately needed for airfields by Allied air commanders and their squadrons back in England. It remained in German hands. According to the Editors of Eisenhower's Papers: "By June 30, the British army had not captured Caen, and now Montgomery issued his first directive that showed *an intension of holding on the left and breaking through on the right*. He directed the British forces to contain the greatest possible part of the enemy forces. This was a correct evaluation, brought about by the German reaction at Caen."[42] With the British Army stalled in front of Caen, there was little likelihood that they were going to take Falaise or Argentan anytime soon.

Eisenhower and Bradley had been looking at other options. They ". . . began to study intensively breakthrough possibilities within the American sector as early as June 20."[43] Once Bradley had taken Cherbourg, he could turn his Army around, and get all his divisions pointed south. There was a problem; Bradley's army was heading into the heart of the hedgerow country. By July 3, Bradley had his divisions sorted out in four corps: Troy Middleton's VIII, Joe Collins' VII, Pete Corlett's XIX, and Leonard Gerow's V. Generals Middleton and Collins, on the extreme right by the coastline, ". . . would deliver the hammer blow in an all-out drive down the west coast of the peninsula toward Avranches."[44] General Corlett would attack in severe hedgerow country toward St. Lo. On the extreme left, Leonard Gerow would

---

[41] Bradley, *A General's Life*, 251.
[42] Alfred D. Chandler Jr., Editor, *The Papers of Dwight David Eisenhower, Vol. III*, (Baltimore: The Johns Hopkins Press, 1970), 1969. Italics in the original.
[43] Chandler, (Ed.), *The Eisenhower Papers, Vol. III*, 1969.
[44] Bradley, *A General's Life*, 269.

protect Montgomery's flank near Caumont. Despite high hopes for Bradley's attack, it failed to break through stout German defenses.

The Germans moved Panzer Lehr Division into the line opposite the Americans. Pete Corlett's attack with XIX Corps went in on July 7 against the German center. It met fierce resistance and horrible weather. Bradley's blitz to Avranches had failed. "It failed," wrote Bradley, "in part because I bowed to pressure from above and allowed it to go too soon. I should have given Collins more time to redeploy from Cherbourg. It failed in part because of the bad weather."[45] Bad weather meant no air support and poor road conditions for Bradley's mobile divisions. As always, there was the *bocage* in the back of everyone's mind, the *bocage* where hedgerow after hedgerow seemed to stifle every attempt to put in an attack.

By mid-July the Allied Armies were stuck in Normandy. The nasty phrase 'stalemate' hung over Allied ground operations like a cloud, a reminder of the horrible casualties both sides suffered during World War I. Intelligence officers were predicting a German withdraw at any moment. The Allies knew, through *ULTRA*, that the Germans were short of everything, they had not been getting reinforcements to replace their personnel losses and they were short of ammunition, fuel, spare parts, and transportation. Yet German resistance seemed to be as stout as ever.

After some delay, the British launched Operation *Goodwood* on July 18. The attack was preceded by Allied bombers that dropped 7,000 tons of bombs in the Caen area. The British attack gained seven miles at its deepest penetration and served to retain the bulk of German armor on the Allied right flank, near Caen. Yet the operation did not live up to the expectations of many senior officers at Supreme Allied Headquarters (SHAEF), including General Eisenhower, who expressed disbelief that the Allied Armies could expect to blast their way through France at the rate of 1,000 tons of bombs per mile.[46]

Operation *Goodwood* was called off on July 20 due to heavy rains and severe losses in British armored divisions. Allied interest then shifted to the left flank, where US VII Corps under Major General "Lightning Joe" Collins was preparing an attack near St. Lo as a complement to Montgomery's right hook at Caen. After sloshing their way through the swamps of the Carentan peninsula and the Normandy hedgerows, the Americans had only days before secured relatively open, dry ground along the St. Lo-Periers road.

---

[45]   Bradley, *A General's Life*, 271.
[46]   Butcher, 617.

Eisenhower wrote to Montgomery on July 21, "Now we are pinning our immediate hopes on Bradley's attack, which should get off tomorrow or on the first good day."[47]

Bradley's offensive was called Operation *Cobra*. It was led by J. Lawton Collins, commanding US VII Corps. Collins had been given the name "Lightning Joe" for his exploits in the Pacific Theater. He had three infantry divisions assigned for the initial assault: 4th, 9th, and 83rd. Allied medium and heavy bombers were to saturation bomb a rectangle-shaped area one mile deep by three miles wide just south of the St. Lo-Periers highway. The bombing was to be immediately followed up with an infantry attack through the hard crust of German defenses to vital road junctions in the German rear. Once the main defensive positions had been silenced and the road junctions occupied by the infantry, General Collins planned to unleash his armored divisions to begin the exploitation phase of the operation.

After one day's delay due to bad weather, *Cobra* began on July 25. The attack began with a devastating display of Allied airpower. Over 2,430 Allied heavy, medium, and fighter bombers dropped more than 4,000 tons of bombs on a 2,500 by 6,000 yard area south of the St. Lo-Periers road.[48] Just like the day before, some bombs fell short and into American lines. The 30th US Infantry Division suffered most of the casualties. General Lesley McNair went forward with the troops to watch the bombing. He was killed by one of the short bombs.

Despite the devastation wrought by Allied bombing, German resistance at the point of the attack remained strong. The 9th US Infantry Division met fierce resistance as it headed to the town of Marigny. 4th Infantry found the same resistance on their way to La Chapelle. Although the early infantry attacks did not secure their objectives, their attacks did clear enough of the critical access roads to St. Giles and Marigny for General Collins to get a reasonably accurate picture of the German defenses. General Collins later wrote, ". . . noting a lack of coordination in the German reaction, particularly their failure to launch prompt counterattacks, I sensed that their communications and command structure had been damaged more than our troops realized."[49] Late that afternoon, Collins alerted 1st Infantry, CCB

---

[47]   Chandler, (Ed.), *The Eisenhower Papers, Vol. III*, 2019.

[48]   Bradley, *A General's Life*, 280.

[49]   J. Lawton Collins, *Lightning Joe, An Autobiography*, (Novato, CA: Presidio Press, 1994), 242.

[Combat Command B] of Third Armored and General Brook's 2nd Armored Division to be ready to join the attack on the morning of the 26th.

German commanders soon learned that the Americans had hit the center of their line near St. Lo and were moving south of the St. Lo-Periers highway. Generalleutnant Dietrich von Choltitz, commander of the German LXXXIV Corps, committed his reserve, a reinforced regiment of the 353rd Infantry Division near Periers and ordered it to attack toward La-Chapelle-en-Juger. At about the same time, German Seventh Army Commander, Generaloberst Paul Hausser, ordered one regiment of the 275th Division toward Chapelle where they were directed to contact Panzer Lehr and reform a line of defense.[50] Although Hausser and Choltitz were not in contact with each other, their attempt to deny the Americans the road net at Chapelle was the same.

Unfortunately, those German reinforcements rushing to La Chapelle did not know that the Allied bombing had shattered Panzer Lehr. General Bayerlein's division was no longer capable of organized resistance. The Regiment from the German 275th Infantry Division had been traveling in daylight when they were caught out in the open by Allied fighter-bombers. A combination of Allied fighter-bombers and American infantry soon decimated the regiment. "The regiment lost all semblance of organization and at the end of the day would be able to find only 200 survivors."[51] Loss of this regiment left the 352nd Division's western flank wide open. The 352nd was defending the Vire River and the village of Hebecrevon. That night von Kluge reported to Hitler's headquarters, ". . . As of this moment, the front has burst."[52] The flanks were still holding, but the Americans were pouring through a three-mile wide hole in the center of the German lines where Panzer Lehr had been crushed.

The Americans had only penetrated the German lines to a depth of about three miles. The crossroads on the St. Lo-Periers road remained in the hands of German paratroopers. The following day, German resistance began to crumble. Major General Edward H. Brooks commanded 2nd US Armored Division. His division was to protect the right flank of the COBRA Operation by taking the high ground and road junctions. General Maurice Rose's Combat Command A led the division toward St. Gilles over

---

50   Martin Blumenson, *The Duel for France, 1944,* (Cambridge: Da Capo Press, 2000), 99.
51   Blumenson, *The Duel*, 100.
52   Blumenson, *The Duel,* 100.

terrain pockmarked by bomb craters. Rose's column met little resistance. By mid-afternoon on July 26th CCA was rolling through St. Gilles to the high ground five miles south. The pace of the offensive suggested that a breakthrough might be at hand.

At the west end of the American attack, near Periers, the 330th Infantry Regiment found the going tough; they were not able to secure the critical crossroads on the St. Lo-Periers highway from the German paratroopers. However, elements of the 4th US Infantry Division took La Chapelle and drove forward three miles into the German center. By mid-afternoon, the US 30th Infantry was moving forward against weak opposition. General Collins was now convinced that *Cobra* had broken through the main German defenses; their counterattacks were weak and uncoordinated, ". . . he told the infantry divisions to continue their attacks through the night."[53]

CCB of 3rd Armored Division was attached to 1st US Infantry Division for *Cobra*. They encountered slight, uncoordinated resistance between the St. Lo highway and Marigny. They were supposed to clear the road to Marigny and then veer off on the road to Coutances. But at Marigny they ran into elements from the German 353rd Division and two companies from the 2nd SS Panzer Division. Marigny was not cleared until the morning of the 27th. By midnight, they had advanced five miles down the Coutances road.

Major General Troy H. Middleton commanded the US VIII Corps. There were four infantry divisions initially assigned to his Corps: 8th, 79th, 83rd and 90th. Middleton's corps met strong enemy resistance when they jumped off on the morning of July 26. By the next morning the Germans had gone, all they found on their front were huge mine fields and assorted booby traps left behind by the enemy. The four divisions advanced against light opposition. The 90th US Infantry Division took the town of Periers. The 8th and 79th Divisions had moved forward nearly ten miles and were close to Coutances.

On July 27, late in the morning, US 2nd Armored Division committed CCB, commanded by Brigadier General Isaac D. White. White's mission was to drive hard for the coastline behind the Germans, hoping to trap a large number of the withdrawing Germans. CCB's reconnaissance battalion took the lead and made excellent progress until they ran into a German roadblock southwest of Canisy. With help from a mobile battery of artillery and a flight of Allied fighter-bombers attacking strong points on a German-held ridge line, the resistance was overwhelmed. CCB continued their advance the following day and arrived at Cerences, deep in the German rear. It slowly

---

[53] Blumenson, *The Duel,* 101.

became apparent to the Americans that they had trapped a huge enemy force near the town of Roncey.

By July 28, the lack of communications had created much confusion within the German high command. According to Martin Blumenson, ". . . in the LXXXIV Corps coastal sector . . . communications were virtually nonexistent. The corps headquarters had hardly any contact with its divisions . . . Some troops found Americans already behind them."[54]

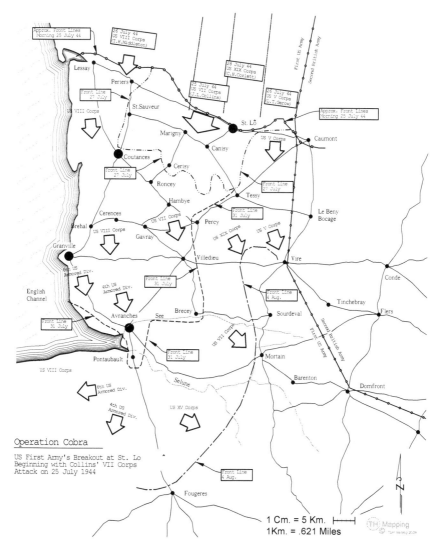

54   Blumenson, *The Duel*, 117,118.

An armored car fired on General Hausser near Gavray. An American reconnaissance patrol killed Christian Tychsen, the Commander of the 2nd SS Panzer Division, near his headquarters.[55] Hausser thought they should be able to break out of the trap by attacking southeast toward Percy.

On July 29, flights of P-47s from the 405th Fighter-Bomber Group found an "airmen's dream" over what became known as 'the Roncey pocket.' P-47 pilots, flying in stacked columns above the town, took turns unleashing their 3.5-inch rockets into the mass of German infantry, tanks, artillery, and assorted vehicles. CCB's tanks and artillery lobbed their shells into this roiling caldron of smoke and fire. The Allied air and artillery attack at Roncey lasted over six hours. According to Martin Blumenson, "More than 100 German tanks and over 250 vehicles were later found in various stages of wreckage; others had been abandoned intact . . . (US) intelligence officers guessed that fuel shortages had caused the Germans to abandon their equipment, but the fact was that the Germans had fled on foot to escape the devastating fire rained down upon them."[56]

On Bradley's left flank, just south of St. Lo, Major General Charles H. Corlett's XIX US Corps was supposed to join the attack one day after the main attack went forward. Initially, only Major General Paul W. Baade's 35th Infantry Division participated in a limited offensive. They shelled the ridges south of St. Lo on July 26. By the next day, it was obvious that the Germans were withdrawing. General Baade received permission from General Corlett to mount a regular attack and easily secured the ridgelines and several Vire River bridges south of St. Lo.

Field Marshal Guenther von Kluge had taken additional steps to plug the hole in the center of his Seventh Army line opposite the Americans. He created the XLVII Panzer Corps out of the 2nd and 116th Panzer Divisions with orders to assemble on the west bank of the Vire River and prepare to attack northwest from the vicinity of Tessy-sur-Vire. These divisions were taken from General Heinrich Eberbach's Panzer Group West near Caen.

As von Kluge was assembling his forces, Major General Charles Corlett was ordered to move XIX US Corps to the west bank of the Vire River. On July 28, Corlett had assembled the 28th, 29th, and 30th Infantry Divisions on the west bank of the Vire River. He also had CCA (Combat Command A) of the 2nd Armored Division available for offensive operations. It was reinforced

---

55   Blumenson, *The Duel,* 118.
56   Blumenson, *The Duel,* 122.

by one infantry regiment. The 30th Infantry Division would secure the Vire River bridges while CCA of 2nd Armored probed forward in the direction of Tessy-sur-Vire. 30th Infantry and CCA of 2nd Armored ran into von Kluge's 2nd Panzer Division and came to an immediate stop. 29th US Infantry arrived just in time to engage the 116th Panzer Division. By the time the green 28th Infantry Division arrived, the battle had become a slugging match. It lasted for four days. "It's a madhouse here," von Kluge screamed into his phone during the morning of July 31, "You can't imagine what it's like . . . Commanders are completely out of contact with their troops."[57] Although the Americans took Tessy on August 1, they were far behind schedule.

Delay for the Americans meant that XIX Corps would be a few days late in taking Tessy-sur-Vire. Delay for the Germans meant that the six-mile gap in their front had become a 12-mile gap. The German left flank from St. Lo to the coast was now wide open. Pete Corlett's XIX Corps had done some hard fighting so that Collins' VII Corps could continue their drive south. By July 31, VII Corps had reached the base of Cotentin peninsula, which was over 30 miles south of St. Lo. The exploitation phase of *Cobra* was over for VII Corps.

American eyes now fixed on the right flank along the coast, where Troy Middleton's VIII Corps was driving hard for the road net at Avranches and the bridges over the See and Selune Rivers. Major General John S. Wood's 4th Armored and Major General Robert W. Grow's 6th Armored Divisions now moved forward to spearhead VIII Corps' drive into Brittany. Neither division had gained much ground on July 29, but 4th Armored took 125 prisoners and seemed to be in a better position to take Avranches.

The handling of prisoners was becoming a problem. Armored spearheads are not supposed to stop. Therefore, they developed a new procedure for handling the increasing number of Germans who chose to surrender. The new procedure was to disarm the prisoner and send him to the rear without guards. "The 4th and 6th Armored Divisions together had taken more than 4,000 prisoners on July 31. The 79th and 8th Infantry Divisions moving behind the armor on the back country roads had done little more than process an additional 3,000 prisoners, some of them so happy to be out of the war they were giggling in delight."[58]

In spite of their dire situation, small battle groups of Germans were still trying to escape to the east. "During the night of July 29-30 . . . some 1,200 men from the 2nd SS Panzers and the 17th SS Panzer Grenadiers, supported by

57   Blumenson, *The Duel,* 135.
58   Blumenson, *The Duel,* 143,144.

about ninety tanks, assault guns, and other armored vehicles surviving from the Roncey concentration, pierced the cordon of the 3rd Battalion, 67th Armored Regiment just north of St. Denis-le-Gast."[59] The Germans overran the American command post and most of them escaped. But they did leave behind some 500 prisoners. Another group of 2,500 Germans from the 2nd SS Panzer Division hit American defensive positions near Cambry. After a six-hour battle, 1,000 Germans were captured and 100 German vehicles destroyed.[60]

CCB 4th US Armored Division, commanded by Brigadier General Holmes E. Dager, entered Avranches on the evening of July 30. They found the city undefended and two bridges over the See River still intact. Several large bodies of German stragglers passed through Avranches during the night of July 30. At one point, the Germans briefly regained control over one of the See River bridges, but they were more interested in escaping than in controlling the bridge and disappeared just as quickly as they came.

Kluge was desperate. He could not contact either Hausser or von Choltitz, communications with other German officers who were in a position to influence the events at Avranches was nearly impossible. "As the rout gathered momentum, it became quite evident that Kluge was unable to find out what was going on. His signals to Hausser's Seventh Army, demanding information, remained unanswered, but Hausser couldn't help much himself . . . On the 31st [of July] Kluge was finally able to signal to Hitler that the Americans . . . occupied Avranches . . . and had ripped open the whole Western Front."[61]

Finally von Kluge got in touch with General Wilhelm Farmbacher, Commanding the 15th German Corps in Brittany. The situation at Avranches was critical. Von Kruge asked Farmbacher what he could do to help. Farmbacher was not sure, but he later telephoned von Kluge with the message that Colonel Rudolf Bacherer and elements of the German 77th Infantry Division were on the road toward Pontaubault. Along the way, Colonel Bacherer was able to find some additional field artillery and remnants of the 5th German Parachute Division.[62]

---

[59] Russell F. Weigley, *Eisenhower's Lieutenants: The Campaign of France and Germany 1944-1945,* (Bloomington: The Indiana University Press, 1990), 160. Also Blumenson, *The Duel,* 122, 123.

[60] Blumenson, *The Duel,* 122, 123. Also Paul Hausser, *Seventh Army in Normandy*, *(25 Jul-20 Aug 44)*, (Europe: Historical Division, Headquarters US Army, undated), 14-24.

[61] F.W. Winterbotham, *The Ultra Secret,* (New York: Harper & Row, Publishers, 1974), 147.

[62] Blumenson, *The Duel*, 143. Also, see Eddy Florentin, *The Battle of the Falaise Gap*, translation, Mervyn Savill, (New York: Hawthorn Books, Inc., 1967, First

On the morning of July 31, just west of Pontaubault, Colonel Bacherer ran into General Dager's CCB from 4th Armored. The weather was terrible; it was raining with heavy cloud cover. Ideal weather for the Germans because it hampered allied air cover. Using artillery hidden along the mountainous, switchback roads and the villages of Saint-Quentin and Saint Martin, Bacherer's forces drove CCB back. After four hours of heavy fighting on the road switchbacks, the issue was far from decided; in some places it was bloody hand to hand combat. Then, just before noon the skies cleared and one of CCB's red target indicators was seen by a squadron of P-47 fighter-bombers. Within fifteen minutes Bacherer's tanks, artillery and thin skinned vehicles were a smoldering mass of twisted steel. The result, wrote Eddy Florentin, was, ". . . an indescribable chaos and carnage . . ."[63] The sudden arrival of Colonel Bruce C. Clarke's CCA, 4th Armored, sealed Bacherer's fate. All three bridges at Avranches and Pontontaubault were captured intact and were now held with considerable force.

The outcome of *Cobra* was beyond anything Bradley or Collins could have hoped for "The LXXXIV Corps was smashed, the II Parachute Corps beaten, and the Seventh Army defeated. The way was open to even greater German disaster . . . incalculable results. Brittany was at hand, and Paris was within reach. Prospects for the future were unlimited."[64]

The war in Europe had entered a new phase. Gone were the swamps and bloody hedgerows of the Carentan, where a carefully planned and executed attack might gain a few hundred yards at terrible cost. Gone too was the war of the sergeants, the lieutenants and captains. Suddenly, daily gains were measured in miles. Advances of ten, twenty, and even fifty miles a day would become the new standard. Before COBRA, Montgomery's and Bradley's plans had been broken by stout German defenders and bad ground. Suddenly a wealth of tactical opportunities presented themselves. Ralph Ingersoll later wrote, "Armed forces are like that; they are at the mercy of the decisive reactions of their commanders. Without the necessary orders, nothing happens—regardless of how alert and able the junior commanders and their forces may be."[65] Now, for the first time since the invasion, what the generals did or did not do would become extremely important.

American Edition), 13.

[63] Florentin, 13, 14.

[64] Blumenson, *The Duel*, 150.

[65] Ralph Ingersoll, *Top Secret*, (New York: Harcourt, Brace, 1946), 153.

With the Normandy invasion and the battle of the hedgerows behind him, General Bradley could look forward to a more mobile phase of operations with a new confidence in the men he led. On August 1, Bradley gave up Command of the First Army to assume Command of the new 12th US Army Group. General Courtney Hodges was given Command of First Army. A new US army was created by adding VIII US Corps to the newly arriving XII, XV, and XX Corps. The new Army was the US Third, and its commander was, according to General Bradley, ". . . the strangest duck I have ever known."[66]

General George S. Patton Jr. was patiently awaiting his turn on the stage. He was about to prove to General Bradley why George Marshall and Dwight Eisenhower felt this particular loud mouthed, profane, arrogant son-of-a-bitch was worth saving.

George Patton had spent nearly a year in his commander's doghouse for two slapping incidents in Sicily and an inappropriate political assessment of post-war global domination by Great Britain and the United States. This was the so-called Knutsford Incident, where, in a public speech, Patton supposedly had forgotten to mention the Russians.[67] Lacking command authority, Patton had been helping Troy Middleton with VIII Corps since the beginning of *COBRA*.

Now, on August 1, Patton took command of Third Army. He would provide something the Americans had lacked in Normandy: a sense of urgency, an audacity, and a ruthless driving power. The result for the US Army in Europe was a variation of the German blitzkrieg operating under the protective cover of the most effective fighter-bombers built during the war: Thunderbolts, Mustangs, and Typhoons. Within a few days, Eisenhower was giving his boss in Washington the good news, news he knew would please the chief: ". . . Patton is . . . on the marching wing of our forces."[68]

With Hodges at First Army, Patton at Third Army, and Bradley at the newly created US 12th Army Group, the new chain of command was nearly complete. There was one General who was less than pleased with these developments; that was British General Bernard L. Montgomery. Additionally, it had been decided before the invasion, that when Bradley became Army Group Commander, General Eisenhower would step up and take Command of Allied Ground Forces.

---

[66] Bradley, *A General's Life*, 98.

[67] Farago, 417, 418.

[68] Alfred D. Chandler Jr., Editor, *The Papers of D. D. Eisenhower, Vol. IV*, (Baltimore: The Johns Hopkins Press, 1970), 2062.

In other words, he would take Montgomery's job. Citing poor communications at his headquarters near Granville, code named *SHELLBURST*, Eisenhower declined to take command on August 1.

Patton, under orders from General Bradley, rushed his people into Brittany. Getting through the restricted road net at Avranches-Pontaubault was a stroke of genius. Patton put five divisions across the one bridge at Pontaubault in less than seventy-two hours. ". . . (We) are cutting the 90th Division through the same town and on the same street being used by two armored and two other infantry divisions. There is no other way of doing it at this time."[69] Patton had sent Robert Grow's 6th Armored Division heading for Brest and John S. Wood's 4th Armored Division to Vannes. General Wood later said, "It was one of the colossally stupid decisions of the war."[70] Wood was right; 4th and 6th Armored Divisions should have moved north onto the open German flank. General Patton had no hand in determining allied strategy in this phase of the war. He was simply following Bradley's orders.

Patton's gift for speed did not fail him, but the Allies were following an outmoded plan. The German left flank had disappeared; France lay open to Patton's tanks. The Brittany ports Grow and Wood were rushing toward would shortly become useless. It was August 2nd before Bradley and Montgomery realized they were heading in the wrong direction. Patton had sent Wood's Division to Vannes to seal off the base of the Brittany peninsula. Sending all of Patton's Third Army into Brittany to open up the ports had been part of the original plan, but the collapse of the German left flank created opportunities in central France that banished Patton's Brittany operations into history's dustbin.

Bradley told Troy Middleton on August 2, "I don't care if we get Brest tomorrow—or ten days later. Once we isolate the Brittany Peninsula we'll get it anyhow."[71] Bradley later told Patton they persisted in the Brest attack, and spent so many Americans lives on it to maintain the illusion that the US Army never lost a battle. Unfortunately, Brest, Lorient, and the other Brittany Ports were all useless; none were ever used to supply Allied forces. John Wood's 4th Armored barely made it out of Brittany in time for the last battle in Normandy, arriving at Le Mans on August 13. Grow's 6th Armored didn't make it out in time; they took the scenic route to Brest. Brest finally fell to the Americans

---

[69]   Blumenson, (Ed.), *The Patton Papers 1940-1945*, 495.

[70]   Liddell Hart, *History of the Second World War*, 557. From Eric Larrabee, *Commander in Chief*, (New York, Simon & Schuster, Touchstone, 1988), 466.

[71]   Farago, 489.

after a three-division assault on September 15. "The port, captured at the cost of 10,000 American casualties, was not put back in operation."[72]

Hitler insisted that his generals defend every yard of French territory. Clearly, the Germans had overstayed their welcome. "The failure of the Germans to withdraw in textbook fashion," Bradley wrote, "began to suggest to us a fabulous opportunity. We might be able to trap the Germans west of the Seine . . . Since this opportunity had not been anticipated in the Overlord plan; it required some hasty and rather radical revisions in our thinking."[73] At this time, the Allies were still following the original plan that detailed a power drive to the Seine by three Allied Armies: First Canadian, Second British, and First US. This was the "wide envelopment plan." Bradley's new plan would move the Allied pivot into the American sector between Vire and Mortain, and change the objective to some area 'west of the Seine.' Montgomery's second British Army was still only a few miles south of Caen. Caen was their D-day objective.

While the Allies were mulling their options, Hitler and his generals in East Prussia saw an opportunity to rebuild their defenses in Normandy. What they feared most was a mobile battle for France. With superior Allied mobility and complete control of the air over France, it was a battle the Germans knew they would not win. If the Allies broke out of Normandy, the Germans knew the battle for France was already lost.

Looking at a map, Hitler saw an opportunity to drive through Mortain to Avranches and the sea, cutting off Patton's Third US Army, and letting it wither on the vine. If they could concentrate their armored divisions near Mortain, Hitler was convinced an attack could breakthrough to the coast, cutting off Third Army. According to *ULTRA* Messages XL 4405 and XL 4426 plans for the German attack into the American flank at Mortain, Operation *Luttich [*misspelled *Luettwitz]*, were already being implemented by August 2. The Allies knew the name of the German operation, *Luttich*, they knew it involved withdrawing certain armored divisions from the front near Caen, but they did not know specifically what *Luttich* was or where it would take place. Unfortunately for the Germans, those flags for divisions Hitler and his generals were moving around on battle maps in East Prussia bore little resemblance to the armored divisions Hitler had sent to war in 1940 and 1941.

---

[72]   Geoffrey Perret, *There's A War to be Won: The United States Army in World War II,* (New York: Ballantine, 1997), 344.

[73]   Bradley, *A General's Life,* 290.

In most cases, they were little more than shells of divisions, humbled by their experiences on the eastern front and soundly hammered by the British at Caen.

General Bradley must have appreciated the good old pre-*ULTRA* days. He wrote, "Recently some historians have begun to write that Ultra alerted us to this counterattack almost at inception . . . My recollection is in sharp variance. In this instance, Ultra was of little or no value . . . (Ralph) Bennett states categorically that Ultra 'knew nothing' of Hitler's August 2nd order, and did not detect the offensive until mere hours before it was launched."[74] This, of course, is simply not true. XL 4405 had warned the Allies about *Luttich* on August 2, but contained no specific information about the operation, what it was or where it would take place. F.W. Winterbotham suggested that the Allies knew about *Luttich* from that same date, August 2, and planned for both the defense at Mortain and the short envelopment from Le Mans-Argentan-Falaise beginning at that time.[75]

Bradley's suggestion that *ULTRA,* ". . . did not detect the operation until mere hours before it was launched,"[76] is also problematic. Bradley was probably referring to *ULTRA* message XL 4991, which was not released to Allied officers until 1912 hours on August 6. In that case, Bradley is right, he had only a few hours to prepare for the German attack, and probably could not have done much more than alert his units to move to the area involved. But there was another *ULTRA* message that Bradley fails to mention. *ULTRA* message XL 4913 was released to Allied officers at 0624 hours on August 6. XL 4913 was very specific and its wording could not have confused anyone: "REPORTED BATTLE GROUP ASSEMBLING . . . RECCE FORCES BEING SENT OUT TO SOUTHWEST. COVERING LINE AT SOUTH EDGE FORET DE MORTAIN (&) FORET DE MORTAIN . . . OTTE PREVIOUSLY WITH ONE SEVEN SUGAR SUGAR DIVISION. FOR AMALGAMATION TWO SUGAR SUGAR AND ONE SEVEN SUGAR SUGAR DIVISIONS."[77] XL 4913 described a battle group of the 2nd and 17th SS Divisions assembling near the forest at Mortain. This could mean only one thing, a German attack through Mortain to Avranches. If German armor was going to cover an infantry withdraw from Normandy, they would be deployed much further north and east. The concentration of German armor this far west had to mean a German attack in the Mortain sector. Allied intelligence could not have missed it.

---

[74] Bradley, *A General's Life*, 291.
[75] Winterbotham, 148-150.
[76] Bradley, *A General's Life,* 291.
[77] *ULTRA* Intercept # 4913.

General Dwight D. Eisenhower, Supreme Commander, Allied
Expeditionary Force

General D. D. Eisenhower, the Supreme Allied Commander and
General O. N. Bradley, Commanding, 12th US Army Group

Left to right: Generals Omar N. Bradley, Commanding, First US Army, Dwight D. Eisenhower, the Supreme Allied Commander, Leonard T. Gerow, Commanding, US V Corps and J. Lawton Collins, Commanding, US VII Corps

J. Lawton Collins, Commanding, US VII Corps

ZZ

XL 4405 £ 4405 SH 80 £ 80 SHA 27 £ 27 AG 19

19 FU 65 £ 65 AGA 39 £ 39 ON CR YK ZE RF 35 £

; TA 74 £ 74 %

NZER GRUPPE WEST STATED)) THAT LAST PANZER

OMPANY WOULD LEAVE NOT £ NOT LATER THAN

VENTYNINTH JULY FOR LUETTWITZ £ LUETTWITZ.

COMMENT GOC £ GOC TWO PANZER DIVISION)

ELC/AHW/JB   020612Z/8/44

REF. CX/MSS/T267/146.   XL 4913.

((XL 4913 £ 4913 SH 48 £ 48 SHA 93 £ 93 TG 60 £ 60 BV 87 £
87 ON YK XX ZE EF 89 £ 89 ST 53 £ 53 DL 52 £ 52 ?

FLIVO OTTE IM KAMPE £ OTTE IM KAMPE (ABLE) ORDERED ONE SIX
THREE NOUGHT HOURS FIFTH TO)) PROCEED IMMEDIATELY TO EIGHT
FOUR DIVISION.   INFORMATION ON OPERATIONAL AREA TO BE
OBTAINED FROM CORPS AND ARRIVAL AT NEW HOW QUEEN TO BE
REPORTED.   (BAKER) AT ONE EIGHT ONE FIVE HOURS FIFTH
REPORTED BATTLE GROUP ASSEMBLING AREA LE FRESNE PORET £ LE
FRESNE PORET RECCE FORCES BEING SENT OUT TO SOUTHWEST.
COVERING LINE AT SOUTHERN EDGE FORET DE MORTAIN £ FORET DE
MORTAIN.   COMMENT. FLIVO OTTE £ OTTE PREVIOUSLY WITH ONE
SEVEN SUGAR SUGAR DIVISION.   FOR AMALGAMATION TWO SUGAR
SUGAR AND ONE SEVEN SUGAR SUGAR DIVISIONS ON SECOND SEE XL
£ XL FOUR SIX THREE NINE.   HOW QUEEN TWO SUGAR SUGAR
DIVISION LE FRESNET PORET £ LE FRESNET PORET ON FIFTH SEE
XL £ XL FOUR EIGHT NOUGHT ONE.   SUGGEST (BAKER) STILL
REFERS ONE SEVEN SUGAR SUGAR DIVISION/

APGP/AHW/HB   060624Z/8/44.

CX/MSS/T268/71   XL 4991

ZZZZ

((XL 4991 £ 4991 SH 1 £ 1 SHA 46 £ 46 TG 2 £ 2 BY 29
£ 29 ON YK ZE RF 39 £ 39 ST 87 £ 87 DL 72 £ 72
AD 63 £ 63 %

ONE FOUR HOURS SIXTH SECOND SUGAR SUGAR DIVISION
REQUESTED NIGHT FIGHTER OPERATIONS FOR PROTECTION
OF OWN ATTACK OVER AREA SAINT CLEMENT £ SAINT
CLEMENT TARE SIX TWO ONE THREE - SAINT HILAIRE
£ SAINT HILAIRE (STRONG INDICATIONS TARE FOUR
SEVEN NOUGHT THREE), AND DAY FIGHTERS ON SEVENTH
OVER SAME AREA

WM/HYD/BMF   0619 12Z/8/44

Patton confirms the *ULTRA* warning in an August 7th Diary entry: "We got a rumor last night from a secret source that several panzer divisions will attack west from . . . Mortain . . . on Avranches. Personally, I think it is a German bluff to cover a withdraw, but I stopped the 80th, French 2nd Armored, and 35th (Divisions) in the vicinity of St. Hilaire just in case something might happen."[78] Patton would not have had time to deploy those divisions if he had received no warning. Bradley's memory about *ULTRA* and the German counterattack at Mortain must have failed him.

The Germans attacked during the night of August 6/7, with three panzer divisions near Mortain and initially drove the Americans back. The 2nd SS Panzer Division and elements from the 17th SS Panzer Grenadiers, ". . . advanced against the 30th (Division) in two columns, overran Mortain from north and south, and plunged on southwestward almost to St. Hilaire by noon."[79] They took Mortain but could not take Hill 317. There, the 2nd Battalion, along with Company K of the 3rd Battalion, 120th Infantry Regiment, was surrounded on a rocky outcropping just east of town. They succeeded in calling down extremely accurate artillery barrages on the attacking Germans, with an excellent view of ". . . the whole area of the counterattack, the Selune River valley from Domfront twenty-five kilometers eastward, to the Bay of Mont St. Michel beyond Avranches thirty-two kilometers to the west . . . all the columns of the 2nd SS Panzer Division."[80]

For the next five days, men from the 2nd Battalion remained surrounded. They refused repeated demands for their surrender and remained a huge problem for the Germans until their relief. Barely 400 of the original 700 men holding Hill 317 walked off when they were relieved, the rest were dead, wounded, or captured.[81] But the Germans paid a price too, "When they (2nd Battalion) were relieved on August 12 their positions were ringed with heaps of German dead."[82]

An attack around sunrise by the 2nd Panzer Division enjoyed more success. They struck north of St. Barthelemy west toward Le Mesnil Tove, ". . . overrunning two companies of the 30th Division's 117th Infantry and almost encircling the rest of the regiment before American artillery forced the Germans to halt . . ."[83]

---

[78]   Martin Blumenson (Editor), *The Patton Papers, 1940-1945,* (Boston: Houghton Mifflin, 1974), 503.

[79]   Weigley, *Eisenhower's Lieutenants,* 196.

[80]   Weigley, *Eisenhower's Lieutenants,* 196.

[81]   Weigley, *Eisenhower's Lieutenants,*.200.

[82]   Perret, 349.

[83]   Weigley, *Eisenhower's Lieutenant's,* 197.

Once the morning fog cleared, Allied fighter-bombers discovered the leading columns of 2nd SS Panzer near Le Coudray and stopped them cold.[84] US 3rd Armored Division's CCB ran into 1st SS Panzer just west of St Barthelemy and checked their advance. Meanwhile, the Commander of the German 116th Panzer Division complained that his division was too heavily engaged to put in a proper attack. His division arrived very late in the afternoon, and after a cursory attack, ". . . was stopped dead by an American anti-tank screen."[85]

Two US armored divisions played a huge part in spoiling von Kluge's offensive by sealing off the flanks of the German penetration. Leland Hobbs, commanding 30th Infantry, was given CCB from 3rd Armored Division. He directed it to the south bank of the See River to seal off the northern flank. CCA from 3rd Armored and elements from 30th Infantry had launched a pre-dawn attack toward Barenton from the west, when they ran into the left flank of German attack and elements of the 2nd SS Panzers and the 17th SS Panzer Grenadiers.

Major General Edward H. Brooks and his 'Hell on Wheels' 2nd US Armored Division just happened to be in the area. As the senior officer, Brooks was given command of 3rd Armored's CCA and those elements of 30th Infantry in the vicinity of Barenton. "With considerable chunks of both of the big, old-style armored divisions, he had collected a strong holding force on the southern flank."[86] Just to make sure about the southern flank, Bradley gave Collins Major General P. W. Baade's 35th Infantry Division, which had been on its way to join Patton's Third Army south of Avranches. By that evening Baade had his division off, ". . . the Mortain-Barenton road just south of Hill 317."[87]

It was obvious to generals on both sides that the German attack was not going to succeed. Bradley had more forces in the Mortain vicinity than he needed, so he sent Wade Haislip's XV Corps northeast toward Le Mans.[88] On the evening of August 7, Bradley was thinking about the Canadian attack toward Falaise and the German attack at Mortain when it struck him. "If the Canadians could push into Falaise and beyond to Argentan, and if I turned Haislip due north from Le Mans toward Argentan, there was a good chance

---

[84]   Hastings, *Overlord*, 285.

[85]   Hastings, *Overlord*, 285.

[86]   Weigley, *Eisenhower's Lieutenants*, 198.

[87]   Blumenson, *The Duel*, 230.

[88]   Bradley, *A General's Life*, 293.

that we could encircle and trap the whole German force in Normandy in a matter of a few days."[89] Bradley's plan would later be called 'the short envelopment.'

It was a sound tactical plan, literally leaping off the map. It was also far superior to Montgomery's wider 'Seine envelopment' because, as Bradley said, ". . . the 'wheel' would be smaller, we could go immediately, without waiting for logistical buildup."[90] Bradley's plan took advantage of the German's ill-advised attack at Mortain; Montgomery's wide envelopment did not. The plan did have one drawback. It was not General Montgomery's plan, and everyone knew how General Montgomery liked his own plans.

[89]   Bradley, *A General's Life,* 294.
[90]   Bradley, *A General's Life,* 294.

Chapter 2

General Bradley at the Falaise Gap

"I believe that the (halt) order . . . emanated from the 21st Army Group, and was either due to [British] jealousy of the Americans or to utter ignorance of the situation or to a combination of the two. It was very regrettable that the XV Corps was ordered to halt, because it could have gone on to Falaise . . . and definitely and positively closed the escape gap."[91] G.S. Patton Jr., Diary entry made August 16, 1944.

The more he thought about it, the better the plan looked. Bradley presented the plan to his staff; they liked it. He tracked down Eisenhower on the battlefield and went over the basics of the plan in the back seat of Eisenhower's Packard.[92] Eisenhower liked the plan so much they returned to Bradley's headquarters to go over it in detail. After a fuller explanation, Eisenhower approved the plan. Bradley later wrote, "While Ike was still at my CP, I telephoned Patton and told him to alert Haislip to a move north, from Le Mans toward Argentan."[93] Patton preferred the wider envelopment to the Seine, but quickly saw an excellent opportunity in Bradley's short hook at Argentan. Bradley then called Montgomery, who was worried about the German attack at Mortain, but Bradley convinced him that Hodges and Collins had that attack well in hand. After his concerns about Mortain were satisfied, Montgomery readily agreed to the plan. On August 8, General Bradley had good reason to believe that everyone agreed on the tactical plan. He thought he had all the principals on board: Eisenhower, Montgomery, Patton, and his staff. Everyone agreed the plan held great possibilities. George Patton wrote to his wife, "We may end this in ten days."[94]

The Allied commanders had agreed to implement Bradley's 'short envelopment plan.' It was critical that the Germans now seize the moment

[91] Blumenson, (Ed.), *The Patton Papers 1940-1945*, 508, 509.
[92] For a different explanation of the events about the Allied decision to turn Patton north at Le Mans see F.W. Winterbotham's, *The Ultra Secret*, pages 148 to 158 inclusive.
[93] Bradley, *A General's Life*, 294.
[94] Blumenson, (Ed.), *The Patton Papers, 1940-1945*, 504.

and retire to the Seine while there was still time. The Germans could still conduct an orderly withdraw from Normandy, but that window of time was closing fast. Unfortunately, the German commanders in Normandy were getting unwelcome advice from Hitler. When von Kluge complained that the panzer forces were not up to the task demanded of them at Mortain, Hitler told von Kluge that he had gone in too soon, that he should have waited longer to assemble more tanks and assault guns. Von Kluge may have protested that waiting was becoming a dangerous game; the Americans were pouring through and around his southern flank, heading for Le Mans. If the Americans got to La Mans and turned north every German in Normandy was in danger of encirclement. But Hitler insisted the front at Mortain was to be held at all costs because OKW remained convinced that the Mortain counterattack was still the best way to avoid a mobile battle for France.

George Patton would have liked to widen Bradley's envelopment to the Seine, but once Bradley had given the order Patton immediately saw the advantages in the short envelopment plan. He later wrote, "When I got back [to 3rd Army Headquarters] I wrote an order for the attack of the XV Corps. Hughes and Kenner said it was historic—I hope so."[95] Patton told Haislip on August 4 to attack toward Mayenne and Laval.[96] By the next day, Haislip was in Mayenne. Allied intelligence units on the open German flank were all having the same problem; no one knew where the Germans were. There was little information on the Germans to share. Ladislas Farago wrote, "He did not have to bypass any (Germans). There was no resistance. Nobody knew anything about the enemy simply because there were so few Germans left in Haislip's path."[97]

Patton's enthusiasm was contagious; Haislip had caught it. He issued the following order to all officers of XV Corps: "Push all personnel to the limit of human endurance . . . action during the next few days might be decisive for the entire campaign in Western Europe."[98] The following day, one of Haislip's divisions took Laval; on August 8th they entered Le Mans. Major General Walton Walker's XX Corps was already at the Loire River.

[95]   Blumenson, (Ed.), *The Patton Papers, 1940-1945*, 504.
[96]   Martin Blumenson, *The Battle of the Generals: The Untold Story of the Falaise Pocket—The Campaign That Should Have Won World War II*, (New York: Quill, William Morrow, 1993), 166.
[97]   Farago, 527.
[98]   Farago, 528.

The Germans had sought reinforcement from southern France, but their divisions were arriving late and in little bits and pieces. The German 9th Panzer Division was partially motorized, but the 708th Infantry was horse drawn and on foot. Seventh Army headquarters had recruited the LXXXI Corps from the Seine Sector to buildup a southern flank in the Laval-Le Mans sector, protecting vital German administration and supply installations at Le Mans and Alencon. Haislip's speed caught the Germans completely by surprise; the Americans took Laval almost without firing a shot. This forced LXXXI Corps to commit elements of the 708th Infantry and 9th Panzer as soon as they arrived, without properly organizing either of the units involved or drafting a defensive plan.[99] The Germans were forced to evacuate the administrative offices in Le Mans.

The US 90th Infantry Division joined the 79th Infantry in the rush to Le Mans. Advancing in separate columns, 90th Division elements brushed aside a smaller German force which then retreated into a forest. "Although the Americans judged that only minor forces were present, the 90th Division took 1200 prisoners and destroyed a large part of the reconnaissance battalion of the 9th Panzer Division and a regiment of the 708th. Was this the same 90th Division that had stumbled in the Cotentin?"[100] The record of the 90th Infantry Division showed a marked improvement after Bradley gave command of the 90th to Major General Raymond S. McLain. By the evening of August 8, all three of Haislip's divisions (79th and 90th Infantry and 5th Armored) were approaching Le Mans, by the following morning they controlled all access roads into Le Mans.

Most of August 9 was taken up in reorganization for the drive north toward Argentan, resting, refueling, and resupply. Patton moved the green 80th Infantry Division into the Mayenne-Le Mans gap and assigned it to Haislip. He also assigned the newly arrived (August 1) 2nd French Armored Division to Haislip, giving Haislip a total of four divisions, with one, Major General Horace L. McBride's 80th Infantry, in Corps reserve. French 2nd Armored was commanded by the very able but undisciplined Major General Jacques Leclerc. The French Division had gained combat experience fighting the Germans in North Africa and Italy. Patton advised Haislip to lead with his armor and, since both his flanks were going to be wide open, Patton suggested he attack in depth.

---

99   Blumenson, *The Duel*, 207.
100   Blumenson, *The Duel*, 207.

The plans Patton and Haislip devised sent two armored divisions abreast north toward Argentan. 2nd French Armored was on the left, they would drive through Carrouges and head for the inter Army Group boundary just two miles south of Argentan and west to Ranes. 5th US Armored Division was on the right, they were ordered to proceed north to Sees and then to the road junction town of Argentan and cover the inter Army Group line toward St. Leonard and Gace. Patton and Haislip had borrowed trucks to mobilize two of Haislip's infantry divisions: the 79th and 90th 2nd French Armored Division was supported by McLain's 90th Infantry Division on the left flank; they were given permission to use roads N 12 and N 24 *bis*. On the right flank, the newly motorized 79th Infantry joined 5th Armored in using road N138 *bis* toward Sees.[101]

Patton's plans for protecting Haislip's flanks also involved two new corps: Major General Walton Walker's XX Corps and Major General Gilbert R. Cook's XII Corps. Patton was trying, unsuccessfully so far, to get Bradley to release 35th Division from First Army and Wood's 4th Armored Division from Brittany. He planned to form XX Corps from 7th Armored and 35th Infantry Divisions. He wanted to form Cook's XII Corps from the 4th Armored and 5th Infantry Divisions. He also planned to send XX Corps north on the left flank of Haislip's XV Corps, and XII Corps north on the right flank.[102] Due to changes in the divisions available to Patton on 13 August, these plans were slightly changed.

Haislip's attack began on August 10 and met scattered resistance; very little was known about the Germans in their path. In a series of short, sharp, running battles, they met elements of ". . . the German 708th Infantry Division on the left, the 9th Panzer Division in the center and the 354th Sichrung Regiment on the right."[103] The 708th disintegrated almost on contact, it was, one writer observed, "of poor quality." The 9th Panzer was a tougher unit, and they were well trained. Still, they experienced problems coordinating their defensive plans. One section of the 9th Panzer ended up on the west bank of the Sarthe and the rest of the division was on the east bank; they never succeeded in coordinating their efforts.

---

[101] Florentin, 96.

[102] George S. Patton Jr., *War As I Knew It,* (Boston: Houghton Mifflin, 1975), 104, 105.

[103] Lt. Col. Emmanuel S. Cepeda and others, Committee 2, *The Fifth Armored Division in the Falaise-Argentan Sector*, (Fort Knox, Kentucky: The Armored School, 1950), 52.

Patton estimated that the 9th Panzer destroyed some forty Allied tanks on August 10, but it did not slow Haislip down.[104] The effect of those battles on 9th Panzer was more serious. General Heinrich Eberbach, Commander of Panzer Group Eberbach, later wrote that the 9th Panzer had reported the strength of, ". . . a battalion of infantry, a battalion of artillery, and perhaps a dozen tanks."[105] 9th Panzer Division did survive, but at greatly reduced strength.[106] The German 708th Infantry Division was not so fortunate. The division had been so badly hurt the survivors were judged "ineffective." They were subsequently sent out of the combat zone to rest and recover.[107]

Allied intelligence officers were reading *ULTRA* intercepts of German radio traffic. They witnessed an argument unfolding at the highest levels of the German command. In Normandy, Generals Eberbach and von Kluge agreed that it was not possible to mount a successful attack through Mortain.[108] Hitler's headquarters, OKW, kept insisting that the Mortain counterattack must be carried out with the maximum force available. Messages flew back and forth between Normandy and Germany. Von Kluge was desperate; the Americans had turned north at Le Mans and were heading for Alencon and the German's Seventh Army supply depots. There was little, von Kluge warned, to impede the American advance. Finally, late on the evening of August 11 Hitler relented. Von Kluge could consolidate his front at Mortain and withdraw enough armor to deal with the Americans driving north from Le Mans. He was given permission to attack XV Corps western flank, halting the American advance, as a prerequisite to returning to the Mortain offensive, which Hitler still insisted upon.[109] This was all duly noted by Allied intelligence officers through *ULTRA* and forwarded to Allied Commanders in the field. Eisenhower, Montgomery, and Bradley knew exactly what the Germans were going to do in Normandy, in some cases, before the German commanders in Normandy knew what their orders were going to be.[110]

---

[104]   Patton, 103.

[105]   Blumenson, *The Duel*, 254.

[106]   Heinrich Eberbach, *Panzer Group Eberbach and the Falaise Encirclement*, (Europe: Historical Division, Headquarters, US Army, no date given), 16.

[107]   Blumenson, The *Duel*, 255.

[108]   Eberbach, 11, 13, 14.

[109]   Blumenson, *The Battle of the Generals*, 201; Also see Hastings, *Overlord*, 288 and Weigley, *Eisenhower's Lieutenants*, 203.

[110]   Winterbotham, 150.

As the soap opera was being played out for the *ULTRA* code-breakers at Bletchley Park, General Montgomery decided, on his own, to help Bradley prepare for the "wider, Seine envelopment." "I have instructed BRADLEY," Montgomery telegrammed Brooke on the evening of August 11, "to collect a fresh army Corps of three divisions in the LE MANS area and to hold it ready to push quickly through toward CHARTRES if and when we suddenly put M517 [wide envelopment] into operation."[111] This order must have come as a complete surprise to Bradley. He and Patton intended to use those divisions forming US XII and XX Corps to protect Haislip's flanks.[112] Montgomery's order was doubly disturbing because the Allies had just learned, through *ULTRA*, that the Germans intended to attack Haislip's open western flank.[113]

This was Bradley's first clue that Montgomery was less than pleased with his "short envelopment plan," although Montgomery said nothing in his order that would indicate he intended to cancel the short envelopment at Argentan-Falaise. Bradley must have protested the order, because the disagreement is documented the following day in Chester B. Hansen's diary notes: "There is some discussion now concerning an alleged disagreement in strategy between Brad and Monty concerning the timing for this northward movement. I am told that Monty is anxious that the continued movement toward Paris (the wide envelopment) in seizure of more terrain while Brad is equally insistent that we turn north now at Le Mans and trap the German army . . ."[114] It seems likely the disagreement between Bradley and Montgomery began the minute Bradley received Montgomery's order to retain three divisions at Le Mans. Hansen has faithfully recorded Bradley's position.

There were no discussions at this time between Patton and Haislip or any of the division commanders about the boundary line between US 12th and British 21st Army Groups. Because it was changed five times during the battle, there has been a great deal of historical confusion about the boundary line and the timing of the changes Montgomery directed.[115]

The arbiter of the Army Group boundary line was the Allied Commander of Ground Forces, General Montgomery. The original (pre-invasion) Army

---

[111]   Hamilton, *Master,* 784.
[112]   Patton, 104.
[113]   Bradley, *A General's Life,* 297.
[114]   The Chester B. Hansen Papers, August 12, 1944.
[115]   Francis De Guingand, *Operation Victory,* (London: Hodder and Stoughton, November, 1947), 407, 408. Also, see Bradley, *A General's Life,* 295, 303.

Group boundary showed the line, beginning at its northern most point on the coast, five miles west of Arromanches, south to four miles west of Bayeux, south to one mile west of Caumont, south to one mile east of Vire, south to Domfront and then east to Alencon. The north-south line from Arromanches to Vire remained constant throughout the Normandy campaign, but the southern extension of the boundary line kept shifting north into the area reserved for Montgomery's British 21st Army Group.

On August 3, Montgomery adjusted the boundary line north 14 miles to a line Ranes-Sees. On August 8, as they were discussing the short envelopment, Bradley and Montgomery adjusted the boundary north to just two miles south of the line Argentan-St. Leonard-Evreux. On August 16, after discovering through *ULTRA* that the Germans were still in the Falaise Pocket, Montgomery adjusted the Army Group boundary for the fourth time, by allowing Bradley's forces to penetrate the British zone at Argentan and St. Leonard so they could meet the Poles at Chambois. As soon as the battle was over, Montgomery switched the boundary line back to give his British troops the critical road net of Argentan-St. Leonard-Evreux.[116] It was the last boundary change, the fifth, switching the boundary line back, south of the Argentan and St. Leonard highway, which created a lot of confusion within the Falaise pocket.[117]

After battles with the German 708th Infantry and 9th Panzer Divisions, there was little resistance to Haislip's XV Corps between Le Mans and Argentan. One writer suggested, "As far as delays were concerned, traffic jams were about as bad a nuisance as the Germans."[118] General Haislip, ". . . on the evening of August 11 established Argentan as the new corps objective."[119] By the morning of August 12, the French 2nd Armored was in Alencon. They found the town undefended and captured the bridges over the Sarthe intact. US 5th Armored drove east of Alencon, ". . . rushed through Mamers, and captured Sees."[120] Sees was defended by a bakery company, elements of the struggling 9th Panzer and elements of 116th Panzer were rushed east from the Mortain sector.[121]

---

[116] Chester Wilmot, *The Struggle for Europe*, (Connecticut: Greenwood Press, 1972), Map, The Falaise Pocket, facing p. 417, also see De Guingand, 407.

[117] De Guingand, *Operation Victory*, 408.

[118] Weigley, *Eisenhower's Lieutenants*, 202.

[119] Blumenson, *The Duel*, 254.

[120] Blumenson, *The Duel*, 254.

[121] Eberbach, 16.

With Alencon occupied, the supply depots of the German Seventh Army were now in American hands. Henceforth, Seventh Army would have to rely on Fifth Panzer Army for their daily rations of food, fuel, and ammunition. This was an immediate problem because there were only a few good east-west roads still under German control. Moreover, those roads were usable only during the eight hours of summer darkness due to the omnipresent Allied fighter-bombers.[122] Surface damage and traffic jams on the few available roads reduced vehicle movement to little more than walking speed.

Bradley later wrote that his decisions during the battle of the Falaise Gap were influenced, at least in part, by ". . . the troops under Haislip's command, wishing they were more battle-wise."[123] Bradley points out that Haislip's two armored divisions were inexperienced. This was true of US 5th Armored, but not the French, who had experience in Africa and Italy. Bradley was correct that Leclerc was "notoriously undisciplined and did not speak English."[124] Bradley said he had concerns about I.T. Wyche, commanding 79th Infantry and McLain of the 90th Infantry. Both concerns turned out to be terribly misplaced. In fact, McLain was so good that in a few months he would be commanding a corps. Bradley was correct about the 80th Infantry being green, but then nearly all divisions coming from the US at this time of the war were green. But green is an indication of inexperience, not incompetence. Major Generals Wyche of the 79th Infantry and McBride of the 80th commanded their divisions with honor and distinction throughout the war. Neither general was relieved for incompetence.

The 2nd French Armored Division drove on to Carrouges. Fifth US Armored Division cleared Sees and headed north to Argentan. The southern access to Argentan was compromised by a huge forest, the Foret d' Ecouves. Haislip assigned the roads west of the forest, N 12 and N 24 *bis* to 2nd French Armored and the road east of the forest, N 138 *bis* to 5th Armored Division.[125] Haislip did not recommend anyone use the road through the forest due to the possibility of a German ambush. The forest was a good place for Germans to hide from Allied fighter-bombers. General Leclerc decided that 2nd French Armored should beat the Americans into Argentan and would therefore require all three roads. The 2nd French Armored blocked the refueling efforts of 5th Armored's Combat Command A.

---

[122] Eberbach, 17.
[123] Bradley, *A General's Life*, 297.
[124] Bradley, *A General's Life*, 296.
[125] Florentin, 96.

Blumenson wrote, ". . . an American combat command north of Sees—five miles short of Argentan—had to postpone its attack for six hours until the French cleared the road. Only then could gasoline trucks . . . come forward to refuel the American tanks."[126]

As the Americans and French closed on Argentan, enemy resistance stiffened. CCA, 5th Armored continued their advance with excellent air support and close coordination with 5th Armored's artillery. CCA commander, Brigadier General Eugene A. Regnier wrote: "By August 12, 1900, CCA was in that portion of Argentan . . . south of the Orne River. Here I halted the advance. The command had accomplished its assigned task to wit: Blocking of the escape routes—south and east of Argentan . . ."[127] Fifth Armored's CCR had one task force near the inter-Army Group boundary line at Exmes and another task force near Gace.[128] The following afternoon, the French would send a small reconnaissance force of infantry into Argentan; they would stay a few hours before leaving the town to the Germans, whose tank support proved decisive. No one was quite sure what to make of the Army Group boundary, or road N 24 bis on their map of Normandy.[129] Fifth Armored's CCB remained in division reserve near Freneaux.

Eisenhower stopped by Bradley's headquarters late on the afternoon of August 12, and stayed for supper. "With Ike's approval," Bradley wrote, "I took steps to reinforce Haislip with the best troops I had in my command: Collins VII Corps. That afternoon I ordered Collins to go all out to the northeast, inserting his corps between Haislip and the bulk of the Germans withdrawing from Mortain."[130] This would protect Haislip's left flank from the German attack *ULTRA* had predicted. The Americans had closed on the inter-Army Group boundary line late on August 12th.

Unfortunately, the British/Canadian drive toward Falaise had stalled again. In the Canadian First Army area, only limited objective attacks down the Laize River valley were planned for the next day.[131] They were still ten miles north of Falaise, barely twelve miles south of Caen, which was their D-day objective.[132] The second big Canadian attack, Operation *TRACTABLE*, was scheduled for the afternoon of August 14.

---

126   Blumenson, *The Duel*, 255.
127   Cepeda, 67.
128   Cepeda, 43.
129   Florentin, 124.
130   Bradley, *A General's Life*, 298.
131   Hastings, *Overlord*, 301.
132   Bradley, *A General's Life*, 297.

There appeared to be no sense of urgency from the British Commander. General Montgomery took no steps to reinforce the Canadians and Poles in their critical attacks toward Falaise. Chester B. Hansen wrote in his diary "The British effort from the north aimed at Falaise has moved slowly despite their efforts to push forward . . . It is possible that Montgomery has subscribed to the vice of extreme over-caution and has made the error of many commanders in denying sound tactics for the prestige value of objective."[133]

At 2000 hours on the evening of August 12, Patton's Chief of Staff, Major General Hugh J. Gaffey, sent a message to Commanding General, XV Corps: "UPON CAPTURE OF ARGENTAN PUSH ON SLOWLY DIRECTION OF FALAISE ALLOWING YOUR REAR ELEMENTS TO CLOSE. ROAD: ARGENTAN-FALAISE YOUR LEFT BOUNDARY INCLUSIVE. UPON ARRIVAL FALAISE CONTINUE TO PUSH ON SLOWLY UNTIL YOU CONTACT OUR ALLIES."[134]

After a staff meeting at Third Army Headquarters the following morning at 0900 hours, new orders were prepared for Haislip's XV Corps. These new orders directed XV Corps, ". . . to hold in position generally SEES-ARGENTAN-COURRAGES, prepared for movement upon Army order . . ."[135] This new order was not a definitive halt-order; it did leave open the possibility of further movement to the north, but only ". . . upon Army order."

If these orders sounded confusing at the Corps level, it was worse on the front line. Committee 2 [at the Armored School, Fort Knox] wrote ". . . orders [to 5th Armored] were changed and changed again. Initially the division ordered CCA to withdraw all elements from ARGENTAN. This order was no more than accomplished when new orders were received to the effect that CCA was to seize ARGENTAN, and push up the ARGENTAN-FALAISE road to join the Canadians . . . CCA moved out . . . when suddenly a slight change of orders was received. Instead of seizing ARGENTAN, CCA would bypass this city and push north to join the Canadians. Before CCA's staff could plan and implement this change, the entire order was cancelled. Confusion was certainly present . . ."[136]

The final decision on the northern limits of XV Corps' advance was not made until 1130 hours, August 13. It was relayed to Patton in a telephone call from Bradley's Chief of Staff, Major General Leven C. Allen. Patton's Chief

---

[133]   The Hansen Papers, August 13 and 14, 1944.
[134]   Hobart R. Gay, Diaries, August 13, 1944.
[135]   Hobart R. Gay, Diaries, August 13, 1944.
[136]   Cepeda, 61 & 62.

of Staff, Major General Hugh J. Gaffey answered the phone. General Allen told Gaffey, ". . . by order of General Bradley the Anglo-American boundary in the Falaise-Argentan area was not to be crossed under any circumstances and that the advance of XV Corps was to halt forthwith on the Argentan-Sees line."[137] When Gaffey told him about Bradley's halt-order, Patton's response was, "You're kidding."[138] Patton tried to get the halt-order overturned. He made several telephone calls to Bradley and Eisenhower's headquarters without talking to either general. Bradley left his own headquarters about 1030 hours that morning to visit Eisenhower, before their afternoon lunch and strategy meeting with Montgomery. Bradley chose not to talk to Patton for the rest of the day.

The halt-order was controversial as soon as it was issued. Patton sensed it immediately. He told General Gaffey, "The question why XV Corps halted on the east-west line through Argentan is certain to become of historical importance. I want a stenographic record of this conversation with General Allen included in the history of the Third Army."[139] Unable to convince anyone of Haislip's ability to close the gap and keep it closed, Patton directed his Chief of Staff to issue the orders to XV Corps: ". . . to stop further movement to the north, not to go beyond Argentan, and to recall at once any elements that might be in the vicinity of Falaise or to the north of Argentan."[140] As usual, Patton advised XV Corps to be alert for offensive movement in a different direction.

Bradley later wrote about the halt-order, suggesting he gave the order on the evening of August 12 during a phone call with Patton. Bradley wrote, "You're (Patton) not to go beyond Argentan. Just stop where you are and build up on that shoulder. Sibert tells me the German is beginning to pull out. You'd better button up and get ready for him."[141] Bradley also said that his orders were, ". . . so uncompromising . . . George (Patton) recalled Haislip's troops without a word."[142] Bradley later changed both the timing of his halt-order to Patton and the willingness with which Patton accepted the order, neither of which agreed with Third Army's historical record of the event.

Allied intelligence was another problem area. Very little accurate intelligence seems to have been available to the Allies during the Battle of the

---

[137] Farago, 539.
[138] Farago, 539.
[139] Farago, 540.
[140] Farago, 541.
[141] Omar N. Bradley, *A Soldier's Story*, (New York: Rand McNally, 1978), 376.
[142] Bradley, *A Soldier's Story*, 376.

Falaise Gap. But the Allies were conducting unrestricted air reconnaissance of the battlefield. They had literally dozens of ground reconnaissance units active and were receiving a 'treasure trove' of *ULTRA* radio intercepts.

In light of all the available intelligence sources, it seems odd that Allied intelligence got it wrong. Montgomery's British intelligence officers at 21st Army Group Headquarters controlled Allied Intelligence estimates concerning the strength and plans of the German Army. During the Battle of the Falaise Gap, British intelligence was reading secret German radio transmissions [*ULTRA*] almost as fast as the Germans were sending them.[143]

Allied intelligence had begun to detail accounts of the Germans withdrawing from Normandy on August 11. By the time Eisenhower and Bradley met at Montgomery's headquarters on August 13, ". . . the general estimate was that too many (Germans) had already escaped."[144] A few days later, when the presence of the Germans in the pocket could no longer be denied, Bradley wrote, "To our astonishment it was now reported that the Germans had not yet withdrawn after all."[145] This was indeed astonishing intelligence.

Bradley also says he sent six of Patton's divisions northeast on his own late in the afternoon of August 14. He later wrote, "If Montgomery wants any help in closing the gap, I thought, then let him ask for it. Since there was little likelihood of his asking, we would push on to the east."[146] But Montgomery had already ordered Bradley to retain a corps of three divisions in Le Mans expressly for that purpose. It seemed unlikely that Bradley would surprise Montgomery by implementing Montgomery's plans. Bradley corrected his error when, in 1983, writing *A General's Life* with Clay Blair, he published a letter he had received from Montgomery on the afternoon of August 14. Montgomery wrote to Bradley, in part, ". . . I think your movement of 20 Corps should be N.E. toward DREUX. Also any further stuff you can move around to LE MANS, should go N.E."[147] Bradley's bravado in sending Patton's divisions northeast without clearing it with Montgomery turned out to be little more than chest thumping. He was simply following Montgomery's orders.

---

[143] Winterbotham, 150.
[144] Bradley, *A General's Life*, 299.
[145] Bradley, *A General's Life*, 303.
[146] Bradley, *A Soldier's Story*, 378, 379.
[147] B.L. Montgomery, letter to General Bradley dated 14 August 1944 from the Bradley Papers, US Army Military History Institute, Carlisle Barracks, Pa.

Eisenhower and Bradley shared their concern for a, ". . . calamitous battle between friends . . ."[148] They professed having great concern for the lives of Allied soldiers due to accidental shelling or bombing while closing the trap. As Bradley put it, "With Haislip pushing north and the Canadians pushing south to close the jaws of the trap, we had to be extremely careful in joining these forces."[149] Bradley was also concerned about an impending German attack against Haislip's left flank they had learned about through *ULTRA*.

Although General Bradley acknowledged that he made several errors in 1951, he was adamant that the decision to halt Patton at Argentan was his and his alone. "Some writers have suggested that I appealed to Monty to move the boundary north to Falaise and he refused," Bradley wrote in 1983, "but, of course, that is not true. For all the reasons I have stated, I was determined to hold Patton at Argentan and had no cause to ask Monty to shift the boundary."[150]

Unfortunately, none of the reasons Bradley selected for halting Patton at Argentan hold up to serious inquiry. Instead, Bradley's reasons appear to have been created after the fact in an attempt to hide what actually happened. Given Bradley's outstanding record of service, this is a damning accusation. As Bradley suggests, Eisenhower gave him his full support. Eisenhower places himself at the scene when the critical halt-decision was made: "I was in Bradley's headquarters when messages began to arrive from commanders of the advancing American columns, complaining that the limits placed upon them by their orders were allowing Germans to escape. I completely supported Bradley in his decision that it was necessary to obey the orders, prescribing the boundary between army groups, exactly as written; otherwise a calamitous battle between friends could have resulted."[151] Eisenhower was at Bradley's headquarters on the evening of August 12th, in fact, he stayed for dinner. Eisenhower's explanation fits nicely with the version of events Bradley created in 1951 for *A Soldier's Story*, when Bradley suggested he gave Patton the halt-order that evening.

Unfortunately, Eisenhower's version of events does not fit well with Bradley's amended account published in 1983, when he suggests the halt-order was given early on the morning of August 13th. Eisenhower

---

[148] Bradley, *A General's Life*, 297.
[149] Bradley, *A General's Life*, 297.
[150] Bradley, *A General's Life*, 301.
[151] Eisenhower, *Crusade*, 278, 279.

was at his own headquarters on the morning of August 13th. [152] It seems likely that any discussions Bradley and Eisenhower had on the evening of August 12th were dominated by Allied efforts to close the Falaise Gap. As Eisenhower suggested, US commanders were calling in asking for guidance on the boundary just south of Argentan.

Bradley and Eisenhower met again the following morning at Eisenhower's headquarters, from about 1030 until they had to leave to go to Montgomery's headquarters for an afternoon conference, probably around noon or shortly thereafter. The halt-order was not issued to Patton's Third Army until 11:30 a.m. on the same day. Patton made sure a record was kept of the events surrounding the decision to stop Third Army south of Argentan.

That afternoon Montgomery was host to a luncheon, an award ceremony, intelligence briefing, and a strategic planning session. Bradley never mentioned the medal he received at 21st Army Group Headquarters. Nigel Hamilton kindly includes a photograph of the award ceremony in his book [*Master of the Battlefield*], apparently to show that although the Americans left Montgomery's headquarters that afternoon badly bruised, they did not leave empty-handed.[153] It was a long day for General Bradley. He later wrote, ". . . Sunday, August 13, was one of the most taxing [days] I would ever experience."[154] Generals Patton and Hodges would probably agree.

[152]   Farago, 540.
[153]   Hamilton, *Master,* photo between 736 and 737.
[154]   Bradley, *A General's Life,* 298.

Chapter 3

General Bradley's Dilemma

"During the previous night, (August 12/13) Haislip's forces had closed to the 'boundary' at Argentan. The Canadians were still bogged down six miles short of Falaise; there was thus a gap of about nineteen miles between our forces."[155] General Bradley

Generals Eisenhower and Bradley and Field Marshal Montgomery each had an opportunity to explain the halt-order given to General Patton on August 13. In his book, *Crusade in Europe,* Eisenhower described both the short envelopment Bradley was conducting at Argentan and ". . . the opportunity for . . . an even wider envelopment toward the crossings of the Seine River."[156] Eisenhower later wrote, "Mix-ups on the front occurred," so Bradley's forces had to be halted in place, ". . . even at the cost of allowing some Germans to escape."[157] Eisenhower suggested it was difficult to coordinate tactical maneuvers between the two Allied army groups. He added that the decision to halt the Americans was not his, but Bradley's. "I completely supported Bradley," Eisenhower wrote, "in his decision that it was necessary to obey orders, prescribing the boundary between army groups, exactly as written, otherwise a calamitous battle between friends could have resulted."[158]

Bradley would have received his boundary instructions from Montgomery, not Eisenhower. In spite of his denials, there were strong indications that General Bradley sought to have the boundary line moved north to allow an American thrust toward Falaise on the evening of August 12.

In *Normandy to the Baltic* published in 1946, Montgomery hardly mentions the Americans stopping at Argentan or Germans escaping the trap. For Montgomery, "The outstanding point about the Battle of

[155]   Bradley, *A General's Life*, 298.
[156]   Eisenhower, *Crusade*, 276.
[157]   Eisenhower, *Crusade*, 278.
[158]   Eisenhower, *Crusade*, 279.

Normandy is that it was fought exactly as planned before the invasion."[159] There were, Montgomery suggested, too many Germans and too few good roads. In his *Memoirs,* published in 1958, Montgomery does not mention the battle of Falaise-Argentan at all. Mistakes sometimes disappear into the fog of battle.

In 1948, Omar Bradley succeeded Eisenhower as US Army Chief of Staff. He was later appointed Chairman of the Joint Chiefs. General Omar N. Bradley had become his nation's number-one soldier. It was from this lofty perch Bradley wrote *A Soldier's Story* in 1951. His book dealt exclusively with events during the Second World War. He enthusiastically took responsibility for all command decisions involving US forces made at the Falaise Gap. Bradley recalled a telephone conversation he had with George Patton on the evening of August 12. Patton told Bradley that he already had forward elements in Argentan, and asked for permission to continue the operation toward Falaise. Bradley remembered telling Patton, "Nothing doing, you're not to go beyond Argentan. Just stop where you are and build up on that shoulder . . . the German is beginning to pull out. You'd better button up and get ready for him."[160] Bradley also added Eisenhower's main concern, "I was fearful of colliding with Montgomery's forces." Bradley said that his instructions to Patton were, ". . . so uncompromising . . . that George recalled Haislip's troops without a word."[161]

Bradley's boss was British officer, General Bernard L. Montgomery. According to Bradley, he was not a factor in his decisions. ". . . Monty had never prohibited and I never proposed that US forces close the gap from Argentan to Falaise. I was quite content with our original objective and reluctant to take on another."[162] Bradley added, "I much preferred a solid shoulder at Argentan to the possibility of a broken neck at Falaise."[163] Leaving little room for doubt, Bradley goes on to repeat his disclaimer: "In halting Patton at Argentan, however, I did not consult with Montgomery. The decision to halt Patton was mine alone; it never went beyond my CP."[164]

With the gap between Argentan and Falaise still not closed on August 14, the general who had too few troops to go the twelve miles between

---

[159] Bernard L. Montgomery, *Normandy to the Baltic*, (London: Hutchinson, 1946), 112.

[160] Bradley, *A Soldier's Story*, 376.

[161] Bradley, *A Soldier's Story*, 376.

[162] Bradley, *A Soldier's Story*, 377.

[163] Bradley, *A Soldier's Story*, 377.

[164] Bradley, *A Soldier's Story*, 377.

Argentan and Falaise just one day earlier, now discovers he has too many divisions sitting behind an arbitrary army group boundary. General Bradley decided to review his options. One option was to do nothing, to continue holding the shoulder at Argentan until the British arrived or all the Germans escaped, whichever came first. The second option was to ask Montgomery's permission to take the high ground northeast of Argentan or the road net between St. Leonard and Chambois, shutting off the southern half of the German escape route. The third option was to divide his forces in the Mortain-Le Mans-Argentan triangle, leaving enough divisions behind to hold the Argentan shoulder, while sending six of Patton's divisions north east to Dreux, Chartres, Orleans, and the Seine. Patton and Bradley had been working on similar plans. Their plans bear an obvious resemblance to Montgomery's Plan M517, the wider Seine envelopment.

By late evening on August 14, Patton had, with Bradley's approval, three corps heading individually for Dreux, Chartres, and Orleans. Again, Bradley suggests that he acted without Montgomery's knowledge or approval, "If Montgomery wants help in closing the gap, I thought, then let him ask for it. Since there was little likelihood of his asking, we would push on to the east."[165] Bradley recalled that Montgomery was very surprised when told that Patton was heading for the Seine.

By the 1980s, a lot had happened since Bradley published *A Soldier's Story* in 1951. Patton's biography by Ladislas Farago, *Ordeal and Triumph,* was published in 1964. *The Patton Papers*, by Martin Blumenson, documents released by the Freedom of Information Act, and previously secret British *ULTRA* information all became available to the public during the 1970s. The 1970s were very cruel to Omar Bradley's account of the events at the Falaise Gap. New information raised questions about the veracity of Bradley's earlier account. Bradley resolved to try again, to set the record straight. His autobiography, *A General's Life*, written with Clay Blair, was published in 1983.

In his autobiography, while recalling the events of August 8, Bradley made it clear that the idea to turn Patton north at Le Mans, the so-called short envelopment, was his. No one has ever successfully challenged Bradley on this point, although Montgomery liked to take credit for all successful troop movements within his command, even if he had to do so

---

[165]   Bradley, *A Soldier's Story*, 378, 379.

after the fact.[166] When Eisenhower, who had also seen the possibility of a short envelopment, visited Bradley on August 8, he found that Bradley, ". . . had already acted on this idea . . ."[167] From August 8 through August 21, the date the gap was finally closed, Allied Commanders understood that the short envelopment through Argentan to Falaise involved the meeting of Patton's Third US Army and Crerar's First Canadian Army. The place the two Allied pincers came together was not important, as long as it trapped most of the Germans in Normandy. But the timing was important. It was critical that the two Allied armies met before the Germans escaped.

Bradley was terribly enthusiastic about the opportunity presented by the German counterattack at Mortain. It was, he wrote, ". . . nothing short of fantastic."[168] On August 9, he told visiting United States Secretary of the Treasury, Henry Morgenthau, "This is an opportunity that comes to a commander not more than once in a century. We're about to destroy an entire hostile army."[169] It all depended on the Germans continuing their attack at Mortain until the Allies were in position to close the trap.

With the publication of *A General's Life* in 1983, it was obvious that General Bradley had become a more cautious historian. His enthusiasm for commanding the American forces at Argentan was now dampened by a host of concerns he had forgotten to share with his readers in 1951. First, he was concerned about the experience and quality of the divisions in Wade Haislip's XV Corps. Major General Oliver's 5th Armored Division was new to combat. The 2nd French Armored's commander was General Jacques P. Leclerc. Who was, according to Bradley, ". . . notoriously undisciplined and did not speak English."[170] Bradley had reservations about the commander of the 79th US Infantry Division, Major General I.T. Wyche. The 90th US Infantry Division had a series of problems in Normandy and had gone through several commanders. However, they were now commanded by the very able Major General Raymond McLain. The 80th US Infantry Division was "utterly green." Bradley later wrote, ". . . my decisions would, in part, be influenced by the misgivings I had about these five divisions."[171]

---

[166] Montgomery, *Normandy,* (taking credit for the short envelopment), 99. Also, see Winterbotham, pages 148 to 158 inclusive.

[167] Ambrose, *Eisenhower,* 330.

[168] Bradley, *A General's Life,* 296.

[169] Bradley, *A General's Life,* 296.

[170] Bradley, *A General's Life,* 296.

[171] Bradley, *A General's Life,* 297.

Bradley was also concerned about the exposed left flank of Haislip's XV Corps. Patton had planned to put Walton Walker's XX Corps on Haislip's left flank, and Gilbert Cook's newly formed XII Corps on Haislip's right flank. But amazingly neither of those corps moved from the vicinity of Le Mans until the evening of August 14, and then Walker was headed to Chartres and Cook was headed to Orleans—both advancing northeast, away from the Falaise Pocket. Bradley later wrote that he lacked the strength to close the gap at Falaise. Did he forget that these four divisions were uncommitted near Le Mans?

The reason for Bradley's concern about Haislip's left flank was an *ULTRA* message detailing Hitler's instructions to German commanders in the Falaise pocket. On the evening of August 11, Hitler allowed his generals to shorten the defensive line at Mortain, releasing some panzer units so they could deal with the threat posed by XV Corps near Le Mans. Bradley wrote that ". . . von Kluge was only too happy to oblige. An eastward attack on Haislip's flank would set the stage for a fighting withdraw from the whole dangerous pocket."[172] On the afternoon of August 12, Bradley ordered General Joseph Collins to disengage his VII US Corps at Mortain and drive northeast to cover Haislip's left flank. Eisenhower, who was visiting Bradley's headquarters at the time, agreed with Bradley's decision.[173]

Bradley said that he gave Patton the halt-order on the morning of August 13. "I had a sharp telephone exchange with Patton that morning . . . You're not to go beyond Argentan. Just stop where you are and build up on that shoulder."[174] Later that day, Bradley said he met Ike and Monty at Montgomery's Headquarters, ". . . for lunch and a full afternoon of discussion of the strategic and tactical situation."[175] Montgomery's idea of a discussion was to lecture the Americans on how to manage a war, and then propose his own strategic plan for the future conduct of all Allied ground forces in the European theatre. Bradley complained that Montgomery's strategic plans would undermine the American command, subordinating it to British control. "It was," Bradley concluded, "a distinctly uncomfortable afternoon."[176] To recover, Bradley spent the remainder of that Sunday afternoon and most of the evening at Eisenhower's Headquarters. Eisenhower's Naval Aide,

---

[172] Bradley, *A General's Life,* 297.
[173] Bradley, *A General's Life*, 298.
[174] Bradley, *A General's Life*, 298.
[175] Bradley, *A General's Life*, 299.
[176] Bradley, *A General's Life*, 299.

Captain Harry C. Butcher remembered, ". . . Bradley was here playing bridge as calmly and as peacefully as if he had just come off the golf course on a Sunday afternoon."[177]

The estimates British intelligence presented that Sunday afternoon at Montgomery's Headquarters suggested the German withdraw from the pocket was already in progress. Bradley later wrote the German withdraw was proceeding, ". . . with or without Hitler's authorization," adding that, "This news was a shattering disappointment—one of my greatest of the war. A golden opportunity had truly been lost." [178] Bradley blamed Montgomery for the failure to close the gap. His forces were on the boundary at Argentan in time, but Montgomery's forces still hadn't taken Falaise, twelve miles to the north. Bradley added a footnote about the erroneous British intelligence estimates: "Our [intelligence] estimate that afternoon is reflected in several contemporary documents, all written or dated the following day, August 14." [179] Bradley later acknowledged the intelligence mistake, "We still had it within our power to close the trap, but we did not know it."[180]

One of the intelligence estimates Bradley referred to in his footnote was a handwritten letter in the clipped writing style of B.L. Montgomery. The letter, dated August 14, contains the same estimate of German status within the pocket that was given to Eisenhower and Bradley on the afternoon of August 13 by British intelligence. "A good deal (of Germans) may have escaped," Montgomery wrote, "I think your movement of 20 Corps should be N.E. toward Dreux."[181] Montgomery also told Bradley that any other units he could bring through Le Mans should also go northeast.

Bradley repeated his earlier statement that the halt-order to Patton came from his Headquarters. "Some writers have suggested that I appealed to Monty to move the boundary north to Falaise and he refused, but, of course, that is not true. For all the reasons I have stated, I was determined to hold Patton at Argentan and had no cause to ask Monty to shift the boundary."[182]

On August 15 Bradley attended a meeting at Montgomery's Headquarters where he discovered that Allied intelligence had reversed itself. The Germans were still in the Falaise Pocket. "To our astonishment it was now reported

---

[177]   Butcher, 640.
[178]   Bradley, *A General's Life*, 299.
[179]   Bradley, *A General's Life,* 299.
[180]   Bradley, *A General's Life*, 300.
[181]   Bernard L. Montgomery letter to General Bradley, dated August 14th, 1944.
[182]   Bradley, *A General's Life*, 301.

that the Germans had not yet withdrawn after all. Elements of at least five panzer divisions were at or approaching Argentan."[183] Bradley must have been shaken; he hurried from Montgomery's Headquarters to Patton's, where he delivered his second halt-order in two days. Patton recorded Bradley's visit in his diary: "Bradley came down to see me suffering from nerves. There is a rumor, which I doubt, that there are five panzer divisions at Argentan . . ." [184] Concerning his decision to send Patton north on August 14, Bradley later wrote that he had been misled by British intelligence.[185]

The Germans received permission to withdraw from the gap on August 16; British intelligence immediately decoded the *ULTRA* intercept and forwarded it to Allied commanders in the field. Montgomery finally decided to take steps to secure the short envelopment in Normandy. He called Bradley and asked for help in closing the trap on the Germans at Chambois.[186] Montgomery wanted to enlarge the Allied trap by meeting Bradley's forces at Chambois. He told the Canadians, who had just taken Falaise, to drive through Falaise to Trun and Chambois. While the Canadians were still clearing the roads in Falaise the next day, Montgomery's patience was wearing thin. Orders thundered down to the First Canadian Army from 21st Army Group Headquarters couched in unmistakable terms: ". . . It is absolutely essential . . . at all costs . . . and as quickly as possible."[187] British divisions were resting on the west end of Montgomery's front near Vire, but they were not used to reinforce the Canadians. Montgomery did every thing he could to get the Canadians moving except commit his tired British divisions to battle.

Bradley later wrote, "I did not sleep very well that night."[188] The only force he had available to meet the Canadians at Chambois was the three divisions Patton's XV Corps had left behind: the 80th and 90th Infantry Divisions, and the 2nd French Armored Division. This was to become Leonard Gerow's new V Corps, but Gerow had not yet taken command. Fifth Corps' prior mission had been completed on August 15, when they occupied Tinchebray. In the confusion of battle, Bradley had not yet alerted Gerow to the change in divisions he was assigning to V Corps.

[183]   Bradley, *A General's Life*, 303.
[184]   Blumenson, (Ed.), *The Patton Papers, 1940-1945*, 511.
[185]   Bradley, *A General's Life*, 303.
[186]   Bradley, *A General's Life*, 303.
[187]   Hastings, *Overlord*, 303.
[188]   Bradley, *A General's Life*, 303.

The gap was initially closed on August 19 when the 359th Infantry Regiment of 90th Division met Polish Lancers from the 10th Dragoons of the First Polish Armored Division. But the Poles northern flank was stretched very thin and the Germans broke through their line surrounding fifteen-hundred Polish soldiers on Mont Ormel.[189] The northern pincer was finally secured on August 21. By then, Patton had crossed the Seine at Mantes and kept going. Patton wrote his wife, "We jumped seventy miles today and took Sens, Montereau, and Melun so fast the bridges were not blown . . . We are going so fast that I am quite safe. My only worries are my relations, not my enemies." [190]

There are several discrepancies in General Bradley's account of the halt-order to Patton. *The first problem with Bradley's account concerns the timing of the halt-order.* It is important to understand exactly when the halt-order was given. Unfortunately, when discussing the timing of the halt-order, Bradley is his own worst enemy. By his own account, Bradley got the timing of the halt-order wrong in 1951.

In 1951, Bradley wrote that he gave Patton the halt-order on the evening of August 12, so strict and uncompromising were Bradley's instructions, ". . . that George (Patton) recalled Haislip's troops without a word."[191] By 1983, Bradley moved the timing of the halt-order to the morning of August 13, "I had a sharp telephone exchange with Patton that morning."[192] Bradley's suggestion that Patton complied with his order, ". . . without a word" . . . has also disappeared. In fact, the halt-order made Patton hopping mad. Bradley later admitted, "All that afternoon . . . Patton had been stewing over my decision to halt Haislip at Argentan . . . trying to get the decision overturned so that Haislip could attempt to take Falaise."[193]

Bradley's 1983 explanation for the timing of the halt-order is closer to the truth, but was still not entirely accurate. The *Hobart R. Gay Papers* provide a different picture of the events at Third Army Headquarters that morning. "Sunday, August 13, 1944 . . . Army Commander received a directive from Commanding General, Twelfth US Army Group, to the effect that XV Corps would hold in position generally SEES-ARGENTAN-COURRAGES, prepared for movement upon Army order . . ." [194] Whatever it was that Patton

[189]   Weigley, *Eisenhower's Lieutenants*, 213.
[190]   Blumenson, (Ed.), *The Patton Papers 1940-1945*, 524.
[191]   Bradley, *A Soldier's Story*, 376.
[192]   Bradley, *A General's Life*, 298.
[193]   Bradley, *A General's Life*, 301.
[194]   The Hobart R. Gay Papers, Sunday, August 13, 1944.

and Bradley discussed on the telephone, it did not include a halt-order. That came later, and not from General Bradley, but from Major General Leven C. Allen, Bradley's Chief of Staff.

At 11:30 a.m. on August 13, Major General Leven C. Allen called General Hugh J. Gaffey at Patton's Headquarters. General Allen told General Gaffey, ". . . by order of General Bradley the Anglo-American boundary in the Falaise-Argentan area was not to be crossed under any circumstances and that the advance of XV Corps was to halt forthwith on the Argentan-Sees line."[195] Patton was in his trailer when Gaffey gave him the news. Patton's reply was, "You're kidding."[196]

Patton believed that Haislip could have easily taken Falaise, and was deeply troubled by the halt-order. He called Bradley's headquarters to speak to Bradley, but Bradley was not there. He had left for Eisenhower's headquarters near Tournieres. Patton called Eisenhower's headquarters, but could not get Bradley to come to the phone. He called Bradley's Headquarters again, and explained to General Allen it was ". . . perfectly feasible for XV Corps to continue the operation."[197] In the meantime, General Allen had talked with General Bradley again, and told Patton, "The answer is still no."[198]

The halt-order given to General Patton was not delivered by Bradley, as he suggests, but by his Chief of Staff, General Level Allen. The timing of the halt-order was not early Sunday morning, "When I learned what had happened during the night . . ." but at 11:30 a.m., nearly midday.[199] The halt-order at Argentan was sure to be controversial the minute it was issued. It is not very likely that the man who issued the order would forget when it was issued and who gave the order to General Patton.

Bradley further complicates the historical record by suggesting that he left his headquarters and drove directly to Montgomery's headquarters for an afternoon meeting. He wrote, "I met Ike and Monty at Monty's CP for lunch . . ."[200] This was not true either. Bradley left his headquarters between 10:15 and 10:30 a.m., probably right after the call from First Army telling him that Collins had closed the gap on Haislip's left, and drove directly to

[195] Farago, 539.
[196] Farago, 539.
[197] Farago, 540.
[198] Farago, 540.
[199] Farago, 539.
[200] Bradley, *A Soldier's Story*, 299.

Eisenhower's headquarters at *Shellburst*. He was at *Shellburst*, in discussion with Eisenhower when Patton tried to contact him about the halt-order.[201]

The second problem with Bradley's account of the events is his concern for Haislip's open left flank. General Patton had originally hoped to cover Haislip's flanks with Walker's XX Corps on their left and Cook's XII Corps on their right as XV Corps drove toward Argentan. Unfortunately, neither one of these Corps was available to protect Haislip's flanks when the time came.

The non-appearance of XII or XX Corps on Haislip's flanks was one of the great mysteries of the Falaise Gap. What happened to those two corps? Walker's XX Corps remained in the vicinity of Le Mans throughout the period, August 12-14. "On August 13," Patton complained that, "it became evident that the XX Corps was hitting nothing, so we moved it northeast of Le Mans . . ."[202] On the thirteenth Patton also formed Cook's XII Corps with Major General Wood's 4th Armored Division arriving from Brittany and Major General Baade's 35th Infantry Division. Cook joined Walker camping out in the French countryside.

The historical record on these two corps during this period is deficient; very little information is available from normal sources. Historians are left with the curious image of General Bradley looking unsuccessfully for additional US forces at Argentan on August 13, while barely sixty miles away, at Le Mans, four US divisions in two corps are camping out in the French countryside. Either of these Corps could have been on Haislip's eastern flank within a few hours. Of course, that would have compromised Montgomery's August 11th order to prepare for the wide envelopment by holding those divisions near Le Mans.

A few days earlier, on August 11, British intelligence had decoded an *ULTRA* message authorizing a partial withdraw of German armor from the Mortain front, to deal with Haislip's thrust into the southern German flank. By the afternoon of August 12, Bradley had decided to replace Cook and Walker's corps on Haislip's flanks with Joe Collins' VII Corps. Bradley later wrote, "I was now gravely concerned about the impending German attack on Haislip's left flank. With Ike's approval, I took steps to reinforce Haislip with the best troops I had in my command: Collins' VII Corps."[203]

---

[201]   Farago, 539.

[202]   Patton, 104.

[203]   Bradley, *A General's Life*, 298.

During the night of August 12/13, Patton ordered Haislip to continue his advance past Argentan toward Falaise, disregarding the Army Group boundary south of Argentan. "When I learned what had happened during the night," Bradley wrote, "I was furious."[204] Bradley was mad at Patton for violating the boundary line and because, "He had extended Haislip's vulnerable left flank even further, knowing full well that *ULTRA* had forecast a German counterattack on that very day."[205] Bradley does not inform the reader that Collins closed the gap on Haislip's left flank until he is discussing events a full day later, on August 14. Did it really take Joe Collins two days to move VII Corps 30 miles? Bradley's wording is crafty, he wrote, ". . . Joe Collins had closed the gap and blazed north twenty miles on Haislip's left *the day before* against light resistance . . ." [206] '*The day before*,' means that Collins closed the open flank on August 13, but when on August 13?

Major William Sylvan's Diary provides the answer: Diary entry for August 13, "At ten, General Collins called asking for more territory to take.'"[207] Given the light resistance he had faced driving to Ranes, Collins was convinced that he could drive through Argentan to Falaise. First Army Commander, Lieutenant General Courtney Hodges endorsed Collins' request and telephoned Bradley's headquarters to get approval. Hodges' request, like Patton's, was turned down, ". . . the sad news came back that First Army was to go no further than at first designated . . ."[208]

Now we know that Haislip's open left flank could not have been a factor in Bradley's decision to halt Patton at Argentan. Bradley knew that General Collins' VII Corps had covered Haislip's open flank at around 10:00 AM that Sunday morning. First Army's diary recorded the call. Bradley knew that Haislip's flank was covered, at least by reconnaissance elements, one and a half hours before he issued the halt-order to Patton. *The Sylvan Diary* confirms that Collins notified First Army that his mission was substantially complete at ten, and that First army immediately called 12th Army Group with the news.[209] We also know that Patton did not receive the halt-order until 11:30 a.m., a full one-and-a-half hour later. Hobart R. Gay at Third Army Headquarters recorded that call.[210] There

204 Bradley, *A General's Life*, 298.
205 Bradley, *A General's Life*, 298.
206 Bradley, *A General's Life*, 302. Italics added.
207 Major William Sylvan's Diary, Sunday, August 13
208 Major William Sylvan's Diary, Sunday, August 13
209 Major William Sylvan's Diary, Sunday, August 13
210 Farago, 539.

was plenty of time between First Army's request for a boundary change at approximately 10:15 a.m. and the halt-order to Patton at 11:30 a.m., for a heated conversation between Bradley and Eisenhower at Eisenhower's Headquarters. Bradley and Eisenhower decided to issue the halt-order to General Patton, but delegated the actual telephone call to Bradley's Chief of Staff, Major General Leven Allen.

Bradley did not make the phone call to Patton. Nor did he visit Patton's headquarters to explain the halt-order because he knew Patton was in bitter disagreement with the decision. Bradley did not explain his halt-decision to First Army either. In the event of disagreement between commands, the higher command is bound by US Army protocol to personally visit the lower-ranking commander to address their mutual disagreement. That did not happen on August 13. In fact, General Bradley remained out of touch with both Third and First Army headquarters all day. He spent the afternoon at Montgomery's headquarters going over the latest intelligence reports and discussing long-term allied strategy with Eisenhower and Montgomery. He spent the evening at Eisenhower's eating supper and playing bridge.

How dangerous was Haislip's open flank? XV Corps was attacking directly north from Le Mans with two armored divisions abreast. Second French Armored was on the left; it attacked through Alencon and Carrouges to the Army Group boundary line from Argentan west to Ranes. Fifth US Armored was on the right; it attacked past Alencon to Sees and the Army Group boundary near Argentan then east to L'Aigle. US 90th Infantry was in close support of the 2nd French Armored and 79th US Infantry was in close support of 5th US Armored.[211] Haislip and Patton had taken the precaution of having one regiment in each infantry division fully motorized, so the infantry could keep up with the armor. Haislip's drive north from Le Mans was conducted in depth, with an infantry division echeloned behind each armored division. If one of Haislip's armored divisions had been attacked, the attacker would soon find his flank under assault by Haislip's motorized infantry, which was right behind the armor. Patton and his generals would use this formation with great success when they drove across France in late August and early September with both flanks wide open.

Close tactical air support was another important factor in securing Haislip's open flanks. Allied pilots had a host of targets to choose from during the last two weeks of the battle in Normandy, when the Germans

---

[211]   Florentin, 96.

were forced to move units during the daylight hours. Brigadier General C.A. Regnier, Commanding 5th Armored Division's CCA commented on the air support his unit received: "Never . . . were we without air support in daylight during any of the critical phases of this operation . . . Let me assure you that these operations could not have been accomplished without the generous and whole-hearted support of the Air Corps."[212] Patton and Haislip had done everything in their power to mitigate the dangers inherent in an open flank. While some risk existed, Haislip's open flank was never as dangerous as Bradley's excessive hand-wringing would suggest, nor was it a factor in Bradley's decision to issue the 'halt-order' to Patton at Argentan.

General Bradley wrote that the *ULTRA* message which alerted him to the impending German attack on Haislip's flank, also warned him about the German withdraw from Normandy. "An eastward attack on Haislip's flank," Bradley wrote, "would set the stage for a fighting withdraw from the whole dangerous pocket."[213] This simply was not true. The *ULTRA* message, which had alerted the Allies to an attack on Haislip's flank, was decoded on August 11. It also told the Allies that Hitler viewed the attack on Haislip as necessary distraction to the main German attack at Mortain, which Hitler still insisted on after Haislip's threat was eliminated.[214] Since Bradley was aware of the impending German attack on XV Corps through *ULTRA,* he was also aware of Hitler's determination, despite the protests of his generals, to renew the Mortain offensive.

The third problem with Bradley's account of events at the Falaise Gap is his stated concern about the accidental meeting of two armies, with allied armies shelling each other. Bradley shared Eisenhower's concern about the accidental meeting of George Patton's Third US Army and Henry Crerar's First Canadian Army. "Without utmost care," Bradley wrote, "I could foresee our armies accidentally shelling one another . . . nothing is more demoralizing to troops than to see men killed by friendly fire."[215]

Bradley liked to portray himself as just another common soldier. Unlike Patton and Montgomery, Bradley wore strictly G.I. issue clothes. In those pictures from World War II showing famous generals, Bradley is the frumpy-looking officer, who somehow stumbled into a room full of great men. His face, his bearing, and his clothing were nondescript, and he

---

[212] Cepeda, 68.
[213] Bradley, *A General's Life,* 297.
[214] Eberbach, 14.
[215] Bradley, *A General's Life,* 297.

loved the impression it left. Bradley was the general who loved to discuss the welfare of his troops. This was all great stuff for the reporters; it made wonderful copy back in America. Bradley was very popular with *Stars and Stripes* cartoonist Bill Mauldin, whose cartoon of Bradley talking to enlisted soldiers in Africa was included in Bradley's first book.[216]

There was a host of measures Bradley and Montgomery could have taken to prevent their armies from shelling each other. They might have picked a prominent geographical feature such as a town, a road junction, a river, or even high ground, and used it as a no-fire zone for their meeting place. They might have used colored smoke flares, artillery or mortar rounds for unit identification. H. Essame, British military historian, suggests, ". . . parallel axis of advance . . . thus cutting the German escape routes in two places instead of one."[217] Essame also suggests a lack of radio security, "Wireless security too was deplorably bad . . . The air in fact was a never-ending babble of Allied voices. No one could possibly have remained long in ignorance of the near approach of friends."[218]

The actual meeting of Allied armies took place at Chambois on the evening of August 19 at 5:55 p.m. It had been done in a hurry since Montgomery's phone call to Bradley on August 16. Other than the location of the town, Chambois, there were no plans made for the meeting. It was rush, rush. Soldiers from Company G, US 359th Infantry Regiment, commanded by Captain Laughlin E. Waters met Poles from the 10th Regiment of Dragoons of the First Polish Armored Division, commanded by Major Zgordzelski.[219] There were no reports of friendly fire casualties when Company G met elements from the 10th Polish Dragoons in Chambois.[220] All of Bradley's concerns, his worrying, and hand wringing had come to naught. H. Essame was right, "He [Bradley] would have done well not to make this excuse."[221]

The fourth problem with Bradley's account of the events in the Falaise Gap is his reluctance to go beyond the inter-Army Group boundary south of Argentan; and his insistence that he either go all the way to Falaise or stop on that army group boundary line. Boundary lines between units are an operational and tactical necessity. It is important to know which roads

---

[216]   Bradley, *A Soldier's Story*, xviii.

[217]   H. Essame, *Patton, A Study in Command,* (New York: Charles Scribner's Sons, 1974), 169.

[218]   Essame, 170.

[219]   Florentine, 240,241.

[220]   Weigley, *Eisenhower's Lieutenants*, 213.

[221]   Essame, 169.

are available when planning an attack. A successful operation depends on a road net sufficient for all the assaulting forces and their re-supply vehicles. An attack that cannot be fully deployed or re-supplied will never develop its full offensive potential. Several of Montgomery's offensives failed for this reason. Patton, on the other hand, was a genius with large unit offensives. He seemed to know, almost instinctively, which roads would be required by a particular unit for any offensive.

There were five separate northern boundary lines assigned to Bradley's 12th Army Group in Normandy. The original boundary line was drawn by pre-invasion planners. It ran through Domfront and Alencon. The second boundary was given on August 3rd. It was moved slightly north to Ranes-Sees. The third boundary is implicit in Bradley's short envelopment discussion with Montgomery on August 8. It was just south of Briouze-Argentan-St. Leonard. The fourth boundary change was communicated to Bradley in a Montgomery telephone call on the evening of August 16. He asked for Bradley's help closing the gap and allowed American penetration of the British zone at Argentan up to Chambois. The fifth change occurred when Montgomery shifted the boundary back to the line Briouze-Argentan-St. Leonard after the gap had been closed. It retained the Argentan-Evreux highway in British possession. Montgomery planned to use that highway for British XXX Corp's egress from Normandy.[222]

---

[222]   De Guingand, 407, 408. Also, see Wilmot map facing p. 417.

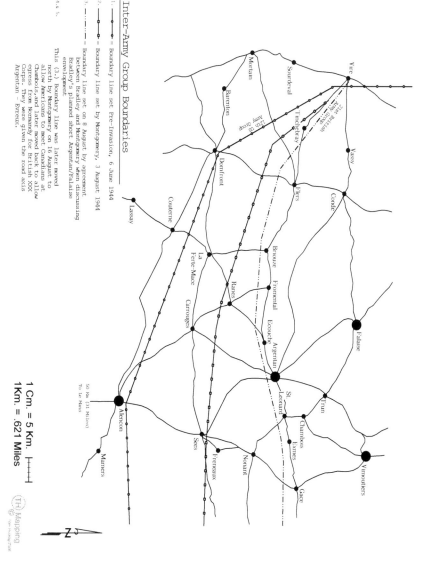

Inter-Army Group Boundaries

1: ●——● = Boundary line set Pre-Invasion, 6 June 1944

2: □——□ = Boundary line set by Montgomery, 3 August 1944

3: —·—·—· = Boundary line set on 8 August by agreement
between Bradley and Montgomery when discussing
Bradley's planned short Argentan/Falaise
envelopment.

4, & 5. This (3.) Boundary line was later moved
north by Montgomery on 16 August to
allow Americans to meet Canadians at
Chambois,and later moved back to allow
egress from Normandy for British XXX
Corps. They were given the road axis
Argentan - Evreux.

1 Cm. = 5 Km. |—·—|
1Km. = .621 Miles

This was the boundary change that created so much confusion within the pocket, and was necessary only because the Allied Ground Forces Commander [Montgomery] lacked a firm grip on the battle. The master of the set-piece battle had created a tactical mess in Normandy.

General Bradley learned his tactics at Fort Benning. He was a protégé of George Marshall and Joseph Stilwell. General Marshall had been stationed in China between the wars. He once ran a training exercise for younger officers, when one bright young officer was unable to handle an unexpected change.[223] When Marshall learned that this officer had finished first in his Infantry Training Class at Fort Benning, he knew that changes would have to be made. "In the present Army, there were cut-and-dried answers to almost every problem. In the Army, he [Marshall] envisaged, there would be clear answers to almost nothing."[224]

Marshall demanded that infantry training stress the inevitable changes and confusion officers found on the battlefield. To achieve confusion, Marshall ordered more exercises conducted at night, orders were often vague and inconclusive, orders were changed in the middle of the exercise, and commanding officers were changed without warning. Marshall also published to the class any unusual or creative solutions to problems that ran counter to the approved solution. After Marshall had reformed Benning, an officer had to learn to think on his feet, to accept change and confusion as a normal result of battlefield conditions. Bradley excelled at Benning under Marshall and Stilwell. He impressed his superiors so much that they asked him to stay on as an instructor.[225]

Reviewing his tactical options on August 13, Bradley wrote, "I much preferred a solid shoulder at Argentan to the possibility of a broken neck at Falaise."[226] Bradley has reduced his tactical options to just two: either he sends Haislip's XV Corps north to Falaise to close the gap, or he halts Haislip's Corps behind an arbitrary inter-Army Group boundary just south of Argentan. Of course, this begs the question: were there any objectives worth taking between the boundary line south of Argentan and Falaise? And if there were, and Montgomery never prohibited his northward movement, why didn't General Bradley try to take them?

---

[223]   Forrest C. Pogue, *George C. Marshall, Education 1880-1939*, (London: MACGIBBON & KEE, 1964), 268.

[224]   Perret, 13.

[225]   Bradley, *A General's Life*, 67.

[226]   Bradley, *A Soldier's Story*, 377. Also see Bradley, *A General's Life,* 298, 299.

In 1950, Committee 2 of the Armored Officers Advanced Course at Fort Knox, Kentucky, published a Research Report entitled *The Fifth Armored Division in the Falaise-Argentan Sector*. Lieutenant Colonel Emmanuel S. Cepeda was the ranking officer on Committee 2. The officers on Committee 2 wanted to make it very clear that they would not be critical of any prior decisions made on the field of battle. They wrote, "No attempt is made here to determine whether or not the higher strategy in the Argentan-Falaise Sector was correct. It is felt that any 'second guessing' as to whether or not the gap could have or should have been closed in this area, is out of order in this report."[227]

Having protected their careers, Lieutenant Colonel Cepeda and his fellow officers proceeded to destroy Bradley's either/or tactical options on August 13. They wrote, "The decision to close from the south was made and then changed many times during the actual battle, and the reports written by higher commanders involved bring to light difference of opinion even at this late date. We do feel however that on the 12th of August, the 5th Armored Division could have and should have denied ARGENTAN to the enemy."[228] The road net at Argentan was just a few miles inside the army group boundary. Committee 2 also cites an order issued on August 11 at 2317 hours to CCA, 5th Armored, ". . . instructions for movement (of) CCA to new obj. CCA move so as not to interfere with CCB and CCR onto Route 158 at Sees . . . Sever RR at NW ARGENTAN. Lose no time. Go into bivouac for aggressive defense . . ." [229] They concluded, ". . . the above order and subsequent action was meant to deny the enemy the high ground north and northwest of ARGENTAN. Such action would have prevented the use of this critical terrain feature as a 'shoulder' of the escape gap." [230]

No fewer than eight major roads enter the town of Argentan. The Germans found five roads entering Argentan from the west and three roads leaving to the east. The road net at Argentan controlled the entire southern sector of vehicle traffic through the Falaise Gap. The high ground northeast of Argentan is where the Germans placed the artillery they used to shell 5th Armored on the afternoon of August 13. The Germans used the same high ground to shell the 80th US Infantry Division on the morning of August 18.

---

[227]   Cepeda, 65.
[228]   Cepeda, 66.
[229]   Cepeda, 66.
[230]   Cepeda, 66, 67.

When the 90th US Infantry Division finally got permission to cross the boundary on August 17/18, their division artillery on ". . . the le Bourg-St. Leonard ridge was enjoying an 'artilleryman's dream' against every conceivable kind of motorized or horse-drawn vehicle passing through its sights."[231] The le Bourg-St. Leonard ridgeline, like the town of Argentan, was only a few miles inside the army group boundary. Yet this critical terrain feature remained in German hands for over a week.

Bradley deliberately phrased his options on August 13 as an either/or situation, so that he would not be required to answer questions like those raised by Committee 2. Russell Weigley agreed with Lt. Colonel Cepeda, ". . . the true reason why the German front held at Argentan was the halt-order."[232] The Americans remained inactive south of the army group boundary line for nearly a week, allowing the Germans to occupy the high ground northeast of Argentan, the ridgeline at St. Leonard and the critical road net at Argentan. An American advance of only a few miles past the inter-Army Group boundary would have secured these critical tactical objectives and saved Allied lives. Bradley's failure to secure the objectives, especially the high ground, left his troops at a clear tactical disadvantage for over a week. His reputation as 'the G.I.'s General' must suffer as a result. Unless, of course, General Bradley was ordered to hold Patton's Third Army south of Argentan.

The fifth problem Bradley created while explaining events in the Falaise Gap concerned his treatment of subordinate Third Army Commander, Lieutenant General George S. Patton Jr. They were oil and water. Patton, six years older, was Bradley's commanding officer in North Africa and Sicily. Bradley, the junior officer until his appointment to command First US Army during the Allied invasion of Europe, was now the boss. Patton was profane, high strung, nervous, a braggart and an impeccable dresser. He was always attired in a freshly pressed uniform with highly polished riding boots. Bradley was relaxed, calm, seldom showed his temper or swore in public. He dressed casually and non-pretentiously in a G.I. issue uniform. Patton suffered from dyslexia; most of his efforts at learning, especially reading, were a terrible chore. After being turned back in his first year, Patton got through West Point on sheer will power. Bradley was a natural, gifted student; he excelled at math. He worked mathematical problems in his head as a form of relaxation. Patton loved horses. Bradley hated horses.

---

[231] Weigley, *Eisenhower's Lieutenants*, 213.
[232] Weigley, *Eisenhower's Lieutenants*, 207.

Patton and Bradley were about as different as two men in the same occupation can become. Yet, for nearly a year, they worked together, at times very closely, in a vain attempt to counter Montgomery's powerful influence on Allied strategy. Even working in harmony they were no match for cabal of Montgomery, Brooke, Churchill and the British officers at SHAEF. "My own feelings on George (Patton)," Bradley wrote, "were mixed. He had not been my choice for Army commander and I was still wary of the grace with which he would accept our reversal in roles."[233] Yet, in spite of their obvious differences and Bradley's initial reluctance, Bradley and Patton went on to form one of the most productive teams in the Allied command. In *A Soldier's Story,* Bradley wrote, "Before many months had passed, the new Patton had totally obliterated my unwarranted apprehensions . . ."[234]

From mid-August 1944, through the end of the war, the Bradley-Patton relationship was, with few exceptions, one of complete cooperation. Whenever friction between the Allies threatened 12th Army Group's mission, Bradley increasingly turned to George Patton as a buffer to the powerful influence Montgomery was capable of exercising over Eisenhower and his British minions at SHAEF. Russell F. Weigley wrote, "Patton's dramatic transformation in less than two months from bete noire to hero among Bradley's staff was a direct function of the correspondingly swift decline of the hero of El Alamein; that Patton, so recently loathed in these quarters, could now be welcomed so enthusiastically implies much about the amount of poison that had so quickly seeped into the relationship between the two army groups."[235] Bradley's relationship with Eisenhower also became strained. After the Battle of the Bulge, Bradley, in a fit of anger, threatened to resign if Eisenhower ever put Montgomery in command of 12th US Army Group.

Ladislas Farago's biography of Patton, *Ordeal and Triumph,* was the book on which the movie "Patton" was based. General Bradley served as technical adviser on the film. Although he must have enjoyed the work, and having his opinions considered, he could not help but notice that the film was about George Patton and not Omar Bradley. That film, and a host of newly published books, enhanced Patton's reputation. They were an indication that the public's opinion of George Patton was changing. Bradley

[233]   Bradley, *A Soldier's Story,* 355.
[234]   Bradley, *A Soldier's Story,* 355.
[235]   Weigley, *Eisenhower's Lieutenants,* 210.

must have sensed the change; he was there at the beginning. He had helped make the movie.

The improvement in George Patton's military reputation has been accompanied by a corresponding decline in the reputations of Bernard Montgomery and Omar Bradley. Assisting Clay Blair with *A General's Life* in 1983, Bradley could not help himself; he could not resist the opportunity to make a few derogatory remarks about his old friend. Bradley blamed Patton for ordering Haislip to go past the Army Group boundary at Argentan. Bradley suggested that Patton, ". . . knowingly and willfully violated an Allied agreement." Bradley added, ". . . I was furious . . . He (Patton) had placed his troops in 'no man's land.' . . . exposed to Allied air attack. He had extended Haislip's vulnerable left flank ever further . . ." [236]

Bradley's descriptions of Patton's actions at the Falaise Gap helped to confirm the public's perception of Patton as a reckless, wild-eyed renegade, the general who would do anything, including sacrificing the lives of his men just for a headline in tomorrow's newspaper. There were more than a few facts Bradley forgot to include in his autobiography.

Bradley's criticism of Patton for sending XV Corps past the Army Group boundary on the night of August 12/13 has led several historians to conclude that Patton disobeyed Bradley's orders. This was not very likely. Patton knew he was not Bradley's choice for Third Army commander. He knew Bradley had reservations about his behavior in Sicily, among other things. On August 12, Patton had been Bradley's Army Commander for less than two weeks. Patton would not have risked his new command by deliberately violating an order from Bradley or anyone else. He knew he was on Eisenhower's short leash. Patton's name had not yet been released to the American press.

Bradley's vagueness in describing the events on August 12 and 13 was confirmed by the confusion in orders drawn up at Patton's headquarters. Martin Blumenson tried to read Bradley's thoughts: "Perhaps Bradley seemed to equivocate . . . Perhaps he said he would see in the morning. Perhaps he uttered . . . a tentative or qualified okay . . . there must have been something. For Patton, contrary to popular legend, never violated instructions, never deliberately disobeyed orders."[237]

Patton's, "You're kidding" response to Gaffey when informed about the halt-order, was not the response one might expect from a commander

[236] Bradley, *A General's Life*, 298.
[237] Blumenson, *The Battle of the Generals*, 208.

who had just been caught exceeding his authority.[238] It was a response one might expect from a general who had an entirely different understanding of his mission. Patton was surprised by Bradley's halt-order. He had clearly expected to receive permission to continue the operation, so he spent the next several hours trying to get the halt-order overturned. Not the behavior one might expect from a general recently out of Eisenhower's doghouse who had been caught disobeying orders.

Bradley also ignored the simple fact that all the senior Allied commanders on the southern flank of the Falaise Gap agreed with George Patton, not Omar Bradley. The following officers argued in favor of continuing to close the gap by driving north of the Army Group boundary: Jacques P. Leclerc, Commanding 2nd French Armored, Wade Haislip, Commanding XV Corps, Joseph Collins, Commanding VII Corps, Courtney Hodges, Commanding First Army, and George Patton of Third Army. The only senior American officer who opposed the operation on its merits was Omar Bradley. Interestingly, it was General Bradley who had proposed the operation on August 8. General Eisenhower also said he opposed the operation, but he was never directly involved in tactical decisions.[239]

Bradley blamed Patton for selecting Falaise as one of the objectives of XV Corp's northward attack. He wrote, "Falaise was a long sought British objective and, for them, a matter of immense prestige. If Patton's patrols grabbed Falaise, it would be an arrogant slap in the face at a time when we clearly needed to build confidence in the Canadian Army."[240] Patton did mention Falaise as an objective on the night of 12/13 August in communications with XV Corps.

But the first mention of Falaise as an objective for Third Army was from General Eisenhower. Eisenhower wrote to George Marshall on August 9, ". . . Patton has the marching wing which will turn . . . northeast from . . . Le Mans and just to the west thereof marching toward Alencon and Falaise."[241] Eisenhower had not spoken to Patton since Patton took Command of Third Army on August 1. However, Eisenhower was in almost daily contact with Bradley during this time. Eisenhower's letter to Marshall comes just one day after he and Bradley met on August 8 to discuss the so-called short envelopment through Argentan-Falaise. Eisenhower's awareness that Falaise

---

[238]   Farago, 539.
[239]   Eisenhower, 278, 279.
[240]   Bradley, *A General's Life*, 298.
[241]   Chandler, (Ed.), *The Eisenhower Papers, Vol. IV*, 2062.

was an objective for Patton's Third Army must have come from Bradley, since it could not have come from George Patton.

It was terribly disingenuous of Bradley to accuse Patton of following his orders. Again, the success of the envelopment depended on its timing, not its location. The truth is that Patton would have preferred the wider envelopment, which he thought would trap more Germans. Bradley later admitted, "He (Patton) leaned toward my idea of the day before—the deeper and wider envelopment along the Seine . . ."[242]

The idea for the short envelopment and the location of the southern pincer through Argentan to Falaise was Bradley's. It was a poor selection both because it was too close to the fighting south of Caen and because the town of Falaise had appeared on several of Montgomery's plans as an objective for British/Canadian offensives from the north. Montgomery would have been sensitive to any operation which looked like the Americans had come to rescue the British stalled at Falaise. Bradley admitted as much after the fact, but then tried to blame Patton for his decision to close the gap at Argentan-Falaise.

A far better axis for the American advance would have been to extend it eastwards to Gace or L'Aigle and then north to Bernay or Lisieux. This operation would have removed the fighting from the congested area between Falaise and Argentan, entrapped more Germans, given the Allies additional north-south roads and still have been close enough so that logistically it could have been conducted in the same time frame as Bradley's earlier proposal.

In two attempts, Bradley has failed to provide a rational explanation for the events at the Falaise gap. Instead, his two autobiographies contain a series of deliberate distortions, half-truths, and outright lies for purposes the author never shares with his readers. It is apparent from the information he provides that Bradley is trying to cover up something.

Historians have usually given General Bradley the benefit of the doubt. He was such a decent man and competent officer. It may seem appropriate to assign his historical gaffs to a faulty memory or to unreliable sources. But in Bradley's case, that does not seem to be an adequate solution. Chester B. Hansen, William Sylvan, and George Patton's memories and their diaries were explicitly accurate; and no one had better access to Army historical information than a former Army Chief of Staff.

---

[242] Bradley, *A General's Life,* 294.

Bradley is also a participant in the events he is describing. Given the controversial nature of his decision to halt Patton, it does not seem likely that he forgot who gave the order, when it was given, and under what circumstances the halt-order was issued. It also seems unlikely that a general would give up so easily on ". . . an opportunity that comes to a commander not more than once in a century."[243] The opportunity of a lifetime, gone, and barely a whimper came from the commander whose reputation would have been greatly enhanced had the operation succeeded. The so-called short envelopment through Argentan to Falaise was, after all, Bradley's plan. It does not make any more sense today than it did sixty-odd years ago.

---

[243]   Bradley, *A General's Life*, 296.

Chapter 4

Astonishing Intelligence

"... The very next day, August 15, intelligence reversed itself. To our astonishment it was now reported that the Germans had not yet withdrawn [from the Falaise Pocket]."[244] Omar Bradley

It was the best-kept secret of the war. It was, perhaps, the best-kept secret of any war. *ULTRA* was the code name for the interception of German radio traffic encoded on an *ENIGMA* cypher machine, its decoding at Bletchley Park, just outside London, and subsequent delivery to government officials and high-ranking British and American officers on the battlefield. Hundreds of people swore a wartime oath of secrecy about *ULTRA;* all fulfilled their oaths. President Roosevelt, Prime Minister Churchill, their staffs, the Chiefs of Staff of the armed forces of Great Britain and the United States, and senior commanders were all privy to *ULTRA* messages. It was the Allies' most closely guarded secret of the war.

F.W. Winterbotham received permission from the British government to publish *The Ultra Secret* in 1974, but he did so without access to official documents. Those "... hundreds of signals ..." which, says Winterbotham, "... I left locked in the vaults of Whitehall."[245] In 1977 the British government agreed to release, "... a substantial number of the actual *ULTRA* signals."[246] Three excellent books on the subject followed in quick succession: Ronald Lewin's *Ultra Goes to War* (1978), Ralph Bennett's *Ultra in the West* (1979), and Peter Calvocoressi's *Top Secret Ultra* (1980). By the mid-1980s, microfilm tapes of actual *ULTRA* messages were available for public viewing at the US Army Military History Institute at Carlisle Barracks, Pennsylvania.

The idea or concept for the enigma-encoding machine came from Holland. Hugo Alexander Koch registered his patent for the basic design in 1919. Dr Arthur Scherbius, a German engineer, took Koch's ideas and

---

244   Bradley, *A General's Life*, 303.
245   Winterbotham, *The Ultra Secret*, Preface, vii.
246   Ronald Lewin, *ULTRA Goes to War,* (New York: McGraw-Hill, 1978), 18.

incorporated some of his own to create an encoding machine he called Enigma. Dr Scherbius was a manager of the German firm Cipher Machines Corporation, which produced and marketed the new encoding device in 1924. US diplomats bought one of these machines in 1927 for $144, plus shipping. It was shipped back to the United States via the SS *President Harding* and delivered to the US Army Signal Corps in May 1928.[247]

ULTRA proved one of the outstanding intelligence coups of the war. "The breaking of Enigma ciphers played a significant part in the second World War. The value of its contribution varied from time to time . . ." wrote Peter Calvocoressi, "But without doubt Ultra made a big difference, sometimes a vital one."[248] This was especially true in the August 1944 period, when German commanders in France were forced to use radio traffic almost exclusively for communication. Ralph Bennett estimates that twenty-five thousand *ULTRA* messages went from Hut 3 at Bletchley Park, where the German radio traffic was decoded, to the Allied Commander in the field, General Eisenhower, between January 1944 and the end of the war.[249] Eisenhower wrote a letter of thanks after the war had ended to General Stewart Menzies, Chief of the British Secret Service. In the letter Eisenhower asked Menzies to give his staff, ". . . my heartfelt admiration and sincere thanks for their *very decisive contribution to the Allied war effort.*"[250]

Peter Calvocoressi wrote, "Essentially Enigma was a transposition machine. That is to say, it turned every letter in a message into some other letter."[251] The transposition of the twenty-six letters in the alphabet was the basic idea behind Enigma, but it was far more complicated than that. Enigma looks like two typing machines. Intricate electrical wiring is the secret to Enigma's seemingly endless number of alphabetical settings. The lower set of letters [there were no numbers or punctuation marks] appear on regular typewriter keys; the upper set of letters appear behind round, clear plastic covers and light up whenever that electronically keyed letter is typed on one of the regular keys below. The letters are never the same. If you type an "A," an "L" may light up on the upper set of letters. The electrical current

---

[247] Lewin, *ULTRA*, 27.

[248] Peter Calvocoressi, *Top Secret ULTRA*, (New York: Pantheon, 1980), 4.

[249] Ralph Bennett, *Ultra in the West, The Normandy Campaign 1944-45,* (New York: Charles Schribner's Sons, 1980), xiii.

[250] Winterbotham, 2.

[251] Calvocoressi, 23.

created by pressing a key goes from the keyboard to the selected electrical contacts inserted into one of twenty-six holes in a plug board. From the plug board the electric current enters one of three (later four and five) round drums mounted on a spindle. It passes through each of the three drums, off a reflector, back through the drums to the plug board again and finally to the top keyboard, where one letter lights up. Each drum has fifty-two contact points, twenty-six on each side of the drum for the twenty-six letters in the alphabet; wiring within the drum to each contact point is random. "A" on the right side of the drum may be connected to any letter but "A" on the left side of the drum. Each time a letter is depressed electricity flows through that contact point, causing the right hand drum to rotate one click. After the right hand drum has rotated twenty-six clicks, it stops rotating and the center drum begins to rotate one click, etc. If you typed an "A" in the message and got an "L" the first time, the second time you pressed the "A" key you might get a "G," depending on the machine's settings. But you would never get the same letter in succeeding key depressions because the drum rotation produces a different electrical contact point with each new letter displayed.[252]

The key to deciphering messages created on the Enigma machine was to uncover the original settings used in creating the message. Calvocoressi wrote, ". . . the machine [enigma] had a number of manually adjustable parts and the cryptographer needed to know not only how the machine was constructed and how it worked, but also how these various movable parts were set by the operator at the moment when he began transmitting each particular message."[253] In early August 1944, the Allies were once again very lucky. An air supply drop, intended for the besieged Germans holding out in Brest, fell short of its intended target and into allied lines. The parcel contained a packet of Iron Crosses for the brave defenders of Brest and, ". . . the current Enigma-setting for a substantial period ahead: this gift of the daily Enigma settings for the coming weeks was true treasure-trove."[254] Possession of the daily Enigma machine settings allowed allied intelligence officers at Bletchley Park to read secret German radio transmissions almost as soon as they were recorded.

---

[252] Calvocoressi, 24-31 inclusive. An explanation of how the ENIGMA machine worked.
[253] Calvocoressi, 23, 24.
[254] Lewin, *ULTRA*, 341.

The ULTRA Message Explained

ZZZZ message priority.
One Z is low priority,
five ZZZZZ's is the
highest priority.

XL 6330
ULTRA Message Number

XL 6330

ZZZZ

((XL 6330 £ 6330 SH 11 £ 11 SHA 55 £ 55 TG 71 £ 71

BV 98 £ 98 BVA ON CR YK ZE EF 83 £ 83 ST 95

£ 95 DL 75 £ 75 % — Decoded ULTRA Message was sent to these offices or headquarters.

EBERBACH £ EBERBACH ONE SIX ONE FIVE HOURS FOURTEENTH

TO (FAIR INDICATIONS ONE ONE SIX PANZER DIVISION)

COLON TWO BATTLE GROUPS)) OF TWO SS £ SS PANZER

DIVISION WOULD REACH BAILLEUL £ BAILLEUL THAT NIGHT.

TWO PANZER DIVISION WOULD TAKE ECOUCHE £ ECOUCHE

MORNING FIFTEENTH. ARGENTAN £ ARGENTAN THEREFORE

TO BE HELD AT ALL COSTS. PANTHER £ PANTHER ABTEILUNG

BEING SUBORDINATED TO (STRONG INDICATIONS TWO

SS £ SS) PANZER DIVISION

PCP/AHW/DJM

Initials of officer who drafted the signal and the Hut 3 Duty Officer who approved it.

151001Z/8/44

Day, hours and date this message was sent from Bletchley Park to Allied officers in the field. This message was sent on the 15th, at 1001 hours, August, 1944.

An explanation of the ULTRA Message:
Source, from photograph between pages 86 and 87:
Peter Calvocoressi, *Top Secret Ultra*, (New York: Pantheon Books, 1980).

When the Americans broke through the German western flank in July, the Germans could no longer rely on telephonic communications. They were forced to rely almost exclusively on radio messages. Telephone wires to unit headquarters had been destroyed by the massive bombing and the swiftness of the American advance did not allow the Germans time to relay the wires needed to reestablish telephone communications.

Panzer Group Eberbach, the new German armored headquarters, was created to deal with the American break out at St Lo. On August 2, Hitler ordered armored units to move from their positions between Vire and Caen to the Mortain area in an attempt to head off the Americans at Avranches.[255] The German radio message sent on that date required ". . . two whole sheets of my [Winterbotham's] *ULTRA* paper . . ."[256] If Winterbotham's account is to be believed, and there is no reason to doubt it, the Allied commanders knew at some point during the 2nd of August that Hitler ordered Kluge to ". . . collect together four of the armored divisions from the Caen front with sufficient supporting infantry divisions and make a decisive counterattack to retake Avranches and this to divide the American forces at the base of the Cherbourg peninsula."[257] Winterbotham suggests that Eisenhower considered this message so important, that he asked his Assistant SHAEF Commander, Air Marshal Arthur Tedder, to call British Intelligence and make certain that the message was not a bluff.[258] It wasn't. The next day Kluge sent a reply message to Hitler pointing out the logical consequences of an aborted attack so far west, and the very real possibility that the German force involved could be cut off and destroyed by the Allies. The Allies had at least three days warning before the German attack at Mortain. The Allies had so much time to prepare that Bradley was warned not to make his defense so stout at the point of attack lest he give away the secret that the Allies were reading German radio messages.[259]

In the chaos of fighter-bomber attacks and constant movement, it became impossible for German signalmen to lay telephone wire connecting the various headquarters. Shortages of all types of materials necessary for the conduct of military operations, particularly gasoline and ammunition, were a constant impediment for the Germans. German headquarters units had to

---

255   Winterbotham, 148.
256   Winterbotham, 148.
257   Winterbotham, 148.
258   Winterbotham, 149.
259   Winterbotham, 152.

rely on their Enigma machines, both for receiving orders and transmitting operational reports. *During the period of the Battle of the Falaise Gap, Allied cryptographers, with the daily ULTRA settings in hand, were reading secret German radio transmissions almost as fast as the Germans.*

As the battle of the Falaise Gap raged from August 8 to August 21, allied fighter-bombers took a fearful toll of thin-skinned command cars and light trucks used to transport radios and Enigma-encoding machines. Many German commanders in the Falaise pocket lost their radios and had to resort to the World War I technique of using runners to establish contact with other units. Many senior officers were out of touch with their units for extended periods. General Paul Hausser, Commanding German Seventh Army, reported that he was out of contact with both Panzer Group Eberbach and LXXIV Corps during the final stages of the battle in Normandy.[260]

Possession of the daily settings for the Enigma machine during the Battle of the Falaise Gap was an intelligence coup of the highest order. It was not unlike the American code breakthrough just before the Battle of Midway. "These were some of *ULTRA'S* most prolific days of the whole war; unprecedented amounts of Enigma traffic were being intercepted, and most of it was decoded with such rapidity that signal after signal could be prepared so close to the German time of origin that each seemed more urgent than the last . . . (Enigma traffic) was so great that for the period of the Falaise pocket a mere selection . . . to show how *ULTRA* depicted the confusion as a swift and terrible fate overtook Hitler's armies in Normandy."[261] F.W. Winterbotham agreed with the short time Bennett suggests it took for *ULTRA* decoding and transmission to high government officials and military officers. Winterbotham wrote, "Churchill was quite evidently elated . . . *his voice sounded almost gay; he was getting Hitler's signals in London within an hour of Hitler dispatching them.*"[262]

Almost never in the recorded history of warfare had one army so successfully penetrated their enemy's most intimate operational secrets, their plans, their orders for carrying out those plans, an order of battle, locations for headquarters, and unit operational boundaries. From August 10 through August 16, 1944, Hitler's arguments with Kluge over his planned counterattack against the Americans at Avranches were laid out for Allied generals in excruciating detail. British Intelligence officers reading

---

[260]   Hausser, [German] *Seventh Army in Normandy*, 56, 65.
[261]   Bennett, 119.
[262]   Winterbotham, 150.

the *ULTRA* messages bantered back and forth about who would win the argument: Kluge or Hitler. F.W. Winterbotham wrote, "My money was on Hitler."[263] He was right.

Major General Elwood R. (Pete) Quesada [Bradley's Tactical Air Commander] related the story during the battle of the Falaise Gap of how he and General Bradley once stood facing each other, clutching the latest *ULTRA* intercepts, grinning like school boys, saying, "We've got them."[264] Allied commanders would have two weeks from August 2 to close the trap.

Each US armored division in Normandy contained one Cavalry Reconnaissance Squadron; each Reconnaissance Squadron contained four Cavalry Reconnaissance Troops of five officers and 140 enlisted men.[265] This meant that each of the three Combat Commands, CCA, CCB, and CCR (reserve) had their own Reconnaissance Troop, with one Troop left over for Division Headquarters. The Squadrons also contained one Assault Gun Troop with four Assault Gun Platoons, one Light Tank Company with three Light Tank Platoons, in addition to Squadron Headquarters Troop and attached service units. The total assigned strength, from July 1944, of each Squadron was forty-two officers and 852 enlisted men, about the size of a regular infantry battalion.[266] Each US infantry division contained one Cavalry Reconnaissance Troop. Independent Cavalry Reconnaissance Squadrons were also assigned to each US Corps Headquarters, but they had three, not four, Reconnaissance Troops.

General Patton was determined that his Third Army should advance further and faster than any other Army in Europe. Patton never cared that his flanks were wide open, but he desperately needed timely intelligence about the Germans. There was no reconnaissance force attached to his Army Headquarters, so he had to improvise. He talked Bradley into assigning Colonel Edward M. Fickett's 6th Cavalry Group to Third Army. Colonel Fickett's men were reorganized into a unit called Army Information Service (AIS), with the double task of reconnaissance and communications. The reconnaissance platoons, with two officers and twenty-eight men each, were ". . . to report all activities in the areas they covered. Their reports were

---

263   Winterbotham, 149.
264   Lewin, *ULTRA*, 339.
265   Bradley, *A Soldier's Story*, Appendix.
266   Bradley, *A Soldier's Story*, Appendix, also see US Cavalry Recon. Squadron Mech. From   http://www.bayonetstrength.150m.com/Reconnaissance/united_states_cavalry_reconnaiss . . . 10/22/2006

condensed into teletype messages and sent to Third Army's advance CP."[267] Fickett and his men soon gained fame as 'Patton's Household Cavalry.' They were Patton's eyes and ears on the battlefield, often making Patton better informed about enemy dispositions than the commanding officers in other units, closer to front line action.

From August 10 through 14, there were five US Armored and eight US Infantry Divisions, four US Corps Headquarters (the VII, XII, XV, and XX), and two Army Headquarters (First and Third) carrying out offensive operations in the triangle formed by Mortain-Le Mans-L'Aigle. The total number of reconnaissance patrols conducted within that triangle during those five days would have been staggering. They came to the same conclusion as 3rd Squadron's report to XX Corps: "The 3rd Squadron, reinforced by the light tanks of the 43rd squadron was dispatched to patrol north and make contact with First US Army units around MAYENNE. The cavalry made contact and was ordered to make an area reconnaissance east. In a three-day action it struck east on an approximately eighty-mile front and as a result of the area reconnaissance which carried them east to a north-south line, SEES to BLOIS, it was determined that the left flank of the Seventh German Army was lightly held and the moment opportune for an encirclement."[268]

Forty-third Squadron's three-day reconnaissance ended on August 13, when they reported back to XX Corps. According to a XX Corps' Operational Report, "By August 13, it was apparent that the majority of Seventh German Army was trapped."[269] The same day US reconnaissance units were reporting that the Germans were trapped in Normandy, British intelligence officers at Montgomery's 21st Army Group headquarters gave an extensive intelligence briefing which concluded that too many Germans had already escaped the Allied trap. Who was right?

General George Patton's flamboyant reputation has provided some historians, including General Bradley, with a convenient scapegoat for the events in the Falaise Pocket.

If there was an American commander out of step with what was happening at the Falaise Gap, his name was not George Patton, it was Omar Bradley. With opportunities literally leaping from the maps at

---

[267] Farago, 492.
[268] XX Corps, United States Army, *An Operational Report, The Campaigns of Normandy and France, 1 August-1 September, 1944,* 5.
[269] XX Corps, *Operational Report,* 5.

Third and First Army Headquarters, Bradley decided to take the day off. It was, after all, a Sunday. He spent part of the morning at Eisenhower's headquarters, the afternoon at a luncheon, a briefing, and a review of the Allied situation in the Falaise Gap. By that evening, Bradley was back at Eisenhower's, ". . . playing bridge as calmly and peacefully as if he had just come off the golf course on a Sunday afternoon."[270] Patton and Hodges never saw Bradley that Sunday. They were left to ponder, 'what might have been.'

Bradley was apparently unconcerned about closing the Falaise Gap. In the event of a disagreement between officers, the senior officer is required [by US Army protocol] to go down the chain-of-command to solve the problem. Bradley did not do that on August 13. He refused to discuss the halt-decisions that day with either Patton or Hodges at their headquarters, as army protocol demanded. General Patton confirmed this requirement in a list of "Fighting Principles" he drew up. He wrote, [It is], ". . . always easier for the senior to go up (to the front) than for the junior to come back."[271] But Bradley later insisted that his decision was correct, "My proper place that day was where I spent it, with Ike and Monty."[272]

In addition to *ULTRA* and recent ground reconnaissance reports, the allies enjoyed absolute air supremacy over the Normandy battlefield. The allies also had the good fortune of being able to read *ULTRA* messages almost as soon as they came in. On August 11, *ULTRA* message XL 5728 was released to allied commanders at 2328 hours: *ONE ONE SIX PANZER DIVISION TAKEN OUT OF LINE AND)) COLLECTING IN AREA ST. SAUVEUR DE CHAULIEU & ST. SAUVEUR DE CHAULIEU (SOURDEVAL & SOURDEVAL EXCLUSIVE) . . . ACCORDING ((FLIVO)) SEVENTH ARMY NOUGHT SIX HOURS ELEVENTH)).*[273] A rough translation is, "The German Seventh Army reported that 116th Panzer has been removed from the line and is assembling near Sourdeval."

On August 12, *ULTRA* message XL 5845 reported: "FOUR SEVEN CORPS NOUGHT SIX HOURS TWELVTH COLON WITHDRAW)) MOVEMENT BEGAN TWO ONE HOURS ELEVENTH. TWO PANZER DIVISIONS OCCUPIED MAIN DEFENSE LINE IN LEFT SECTOR.

---

[270]   Butcher, 640.

[271]   Blumenson, (Ed.), *The Patton Papers, 1940-1945*, 424.

[272]   Bradley, *A General's Life*, 301,

[273]   ULTRA Message # 5728.

ONE ONE SIX PANZER DIVISION ON THE MOVE WITH ALL
ELEMENTS DIRECTION ALENCON & ALENCON."[274]

REF. CX/MSS/T.273/108   XL 5728

ZZZZ

((XL 5728 £ 5728 SH 1 £ 1 SHA 45 £ 45 TG 29 £ 29

BV 56 £ 56 ON YK ZE EF 9 £ 9 ST 82 £ 82 DL 12 £ 12 %

ONE ONE SIX PANZER DIVISION TAKEN OUT OF LINE AND))

COLLECTING IN AREA ST.SAUVEUR DE CHAULIEU £ ST.

SAUVEUR DE CHAULIEU (SOURDEVAL £ SOURDEVAL EXCLUSIVE)

AND LE FRESNE PORET £ LE FRESNE PORET ACCORDING

((FLIVO SEVENTH ARMY NOUGHT SIX HOURS ELEVENTH))

TELB/JEM   112328Z/8/44.

---

[274]   ULTRA Message # 5845.

3

REF: CX/MSS/T274/57   XL 5845

ZZZZ   189

((XL 5845 £ 5845 SH 83 £ 83 SHA 28 £ 28 TG 8 £ 8
BV 35 £ 35 ON CR YK ZE EF 89 £ 89 ST 47 £ 47 DL 73
£ 73 %

TWELFTH
FOUR SEVEN CORPS NOUGHT SIX HOURS ~~FIFTEENTH~~ COLON WITH/
WITHDRAWAL)) MOVEMENT BEGUN TWO ONE HOURS ELEVENTH.
TWO PANZER DIVISION OCCUPIED MAIN DEFENCE LINE IN LEFT
SECTOR. ONE ONE SIX PANZER DIVISION ON THE MOVE WITH
ALL ELEMENTS DIRECTION ALENCON £ ALENCON

DB/HDD

1215362/8/44

G B

That same morning, August 12, between the hours of 0845 and 0945, a tactical air reconnaissance mission was flown by Butch Lowndes and Ken Hay-Roe of 430 Squadron, ". . . in the Falaise, Argentan, Sees, Briouze, Domfront area."[275] 430 Squadron was attached to General Miles Dempsey's British Second Army. Writing after the battle, General Richard Rohmer reports, "What Butch Lowndes saw as he flew west out of Argentan along the main highway to Briouze was six German tanks lumbering eastward at Fromentel, only ten miles west of Argentan."[276] Any senior allied officer with access to both *ULTRA* and this tactical air reconnaissance report could easily deduce that these were elements of 116th Panzer heading for Alencon and US XV Corps' open flank.

It seems amazing, in retrospect, that allied commanders even suggested they missed closing the trap on the Germans because of faulty intelligence information. There would appear to be an overwhelming amount of timely and highly accurate intelligence information available to the men who claim to have made the wrong decision, based, they said, on faulty intelligence. Ronald Lewin strongly disagrees, "To recreate for oneself the chaos in the German escape-pocket by reading the (*ULTRA*) signals sent out from Bletchley is to see that whatever else Montgomery and Bradley may have lacked, it was not intelligence about the enemy. *These messages confirm, in fact, that an explanation for the Allies failure to cut off the Germans completely at Falaise must be sought elsewhere.*" [277] If intelligence was not at fault, then what was? Was this a simple case of taking the counsel of one's fears? Did Allied commanders simply lack the boldness that the situation required? Or did British intelligence officers manipulate their estimates to serve some hidden political agenda?

The British government did not release the *ULTRA* secret for nearly 40 years. It took *ULTRA* less than ten years to force major historical revisions of the events in Normandy. The British were the acknowledged Allied intelligence experts in Europe; they had hundreds of years of diplomatic and intelligence experience. Shortly after the war began, they had turned an entire German spy network to work for the Allies. The British also had *ULTRA*.

The Americans, unfortunately, had no intelligence background in Europe; they relied totally on British intelligence. In the Pacific, the

---

275   Richard Rohmer, *Patton's Gap*, (New York: Beaufort Books, 1981), 192.
276   Rohmer, 193.
277   Lewin, *ULTRA*, 342. Italics added.

Americans had their own *MAGIC,* a way to read parts of the Japanese Purple Code. But in Europe, the British ran the show. According to Ralph Ingersoll, "In matters touching the European Theater, the British had a 100 percent airtight, hermetically sealed monopoly on Intelligence about the enemy . . ."[278] When First Canadian Army was activated, the Canadians were also dependent on British intelligence.[279]

The British had produced staff studies on the proposed Allied invasion of southern France code named Operation *Anvil.* Their staff officers manipulated information on the invasion of southern France, hoping to prove to the Americans that it could never succeed. Even if it did succeed, they said, the ports in southern France would never provide the logistical support the Americans expected. British intelligence failed to convince the Americans. Their staff work was subsequently proven wrong on nearly every point. "Later in the war the OPD [Operations and Planning Division] published the British [staff] studies as a book, *The Castigation of Anvil.* It was used in staff officer training as an edifying collection of planning howlers."[280] The British were not only wrong, they were so wrong it was funny. At least the Americans had found a use for the staff work British officers put into their opposition of *Anvil.*

Writing in 1946, Ingersoll's attempted outing of *ULTRA* was thirty years too early: "This is not generally known, and if asked directly the British would deny it, but—and I state this as a positive fact—the British circulated documents among themselves labeled with a code word known only to them. This code word meant for 'eyes of British officers only.'"[281] The code word was *ULTRA.* Ingersoll might have been surprised to learn that his American boss, General Omar Bradley, was also privy to the *ULTRA* secret.

During the long planning phase for *OVERLORD*, the allied code name for the invasion of Europe, Anglo-American cooperation was at its strongest since the early invasions in North Africa. Both sides ignored personal differences and national concerns; British and Americans seemed to grasp the enormity of the challenge before them, and the utter disaster which would have resulted from an Allied defeat on the beaches of Normandy.

---

[278] Ingersoll, 71. Also see Morgan, 45: "The Americans were therefore happy to concede the direction of the intelligence setup . . . to the British."

[279] Paul Douglas Dickson, *A Thoroughly Canadian General, A Biography of General H.D.G. Crerar,* (Toronto: University of Toronto Press, 2007), 265

[280] Perret, 307.

[281] Ingersoll, 71.

* OPD—Operations and Planning Division of the US War Department

Churchill dreamed of the English Channel running red with the blood of British and American soldiers killed during the invasion.[282] The day of the invasion, Eisenhower carried a slip of paper around in his shirt pocket, notes on a speech he would have made to the assembled press corps in the event his invasion forces were thrown back into the sea. Eisenhower would have taken full personal responsibility for the failed invasion. It would have probably ruined his career.

British and American commitments to the Alliance remained strong during the buildup phase of operations. While the potential for defeat remained a possibility, the Allies succeeded in burying the animosity, which had surfaced in North Africa and Sicily. Once the extent of the American victory at St Lo became apparent, British demands on their American allies increased dramatically. Winston Churchill spent most of the day on August 9, berating Eisenhower over Operation *Dragoon* [renamed from *Anvil*], the Allied landing in southern France. Hour after hour Churchill blustered and bullied the Supreme Commander.

The British had no soldiers involved in the *Dragoon* landings; all the divisions involved were either French or American. The British, however, believed they had the right to determine when and where all other Allied soldiers fought. Indeed, Churchill became so agitated during this argument; he threatened to go to the King, and ". . . lay down the mantle of my High Office."[283] In the end, Eisenhower was emotionally and physically drained, but he was powerless to change the landings, scheduled to begin on August 15, barely one week away. Operation *Dragoon* had the firm support of both President Roosevelt and General Marshall. Operation *Dragoon* had also been promised to Marshal Stalin at Tehran in late 1943.[284]

General Montgomery had been working on a long-range strategic plan which would put most of Bradley's 12th Army Group under British Command. Bradley later remarked that Montgomery's plan was, ". . . an unworkable . . . strategic plan that was sure to lead to endless debate and acrimony."[285] Churchill, Brooke, and Montgomery represented the weakest, yet most politically astute and determined member of the Allied Alliance—an unfortunate fact they would go to great lengths to obscure, often at the expense of the naive Americans. The British, always short of

[282]   Sherwood, 590.
[283]   Ambrose, *Eisenhower, Soldier, General*, 330.
[284]   Keith Eubank, *Summit at Teheran*, (New York: William Morrow, 1985), 436.
[285]   Bradley, *A General's Life*, 301.

men, were deeply annoyed that they could no longer determine when and where US soldiers would fight. Politically, the British had far more to lose in Europe than the Americans.

ULTRA, air reconnaissance, and ground reconnaissance were all available to Allied commanders. None of these estimates had an impact on Allied Intelligence estimates about the Germans in the Falaise Pocket. The one thing which did seem to influence Allied intelligence estimates, oddly enough, was the position of General Patton's Third US Army in relation to the Allied inter-Army Group boundary just south of Argentan. It seems odd at first, but as Patton's Third Army closed on the Allied boundary near Argentan, the likelihood that the Germans had escaped from the pocket increased dramatically. Put another way, the chance that the Germans in the pocket got away was inversely proportional to the shrinking distance between Hailsip's XV Corps and the Allied boundary line south of Argentan.

It could be called *Intelligence by Inverse Proportionality*. When, on August 8, orders were given to Patton to turn Haislip north from Le Mans, Montgomery believed, quite reasonably, that the Germans were likely to try to escape the Allied trap. By August 9, if and when the Germans began their retreat from Normandy Montgomery now had a plan. He wrote to Brooke, "Should the Germans escape us here I shall proceed quickly with the plan outlined in M517—the wider envelopment."[286] On August 11, one day after Haislip turned his Corps to the north, Montgomery was so certain that the Germans would try to escape the Falaise Pocket, he ordered Bradley to withhold three US divisions at Le Mans in preparation for the wide envelopment to the Seine, to trap those Germans who may have escaped from Normandy.[287]

By the time Patton's troops reached the inter-Army Group boundary at Argentan during the night of August 12/13, British intelligence insisted, despite a mountain of evidence to the contrary, that so many Germans had already escaped from the Falaise Gap; it was time to begin the wide envelopment to the Seine.[288] This was the basis for those erroneous British intelligence estimates given to Bradley and Eisenhower at Montgomery's headquarters on the afternoon of August 13. Montgomery confirmed them

---

[286]   Hamilton, *Master*, 779.
[287]   Hamilton, *Master*, 784
[288]   Bradley, *A General's Life*, 299, 300.

in a letter to Bradley the following day.[289] Bradley now had official cover, thanks to Montgomery's amazing British intelligence estimates, for the horribly wrong halt-order he gave to Patton and Hodges on the morning of August 13. It gets worse.

Late on the afternoon of August 14, Bradley, following directions in the letter he had just received from Montgomery, sent three corps of Patton's Third Army northeast toward Dreux, Chartres, Orleans, and the Seine River.[290] It is really quite amazing, but the law of *Intelligence by Inverse Proportionality* works a second time. This time the factors involved are the shrinking distance between Patton's Third Army and the Seine River, and the strength of the German Army in the Falaise pocket. That is, the strength of the German Army in the Falaise Pocket will increase in inverse proportion to the shrinking distance between George Patton's Third Army and the Seine River. Less than one day after Patton left the Falaise Gap, August 15, Bradley hurries to Patton's Headquarters, and ". . . suffering from nerves," he brings the astonishing news ". . . that the Germans had not yet withdrawn after all. Elements of at least five panzer divisions were at or approaching Argentan."[291] Bradley also orders Patton to halt his movement toward the Seine until they sort out the mess in the Falaise Pocket. The next day, his nerves apparently settled, Bradley allows Patton to continue his drive northeast.

By August 19, Patton's army was on the Seine at Mantes. Patton had visited the river early that morning. Patton's aid, Major Alexander C. Stiller, made undated notes on General Bradley's visit to Patton's headquarters: "Gen. B. told him how strong the people were in the Falaise pocket and didn't think Gen. P. would be able to contain them . . . they had a big conference and decided that the Third Army shouldn't go beyond . . . Dreux . . . and Chartres . . . (and toward) the Seine . . ."[292] According to Bradley, the Falaise Pocket now contained, ". . . elements of perhaps twelve German divisions, half of them panzers."[293] Patton told Bradley they were already on the Seine; did he want Patton to pull back, and give up ground they had already taken? After some discussion, Bradley agreed that Patton could keep the ground he had already taken, but was to await orders before he advanced any further.

[289]   Bradley, *A General's Life*, 300.
[290]   Patton, 108.
[291]   Bradley, *A General's Life,* 303.
[292]   Blumenson, (Ed.), *The Patton Papers, 1940-1945,* 521.
[293]   Bradley, *A General's Life,* 304.

Patton was given three halt-orders in less than a week: August 13, August 15, and August 19. His mad dash to the Seine made his superiors very nervous, but there was never any great danger, because there were so few Germans around. The Germans were still back in the Falaise Pocket, having magically reappeared. All Patton had to do to confirm their presence in Normandy was to show up at the Seine. If Montgomery did not want Patton anywhere near Falaise, he certainly didn't relish the thought of Patton crossing the Seine and taking Paris.

General Patton was, in fact, the reason for Montgomery's "astonishing intelligence." It had been that damned George Patton all along. Montgomery needed British Intelligence officers to come up with some justification for halting Patton's advance toward Falaise. If the Germans were escaping the trap in Normandy, that would bring his wider envelopment to the Seine back into play. He could then halt Patton at Argentan and later send him on to the Seine. Not an ideal solution, to be sure, but certainly preferable to sending Patton across the gap between Argentan and Falaise and letting him take all the credit for trapping the Germans in the Falaise Pocket.

On August 13 Montgomery wrote to Brooke in England. "There has been considerable enemy movement by day going on but . . . only administrative echelons have so far passed eastward through the gap Falaise-Argentan . . . I am continuing operations on the assumption that the bulk of the enemy forces are still inside the ring as stated by my Intelligence staff."[294] That same afternoon, August 13, Montgomery's Intelligence staff left the Americans with a different impression. General Bradley described that Intelligence briefing: ". . . the general impression conveyed was that the German commanders . . . were already carrying out a substantial withdraw to the east . . . No one was certain how many German divisions had withdrawn or still remained. But the general estimate was that too many had already escaped."[295] Montgomery confirmed that estimate the following day in a letter to Bradley. Montgomery's intelligence staff was quite capable of producing information, which showed both that the Germans had fled the Falaise pocket and that they were "still inside the ring." The hard part was keeping the Americans quiet about an erroneous bit of intelligence that was supported neither by *ULTRA* nor by any other verifiable source. Eisenhower and Bradley apparently said nothing.

---

[294] Hamilton, *Master,* 789.
[295] Bradley, *A General's Life*, 299.

Here was a clear example of British intelligence being used as a tool to politicize what should have been a simple tactical decision. The British had tweaked critical intelligence information for political reasons on both *Anvil* and *Overlord*.[296] Now they manipulated intelligence about the German Armies in Normandy. Montgomery had always preferred the wider envelopment to the Seine. He got the Americans back on the right track with intelligence manipulated to say that, ". . . too many Germans had already escaped."[297] Montgomery forwarded the correct intelligence estimates to Brooke. For the Americans, Montgomery's intelligence staff was probably directed to manipulate the intelligence to say exactly what Montgomery wanted it to say.

There was, as *ULTRA* confirms, no intelligence estimates supporting Montgomery's conclusion. The only intelligence supporting the idea that the Germans had escaped prior to August 16 was the misinformation provided by Montgomery's people at 21st Army Group Headquarters. Indeed, there was a mountain of intelligence saying exactly the opposite. *ULTRA* records a day-to-day dramatization of German generals complaining about their situation in the Falaise Pocket, begging for permission to withdraw. Each day their situation in the pocket grew more desperate than the day before. Hitler later granted grudging permission to shorten the line at Mortain, so that his commanders could withdraw the armored forces needed to deal with Haislip's XV Corps.

Montgomery knew all this and more. He also knew from *ULTRA* that the attack on Haislip's XV Corps was a prerequisite for the renewed German attack at Mortain, deep in the Falaise Pocket, and not preparation for a withdraw from the pocket.[298] It was true that support elements of the German Army [administration, supply, and medical personnel] were leaving Normandy. Montgomery said he wanted to capture all the Germans in Normandy, but that was just a ruse. He was never going to capture all the Germans in Normandy. A few Germans were going to get away no matter what the Allies did. But it was also true that new German divisions were entering Normandy almost daily. Eisenhower wrote, "Five divisions [German] entered the battle area during the week August 5-12 . . ."[299]

---

[296] Ingersoll, 71-73. Also see Perret, 307.
[297] Bradley, *A General's Life*, 299.
[298] Bennett, 118.
[299] Eisenhower, *Crusade*, 278.

The British and Canadians were fighting hard for every mile down the road to Falaise. It was nothing for Patton's Army, operating against fewer Germans in open country to make twenty or even thirty miles a day. Worse, from Montgomery's point of view, the Americans were getting all the headlines.

Most commanders with a map on the wall and a reconnaissance squadron in the field knew the British intelligence estimates were wrong. Eisenhower and Bradley must have known it, and Montgomery probably expected that they knew. Most senior commanders had access to the *ULTRA* intercepts, and *ULTRA* did not lie. The German problem was not that they were leaving too many men behind in Normandy, but that Hitler refused them permission to leave at all. Bradley knew it was not only wrong but dangerous to move Patton's divisions northeast with so many Germans still in the pocket, which was probably why he waited for Montgomery's written instructions on August 14 before sending Patton's three corps northeast.

There was a timing lapse of over thirty hours between the halt-order given to Patton at 1130 hours on the 13th and Patton's instructions for his three corps to move northeast at 2030 hours on the 14th. [300] Bradley could have given this order at any time, once Montgomery's halt-order at Argentan had been confirmed. But he had probably decided not to move any of Patton's divisions without very specific, historically verifiable orders from Montgomery. In this case, Montgomery's usual method of giving his Army Group commanders verbal instructions was not good enough. Bradley had apparently made it clear to Montgomery that all those US divisions sitting on the open German flank would continue to sit there, until he received instructions from Montgomery in writing. It must have been late in the afternoon on August 14 before Bradley got the letter from Montgomery, and for one of the few times during the entire war, Montgomery issued his instructions in writing. Nearly a day-and-a-half had been wasted.

Montgomery's supporters like to paint a picture of Allied harmony and common purpose on August 13, but that was far from the truth. Nigel Hamilton wrote, "Allied tactical policy on August 13 was clear and undivided. It was only on the following day, on 14 August 1944, that doubts began to arise over which portion of the German armies was still entrapped in the pocket—and the accusations began."[301] If Allied tactical policy was clear on August 13, which Allied Army was engaged in trapping the Germans in the

---

[300] Patton, 108.
[301] Hamilton, *Master*, 789.

pocket? There was none. And why were all those Americans on the southern German flank just camping out in the French countryside, didn't they know there was a war on?

The truth was that the military alliance had broken down, just as Eisenhower had predicted in his August 11th letter to Prime Minister Churchill.[302] Future Allied command decisions would be based on the same political bias and professional jealousy that created the debacle at the Falaise Gap. Historian Russell F. Weigley notes the sudden appearance of animosity between Montgomery and Bradley: ". . . that suspicion and dislike had grown so rapidly out of so little apparent controversy indicates sources far deeper than Montgomery's unamiable personality, old distrusts between Americans and British far stronger than the rhetoric of the Grand Alliance."[303]

The Americans never forgave Montgomery for his blatant political decision at the Falaise Gap. American Generals Eisenhower, Bradley, Hodges, and Collins were diplomatically silent at the time, but the bitterness was readily apparent in their behavior and attitudes. August 13 marked a turning point, Patton and Bradley, prior antagonists, became friends and comrades. Montgomery, once admired for his impartial command of the Americans, was now reviled for real and imagined deficiencies. It had only taken a few weeks, but the mood change at Bradley's 12th US Army Group was readily apparent. Through the end of the war in Europe, Montgomery and Bradley would be at odds over military strategy, especially the command of US Army divisions assigned to SHAEF. Bradley, the odd man out, would usually lose the argument.

Eisenhower and Bradley could put on a smiling face for public consumption because George Marshall demanded it. Their correspondence with Montgomery would also retain a measure of polite congeniality, but it can now be said that the veneer of friendship that remained between Montgomery and the Americans was based solely on General Marshall's insistence that American commanders respect the Anglo-American Alliance.

---

[302] Chandler, (Ed.), *The Eisenhower Papers, Vol. IV*, 2065.
[303] Weigley, *Eisenhower's Lieutenants*, 210.

Chapter 5

The Germans in Normandy

"My nerves are pretty good, but sometimes I was near collapse. It was casualty reports, casualty reports, casualty reports, wherever you went. I have never fought with such losses."[304] Field Marshal Erwin Rommel

"The 1 SS Pz Div had never before fought so miserably as at that time. The fighting morale of the German troops had cracked. This I openly reported to Gen Model on August 18, 1944 . . ."[305] General of Panzer Troops, Heinrich Eberbach

If one of something is very good, it does not always follow that two of the same thing is even better. This was true for the German plan, or plan(s) to defend the Atlantic coastline. They called it the "Atlantic Wall."

The textbook solution for defending a long natural barrier was to hold the front with only minimal forces and while creating a powerful mobile force miles behind the front. These forces would be deployed after the assault, when the location of the enemy's main attack was known. Wehrmacht Commander in Chief West, Field Marshal Karl Gerd von Rundstedt favored the textbook solution. So did the Commander of Panzer Group West, General Baron Geyr von Schweppenburg. Neither officer had experience fighting the Western Allies prior to the invasion.

The one Wehrmacht commander who did have combat experience against the British and Americans was Army Group B Commander, Field Marshal Erwin Rommel. Rommel thought that the Allies' absolute control of the air would prevent the panzer reserve divisions from moving quickly to the invasion area. He estimated if the Allies had one or two days in the beachhead, they would become too strong to throw back into the sea.

---

[304] Erwin Rommel, *The Rommel Papers,* Edited by B.H. Liddell Hart with Lucie-Maria Rommel, Manfred Rommel and General Fritz Bayerlein, Translated by Paul Findlay, (New York: Harcourt, Brace, 1953, Fourteenth Printing), 496.

[305] Eberbach, 22.

To prevent this Rommel said, ". . . everything must be directed toward destroying the enemy-landing force while it is still on the water, or at the latest during the landing itself . . . Once they (Allies) have beached and disembarked their troops and weapons, their fighting power multiplies many times over."[306] Rommel was worried about the effect of Allied air power on German reinforcements rushing to the invasion area. Would German reinforcements be able to assemble fast enough, under skies dominated by Allied air power?

Rommel tried to get several panzer divisions moved closer to the Normandy coastline. In May, he asked for permission to move ". . . the 12th SS Panzer Division into the Cotentin peninsula, and the Panzer Lehr Division to the neighborhood of Avranches."[307] Neither request was approved. Rommel predicted that a combination of air and sea power would make a large-scale German attack during daytime nearly impossible. As it turned out, Rommel was right. If Rommel's suggestions had been followed, there was a good chance the Germans would have won the battle of Normandy.

In addition to major motion pictures, *The Longest Day* and *Saving Private Ryan*, the story of the Allied invasion of Europe has been told and retold dozens of times in print and will not be described here. It has been repeated so often that it seems as if Allied success on D-day was almost guaranteed. It wasn't.

The success of the Allied invasion was a very narrow victory, a very close battle. It was a closer run thing than it appears to be in most historical accounts. A whole series of events conspired against the German defenders. The Allies' first stroke of good luck was Operation *Fortitude*; it worked far longer than they could have reasonably expected. This was the Allied ruse that " . . . was designed to make the Germans think that there would be a preliminary attack in Norway, followed by the main assault at the Pas de Calais."[308] Given the location of V-weapon sites on the Pas de Calais and the short distance from England, many German senior officers were absolutely convinced the Allied invasion in Normandy was a feint. Although the Germans did borrow some divisions from this sector as their front in Normandy collapsed, a substantial portion of the Fifteenth Army, nearly

---

[306]   Rommel, 456.
[307]   Rommel, 470. Also see Hans Speidel, *Invasion, 1944*, (New York: Paperback Library, 1964), 79.
[308]   Ambrose, *Eisenhower, Soldier, General*, 290.

100,000 men, remained on the Pas de Calais until Montgomery's forces drove past them on their way to Antwerp in early September.[309]

The weather provided the Allies with another lucky break; it was horrible: cloudy, high winds, heavy seas, and driving rain. From their bases on the continent, it appeared to the Germans that bad weather would last for days. But in England, on the morning of June 5, weather expert and Group Captain J. M. Stagg told Eisenhower and his assembled officers there would be a break in the weather. "The rain that was then pouring down . . . would stop in two or three hours, to be followed by thirty-six hours of more or less clear weather. Winds would moderate."[310] The Germans were unaware of this break in the weather. German Admiral Hennecke read his weather report: "Rough sea, poor visibility, Force 5-6 wind, rain likely to get heavier," and his meteorologists' forecast: "There is little prospect of short-term changes in the weather during the next few days."[311]

Many senior German officers were due at a war games conference set for 1000 hours, June 6 at Rennes. Contrary to orders from Colonel-General Dollman, the Seventh Army Commander, several officers left early for the conference and were not at their posts when the invasion began. "Naval [German] patrols did not put to sea on the evening of June 5 because of 'heavy seas.'"[312]

Rommel took the opportunity to return home to Herrlingen, Germany, on the morning of June 5 for his wife's birthday the following day.[313] He purchased a pair of shoes for her in Paris. He had also planned a meeting with Hitler to discuss command issues and the deployment of OKW's reserve armored divisions. Adolf Hitler preferred to limit the authority of his field commanders; he seldom gave any commander too much control. Rommel did not even command all the Wehrmacht divisions in France. Most of the Panzer divisions were kept in tactical reserve, to be released by Hitler only after reviewing a request from von Rundstedt.

Another tricky command issue for the Germans involved coastal artillery. "The [German] Navy claimed the responsibility for coastal gunnery as long as the invader was sea-borne, but after the landing was made the Army should

---

[309] J.L. Moulton, *Battle for Antwerp*, (London: Ian Allan Ltd., 1978), 46.

[310] Ambrose, *Eisenhower*, 307.

[311] Paul Carell, *Invasion, They're Coming,* Translated by E. Osers, (New York: Bantam Books, 1964), 5.

[312] Speidel, 77.

[313] Carell, 6. Also see Rommel, 470, 471.

take over . . . This led to a disagreement in the planning stages between the tactical artillery principles of the Navy and of the Army, particularly in such matters as the placing of guns and observation posts as well as the actual servicing of the guns."[314]

With a poor, nearly dysfunctional system of command in place, it was amazing the Germans fought as well as they did in Normandy. The unsoundness of the German chain of command, particularly command of the panzer divisions, was a major factor in the German failure to contain and defeat the Allied invasion on June 6. "Rommel demanded orally and in writing that all three services and the Todt Organization in his area be put under his command for one decisive defense effort."[315] His request was denied.

General Patton is supposed to have remarked, 'I'd rather be lucky than good.' The Germans in Normandy were unlucky; they had been tricked by Operation *Fortitude South*, deceived by the weather, and handicapped by their own system of command. Still, the Americans barely held on at Omaha Beach, where they met the 726th, 914th, and 916th Grenadier Regiments of the excellent 352nd German Infantry Division. The issue was in doubt for hours as American dead and wounded piled up on the beach. Only slowly did small groups of men begin to work their way through the beach obstacles and barbed wire up the cliffs, to the source of the terrible automatic weapons fire that had killed so many of their friends. By nightfall, more than two-thousand Americans had become casualties on Omaha Beach, but they scratched out a small bridgehead. The Allies were in France to stay.

Hurrying back to his command post from Germany, Rommel must have sensed time slipping away. Field Marshal von Rundstedt had requested the release of the I SS Panzer Corps, consisting of 12th SS Panzer and Panzer Lehr Divisions early that morning, just after he had received reports of an Allied airborne landing. "The I SS Panzer Corps was finally released that afternoon about 3:00 p.m., but it could not be moved during daylight because of enemy air supremacy . . . It was not until June 9 that the counterattack of the I SS Panzer Corps was carried out."[316] Of course, had OKW and Hitler listened to Rommel a month earlier, the 12th SS Panzer would already be in the Cotentin engaging the left flank of the Americans coming off Utah Beach. With the trouble 1st US Infantry Division had at Omaha, the

---

[314]   Speidel, 45.
[315]   Speidel, 38.
[316]   Speidel, 80.

appearance of just one more German division on the American flank may have been decisive. Once again, the Germans guessed wrong.

The only German attack on June 6 which offered any chance for success was the 21st Panzer Division's attack on the east flank near Caen. Major General Feuchtinger, commanding 21st Panzer, was forming up his division for an attack on the east bank of the Orne ". . . when an order arrived from Seventh Army instructing the division to launch its counterattack on the *west* bank of the Orne."[317] Much time was lost in the ensuing confusion, but eventually one battle group of the 21st Panzer put in the attack, ". . . which did . . . get through to the coast."[318] 21st Panzer was forced to cut the attack short, however, when they discovered British parachute troops in their rear. They withdrew in the direction of Caen to avoid being cut off.

Late on the afternoon of June 6, I SS Panzer Corps began moving to the Allied beachheads in Normandy. They soon discovered that Rommel's warnings about trying to move divisions under skies controlled by Allied air power were fully justified. Movement by day was fraught with extreme danger from Allied fighter-bombers; cratered roads and traffic congestion interrupted movement by night. When the I SS Panzer Corps attack finally went forward on June 9th, they were ordered to attack and push the British/Canadians back from the Caen-Bayeux sector. This was the same area 21st Panzer Division had attacked on D-day with considerable success until British paratroopers got behind the panzers. The Germans now discovered that any large concentration of men and armor preparing for an attack was likely broken up with heavy losses by accurate fire from naval guns, concentrated artillery fire, and Allied fighter-bombers. The attack never really got off. "Saturation bombing and sustained naval gunfire had prevented the I SS Panzer Corps from assembling in time in the area south of Caen. There were heavy German losses in men and material, particularly in signal equipment . . . After local successes, the advance toward the coast was halted."[319]

The next major German attack was planned for the night of June 10/11. It had been planned by General Baron Geyr von Schweppenburg commanding Panzer Group West. Shortly before the attack was to go in, ". . . the headquarters staff of the Western Panzer group was practically wiped out by saturation bombing . . . The Panzer Group lost its Chief of

---

[317]   Rommel, 473. Italics in the original.

[318]   Rommel, 473.

[319]   Speidel, 80, 81.

Staff, General von Dawans, and the IA, its operations officer, as well as other officers. The communications system was put out of commission."[320] The attack had to be called off.

It was over almost before it began. The brief period of Allied vulnerability to German counterattack was gone in less than three days. It had happened just as Field Marshal Rommel predicted it would.

The volume and accuracy of rapid naval gunfire caught the Germans completely by surprise. "Off the five selected landing points there appeared six battleships, twenty-three cruisers, 122 destroyers, 360 motor torpedo boats, and a few hundred frigates, sloops, and patrol boats."[321] Coordination between "forward artillery observers," "artillery control centers" on land and "naval fire control centers" aboard ships in the English Channel had been worked out prior to the invasion. German naval experts had expected a ten to fifteen-mile artillery range from Allied ships in the English Channel. They were taken aback when Allied ships engaged targets as far as twenty to twenty-five miles from the coast.[322] "There was an uncanny precision in the cooperation between the Allied land forces and their air and naval support, as the first three days of the invasion had shown."[323]

The period of danger for the invading Allies had passed, as long as the Allies operated within range of the naval guns, up to twenty miles from the coast. According to Rommel, the Germans were unable to assemble units for an attack within range of those guns. Four days after the invasion, on June 10, Rommel wrote, "The effect of the heavy naval guns is so immense that no operation of any kind is possible in the area commanded by this rapid-fire artillery, either by infantry or tanks."[324] The Allied secret was the placement of naval forward observers with frontline infantry units who were in direct communication with shipboard fire control centers in the English Channel.[325] Thus, in a matter of minutes, Allied infantry units could bring down a rain of highly accurate, large caliber shellfire on their enemy.

The movement of German units in Normandy was becoming increasingly difficult. Units moved forward piecemeal, usually at night, and were rushed into the line to shore up holes in the defensive perimeter. Allied control of the air was allowing the Allies to land forces in Normandy faster than the

---

[320]   Speidel, 85, 86.
[321]   Carell, 55. Also see Rommel, 471.
[322]   Speidel, 45, 46.
[323]   Speidel, 81.
[324]   Rommel, 477.
[325]   Hastings, *Overlord*, 125.

Germans could move their soldiers over land to the battlefield. It proved impossible to mount a large-scale attack against the Allies because of their control of the air and the terrible effect of the naval guns. Both Rommel and von Rundstedt saw the battle slipping away. They believed that ". . . continued persistence in rigid warfare (Hitler's no-retreat policies) was bound, with deadly certainty, to lead within a few weeks to the destruction of Army Group B."[326] A crisis for the Germans in Normandy was at hand as early as the second week in June.

Field Marshal von Rundstedt requested a meeting with Hitler to get Hitler's orders changed before disaster struck. Hitler came west and met with von Rundstedt and Rommel ". . . on June 17, 1944 near Soissons." Rommel opened the meeting with Hitler by, ". . . giving a report on the situation, in which he described how impossible were the conditions under which the German soldier was being forced to fight."[327] Both Rommel and von Rundstedt wanted to conduct ". . . a limited withdraw to be made southward, with the object of launching an armored thrust into the flank of the advancing enemy and fighting the battle outside the range of the enemy's naval artillery . . ."[328] Hitler refused their request. Rommel and von Rundstedt could not change Hitler's mind. For their trouble, Rommel was censured and von Rundstedt was fired.

Historians, faced with a series of conflicting accounts of the battle from mid-June until August, have been free to draw their own conclusions. On the German side, most of the commanding officers complained that they were unable to engage the Allied armies on anything approaching equal terms because of Allied control of the air, the terrible effect of the naval guns, and the Allies vast material superiority. They predicted that unless German strategy was changed or substantial reinforcements rushed to the Normandy front, the unequal battle would not last more than a couple of weeks before the Wehrmacht suffered a total collapse.

On the Allied side, Montgomery was stalled at Caen but insisted the battle was going according to plan. Everyone else, including the SHAEF commander, General Eisenhower, was beginning to worry about a stalemate. It seemed to them that the Germans were winning most battles; Allied casualties were high and the Germans were fighting very hard for every inch of ground. This was especially true on the Allied right flank at Caen;

---

[326] Rommel, 479.
[327] Rommel, 478, 479.
[328] Rommel, 479.

Caen was Montgomery's D-day objective. It still had not fallen by the end of June. The Allies were falling behind their schedule for the tonnage of supplies landed and ground taken in the "lodgement area." The relatively level ground southeast of Caen was desperately needed by the Allied air forces as landing strips for fighter aircraft.

German sensitivity to enemy thrusts toward the critical transportation and communications hub at Caen was apparent in the deployment of their armored divisions. Hitler, through O.K.W., ordered attacks in the Caen sector. The 3rd German Parachute Division required six days to make its journey from Brittany to the vicinity of St Lo under the continuous threat of air attack. Even after fresh German units arrived in Normandy, they were unable to form-up for an attack because of the overwhelming volume of fire from Allied guns.

Field Marshal Guenther von Kluge replaced von Rundstedt as Wehrmacht Commander in Chief West on July 2. Von Kluge had been told by Hitler and others at O.K.W. that Rommel and von Rundstedt were defeatists who had mishandled the invasion. He was led to believe that the only thing needed in France was a commander of his ability to take a firm grip on the battle and kick some butts to turn things around. After a few trips to the front, von Kluge changed his mind. He agreed with Rommel's assessment: "The enemy's command of the air restricts all movement . . . For armored or motorized troops in divisional strength upward, it limits the possibilities of command and maneuver to night or bad weather operations, (or) . . . operations with (a) limited objective. Daylight action is . . . possible . . . (with) A.A. defense—for a small armored combat group."[329]

Under these conditions the huge German counterattack, which the Allies had so greatly feared prior to the invasion and which was the basis of so much of Montgomery's angst in his discussions with Eisenhower, was simply not possible after the first few days of the invasion. This was especially true for any planned German offensive in range of Allied naval guns about twenty miles from the coast. Since Falaise was little more than twenty-five miles from the coastline, Montgomery's 21st Army Group fought nearly all of the Normandy campaign under the protective shield of Allied naval guns. After the first few days of the invasion, there was never any great danger of a calamitous German counterattack on the eastern flank.

On June 29 Colonel General Dollman, German Seventh Army Commander, died of a heart attack; ". . . it was said from bitterness over the

---

[329] Rommel, 485.

interrogations to which he had been subjected after the success of the Allied landings."[330] General of Waffen SS, Paul Hausser, took his Seventh Army Command. Dollman's funeral was held on July 2, the same day Field Marshal von Rundstedt received a letter relieving him of command. Von Kluge had already been named to replace von Rundstedt. Also on July 2, General Geyr von Schweppenburg received a letter relieving him of command of Panzer Group West; his replacement was General of Panzer Troops, Heinrich Eberbach.

Adolf Hitler hoped Hausser and Eberbach were more committed Nazis. Hitler was right about the men he picked, but it really didn't matter. July 2 was also the day Fritz Bayerlein was ordered to move his Panzer Lehr Division west to Saint Lo in the American sector, after leaving behind one-third of his tanks, artillery, and grenadiers to support the infantry division taking his place in the line near Caen.

On July 15, the Commander in Chief of Army Group B wrote his last report to Hitler. It was a devastating letter. "The situation on the Normandy front is growing worse every day and is now approaching a grave crisis . . . As against ninety-seven thousand casualties . . . i.e., an average of two thousand five hundred to three thousand a day—replacements to date number ten thousand, of whom about six thousand have actually arrived at the front . . . we expect that . . . the enemy will succeed in breaking through our thin front, above all, Seventh Army's, and thrusting deep into France."[331] Rommel's conclusion was somber: "The troops are everywhere fighting heroically, but the unequal struggle is approaching its end."[332] Rommel told Hitler he felt, "duty-bound to speak plainly on this point."[333] After visiting a critical section of the front south of Caen on July 17, Rommel was returning to his headquarters at La Roche Guyon shortly after 5:00 p.m. when his Horch staff car was attacked by a British Typhoon fighter-bomber. His driver was killed; Field Marshal Rommel was severely wounded, but he survived.

At 0530 hours on the morning of July 18, the British began an attack near Caen. It was code named Operation *Goodwood*. General Montgomery had planned to ". . . have a real 'showdown' on the eastern flank and to loose a corps of three armored divisions into the open country about the Caen-Falaise

---

[330] Carell, 234.
[331] Rommel, 486, 487.
[332] Rommel, 487.
[333] Rommel, 487.

road."[334] Three waves of British and American heavy and medium bombers dropped over seven-thousand tons of bombs on German defensive positions south and east of Caen. The devastation was overwhelming to those who observed the bombing. Most of the British troops who were waiting for the attack to begin could not see how anything survived the inferno. They were greatly heartened by the carnage.

Unfortunately, Rommel and General Heinrich Eberbach, now Commanding Panzer Group West, had deployed German defenses five belts deep, while leaving the front lines manned by only a token screening force. Allied bombs did considerable damage to the German defenders, but substantial pockets of resistance remained in the third, fourth, and fifth belts of defense. Worse, the Germans knew the timing and direction of the attack. It is not clear whether Sepp Dietrich put his ear to the ground and heard the British tanks approaching, or whether a German intelligence coup provided the early warning. What is clear is that a message from Luftflotte 3 predicted a British attack, ". . . to take place south-eastward from Caen about the night of 17-18."[335]

Operation *Goodwood*, the British attack at Caen, and Operation *Cobra*, the American attack at St. Lo, were set to go at the same time; but Bradley was not ready in time and bad weather delayed his attack for several days.

Operation *Goodwood* was defective in its planning and awkward in its execution, as more than one writer has observed.[336] Planning the movement of men and machines in an attack role was not Montgomery's strong suit. Minefields, bridges, and limited space within the Orne River bridgehead restricted access routes for British armor. Poor infantry-armor cooperation and narrow lanes for British armor through the minefields slowed armored deployment for the main attack. In two days, the British gained seven very tough miles and secured the rest of Caen. In spite of heavy losses in tanks and infantry, Montgomery had served the Allied cause by destroying irreplaceable German armored forces and keeping German attention fixed on their eastern flank at Caen; which, he later implied, was all that he had intended to do from the beginning.

The rains which helped close down *Goodwood* also delayed the American attack. Bradley had been planning Operation *Cobra* for some

---

334   Hastings, *Overlord*, 231.
335   Hastings, *Overlord*, 233.
336   Hastings, *Overlord*, 231. Also, see John Keegan, *Six Armies in Normandy*, (New York: The Viking Press, 1982), 216 to 218 and D'Este, *Decision*, 360 to 367.

time. He wanted to use the good ground at St. Lo as a starting point for his attack, but just getting there was taking longer than he hoped. Bad weather, the hedgerows, and the newly arrived Panzer Lehr and 2d SS Panzer Divisions combined to make things difficult for the Americans. Bradley fired several division commanders because their units had not performed well. He picked his best corps commander to lead the attack, Major General J. Lawton Collins, Commanding US VII Corps.

The attack was set for July 24, but clouds covering the target area forced the attack to be cancelled. Several bombing formations did not get the cancellation in time and dropped their bombs in the area east of St Lo; some fell short into American lines. According to Waffen SS General Paul Hausser, this aborted bombing attack led the Germans to expect, ". . . a decisive (infantry) attack . . . just west of Vire."[337] Germans closer to the action thought they had repelled an American attack. Lieutenant General Fritz Bayerlein, commanding Panzer Lehr, ". . . congratulated himself at the end of the day on the achievement of his troops, who had apparently repelled a major effort and prevented the Americans from crossing the Periers-St. Lo road."[338]

Cobra began the next day, when 2,430 heavy and medium fighter-bombers dropped over four-thousand tons of bombs and napalm in a rectangle one-and-a-half miles deep and three miles wide south of the St. Lo-Periers road. The effect was total devastation within the rectangle-shaped bombing area; it created what some observers called a "moon landscape." According to Martin Blumenson, ". . . a thousand men must have perished . . . The survivors were dazed . . . Three battalion command posts were demolished. A parachute regiment attached to the division virtually vanished. A kampfgruppe attached to Lehr no longer existed."[339] While the bombing was a heady morale booster for the Americans, the devastation it wrought was not complete. Here and there, small groups of Germans survived the bombing. Those Germans outside the target area appeared to be unshaken by what had happened only a few miles away. One of the effects of the Allied bombing was that it cut German communications between the frontline units and rear echelon headquarters.

The Americans were much surprised to find German resistance seemingly undisturbed. Heavy artillery fire greeted the initial waves of

[337] Hausser, 4.
[338] Blumenson, *The Duel*, 92.
[339] Blumenson, *The Duel*, 94.

attacking infantry and stopped them cold. Small groups of US soldiers began making their way forward by going around German strong points. Late that afternoon, General Collins saw, ". . . that their [German] communications and command structure had been damaged more than our troops realized."[340] He decided to commit some of his armored reserve the following morning. Collins was correct. His decision was critical in deciding the battle for Marigny and expanding the flanks of the attack.

The Germans reacted quickly to the American attack. Seventh Army Commander, General Hausser, sent his reinforcements, one regiment of the 275th Division, north from Marigny toward the center of the attack zone at La-Chapelle-en-Juger. Generalleutnant Dietrich von Choltitz, Commanding LXXXIV Corps, also sent a regiment from the 353rd Division toward La-Chapelle. Von Choltitz had hoped that these units could move to the threatened area and attack the forward elements of the American assault. The German counterattack never came off. The regiment from the 275th Division was engaged before it got to La-Chapelle and harassed by Allied fighter-bombers. After a rough encounter with US infantry troops, ". . . the regiment lost all semblance of organization and at the end of the day would be able to find only two-hundred survivors."[341] The regiment from the 353d fared somewhat better, but was so completely engaged it was unable to put in an attack. By nightfall on July 25, the Germans had committed their two reserve divisions and these units failed to hold their positions. The Americans had driven a salient three miles deep into German lines. Von Kluge hoped to shorten his line west of the penetration and withdraw 2nd SS Panzer to reestablish a solid front. That evening, von Kluge prepared his superiors for the worst by telling O.K.W., "As of this moment, the front has burst."[342]

The next day, July 26, the pace of the American attack quickened. On the right flank US 9th Infantry moved forward against the 2nd SS Panzer Division and 91st Infantry Division. By nightfall, General Eddy's troops had advanced two to three miles into German-held territory near Periers. In the center, US 4th Infantry Division had taken La Chapelle, ". . . overran part of the 353rd Division, and put Panzer Lehr artillery units to flight."[343] On the left, after being held up by German artillery fire, the US 30th Infantry

340   Collins, 242.
341   Blumenson, *The Duel*, 100.
342   Blumenson, *The Duel*, 100.
343   Blumenson, *The Duel*, 101.

Division advanced three miles into German lines. Given this success, General Collins saw an opportunity; he ordered that the infantry attacks be continued throughout the night of July 26/27.

At von Kluge's suggestion, General Hausser tried to withdraw 2nd SS Panzer Division from the line to counterattack the Americans, but it was too heavily engaged. He eventually managed to withdraw two battalions, one infantry, and one armor battalion. These units were moved to the center of the German line where American attacks were the strongest. The German 352nd Division fought off flank attacks while withdrawing along the Vire River near St. Lo. Four miles west, the German 5th Parachute Division had given a good account of itself in stopping the US 330th Infantry Regiment. Although they were still in a good defensive position, the paratroopers were already in trouble. ". . . for by this time, between the 352nd and the paratroopers who were holding fast, there was virtually no organized resistance in the four-mile gap, though the German commanders did not seem to know it."[344]

US 2nd Armored Division attacked along the left flank, closest to St. Lo. Their initial assault was slowed by scattered artillery fire and bomb craters in the roads. But by the afternoon of July 26, Brigadier General Maurice Rose's CCA had driven through St. Gilles. A gap several miles wide developed in the German line between Marigny and St. Gilles. Communications with German forces in the LXXXIV Corps sector along the coast had been totally destroyed. With Americans pouring through their line at St. Lo, there was a good chance those German units fighting along the coast near Coutances would be surrounded.

Von Choltitz wanted to withdraw directly south toward Montmartin. General Hausser, the Seventh Army Commander, overruled him; he ordered a fighting withdrawal southeast toward Percy. Choltitz protested that this would leave the German left flank wide open along the coast. Hausser insisted and Choltitz later issued the order. ". . . when Von Kluge learned that Hausser had virtually stripped his coastal positions and thereby jeopardized the entire Normandy defense by inviting American encirclement of the German left flank, he nearly became violent."[345] Due to poor German communications, it probably didn't matter which order was given. An orderly withdraw from the exposed Coutances area had become nearly impossible. German units lacked the ability to communicate and had to resort to runners. It was just

---

[344] Blumenson, *The Duel*, 102.
[345] Blumenson, *The Duel*, 119.

like World War I, except the distance between headquarters was far greater and Allied control of the air made all travel by road in daylight a hazardous undertaking.

By the evening of July 26, Combat Command B from the US 2nd Armored Division was blocking the main roads south and east out of Canisy, shortly after midnight they were in Notre-Dame-de-Cenilly, nearly eight miles south of Canisy. When American tanks rolled past Panzer Lehr headquarters near Dangy, ". . . a shocked Bayerlein reported Panzer Lehr was 'finally annihilated.'"[346] Fifth Army Commander, General Paul Hausser was nearly killed by Americans at Gavray. The Commander of the 2nd SS Panzer Division, Christian Tychsen, fell victim to an American reconnaissance patrol near his headquarters.[347] By July 28, facing only scattered and confused German resistance, reconnaissance elements of CCB 2nd Armored were in Cerences, and the trap was nearly closed.

At first, the Americans thought they might be too late to close the trap on those Germans who had been fighting on the western flank near Coutances and St. Sauvour. Germans retreating southeast began running into roadblocks thrown up by 2nd Armored Division. It soon became apparent that the Americans might still have the time to close the trap behind the German LXXXIV Corps. According to General Paul Hausser, "They [2nd Armored] encountered only weak resistance further south, which enabled them to advance far in the direction of the coast and to reach the Cerences district, which consequently resulted in the encirclement of the LXXXIV Corps."[348] Around mid-day on July 29, Allied fighter-bombers found, ". . . at least five hundred vehicles jammed around Roncey. For six hours that afternoon, the planes attacked what became known as the Roncey pocket."[349] Hausser's LXXXIV Corps was trying to organize a fighting retreat from Roncey southeast toward Percy, but Allied fighter-bombers were giving German armor and thin-skinned vehicles a terrible pounding.

Elements from the 2nd SS Panzer Division, with attached units from the 17th SS Panzer Grenadiers would lead the main attack toward Percy. Surviving elements of the 275th Infantry Division were sent to Hambye, the 243rd Division to Brehal, the 353rd Division to La Baliene, and the 91st

---

[346] Blumenson, *The Duel*, 117.
[347] Blumenson, *The Duel*, 118.
[348] Hausser, 13.
[349] Blumenson, *The Duel*, 121, 122.

to Gavray-Cerences.[350] Hausser suggested that the 2nd SS Panzer suffered the heaviest losses getting to Percy, but they made it easier for the other divisions which got out with acceptable losses.[351] The improvised defensive positions Hausser's LXXXIV Corps took over between Percy and Vire seemed to be holding on July 30 despite the loss of Mount Rubin near Percy to the Americans.

The critically weakened German left flank was another matter. The German flank along the coastline had collapsed and two US armored divisions were heading straight for Avranches at the base of the Brittany peninsula. If they could get to Avranches before the Germans and take control the vital road net and the bridges over the Sees and Selune Rivers, the Americans would have succeeded in turning the German's western flank. By July 31, the situation for German commanders had deteriorated. "It's a madhouse here," Kluge told his chief of staff, General Blumentritt, "You can't imagine what it's like . . . Commanders are completely out of contact with their troops."[352]

German commanders did not know what was happening at Avranches. Their communications system had totally collapsed. "At 9:20 a.m., July 31, Kluge learned definitely that American troops were in Avranches. Other than that, the situation in the Avranches area was 'completely unclear.'"[353] General Hausser was facing a similar dilemma: "It was so very difficult to gain any clear picture of the state of affairs at Avranches. Missioned units [messengers] of the Army staff sent out failed to return. We had to consider it possible that the enemy had reached Avranches."[354]

CCB from 4th US Armored was the first Allied unit into Avranches. They found both bridges over the Sees River at Avranches intact, and managed to secure the bridges despite German counterattacks. The Germans, as it turned out, were more interested in getting away than they were in the bridges at Avranches. Later that same day, CCA of 4th Armored, ". . . raced across the Selune River Bridge at Pontaubault, dispersed a feeble counterstroke, and thus completed assurance that the VIII Corps could burst out of the Cotentin."[355]

To counter the Americans at Avranches, Kluge could only muster remnants of the German 77th Infantry Division (one battalion), some

---

[350]   Hausser, 14.
[351]   Hausser, 16.
[352]   Blumenson, *The Duel*, 135.
[353]   Blumenson, *The Duel*, 141.
[354]   Hausser, 19.
[355]   Weigley, *Eisenhower's Lieutenants*, 174.

paratroopers and artillery.[356] Colonel Rudolf Bacherer and his men gave the Americans a very good fight. The battle raged for over four hours along the narrow mountainous roads and switchbacks. It came down to hand to hand combat. At the end, armored reinforcements and Allied air power turned the battle in the American's favor.[357] Kluge reported the unhappy news to O.K.W., "It's impossible to hold the Americans . . . They have shattered all the strong points which held them in July. It is a blow to the Fuhrer who wants to hold everything at all costs."[358]

The immediate task for the German commanders was to get the cork back into the bottle. If the Americans kept pouring through the road net at Avranches, they would soon become strong enough to threaten the Seventh and Fifth Panzer Armies from the south. The problem was to build up strength in the Mortain sector for a counter attack, especially the armor, without so weakening the Caen-Vire sector that it collapsed. Divisions would also have to be drawn from those forces remaining on the Pas de Calais and those uncommitted divisions in Southern France. All troop movement was hampered by the fact the French transportation system was in chaos and within one hundred miles of the battlefield, movement could take place only during the eight hours of darkness due to the omnipresent Allied fighter-bombers.

A second, but equally serious problem for the German commanders was reorganization. Several German divisions had been in action since early June and were in a desperate condition without large numbers of replacements. General Paul Hausser noted the condition of the divisions under his command: "At the end of the fighting on July 31, seven divisions could be counted as destroyed (Panzer Training Division [Lehr], 352, 275, 243, 77, 91, 5, 5 Para Jg Division); only insignificant remnants gathered together. The 17th SS Panzer Gren Division had only about the same value."[359]

Senior German commanders held a meeting on July 31 at Seventh Army Headquarters near Mortain. In Field Marshal von Kluge's presence, it was decided to try to rebuild the left German flank beginning at Avranches. The Germans still held most of the territory between Mortain and Pontaubault; from there it was only a few miles to Avranches and the coastline. If they

[356]   Blumenson, *The Duel*, 143. Also, see Florentin 13, 14.
[357]   Florentin, 14.
[358]   Florentin, 15.
[359]   Hausser, 24.

could cut off the Americans at Avranches, any forces that had gotten through that road junction would wither as their supply lines were cut.[360]

Hitler quickly adopted the plan for the attack at Avranches as the best means of saving France. The Germans feared that the Normandy battle might become mobile. With their greater mobility and complete control of the air, the Allies would dominate any battlefield on which movement became a tactical requirement. It was 1940 in reverse. For Adolf Hitler, who had always refused to give up ground, the battle for France was going to be won or lost between Mortain and Avranches.

After Panzer Group West headquarters was destroyed by Allied bombers in early June, it was re-designated Fifth Panzer Army and General Geyr von Schweppenburg was subsequently relieved of command. The new Fifth Panzer Army Commander, General of Panzer Troops, Heinrich Eberbach twice told his superiors that he considered the Mortain counterattack impracticable. His objections were dismissed each time. Around August 8 or 9, General Eberbach was relieved of his duties as Fifth Panzer Army Commander and those duties were handed over to SS General Sepp Dietrich. Eberbach was given command of those armored forces preparing for the Mortain counterattack.[361] The new force created for the Mortain attack was named Panzer Group Eberbach.

The transfer of German armored divisions to the Mortain sector had already begun, with *ULTRA* detailing the German troop movements as Operation *Luettwitz*. By the time the attack began on the night of August 6, Eberbach had assembled major elements of, from north to south: 2nd Panzer Division east of Tove and 1st SS Panzer east of St. Barthelemy. The 2nd SS Panzer, 17th SS Panzer Grenadiers and 275th Infantry Divisions were all in positions east of Mortain. Reconnaissance elements from Panzer Lehr covered the southern flank of the attack near Barenton. First SS Panzer could not join in the attack until around noon on August 7. The 116th Panzer Division failed to join the attack until very late in the afternoon on the extreme right (northern) flank of the attack along the north bank of the See River. Gerhard von Schwerin, commanding the 116th, protested that they had been too heavily engaged to put in a proper attack. When they did get going later in the afternoon they ran straight into 9th Infantry Division's artillery and were stopped near their original start line.[362] Within a few days,

---

[360]   Hausser, 27, 28.
[361]   Eberbach, 10, 11
[362]   Weigley, *Eisenhower's Lieutenants*, 198.

". . . the divisions which had taken part in the first offensive on Avranches, 1 and 2 SS Pz Divs, 2 Pz Div, and 116Pz Div, had fallen back to what was practically their starting positions and were being engaged there by the pursuing enemy."[363]

The Germans decided to renew their attack at Avranches, this time, ". . . from the Barenton-St. Hilaire area and from there move to Avranches and Pontaubault."[364] The German High Command at O.K.W. decided that the first attack had gone in too soon, without waiting for the Panzer divisions to be assembled at the start line. 10th SS Panzer Division from the Fifth Panzer Army and 9th Panzer Division from southern France would be added to the attack. Still, the man charged with conducting the attack, gave it little chance of success. General Eberbach noted that the distance from St. Hilaire to Avranches was sixty-five kilometers, but the first attack only had to go forty kilometers. Without proper air cover, which no one expected to materialize, the attack was doomed to failure. General Eberbach wrote, ". . . this longer attack had even less prospect of success than the first one. Our air forces were weaker than ever before . . . the 9 and 10 SS Pz Divs, which were to have been added to the Army were so worn out and battle-weary that of the tanks that took part in the first shorter . . . attack only one-third were now available—120 tanks at the most."[365] General Eberbach continued, "The ammunition and fuel situation at Seventh Army was critical."[366] In a few days, Haislip's XV Corps would overrun the German Seventh Army's administrative offices in Le Mans and their supply depots at Alencon. The German Seventh Army's supply situation would go from critical to catastrophic.

While the Germans were debating the possibility of another attack at Avranches, Haislip's XV Corps was driving north toward Le Mans. A new German Army Corps, the LXXXI Corps from the Seine Sector was moved to Normandy and given authority to defend the German southern flank. On paper, the LXXXI Corps appeared to be sufficient to perform the task it was assigned; but German units lacked the mobility of their American enemy. The 708th Infantry Division and 9th Panzer Division from southern France were added to local anti-aircraft and security units to form the LXXXI Corps.

---

[363] Eberbach, 12.
[364] Eberbach, 13.
[365] Eberbach, 13.
[366] Eberbach, 13.

The speed of the American advance was an immediate problem. The US 79th Infantry took Laval on August 6, almost without firing a shot. On August 7, the US 90th Infantry Division, on its drive toward Le Mans, ran into reconnaissance elements of 9th Panzer and one Regiment from the 708th Infantry Division. After a brief firefight, the 90th brushed past the Germans, having destroyed major elements of the 9th Panzer's reconnaissance battalion and taken one thousand two hundred prisoners.[367] The Germans were arriving late and had been committed to battle without a battle plan.

By the evening of August 8, the German left flank was near collapse. Three US divisions were attacking major road junctions at Le Mans: 79th and 90th Infantry Divisions and the 5th Armored Division. By midnight, the Americans occupied all access roads to Le Mans.[368] The French 2nd Armored had joined Haislip's XV Corps and was clearing the roads leading to Sees-Carrouges.

The German LXXXI Corps had taken up defensive positions protecting Alencon and the German 7th Army supply depots. With 9th Panzer Division anchoring the center of the German defensive positions, the 708th Infantry Division was on their right [west] and the 354th Sichrung Regiment on their left [east].[369]

On August 10, the Germans learned that Haislip's XV Corps was heading due north, straight into their vulnerable southern flank. Eberbach and Kluge were in agreement, they had been arguing with Hitler and O.K.W., trying to explain that the forces available to them in Normandy were no longer sufficient to accomplish what was being asked of them [the attack at Mortain]. It must have been hard to explain the decrease in firepower of individual divisions. No one liked giving Hitler bad news. So it is doubtful that anyone in his headquarters staff explained the reality of the battlefield to him. When he moved a panzer division flag on his map board in East Prussia, he was moving perhaps one thousand to one thousand five hundred men and fifty or one hundred tanks, not the fifteen thousand men and two hundred and fifty tanks they had when they arrived in Normandy. It must have seemed incredible back at O.K.W. that the Americans had so easily absorbed the attack of five panzer divisions at Mortain; surely something must have gone wrong.

---

367 Blumenson, *The Duel*, 207.
368 Blumenson, *The Duel*, 208.
369 Cepeda, *The Fifth Armored Division*, 52.

Finally, the German high command relented, albeit only slightly. Eberbach wrote, "Now . . . even OKW could not close its ears to the necessity of making an immediate attack on the flank of the enemy advancing toward Alencon and Laigle and throwing him back."[370] OKW authorized a slight straightening of the German front at Mortain, so that the necessary Panzer units could be withdrawn from the line to deal with the Americans driving toward Alencon. OKW did not authorize an abandonment of the Mortain offensive. In fact, they insisted that Eberbach and Kluge return to the offensive at Mortain just as soon as the threat to their southern flank had been eliminated. ULTRA confirmed this fact. General Eberbach also confirmed it: "On the contrary . . . OKW did not authorize evacuation of the Mortain 'finger' but, as if hypnotized, kept to the thought of an attack on Avranches."[371]

At last General Eberbach was authorized to deal with the American Corps thrusting itself into the open German flank. On paper, the force being made available to Eberbach was impressive: . . . the LXXXI Corps, XLVII Inf Corps consisted of 116 Pz Div, 1 SS Pz Div, and 2 Pz Div . . . The II SS Pz Corps, consisting of 2 and 9 SS PZ Divs, was to start arriving 15 Aug 44.[372] The first two Corps, the LXXXI and the XLVII were to begin arriving at Argentan on August 12, Eberbach estimated that he would be able to launch his attack on General Haislip's left flank, "As soon as possible, probably on the evening of August 14, '44, XLVII Corps was to attack the enemy flank either south or north of Alencon depending on the development of the situation."[373] Eberbach said he was totally discounting the combat effectiveness of LXXXI Corps [9th Pz Div, 708th Inf Div, one battered security regiment, and one parachute regiment which had not arrived], ". . . nothing could be expected of these units, even for defense."[374]

Eberbach planned to meet his staff at the headquarters of LXXXI Infantry Corps just northeast of Alencon around noon on August 11. Upon arriving at the headquarters Eberbach learned that 9th Panzer Division had been engaged all morning with at least one enemy panzer division. "Late in the afternoon, 9 Pz Div reported that superior enemy forces had broken through. Remnants of the division had assembled at the edge of the woods north of

---

[370] Eberbach, 14.
[371] Eberbach, 14.
[372] Eberbach, 15.
[373] Eberbach, 15.
[374] Eberbach, 15.

Alencon . . . although the strength of the Division was about one infantry battalion, one artillery battalion, and a half-dozen tanks."[375] The Corps commander immediately issued orders for withdraw of his headquarters, ". . . to the region east of Argentan."[376] Just as they were preparing to leave the Alencon area, the sound of tank artillery fire could be heard close by, shells began dropping in the headquarters area, and smoke from burning vehicles limited visibility. Since Allied fighter-bombers made any movement difficult, the headquarters evacuation had to wait until darkness.

By the evening of August 11, the German southern flank was a shambles. Senior officers were again unable to communicate directly with the troops they commanded. *ULTRA* Message XL 5715 released August 11 at 2049 hours discussed the German supply problems: ". . . (84) CORPS) COMPLAINED THAT ITS DEFENSIVE POWER MUST DECREASE CONSIDERABLY, SINCE NO & NO AMMUNITION ALLOCATION FOR TWO DAYS." [377] The roads after dark were choked with stragglers and supply vehicles. Eberbach later wrote, "As we passed through Sees, I noticed a bakery company taking defense positions. All streets were flooded with rear services streaming northward. I sent an officer to 116 Pz Div with the order to push to Sees that night and hold positions there."[378]

The loss of Alencon meant that the German Seventh Army has lost its supply base. Due to the presence of Allied fighter-bombers during the day, German supply vehicles could travel only at night, during the eight hours of darkness. Shortages of ammunition and vehicle fuel were already crippling efforts to mount the attack against the Americans. Now that the Seventh Army was totally dependent on the Fifth Panzer Army for their supplies, fuel and ammunition shortages were bound to get worse. First SS Panzer Division's *ULTRA* Message XL 5835 reported that its supply situation had already reached a critical stage by August 12: ". . . AMMUNITION SITUATION STRAINED OWING FALLING THROUGH OF ALLOCATIONS FROM DEPOT . . . FUEL ONLY JUST ENOUGH TO REACH ASSEMBLY AREA AND NO & NO ALLOCATIONS TO HAND. SPECIAL REQUIREMENTS COLON AMMUNITION ESPECIALLY ARTILLERY AND TWO CM & CM FLAK."[379]

---

[375] Eberbach, 16.
[376] Eberbach, 16.
[377] *ULTRA* Message XL 5715
[378] Eberbach, 16.
[379] *ULTRA* Message XL 5835

3

XL 5715

40

ZZZ

((XL 5715 £ 5715 SH 89 £ 89 SHA 34 £ 34 TG 18 £ 18 .
BV 45 £ 45 ON CR EF 98 £ 98 %   YK/ZE (Proc 6617)

FAIR
IN DAY REPORT ISSUED TENTH (STRONG)) INDICATIONS
84
FIRST SUGAR SUGAR PANZER CORPS) COMPLAINED THAT
ITS DEFENSIVE POWER MUST DECREASE CONSIDERABLY,
SINCE NO £ NO AMMUNITION ALLOCATION FOR TWO DAYS.
(SEE XL £ XL FIVE SIX NINE ONE)

GELC/HDD/JB   1120497/8/44

3

REF: CX/MSS/T274/48   XL 5835

ZZZZ

(-(XL 583δ5 £ 5835 SH 80 £ 80 SHA 25 £ 25 TG 5 £ 5
BV 33 £ 33 ON YK ZE EF 86 £ 86 ST 45 £ 45 DL 71 £ 71 %

2000

SUPPLY SITUATION (FAIR INDICATIONS FOUR SEVEN PANZER))
CORPS) ON ELEVENTH CRITICAL EXCEPT FOR ONE SUGAR SUGAR
PANZER DIVISION. AMMUNITION SITUATION STRAINED OWING
FALLING THROUGH OF ALLOCATIONS FROM DEPOT (COMMENT TO BE
CALLED FERGUSON £ FERGUSON, GERMAN MUENSTER £ MUENSTER) AND
ANOTHER DEPOT UNSPECIFIED. FUELD ONLY JUST ENOUGH TO REACH
ASSEMBLY AREA AND NO £ NO ALLOCATIONS TO HAND. SPECIAL
REQUIREMENTS COLON AMMUNITION XX ESPECIALLY ARTILLERY AND
TWO CM £ CM FLAK. FUEL/MINIMUM OF ONE CONSUMPTION UNIT
                        COLON
EQUALS FOUR ONE NOUGHT OBOE AND FOUR NOUGHT DIESEL

PCP/HDD/MB   121456Z/8/44

The status of Panzer Group Eberbach and the forces he has available to defend the southern German flank at Argentan at midnight 12/13 August 1944.

General Eberbach estimated that the weak security forces, elements from 116th Panzer, 9th Panzer (at the strength of a Company) and parts of an anti-Aircraft Regiment were not sufficient to defend the German front at Argentan. Eberbach said that he had only 80 tanks available to defend the southern flank, he estimated that the Americans and French had 700 tanks. The next day he advised Army Group B that an immediate large scale retreat was necessary to avoid the complete collapse of his Panzer Group.

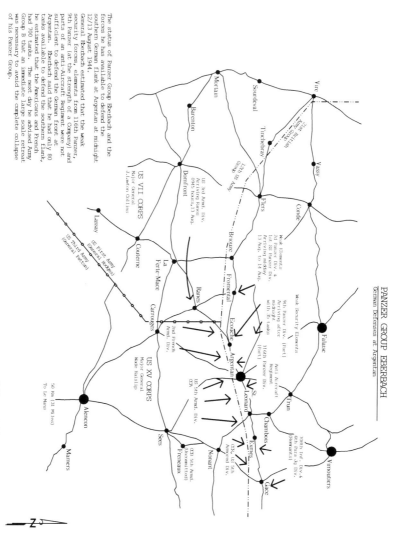

PANZER GROUP EBERBACH
German Defenses at Argentan

1 Cm. = 5 Km.
1Km. = .621 Miles

TH Mapping
© Tom Houlihan

Mortain
Sourdeval
Vire
Barenton
Tinchebray
Vassy
Condé
Dornfront
Flers
US 3rd Armd. Div.
(Arriving Ranes)
0945 hours, 13 Aug.

12th US Army Group 16 N.

Lassay
(US Third Army)
(General Patton)

Coutances

US First Army
(General Hodges)

US VII CORPS
Major General
J. Lawton Collins

La Ferté-Macé

Carrouges

Ranes

Briouze
Fromental
Écouche

Weak Elements
2d Panzer Div. &
1st SS Panzer Div.
Arriving midday
13 Aug. to 14 Aug.

Weak Security Elements

9th Panzer Div. (Part)
Arriving after
midnight
with 35 tanks

116th Panzer Div.
(Part)

Anti-Aircraft
Regiment

Falaise

Argentan

St.
Leonard

Trun

Chambois

Exmes

Vimoutiers

70th Inf., Div.&
6th Para Jg Div.
(elements)

2nd French
Armd. Div.

US XV CORPS
Major General
Wade Haislip

US 5th Armd. Div.
CTR

US 5th Armd. Div.
CTA

CTB, US 5th
Armd Div.

CTB, US 5th
Armd. Div.
(Uncommitted)

Nonant

Fresneaux

Gace

Sées

Alençon

Mamers

50 Km. (31 Miles)
To Le Mans

N

Eberbach drove to the headquarters of the XLVII Corps at Vieux Pont the morning of August 12, about nine miles southwest of Argentan. Here he could finalize plans for the attack on the American divisions thrusting toward Argentan. No information about the defense of Sees reached Eberbach until the afternoon when elements of 116th Panzer Division reported ". . . meeting stiff resistance." Eberbach later wrote, "In a subsequent report which reached headquarters in the evening, we learned that those advancing elements of 116 Pz Div had been destroyed by heavy artillery fire from massed enemy tanks and also that the enemy was forcing his way toward Argentan."[380]

That night, August12/13, Eberbach and the officers of XLVII Corps were forced to relocate their headquarters again. They selected an area near Chenedouil, about fourteen miles west of Argentan. Although the distance between old and new headquarters was barely over twenty miles, Eberbach remarked, ". . . it required six hours to complete it [the trip]."[381] He later wrote, "The entire supply service for one and one-half armies was congested on the few roads between Falaise and Argentan . . . the columns were able to move only during the eight hours of darkness. The huge number of burned-out motor vehicles created many bottlenecks and consequently all roads were congested and traffic was moving at a walk."[382] Remnants of 116th Panzer staggered into Argentan from their most recent clash with the Americans at Sees. Eberbach put them into a defensive line on both sides of Argentan. He later wrote, "Together with the antiaircraft regiment, they [116th Panzer] took up a thin line on both sides of the town and held their positions against heavy attacks of the enemy and put several enemy tanks out of action."[383] These units were joined by, ". . . portions of the 708th Infantry Division and the 6 Para Jg Division . . . [who were] on their way to barricade the area of Gace-Laigle."[384]

During the night of August 12 and the morning of August 13 the defense of Argentan was in the hands of assorted remnants of several badly damaged divisions, elements of the 116th Panzer Division which had just been soundly defeated at Sees and one regiment of antiaircraft guns. According to Brigadier General Gerhard Mueller, commanding 116th Panzer Division,

---

[380]   Eberbach, 17.
[381]   Eberbach, 17.
[382]   Eberbach, 17, 18.
[383]   Eberbach, 18.
[384]   Hausser, 54.

shortly after midnight the 33rd Panzer Regiment from 9th Panzer Division arrived with thirty tanks. This added considerable firepower to weak German defenses in the Argentan sector.[385] These German forces were all that stood between Haislip's XV Corps and Falaise. It was not until noon the following day, August 13, when weak elements of the 1 SS Panzer Division began arriving. The artillery arrived first, but they had no infantry protection, and it was not until much later in the day that the tanks began to arrive. "The mass of infantry did not arrive until the next day [Aug. 14]. Most of the units had been cut to pieces on the march by traffic congestion and air raids."[386]

There was total confusion on the southern German flank. Coordination between units was difficult due to a lack of communications, fuel shortages and traffic congestion. Many commanders were out of contact with their units, communication between headquarters was nearly impossible. Reporting from German Seventh Army Headquarters, General Hausser wrote, "No communication existed with Pz Group Eberbach. It seemed that out ahead of this group, the enemy was pushing ahead in the direction of La Ferte Mace—[Carrouges]—Sees."[387]

From the evening of August 12 until the night of August 13/14 the southern German flank remained wide open. Eberbach later said, "During the night of August 13-14, '44 additional units of the two divisions (Ed: 2 Pz Div and 1 SS Pz Div) arrived and we succeeded in building up a thin front."[388] Eberbach says the attack he planned was never carried out because of the defeat of 9th Panzer Division on August 13.[389] The real reason seems to be that Eberbach knew the forces under his command were utterly incapable of defeating Haislip's powerful XV Corps. Haislip had nearly destroyed most of the German 708th Infantry Division, and so badly handled the 9th Panzer that, ". . . by (the) evening (of August 13) 9 Pz Div had only the strength of a company."[390] The German 275th and 352nd Infantry Divisions were both being withdrawn for reconstitution.[391]

Eberbach had hoped to build his attack force behind a shield created by 708th Infantry, 9th Panzer, and 116th Panzer Divisions east of Alencon, Sees, and Carrouges. This was no longer possible. Eberbach reported, "With

[385] Cepeda, 60.
[386] Eberbach, 18.
[387] Hausser, 56. Spelling is Carouges in the original.
[388] Eberbach, 19.
[389] Eberbach, 15.
[390] Eberbach, 19.
[391] Hausser 52, 54.

the loss of Alencon and Sees, the situation had changed entirely. As the enemy stood close to Falaise in the north, the mouth of the encirclement had a width of only thirty kilometers. The ammunition and fuel situation was dreadfully serious . . . I stressed once again in my report to A [Army] Gp B the necessity of an immediate and quick retreat . . . otherwise a complete collapse was unavoidable."[392] Seventh Army sought to mitigate the fuel problem by issuing the following orders: "According to orders, only vitally important combat vehicles were allowed to be taken along, all other(s) had to be destroyed."[393]

Adolf Hitler was not listening to Eberbach's concerns. On August 14, he directed Eberbach to immediately launch an attack in the general direction of Alencon to remove the threat Haislip's Corps posed to the southern German flank. According to Eberbach, Hitler's order read: "The attack ordered by me [Adolf Hitler] southward past Alencon toward the east is to be effected under all conditions immediately as a preparation for an attack on Avranches."[394] Eberbach thought the order was madness, and would lead to the certain destruction of both the German Seventh and Fifth Panzer Armies. Upon receiving this order from Hitler, Eberbach immediately filed another report with Army Group B. Since he had no working radios or telephones, Eberbach had to use his ". . . last special missions staff officer . . ." to deliver the report.[395] Eberbach's report reads, in part: "Enemy attack with a presumable strength of two panzer divisions and one infantry division . . . Parts of 116 Pz Div annihilated at Sees. Remnants hold against heavy enemy attacks both sides Argentan. Pz Strengths (in tanks): 1 SS Pz Div: 30; 2 Pz Div: 25; 116 Pz Div: 15. The 9 Pz Div still has the strength of a company . . . the fuel and ammunition situation is very serious. Lack of fuel caused 1 SS Pz Div to blow up a number of tanks . . . a quick withdraw from encirclement of Seventh Army imperative in order to avoid catastrophe."[396] General Eberbach was preparing his superiors for the total destruction of those forces under his command.

The same fuel shortages which caused 1 SS Panzer to blow up a number of its tanks began taking a toll on other divisions as well. *ULTRA* Message XL 6136 released on August 14 details the plight of Panzer Lehr Division:

---

[392]   Eberbach, 19.
[393]   Hausser, 59.
[394]   Eberbach, 20.
[395]   Eberbach, 20.
[396]   Eberbach, 20.

"NO & NO FUEL IN DEPOT SPECIFIED, EIGHT FOUR CORPS FUEL ALLOCATING DEPOT NOT & NOT FOUND. PANZER LEHR & PANZER LEHR DIVISION WITHOUT FUEL FOR TWO DAYS. THREE NOUGHT TANKS IMMOBILIZED."[397]

ULTRA Message XL 6128, August 14, reveals how the loss of their ammunition depot affected XLVII Corps: ". . . CONSIDERABLE PERCENTAGE AMMUNITION FOR DIVISIONS LOST . . . AMMUNITION SITUATION NOW & NOW EVEN MORE STRAINED, ALLOCATION URGENTLY REQUIRED. TWO AND ONE ONE SIX PANZER DIVISIONS ARRIVING ASSEMBLY AREA WITHOUT FUEL. COLUMNS FROM PARIS & PARIS UNABLE TO REACH TROOPS FOR THREE DAYS AT EARLIEST. ONE CONSUMPTION UNIT URGENTLY REQUIRED TO INSURE LIMITED MOBILITY."[398]

The plight of Hitler's panzer divisions in Normandy was being read by *ULTRA,* and this information delivered to the Allied commanders while the intelligence information was still fresh. The panzer formations in Normandy had been badly battered. Some, like 9th Panzer and Panzer Lehr would be hard pressed to provide a battalion-sized task force. The Canadians were literally wiping out 12th SS Panzer between Caen and Falaise. Very few members of the Hitler Jugend would survive the Normandy campaign. Nearly all the panzers and their supporting infantry had been on the move since the American breakthrough at St. Lo on July 27. Second SS Panzer and 17th SS Panzer Grenadiers were caught in the American attack, along with Panzer Lehr and 2nd Panzer Division. The 116th Panzer, 2nd Panzer, 1st SS Panzer, 2nd SS Panzer, 17th SS Panzer Grenadiers, and Panzer Lehr Divisions all participated in the abortive German counterattack at Mortain.

Each engagement had left the panzer divisions in a weaker condition. In addition, each time the panzer divisions moved from one front to another, unless they moved at night, they were likely to be attacked by Allied fighter-bombers. The Germans could muster only, ". . . between 120 and 190 tanks for a surprise attack . . ." at Mortain.[399] The same Panzer Divisions, 116th, 2nd Panzer, and 1st SS Panzer were thrown into the line again at Argentan, in a greatly weakened condition, and asked to hold the line. It was too much to ask; even the German soldier had a breaking point.

---

[397]   *ULTRA* Message 6136.

[398]   *ULTRA* Message 6128.

[399]   Blumenson, *The Duel*, 223.

REF: CX/MSS/T275/164   XL 6128

ZZZZ

((XL 6128 £ 6128 SH 71 £ 71 SHA 16 £ 16 TG 62 £ 62
BV 89 £ 89 ON CR YK ZE EF 62 £ 62 ST 84 £ 84 DL 86 £
86   %

FOUR SEVEN CORPS OPS £ OPS EVENING ELEVENTH COLON THROUGH
BLOWING UP OF ARMY AMMUNITION DEPOTS FERGUSON £ FERGUSON
(SEE XL £ XL SIX NOUGHT NOUGHT SIX) AND)) EDGAR £ EDGAR
CONSIDERABLE PERCENTAGE AMMUNITION FOR DIVISIONS LOST
(ESPECIALLY ARTILLERY AND TWO CM £ CM) AMMUNITION SITUATION
NOW £ NOW EVEN MORE STRAINED, ALLOCATION URGENTLY
REQUIRED. TWO AND ONE ONE SIX PANZER DIVISIONS ARRIVING
ASSEMBLY AREA WITHOUT FUEL. COLUMNS FROM PARIS £ PARIS
UNABLE REACH TROOPS FOR THREE DAYS AT EARLIEST. ONE
CONSUMPTION UNIT URGENTLY REQUIRED TO ENSURE LIMITED
MOBILITY. SECONDLY, NOW £ NOW KNOWN THAT MORNING TWELFTH
TWO PANZER DIVISION OCCUPYING MAIN DEFENCE LINE FOUR SEVEN
CORPS IN RIGHT REPEAT RIGHT SECTION OR ((XL £ XL FIVE
EIGHT FOUR FIVE))

TNLB/RFB/NH   1403132/8/44

REF. CX/MSS/T.275/167   XL 6136

ZZZ

((XL 6136 £ 6136 SH 75 £ 75 SHA 20 £ 20 TG 64 £ 64
BV 91 £ 91 YK ZE EF 65 £ 65 ST 88 £ 88 DL 89 £ 89 %

FIVE EIGHT PANZER CORPS COMPLAINED ONE SEVEN)) HOURS
TWELFTH, NO £ NO FUEL IN DEPOT SPECIFIED, EIGHT FOUR
CORPS FUEL ALLOCATING DEPOT NOT £ NOT FOUND.   PANZER
LEHR £ LEHR DIVISION WITHOUT FUEL FOR TWO DAYS. THREE
NOUGHT TANKS IMMOBILIZED

JB/RFB/JEM   1403492/8/44.

The lucky Germans were the ones who got out early. Those prisoners who were captured by 4th and 6th US Armored Divisions back on July 30 and 31, 'giggling with delight' that they no longer had to endure the agony.[400] Eberbach wrote about the German soldier who tired of, ". . . wag(ing) a war of the poor man against an enemy who had everything in abundance, who was fresh while the German soldier had already been engaged in hard fighting for five years . . . suffer(ing) only defeats."[401] It must have been extremely difficult for General Eberbach to watch the disintegration of the German Army, the institution to which he had devoted his life's work. Eberbach wrote, "*'Catch-lines' in rear of the front had to be inaugurated. Even the SS was no exception to this rule. The 1 SS Panzer Division had never fought so miserably as at that time. The fighting morale of the German troops had cracked. This I openly reported to Gen Model on 18 Aug 44 at a meeting in Fontaine L'Abbe, just as I had done face to face to Gen v. Kluge . . .*"[402]

The Germans fought on, not because they were supermen, but because the Allies failed to close the trap. General Dietrich von Choltitz, commanding the German LXXXIV Corps, offered this opinion, "The whole battle is one tremendous bloodbath, such as I have never seen in eleven years of war."[403]

The arguments between Eberbach and O.K.W. concerning the attack on Haislip's XV Corps continued until late on the afternoon of August 16, when Hitler and his advisors finally relented and agreed to a withdraw from the pocket. The following morning, II SS Panzer Corps was placed into Army Group reserve and ordered to proceed to Lisieux, but new orders for the Corps were issued a few hours later which sent them to Vimoutiers instead.

Eberbach later got news that the Americans had driven east of Argentan and taken Le Bourg-St. Leonard. Several enemy artillery battalions on the ridge line at St. Leonard had shut down the roads around Chambois to German traffic. From that ridge line they had what one writer called an "artilleryman's dream," which was an unobstructed view of the eastern end of the Falise pocket. Also on August 17, Eberbach wrote, "Enemy has

---

[400]   Blumenson, *The Duel*, 143, 144.

[401]   Eberbach, 21.

[402]   Eberbach, 22. Italics added.

[403]   Wilmot, 388. Also see Weigley, *Eisenhower's Lieutenant*s, 163. From German Seventh Army's Telephone Log, 2350 hours, July 15, 1944.

broken through southeast of Falaise and is pushing on Trun. The II SS Pz Corps throws enemy back and holds Trun."[404]

That evening, von Kluge was relieved of his Command (Army Group B) and was replaced by Field-Marshal Walter Model. Field-Marshal Model immediately called a meeting of his senior staff officers for the following morning [August 18] at Fontaine l'Abbe. Eberbach later recorded Model's orders: "My intention is to withdraw behind the Seine. For this purpose, we just need a stiffening of the bottleneck at Trun and Argentan with panzer divisions to enable the infantry divisions of Seventh Army to withdraw."[405] While he was in conference with General Model, Eberbach received ". . . a report . . . that Trun was in the hands of British troops. This meant the encirclement was practically completed."[406]

After his meeting with General Model, Eberbach drove directly to II SS Panzer Corps headquarters for a meeting with the commanding officer, Gruppenfuhrer Willi Bittrich, to coordinate his counterattacks between Trun and Argentan. Due to numerous fighter-bomber attacks on his vehicle, Eberbach did not arrive at Bittrich's headquarters until 2200 hours. Bittrich advised Eberbach that his corps was totally unfit for combat, ". . . as a result of night marches and air attacks."[407] Bittrich also told Eberbach, "Although he could not contact any of his division staffs, he knew that his troops had neither fuel, ammunition, food, nor signal equipment. He was unable to say when the Corps would again be ready for action."[408] Eberbach left Bittrich with the understanding that he would launch his attack from Vimoutiers toward Trun as soon as possible.

Eberbach then drove to Fifth Panzer Army headquarters to seek approval for his orders to Bittrich and secure the necessary supplies for the II SS Panzer Corps.[409] Eberbach's orders were approved and the attack of II SS Panzer Corps was set for the night of August 19/20. The Poles in First Canadian Army from the north and the Americans from the south had broken through German lines and met in Chambois late on the afternoon of August 19. Neither Allied force was larger than regimental in size; the Allied defensive positions between Argentan and Trun were therefore paper-thin. Germans

---

404   Eberbach, 25.
405   Eberbach, 26.
406   Eberbach, 26.
407   Eberbach, 26.
408   Eberbach, 26.
409   Eberbach, 26.

trying to escape using the main roads were likely to be captured, but Germans getting off the main roads were likely to make it out of the pocket unmolested.

On the afternoon of August 19, Eberbach visited Bittrich to check on his status. He still had no fuel, and had received only small amounts of ammunition. Sufficient fuel for the attack arrived only the next morning, August 20. By the time the fuel was distributed, etc., it was 1000 hours.[410]

Eberbach and Bittrich decided to divide the 2nd and 9th SS Panzer Divisions into two battle groups, combined, they counted only twenty tanks.[411] Eberbach wrote, "As nearly as I can remember, one kampfgruppe . . . advanced along the route Vimoutiers-Trun and the other kampfgruppe along the road Camembert-St. Lambert."[412] Underneath bad weather which hindered Allied air forces, the two battle groups made excellent progress until they came to a range of small hills between Coudehard, Ecouches, and Champeaux. The hills were finally taken that afternoon, but the battle groups could go no further.[413] They had forced a sizable gap in the Allied encirclement, through which thousands of Germans continued their escape. "During the rest of the day and throughout the night, soldiers with and without arms streamed out of the encirclement. Altogether, about fifty guns and twenty-five tanks might also have gotten out."[414]

It was noon the following day, August 21, when the last German soldiers were able to escape from the Falaise pocket. By then, the Allies had taken back the range of hills. ". . . I considered the task of the Corps fulfilled . . ." Eberbach later wrote, "The withdraw to and over the Seine began."[415] Given their shortages in fuel and ammunition, and Allied control of the air, it seemed amazing that nearly all those Germans who made it out of Normandy, also made it over the Seine.[416]

How many Germans made it out of the Falaise Gap? Good estimates are hard to find. Everyone who gives an estimate is trying to prove a point. It seems likely that the twenty thousand to forty thousand figure most frequently provided by those who participated in the battle is far too low.[417] The figure

---

[410]   Eberbach, 26.
[411]   Eberbach, 26.
[412]   Eberbach, 27.
[413]   Eberbach, 26, 27.
[414]   Eberbach, 27.
[415]   Eberbach, 28.
[416]   Bradley, *A General's Life,* 304.
[417]   Eberbach, 27, 28. Also see Bradley, *A Soldier's Life,* 304, Hastings, *Overlord,* 313, Blumenson, *The Duel,* 310, and Ambrose, *Eisenhower, Soldier, General,* 333.

of three-hundred thousand provided by John Keegan in *The Second World War* is too high.[418] The figure of two-hundred-and-ten thousand provided by Richard Romer in *Patton's Gap* is also too high, but probably closer to the actual number of Germans who managed to escape.[419] The number of Germans who escaped is somewhere between these figures.

Russell Weigley wrote, "Of fifteen divisional commanders in the pocket, only three did not get away. Only one of the five corps commanders did not reach safety. Hausser, Deitrich, and Eberbach all escaped . . . The survival of cadres and headquarters influenced the whole German conception of the battle, with much benefit to German morale . . ."[420] German morale was also given a considerable boost because of the ability of many German officers and NCOs to create order out of chaos. According to Russell Weigley, ". . . these headquarters demonstrated the remarkable rapidity with which they could reconstitute divisions and corps around themselves."[421]

Every German panzer division in Normandy was west of Argentan-Falaise, well within the Falaise Gap on the night of August 12/13, 1944. Ninth and 116th Panzer Divisions were on the edge of the gap near Argentan, but they were under orders to remain in place to protect the southern flank.

All of those German panzer divisions which fought in Normandy were later reconstituted around the cadres of officers and NCOs who had escaped from the Falaise Gap and returned to action. Every panzer division, except one, was reconstituted and put back into action against the Americans during the Battle of the Bulge. These divisions were: 2nd Panzer, 9th Panzer, 116th Panzer, Panzer Lehr, 1st SS Panzer, 2nd SS Panzer, 9th SS Panzer, 10th SS Panzer, and 12th SS Panzer. The only Panzer Division in the Falaise Pocket which did not reappear during the Battle of the Bulge, 21st Panzer Division, was reconstituted and saw action against the Americans in the Saar between September and December 1944.[422]

The Battle of the Falaise Gap lasted so long because the Allied commander, General Montgomery, could not decide how to complete the encirclement. The Germans were very good soldiers, but at Falaise, they broke and ran from the action just like every other soldier suffering a decisive defeat. Even German SS soldiers were running from the battle. Yet

---

[418]   John Keegan, *The Second World War*, (New York: Penguin Books, 1989), 410.
[419]   Rohmer, 213, 214.
[420]   Weigley, *Eisenhower's Lieutenants*, 215.
[421]   Weigley, *Eisenhower's Lieutenants*, 214, 215.
[422]   Duncan Crow, *Panzer Divisions of World War 2, Part 2*, (Windsor, Berks: Profile Publications, no date given), 44-62.

German officers were able to retain a semblance of order during the battle because the Allies had not closed off their escape route. As long as their escape route remained open, German soldiers were honor-bound to make the effort to escape.

From the night of 12/13 August until the 21st of August, the gap between St. Leonard and Falaise/Trun remained open. It was the Allies inability to close the gap and their indecisive tactics which allowed so many Germans to escape the trap in Normandy. As long as an escape route remained, the German soldier was obligated to make the attempt. Once the Allies completed the encirclement and had defeated Eberbach's battle groups between Vimoutiers and Camembert, most of those fifty-thousand Germans remaining in the pocket became willing, probably grateful prisoners.[423]

United States, British, Canadian, and French infantrymen paid a terrible price for the failure of Allied Commanders to complete the encirclement at Falaise. Historian Russell Weigley put it bluntly, ". . . the Allied armies in Europe simply lacked one of the prerequisites of military success, unity of command."[424] The Allies had also lost their best chance to end the war in 1944.

General Eisenhower was supposed to take command of Allied Ground Forces on August 1, when the second American Army was created and General Bradley moved up to Command 12th US Army Group. Eisenhower declined to do so, citing poor communication facilities at his new headquarters near Granville. General Eisenhower's willingness to pamper British political sensitivities had postponed Montgomery's demotion to Army Group Commander for exactly one month, but solved none of the Allies' command problems.

---

[423]   Bradley, *A General's Life*, 304.
[424]   Weigley, *Eisenhower's Lieutenants*, 216.

Chapter 6

A Chronology of Events from
July 18 to September 24, 1944

"I cannot understand why Monty keeps on asking for all four
Armies in the Calais area and then through Belgium, where the
tanks are practically useless now and will be wholly useless this
winter."[425] Patton's Diary entry August 23, 1944

Pre-Invasion plans outlined a vigorous assault for D-day, with Allied
armies getting ". . . a good lodgement . . ." area and quickly moving inland.
At a planning session on May 15 at St Paul's School, Montgomery said,
"We must gain space rapidly, and peg out claims well inland."[426] Later,
Montgomery explained his plans for completion of the lodgement phase
of Allied operations: "Once we can get control of the main enemy lateral
Grandville-Vire-Argentan-Falaise-Caen and the area enclosed in it is
firmly in our possession; then we will have the lodgement area we want
and can begin to expand."[427] Initial plans required British possession of the
Caen-Falaise-Argentan lateral before the second stage of the invasion began.
During the initial phase of operations the Allied offensive would be directed
south toward Argentan-Granville. After build-up and re-supply, the second
phase of Allied operations would involve a pivot with the southern-most
British objective near Alencon redirecting the main Allied offensive to a
north, north-east direction toward Paris and the French interior. The British
Second, Canadian First, and US First Armies would conduct a power drive
to the Seine. US Third Army would be occupied in Brittany, reducing the
German garrisons and opening the Brittany ports for Allied shipping.

Allied planners had also developed a long-term strategy for the drive
into Germany. It was a political compromise that gave both British and
American armies a task. SHAEF planned a double thrust into Germany,

---

[425] Blumenson, (Ed.), *The Patton Papers, 1940-1945*, 527.
[426] Hamilton, *Master*, 588.
[427] Hamilton, *Master*, 588.

one for each Allied Army Group. Montgomery's 21st British Army Group would drive north into Belgium, seize the Belgium airfields, overrun the V-weapon launching sites, capture the port of Antwerp, and then drive north of the Ardennes into Germany. They would continue their drive over the Rhine opposite the Ruhr and destroy the Ruhr industrial area. Bradley's 12th US Army Group was to drive south of the Ardennes past Metz, and the Nancy Gap in France. They would then advance to the Rhine opposite the Saar, cross the Rhine, overrun the Saar, and drive through the Frankfurt Gap onto the central German plateau. Bradley's route into Germany had been the main route used for an invasion of Germany from the west down through history. It was not ideal, but it was certainly preferable to the long way around through the water-logged, heavily forested northern route that the British were attempting to use. The Allied plan had something for everyone, the British and Americans each had their own routes into Germany. Although the British drive was given the classification of "Main" because Antwerp and the Ruhr were both in the British sector, the United States Army would eventually outnumber Montgomery's British Army by a factor of four to one. The question of how many, if any, Unites States Army divisions would be assigned to serve under Montgomery was not addressed in pre-invasion planning.

Most American officers thought giving Montgomery a small US Corps of three or four divisions would be sufficient. Eisenhower told Patton in July that he thought Montgomery might get one small US Army. Both predictions turned out to be wrong. Montgomery's 21st British Army Group had already experienced a manpower crisis in Normandy and had broken up one infantry division and several smaller units to make good their infantry losses. The British were not able to replace their battlefield casualties. During the fall and winter campaign in Europe, Montgomery would do far better with the Americans than even he could have imagined. In his efforts to acquire American troops, vehicles and engineers, Montgomery was ably assisted by General Dwight D. Eisenhower, whose commitment to the Anglo-American alliance has been well documented on both sides of the Atlantic.

Many senior British officers at SHAEF, particularly the Royal Air Force officers, thought Montgomery was the main reason the British Army had failed at Caen. They talked Eisenhower and his Chief of Staff into discussions about firing General Montgomery, the most popular commander in the British Army.

July 18: General Miles Dempsey, Diary: "Sir Ronald Adam, the Adjutant General at the War Office, had come out to Normandy and in a talk in my caravan he warned me that if our infantry casualties continued at the recent rate it would be impossible to replace them, and we should have to 'cannibalize'—to break up some divisions in order to maintain the rest . . ."[428] Max Hastings, writing about Operation *Goodwood* in *Overlord*, makes the same point, adding, "The critical problem of manpower and infantry casualties thus directly influenced an important tactical decision."[429] The British had tanks to spare in Normandy, but they were running out of infantry replacements; therefore, they decided to lead the *Goodwood* attack with armored divisions.

There was a growing fear of World War I-type stalemate in Normandy when Montgomery launched his three armored divisions in an attack near Caen. The attack, codenamed *Goodwood,* followed an air bombardment which dropped seven-thousand tons of bombs on German defenders.

July 19th: US First Army captured Saint Lo.

The British *Goodwood* offensive captured the rest of Caen and advanced seven miles at its deepest penetration. British armored divisions suffered heavy losses, and were eventually replaced with infantry formations. *Goodwood* continued for two more days and was later called off due to heavy rain. Everyone, with the sole exception of General Montgomery, was disappointed with the results. Montgomery told the British press that his army had broken through the German defenses. This turned out to be false, but the British press celebrated the fleeting victory with headlines like: "Second Army breaks through," "British Army in full cry" and "Wide corridor through German front."[430] Of course none of this was true, and when it became apparent, Montgomery toned down his claims for a victory. Montgomery later said that all he really wanted to do with *Goodwood* was draw German reserves and reinforcements onto the British front near Caen, to make things easier for the Bradley and the Americans on the western flank.

British historian Max Hastings commented on the results of *Goodwood*: "The truth . . . which seems self-evident from the course of events, was that

---

[428] The Diary of General Miles Dempsey, source the Liddell Hart Papers. From D'Este, *Decision*, 260.

[429] Hastings, *Overlord,* 238.

[430] Hastings, *Overlord*, 236.

in *Goodwood,* and throughout the rest of the campaign, *Montgomery sought major ground gains for [British] Second Army if these could be achieved at acceptable cost. He forsook them whenever casualties rose unacceptably. This occurred painfully often."*[431] [Italics added]

Harry C. Butcher, diary: [Captain Butcher was a Naval Reservist, a friend, and bridge partner of Eisenhower's before the war. At Eisenhower's request, he was assigned to Eisenhower's personal staff as a Naval Aide. He also handled press relations. Butcher kept a diary and later wrote a book about his wartime experiences]. Telephone call, Churchill to Eisenhower: ". . . the PM called up, boiling mad, saying it would be a cabinet issue, this business of Monty trying to tell the PM where he could and could not go."[432] Montgomery had told Eisenhower not to allow any visitors to his headquarters for a few days and Eisenhower had informed the Prime Minister of Montgomery's request.

Brooke visited Montgomery in Normandy, he advised Montgomery to drop his ban on visitors and ". . . made Monty write a personal invitation to Churchill."[433]

July 20: Assistant SHAEF Commander Arthur Tedder: "On July 20, I spoke to Portal about the Army's failure. We are agreed in regarding Montgomery as the cause."[434]

Telephone call, Tedder to Eisenhower: ". . . the British Chiefs of Staff would support any recommendation that Ike might care to make with respect to Monty for not succeeding in going places with his big three-armored division push."[435]

At an afternoon meeting between Eisenhower and Montgomery at the latter's headquarters, Eisenhower urged Montgomery to continue the attack on the eastern flank at Caen.

July 21: Letter, Eisenhower to Montgomery: "The recent advances near Caen have partially eliminated the necessity for a defensive attitude, so I

---

[431] Hastings, *Overlord,* 239, 240.
[432] Butcher, 617.
[433] Bryant, *Triumph,* 236.
[434] Lord Tedder, *With Prejudice,* (Boston: Little, Brown, 1966), 562.
[435] Butcher, 617. Lord Tedder later wrote that he was misquoted: ". . . although I strongly disapproved of Montgomery's action, it was quite beyond my powers to speak in the name of the British Chiefs of Staff . . . Alan Brooke [C.I.G.S.] gave Montgomery strong support." Lord Tedder, 563.

feel you should insist that Dempsey keep up the strength of his attack . . . We do not need to fear, at this moment, a great counter offensive . . . But while we have equality in size we must go forward shoulder to shoulder, with honors and sacrifices equally shared."[436] The Germans had lost the ability to launch a major counterattack by the second week in June. By June 17 both Rommel and von Rundstedt were in a meeting with Hitler begging him to allow a limited withdraw to get German forces outside the range [25 miles] of Allied naval guns.[437] Eisenhower's reminder to Montgomery that the threat of a great German counterattack no longer existed was strongly supported by *ULTRA* intelligence.[438] Of course, Montgomery knew all of this. He was keeping British Second Army on the defensive not because he feared a German attack but because the British Army could not replace their infantry casualties. Montgomery was letting Bradley's Army lead the way out of Normandy because the Americans could replace their infantry casualties and the British could not. Prime Minister Churchill had also talked to Eisenhower about the problem the British were having with infantry casualties. Churchill called Eisenhower on the telephone and asked him, ". . . if [it was] possible Eisenhower, should avoid too many British casualties." [439]

Arthur Tedder to staff member about Eisenhower's letter to Montgomery: The letter was ". . . Not strong enough. Montgomery can evade it. It contains no order."[440]

Churchill visited Montgomery at his headquarters and was apparently satisfied with Montgomery's explanation of Allied strategy in Normandy.

Captain John Henderson, ADC to Montgomery, on Churchill's visit to Montgomery's headquarters: It was ". . . common knowledge at TAC that Churchill had come to sack Monty. I mean we all knew it. He came in his blue coat with a blue cap, and in his pocket he had the order, dismissing Monty."[441]

Brigadier Charles Richardson, staff officer at British 21st Army Group, in interview with author Max Hastings: "After *Goodwood* we were distinctly worried. We knew Monty put on this impenetrable act of confidence, whatever was happening. But below Freddy de Guingand's level, it was difficult to

---

[436] Chandler, (Ed.), *The Eisenhower Papers, Vol. III*, 2019.
[437] Rommel, 478.
[438] Ambrose, *Eisenhower, Soldier, General*, 321.
[439] Sir Kenneth Strong, *Intelligence at the Top,* (New York: Doubleday, 1969), 203.
[440] Tedder, 567.
[441] Hamilton, *Master*, 739.

judge whether this confidence was soundly based. My feeling was that we were getting into a bigger jam than he was prepared to admit."[442]

July 22: Harry C. Butcher, diary: "Ike said casualties since D-Day had mounted to one-hundred-and-ten thousand of which sixty-eight thousand were American. He figured the Germans had about the same . . ."[443] [Eisenhower's intelligence people were very close on their estimate of German casualties. Rommel estimated German losses at ninety-seven thousand on July 15 and increasing at the rate of two-thousand five-hundred to three thousand a day.[444] Using the three thousand daily figure for the seven days from July 15 to July 22 = 3,000 X 7 = 21,000 + 97,000 = 118,000 German casualties to July 22.]

July 24: Montgomery completed plan #M514, which proposed, "Large scale operation by three or four Arm'd Divs toward Falaise" . . . during the first week in August. This plan retained the bulk of his experienced armored formations on the eastern flank, at Caen.[445]

Harry C. Butcher, diary: ". . . friends at Naval Headquarters said they felt Monty, his British Army Commander, Dempsey, the British corps commanders, and even those of the divisions are so conscious of Britain's ebbing manpower that they hesitate to commit an attack where a division may be lost. To replace the division is practically impossible. When it is lost, it's done and finished."[446]

July 25: Early morning telephone call, Churchill to Eisenhower, Eisenhower's first words were, "What do your people think about the slowness of the situation over there?"[447] Churchill then informed Eisenhower that he had talked with Montgomery and was satisfied that his strategy in Normandy was sound.

Eisenhower, verbal instructions to Harry C. Butcher, ". . . to phone Beetle and to 'Get him out of the meeting if he is in it' and caution him against even hinting at 'the subject we have been discussing.'"[448] The subject

---

[442]   Hastings, *Overlord*, 239.

[443]   Butcher, 621.

[444]   Rommel, 486.

[445]   Hamilton, *Master*, 753.

[446]   Butcher, 622.

[447]   Butcher, 623.

[448]   Butcher, 623.

that Eisenhower was concerned about was removing General Montgomery from Command of Allied Ground Forces.

US VII Corps began Operation *Cobra*, an attack south of the relatively straight St. Lo-Periers road. The attack was preceded by a succession of fighter-bombers, medium bombers, and heavy bombers which conducted the ". . . saturation bombing of a rectangle three-and-a-half miles wide and one-and-a-half miles deep, south of the St. Lo-Periers road . . ."[449]

July 26: General Collins, commanding US VII Corps, decided that German resistance in front of *Cobra* was not coordinated and decided to commit his armor. US 9th and 30th Infantry Divisions assist 1st Infantry, 2nd Armored, and Combat Command B of 3rd Armored through their zones of operation to lead the attack. Combat Command A, 3rd Armored Division, commanded by Colonel Maurice Rose, ". . . rolled through St. Gilles that afternoon, and the exploitation stage of COBRA started . . . The VII Corps had achieved its breakthrough."[450]

Montgomery's view of Eisenhower's July 26 lunch with Churchill and C.I.G.S. Alan Brooke: "It seemed to me that Eisenhower had complained to the Prime Minister that I did not understand what I was doing . . . (H)e (Eisenhower) had told the Prime Minister he was worried at the outlook taken by the American Press that the British were not taking their share of the fighting and of the casualties. The trouble . . . was to grow and develop into storms which at times threatened to wreck the Allied ship."[451]

July 27: Operation *Cobra* was turning into a rout. With Americans pouring through the Marigny-St. Gilles Gap on July 27, the position of those German defenders near the coast was becoming untenable. "There is no alternative but to continue the withdraw along the Cotentin west coast."[452]

Montgomery on Eisenhower's meetings with Churchill and other British senior officers: "I do not think that great and good man, now one of my greatest friends, had any idea of the trouble he was starting. From that time onwards there were always 'feelings' between British and American forces

---

[449]   Bradley, *A General's Life*, 276.
[450]   Blumenson, *The Duel*, 105.
[451]   Bernard L. Montgomery, *The Memoirs of Field Marshal Montgomery*, (London: Collins, December, 1958), 260-263.
[452]   Blumenson, *The Duel*, 108.

till the war ended."[453] Eisenhower had complained to Churchill and Brooke that the British were not carrying their share of the offensive burden in France. Eisenhower's concerns were right on the mark.

Montgomery completed plan #M515. His new plan transferred the experienced British armored divisions from the eastern flank at Caen to the western flank at Caumont. According to Montgomery, "This would sidestep the main panzer formations and more directly help Bradley's Cobra breakout . . .".[454] Plan #515 was based on the sound assumption that the German response to *Cobra's* success will be a series of tactical withdraws from Normandy. But as long as the Germans remained in Normandy, Caen and the eastern flank were the keys to their survival. Montgomery was betting on a staged German withdraw to the Seine River.

Letter, Winston S. Churchill to General Montgomery: "For my own secret information, I should like to know whether the attacks you spoke of to me, or variants of them, are going to come off. *It certainly seems very important for the British Army to strike hard and win through; otherwise there will grow comparisons between the two armies [with the Americans] which will lead to dangerous recrimination* and affect the fighting value of the Allied organization."[455] [Italics added]

July 28: Letter, Eisenhower to Montgomery: "I have just read your M 515 with which I entirely agree . . . I feel very strongly that a three division attack now on Second Army's right flank will be worth more than a six division attack in five day's time . . . let us not waste an hour in getting the whole affair started. Never was time more vital to us and we should not wait on weather or on perfection in detail of preparation."[456] Eisenhower had been complaining to Churchill and Brooke about the slowness of Montgomery's British Army at Caen. Casualty figures were released showing the Americans taking two-thirds of the casualties at a time when the Allied Armies were nearly equal in size.

Brooke to Montgomery, letter: ". . . as a result of . . . the actual situation on your front, *I feel personally quite certain that Dempsey must attack at the earliest possible moment on a large scale. We must not allow German forces*

453   Montgomery, *Memoirs*, 262.
454   Hamilton, *Master*, 753.
455   Winston S. Churchill, *The Second World War, Triumph and Tragedy,* (Boston: Houghton Mifflin, 1953), 29. Italics added.
456   Chandler, (Ed.), *The Eisenhower Papers*, Vol. IV, 2041.

to move from his front to Bradley's front or we shall give more cause than ever for criticism. I shall watch this end and keep you informed, but do not neglect this point . . ." [457] [Italics added]

Montgomery to Brooke, signal M69: "I have ordered Dempsey to throw all caution overboard and to take any risks he likes and to accept any casualties and to step on the gas for VIRE." [458]

July 31: Major General John S. Wood's 4th US Armored Division overcomes weak German opposition and drives through Avranches while securing the bridges over the See and Selune Rivers. The Americans have cracked open the door to Brittany and central France.

Harry C. Butcher, diary: Lack of progress on the British front at Caen has produced BBC news coverage which is almost exclusively American. The British public had become so annoyed at the coverage of events in France that one hostess, ". . . switched off the radio . . . while her American officer guests were listening to the late news."[459]

Harry C. Butcher, diary: "Just how personally Ike has taken command of the ground forces is not yet clear to me. Each time I have suggested he do it, he has belligerently countered, *'Then they will have to get someone to be the Allied Commander* . . . I hope the future will see Ike more definitely and prominently identified with the ground battle."[460] [Italics added]

Letter, Eisenhower to Montgomery: "I learn you have a column in Avranches. This is great news . . . With the Canadian Army fighting intensively to prevent enemy movement away from Caen area Dempsey's attack coupled with Bradley's will clean up the area west of the Orne once and for all. Good luck."[461]

August 1: Elements of 1st and 9th SS Panzer leave the British front at Caen for vicinity of Mortain.[462]

August 2: Meeting, Churchill and Eisenhower: ". . . Ike readily assented to the PM's desire to mention General Morgan as the British officer who

---

[457]   Bryant, *Triumph,* 245. Italics added.
[458]   The Montgomery Papers. From Hamilton, *Master,* 768.
[459]   Butcher, 627.
[460]   Butcher, 627.
[461]   Chandler, (Ed.), *The Eisenhower Papers, Vol. IV,* 2046.
[462]   Hausser, 28.

did the early planning of Overlord with an Anglo-American staff." [463] This would help counter the nearly all-American news coming from Europe on the BBC since the American breakout at St. Lo by giving the British something to brag about.

Allied commanders learned that withdraw of German armor from the eastern flank at Caen was well under way. ULTRA Message XL 4426 was released to field intelligence officers on this date: "*ACCORDING FIRST SUGAR SUGAR CORPS NOUGHT FIVE HOURS SECOND, WITHDRAWAL)) OF ELEMENTS ONE TWO AND NINE SUGAR SUGAR DIVISIONS FROM THE LINE COMPLETED.*" [464]

F.W. Winterbotham in *The ULTRA Secret*: "Then on August the second, in a long signal, which I remember covered two whole sheets of my Ultra paper, Hitler told Kluge . . . to collect together four of the armored divisions from the Caen front with sufficient supporting infantry divisions and make a decisive counterattack to retake Avranches and thus to divide the American forces at the base of the Cherbourg peninsula. He was then to roll the American forces to the north of the armored thrust back to the sea."[465]

Telephone call from Tedder [Asst. SHAEF Commander] to F.W. Winterbotham: The above-detailed *ULTRA* message, ". . . was of such importance that Eisenhower didn't want to take any chances." The message was almost too convenient, Eisenhower directed Tedder to check with *ULTRA* intelligence to make sure the message was not a German ruse intended to deceive the Allies. "I [Winterbotham] phoned Hut 3 to make quite sure that the original German version was in Hitler's own distinct style and language. They told me we had no reason to doubt it on any score, and the signal had without doubt come from Fuehrer headquarters. Tedder was satisfied."[466]

Letter, Eisenhower to Montgomery: "Our armor and mobile columns will . . . want to operate boldly against the enemies flanks and in this situation all of these commanders should be aware of the fact that in an emergency we can drop them supplies by airplane in considerable quantities. I know that you will keep hammering as long as you have a single shot in the locker."[467]

---

[463] Butcher, 632.
[464] *ULTRA* Message XL 4426 dated 2 August 1944.
[465] Winterbotham, 148.
[466] Winterbotham, 149.
[467] Chandler, (Ed.), *The Eisenhower Papers, Vol. IV*, 2047.

Harry C. Butcher diary, Eisenhower to Butcher: "If the intercepts are right, we are to hell and gone in Brittany and slicing 'em up in Normandy."[468]

August 4: Harry C. Butcher, diary: "This morning Ike received a message from the Combined Chiefs directing him to consider plans for pushing out ground forces into the Pas de Calais area." German flying bombs launched from the Pas de Calais are taking a heavy toll on British morale.[469] News coverage of the brilliant American advance was also taking a heavy toll on British morale.

Harry C. Butcher, diary: "At the SHAEF Forward war room last evening, I learned that the Allies had captured some seventy-eight thousand Germans, of which the British got fourteen thousand, the remainder falling into American hands. This was information reported on August 1, since which we have captured an average of four thousand a day."[470] If the British took fourteen thousand prisoners, this meant the Americans had taken sixty-four thousand prisoners. Contrary to what some revisionist historians have suggested about poor American commanders causing higher casualty figures in the hedgerows and swamps of Normandy, these figures seem to suggest that the Americans also did substantially more of the fighting.

First SS Panzer left eastern front at Caen, and was replaced in line by the 89th Infantry Division.[471]

August 5: Eisenhower to Marshall, telegram: "I will not repeat not under any conditions agree at this moment to a cancellation of Dragoon."[472] Eisenhower had learned Churchill was trying to get Dragoon, the Allied landings in southern France, cancelled. The original code name for the operation was Anvil, but Churchill wanted that changed to Dragoon, because he wanted everyone to know he had been 'Dragooned' into it.

A lunch and high-level strategic conference was held at Eisenhower's SHAEF Forward Headquarters in Normandy. Present were: Eisenhower, his Chief of Staff, Bedell Smith, Winston Churchill, British Admirals Cunningham, Ramsay and Tennant, Brigadier L.C. Hollis, and Commander Thompson. Churchill said that Eisenhower would be missing a great

---

[468]   Butcher, 630.
[469]   Butcher, 633.
[470]   Butcher, 632.
[471]   Hastings, *Overlord*, 296.
[472]   Chandler, (Ed.), *The Eisenhower Papers, Vol. IV*, 2055.

opportunity if he did not transfer the landings planned for Southern France to the Brittany ports: Brest, Lorient, and Saint-Nazaire, ". . . or indeed through the Channel ports, where he assumed they could walk in like tourists."[473] According to Harry C. Butcher's diary, "Ike said no and continued saying no all afternoon, and ended saying no in every form of the English language at his command. Ike argued so long and patiently that he was practically limp when the PM departed."[474]

August 6: Montgomery completed Plan #M517. This plan suggested closing off the Chartres-Orleans Gap escape route from Normandy with Airborne and Airportee troops, then destroying all the bridges over the Seine River with Allied air power. Germans retreating from Normandy would be pushed up against the Seine by an Allied power drive out of Normandy with First Canadian, Second British, and First American Armies attacking northeast in one solid front. Patton's Third Army would be busy in Brittany, liberating the much-needed French ports. This plan became known as the "wide envelopment."

Germans counterattack the Mortain hinge on the US-held front lines just before midnight, August 6/7.

August 7: Under the cover of darkness and an early morning fog, the German attack made some initial progress north and southwest of Mortain. Germans captured Mortain while 4th US Infantry was trying to seal off the flanks of the penetration. CCB, 3rd US Armored Division stopped the German spearhead, 1st SS Panzer, near St Barthelemy. When the fog lifted, US Thunderbolts and RAF Typhoons got into the air. They found 2nd German Panzer near Le Coudray and hammered the exposed panzer columns.[475]

Canadian II Corps, Commanded by General Guy Simonds begins offensive, code named *Totalize*, on eastern flank toward Falaise. This represents a return to Plan #M514, except that the number of armored divisions is reduced from three to two, and the divisions given this vital assignment (4th Canadian Armored and 1st Polish Armored) both arrived in Normandy on July 31. The critical drive to Falaise and Argentan had been assigned to two armored divisions with no combat experience. The striking

---

[473] Butcher, 634.
[474] Butcher, 634, 635.
[475] Hastings, *Overlord,* 285.

power of Crerar's Army was in two armored divisions: the 4th Canadian and 1st Polish, both seeing their first combat.

The German counterattack at Mortain was solid evidence that the Germans intended to stay in Normandy. It was a huge gamble, but Hitler had insisted. Caen immediately resurfaced as the most critical pivot on the British front. Montgomery's Plan #515 had been based on the assumption that the Germans would withdraw from Normandy. Plan #515 was now clearly in error, easily corrected, but still an error. All Montgomery had to do was reinforce the new Canadian and Polish armored divisions with one or two of his battle-tested British formations. For whatever reasons, Montgomery failed, from August 7 until August 21, to correct the mistaken deployment he had outlined in Plan #515. Typically, Montgomery was unwilling to admit he had made a mistake, so he left the inexperienced Poles and Canadians on their own in the critical Caen sector.

August 8: Initial reports from First Canadian Army about Operation *Totalize* were good. The Canadians and Poles gained about six miles toward Falaise.

Harry C. Butcher, diary: "Ike keeps continually after both Montgomery and Bradley to destroy the enemy now rather than to be content with mere gains of territory."[476]

Major General Wade Haislip's US XV Corps takes Le Mans.

General Bradley proposes a change in Allied plans. He believes, with the Germans attacking at Mortain, a short envelopment from Le Mans to Argentan will accomplish the same thing as the wider envelopment (Plan #M517) up to the Seine. If the Germans persist long enough in their attack at Mortain, Haislip's XV Corps should be able to close the gap behind them by driving north to meet the British/Canadians at Argentan. Bradley consults with Patton, who would have preferred the wider Seine envelopment; with Eisenhower, who approved it "on the spot"; and with Montgomery, who approved it after his concerns about the German offensive at Mortain were satisfied.[477]

Montgomery later wrote: "*The Situation, August 8,* I have shown that up to this period my plan was to make a wide enveloping movement from the southern American flank up to the Seine about Paris, and at the same time to

---

[476]   Butcher, 636.

[477]   Bradley, *A General's Life*, 294, 295. For another opinion see F. W. Winterbotham, *The Ultra Secret,* 148-158.

drive the centre and northern sectors of the Allied line straight for the river. In view of the Mortain counter stroke, I decided to attempt *concurrently* a shorter envelopment with the object of bottling up the bulk of the German forces deployed between Falaise and Mortain. It was obvious that if we could bring off both these movements we would virtually annihilate the enemy in Normandy."[478] Unfortunately, the two envelopments Montgomery discussed were not tactically compatible. Allied units deployed for the shorter envelopment between Argentan and Falaise will block the roads Montgomery needed to get the First Canadian, First US and Second British Armies quickly to the Seine to prevent the Germans from crossing. In the event, nearly all those Germans who escaped the Falaise Gap, also got safely across the Seine.

On Bradley's directions, Patton wrote the order turning Haislip's XV Corps north at Le Mans to attack in the direction Carrouges-Sees, to the new east/west inter-Army Group boundary which had been drawn along the south bank of the Orne River just two miles south of Argentan.[479]

August 9: Letter, Eisenhower to Marshall: ". . . Patton has the marching wing [of Bradley's Army Group] which will turn in rather sharply to the northeast from the general vicinity of Le Mans and just to the west thereof marching toward Alencon and Falaise. The enemy's bitter resistance in the area between Mortain and south of Caen make it appear that we have a good chance to encircle and destroy a lot of his forces."[480] Eisenhower's assessment was correct.

Meeting at Prime Minister's residence, Eisenhower and Churchill: They have a bitter meeting over Dragoon; the invasion of southern France scheduled to take place on August 15. Churchill wants it cancelled and Eisenhower is equally determined that it must go forward as planned. If he did not get his way, Churchill threatened to ". . . lay down the mantle of my high office." Churchill accused Eisenhower and his government of becoming ". . . a big strong dominating partner . . . indifferent to British interests." Eisenhower later described the meeting ". . . as one of the most difficult of the entire war." Eisenhower explained his position again and again, but nothing he said would satisfy the Prime Minister. "When the meeting broke up, he (Churchill) was still unhappy, indeed had tears in his

---

[478]   Montgomery, *Normandy,* 98, 99. Italics in the original.
[479]   Weigley, *Eisenhower's Lieutenants,* 199.
[480]   Chandler, (Ed.), *The Eisenhower Papers, Vol. IV,* 2062.

eyes."[481] The meeting lasted for hours, leaving Eisenhower physically and emotionally drained, and effectively removed from his duties in Europe for most of the day. *Dragoon* is set to go on August 15, less than a week away. Churchill's motives for beating Eisenhower nearly to death over *Dragoon* are clearly suspect. No British soldiers were involved in the operation.

Canadian 2nd Corps: Operation *Totalize*, the Canadian attack toward Falaise is grinding to a halt, due primarily to a lack of combat experience in the leading armored divisions, and to ". . . (Canadian) staff were exasperated by the persistent delays that appeared to afflict almost every unit movement, the repeated episodes of troops and tanks firing on each other, the difficulty of getting accurate reports from the front . . ."[482] Strong counterattacks mounted by a battle group from the 12th SS Panzer Division hurt the British Columbia Regiment.

Montgomery, signal to Brooke: "Should the Germans escape us here (Falaise-Argentan), I shall proceed quickly with the plan outlined in M517—the wide envelopment."[483]

August 10: German reinforcements move into position opposite the Canadian II Corps. The Canadian advance toward Falaise stalls.

Wade Haislip's XV US Corps begins its attack north from the vicinity of Le Mans toward Argentan with both flanks wide open. Haislip has organized his attack in depth. On the eastern flank, 5th US Armored Division, supported by the 79th US Infantry Division, is ordered to drive through Mamers to Sees. On the western flank, 2nd French Armored Division, closely supported by US 90th Infantry Division, will direct their attack toward Alencon and then to Carrouges. Elements of the German 708th Infantry and 9th Panzer Divisions in sharp but brief defensive actions destroy some forty Allied tanks.[484]

General Adolf Kuntzen, Commanding German LXXXI Corps, in telephone call with von Kluge: "The enemy has started to push north and northeast of Le Mans . . . I have only four battalions at my disposal. I cannot halt the American advance. It is probable that Alencon will fall during the day."[485]

---

[481] Ambrose, *Eisenhower, Soldier, General*, 329.
[482] Hastings, *Overlord*, 299.
[483] Hamilton, *Master*, 779.
[484] Patton, 103.
[485] Florentin, 93.

General Eisenhower inspects the 82nd and 101st Airborne Divisions in England.

August 11th: Harry C. Butcher, diary: "At the moment the Germans are expected again to counterattack near Mortain, where they have amassed five and a half of their seven Panzer divisions . . ."[486]

The Canadian attack toward Falaise has been stalled for several days. General ". . . Simonds ordered his armored divisions to pull out of the line, to be relieved by infantry formations."[487] This ends Operation *Totalize* and effectively shuts down the Canadian attacks toward Falaise until August 14, when Operation *Tractable* is scheduled to begin. With two German Armies immobile in Normandy deployed west of a line Argentan-Falaise, there are no major attacks planned to close the gap from the north for three critical days.

Haislip's XV Corps overwhelms German rearguard defenders and advances toward Sees and Carrouges. The advance is slowed by heavily forested areas and a shortage of good roads. After the initial skirmishes with 9th Panzer and 708th Infantry Divisions, there was little organized German resistance between XV Corps and Falaise. "As far as delays were concerned, traffic jams were about as bad a nuisance as the Germans."[488]

Harry C. Butcher, diary: "Ike has been increasingly concerned about the PM's attitude regarding *Anvil,* and, above all, the feeling that the questioning and apparent dissension might cause a rift in the unity of the Allies at a time when success is almost in our grasp."[489]

Eisenhower to Churchill, letter: "To say that I was disturbed by our conference on Wednesday does not nearly express the depth of my distress over your interpretation of the recent decision affecting the Mediterranean Theater . . . I would feel that much of my hard work over the past many months has been irretrievably lost if we now should lose faith in the organisms that have given higher direction to our war effort, *because such lack of faith would quickly be reflected in discord in our field commands.*"[490]

Montgomery to Brooke, telegram: *"I have instructed BRADLEY to collect a fresh Army Corps of three divisions in the LE MANS area and*

---

[486]   Butcher, 639.

[487]   Hastings, *Overlord*, 300.

[488]   Weigley, *Eisenhower's Lieutenants*, 202.

[489]   Butcher, 639.

[490]   Chandler, (Ed.), *The Eisenhower Papers, Vol. IV, 2065*. Italics added.

hold it ready to push quickly through toward CHARTRES if and when we suddenly put M517 into operation."[491] One day after Montgomery reads *ULTRA* Message 5516, which was released to Allied generals at 1436 hours, August 10, he decides to begin implementing the wider envelopment. It makes no sense. *ULTRA* Message 5516 provides great detail of the order from OKW, German Army Headquarters, to von Kluge in France about returning to the counterattack at Mortain. It mentions the German attack toward Alencon to eliminate XV US Corps' threat to the southern German flank, but the actual attack order is contained in another *ULTRA* message. According to General Heinrich Eberbach, the German Panzer commander charged with carrying out the Mortain attack: "Now, however, even OKW could not close its ears to the necessity of making an immediate attack on the flank of the enemy [Haislip] advancing toward Alencon and Laigle and throwing him back. They agreed to this part of Kluge's proposal.(H) owever, OKW did not authorize evacuation of the Mortain 'finger' but, as if hypnotized, kept to the thought of an attack on Avranches. Thus, Hitler made it impossible for Seventh Army to put the necessary panzer divisions at my disposal immediately."[492]

Montgomery's decision to withhold three US divisions at Le Mans was wrong on three counts. First, he knew through *ULTRA* that the Germans were planning to attack Haislip's XV Corps. He had deliberately weakened the flank protection of an American Corps that was expecting a German attack. Second, his plan totally disregarded the *ULTRA* information that the Germans intended to stay in Normandy. He had read *ULTRA* Message 5516 and he knew that Eberbach's panzer forces must return to the counterattack at Mortain after they destroyed Haislip's corps. Third, Montgomery made his decision to begin implementation of the wider envelopment on August 11th without consulting with either Bradley or Eisenhower. His decision was arbitrary. He was telling Bradley both what to do with his divisions and how to do it. When Bradley complained, Montgomery insisted that too many Germans were already escaping to the east, it was time to reconsider Montgomery's original plan for the wider envelopment to the Seine. They both knew that this was not true.

Eisenhower's letter to Churchill was clearly prescient. The same day he predicts discord in the Allied field commands; Montgomery ignores his prior agreement to conduct the short envelopment at Falaise-Argentan

---

[491]   Hamilton, *Master*, 784. Italics added.
[492]   Eberbach, 14.

without giving the Americans any notice of his change in plan. Eisenhower's pleas to Montgomery to destroy the enemy force in front of him, rather than simply gaining ground, have been totally ignored.

Eisenhower to Marshall, letter: "My entire preoccupation these days is to secure the destruction of a substantial portion of the enemy forces facing us. Patton, on the marching wing of our forces, is closing in as rapidly as possible . . . Within a week there should be real developments on the present front . . . As I have told you, I am extremely hopeful about the outcome of our current operations. If we can destroy a good portion of the enemy's army now in front of us, we will have a greater freedom of movement in northern France and I would expect things to move very rapidly."[493] Eisenhower is again correct; but even the best plans do not always succeed.

August 12: On the northern [British/Canadian] flank, only limited operations of 2nd Canadian Infantry Division in the Laize River valley as preparations for Operation *Tractable* continue.[494] *Tractable* will not begin for two more days.

XX US Corps, An Operational Report: "The 3rd Cavalry Group joined 20 Corps on August 10 . . . The 3rd Squadron, reinforced by the light tanks of the 43rd Squadron was dispatched to patrol north and make contact with First US Army units around MAYENNE. The cavalry made contact and was ordered to make an area reconnaissance east. In a three-day action, it struck east on an approximately 80-mile front . . . east to a north-south line, SEES to BLOIS, *it was determined that the left flank of the Seventh German Army was lightly held and the moment opportune for an encirclement.*"[495] Unfortunately, there was little sense of urgency displayed by the British commander on the northern flank. [Italics added]

Bradley visited Patton's Third Army Headquarters. He agreed with Patton's decision to deploy Lt. General Walton Walker's XX US Corps on the left (west) and Major General Gilbert Cook's XII US Corps on the right (east) of Haislip's XV Corps.[496] But he cannot approve either operation because of Montgomery's order to retain three US divisions at Le Mans in preparation for the wide envelopment to the Seine.

---

[493]   Chandler, (Ed.), *The Eisenhower Papers, Vol. IV,* 2067.
[494]   Hastings, *Overlord,* 301.
[495]   XX Corps, *An Operational Report, 1 August-1 September 1944,* 5. Italics added.
[496]   Gay Diaries, Aug. 12, 1944, 454.

Chester B. Hansen, diary: "There is some discussion now concerning an alleged disagreement in strategy between Brad and Monty concerning the timing for this northward movement. I am told that Monty is anxious that the continued movement toward Paris in seizure of more terrain while Brad is equally insistent that we turn north now at Le Mans and trap the German army containing the hinge of the 1st Army and those elements following the 30 and 12 Corps in the 2nd British Army."[497] This was the result of Montgomery's order to Bradley of the day before; it directed him to withhold three divisions in the vicinity of Le Mans. It was natural for Bradley to dispute an order he disagreed with, especially when he thought he had Montgomery's agreement to conduct the short envelopment on August 8. This is an accurate representation of the events and Hansen's time frame is entirely on the mark. Montgomery's telegram to Brooke on August 11 verifies his decision to begin implementing the wider envelopment on that date.

Late that afternoon, Bradley, with Eisenhower's approval, orders General Joe Collins to drive northeast with his VII Corps through Ranes to contact the left flank of Haislip's XV Corps, sealing off Haislip's vulnerable western flank. Bradley later wrote, "That afternoon I ordered Collins to go all out to the northeast, inserting his corps between Haislip and the bulk of the Germans withdrawing from Mortain. Collins put Huebner's Big Red One, Eddy's 9th and Rose's 3rd Armored in the van, with Barton's 4th in reserve."[498]

Early evening, Eisenhower, who has been visiting Bradley headquarters, decided to stay for dinner. Eisenhower said he was in Bradley's headquarters when calls from commanders came in about the inter-Army Group boundary line just south of Argentan. Did Bradley call Montgomery and ask for permission to move his forces north of that line? Although Bradley denies it, an interview by Forrest C. Pogue with Brigadier Edgar T. Williams, Montgomery's Intelligence Officer, suggests that *Bradley did ask for permission to allow Patton to cross the inter-Army Group boundary at Argentan.* Whatever happened that evening, it is clear no halt-order was issued. [Italics added]

XV US Corps' attack on the southern German flank was still gaining ground. 5th Armored Division captured Sees. 2nd French Armored Division took Alencon. Haislip ordered the attack continued. 5th US Armored

---

[497]   Hansen Diaries, 12 Aug. 1944
[498]   Bradley, *A General's Life*, 298.

headed north toward Argentan, and 2d French Armored attacked toward Carrouges.

That evening 21st Army Group sent a telephone message to First Canadian Army: "1930—Flash: The Yanks are four kilometers south of Argentan and fighting against Pz Division believed to be 9th Pz Division."[499]

Late evening: 2000 hours, message from Third Army to Commanding General XV Corps: "Upon capture of Argentan push on slowly direction of Falaise allowing your rear elements to close . . . Upon arrival, Falaise continue to push on slowly until you contact our allies."[500] It is likely that one or more telephone discussions took place between Patton at Third Army Headquarters and Bradley at 21st Army Group Headquarters. The result of these discussions seemed to be a wait-and-see attitude about crossing the inter-Army Group boundary line just south of Argentan. There was no halt-order given that evening. Patton and Bradley were probably waiting to see what happened with Haislip's left flank. If Collin's VII Corps closed on Haislip's left before the Germans attacked, they may have agreed to ask for permission to continue the attack across the inter-Army Group boundary.

August 13: 0900 hours, message from Twelfth US Army Group to Third Army Commander: ". . . hold (all forces) in position generally *SEES-ARGENTAN-COURRAGES*, prepared for movement upon Army order."[501] Patton directs Haislip to halt at Argentan, but to be prepared to continue the attack toward Falaise or to launch a new attack toward the Seine (northeast). This order was probably based on a telephone call from Bradley or from his Chief of Staff.

1000 hours, Telephone call from General Collins, Commanding US VII Corps to Headquarters, First US Army. First and 9th Infantry and 3rd Armored Divisions had closed the gap on XV Corps's exposed left flank. First Army's diary reports that, ". . . in some places, (they were) on the very boundary itself, and *General Collins felt sure that he could take Falaise and Argentan, close the gap, and 'do the job' before the British even started to move."[502] [Italics added]

---

[499]   War Diary, First Canadian Army, August 12,1944. From D'Este, *Decision in Normandy*, 40.
[500]   Gay Diaries, Copy, Message No. 4 issued 2000 hours, August 12, 1944.
[501]   Gay Diaries, Sunday, August 13, 1944
[502]   William Sylvan's Diary, Sunday, August 13, 58.

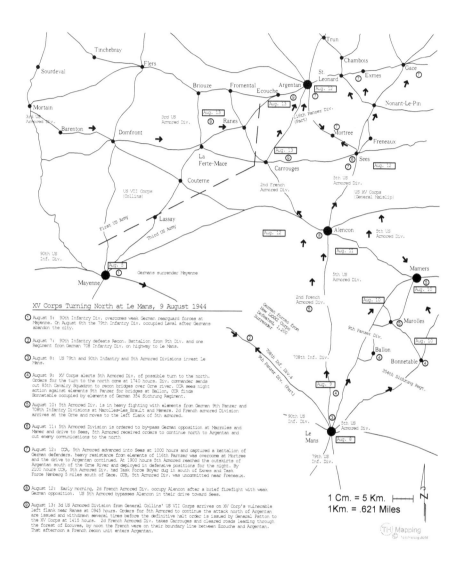

1015 hours, Telephone call from Headquarters, First US Army, General Hodges to Headquarters, 12th US Army Group, General Bradley, recorded by First Army Diary: *"General Hodges immediately called General Bradley, to ask officially for a change in boundaries, but the sad news came back that First Army was to go no further than at first designated, except that a small salient around Ranes would become ours."*[503] [Italics added]

---

[503]   William Sylvan's Diary, Sunday, August 13, 58.

1030 hours, (this call was recorded, but no time given) Bradley ordered his Operations Officer, Brigadier General A. Franklin Kibler, to call Montgomery's Headquarters and request permission to send both Hodges' First Army and Patton's Third Army north of the inter-Army Group boundary. General Kibler talks to Montgomery's Chief of Staff, General De Guingand, who said, "I am sorry Kibler. We cannot grant the permission."[504] Although he later denied it, the historical record clearly indicates that Bradley asked for and was denied permission to allow Patton's Third Army to move north of the inter-Army Group boundary line at Argentan.

1045 to 1145 hours, Bradley left his Headquarters and arrived at *Shellburst,* although Bradley denied he was ever at Eisenhower's headquarters that morning. He suggested he went straight from his headquarters to Montgomery's 21st Army Group. But that was not true. When Patton wanted to protest the halt-order, he was told Bradley was visiting Eisenhower. Neither Eisenhower nor Bradley has revealed what they talked about that Sunday morning. Whatever the two men talked about eventually produced General Bradley's famous 'halt-order' to Third Army's General Patton. Bradley must have placed a telephone call from *Shellburst* back to his own 12th Army Group Headquarters to his Chief of Staff, Major General Leven C. Allen with instructions to deliver the 'halt-order' to Patton. The halt-order was to be issued in his, Bradley's name.

1130 hours, Telephone call from 12th Army Group, Bradley's Chief of Staff, Major General Leven C. Allen, to Patton's Third Army Headquarters, where Patton's Chief of Staff, Major General Hugh J. Gaffey took the call: ". . . by order of General Bradley the Anglo-American boundary in the Falaise-Argentan area was not to be crossed under any circumstances and that the advance of 15th Corps was to halt forthwith on the Argentan-Sees line."[505] When Gaffey gave him the message, Patton's reply was, "You're kidding."[506]

1130 to 1400 hours, General Patton made numerous calls trying to talk to Bradley (Bradley was still at Eisenhower's headquarters but would not take Patton's calls) or anyone else who would listen, attempting to get the halt-order overturned. He was not successful.

---

[504] Farago, 540. Also see, Hastings, *Overlord,* 289 and Weigley, *Eisenhower's Lieutenants,* 206.

[505] Farago, 539.

[506] Farago, 539.

1415 hours, Message from Third Army Headquarters transmitted by General Gaffey, was received by General Haislip of XV Corps. The message directed Haislip to stop any movement north of Argentan and ". . . to recall at once any elements that might be 'in the vicinity of Falaise or to the north of Argentan.'"[507]

1200 to 1700 hours, [approximately], a lunch, intelligence briefing, award ceremony, and meeting to discuss Allied strategy was held at Montgomery's 21st Army Group Headquarters. Those present included: Montgomery, his intelligence officers, Dempsey, Eisenhower, and Bradley. According to Bradley's account, after a ". . . extensive intelligence briefing," the current tactical situation of the 'Falaise Gap' was discussed. Bradley recalls that the intelligence briefing left, ". . . the general impression . . . that the German commanders . . . were already carrying out a substantial withdraw to the east."[508] The intelligence briefing at Montgomery's Headquarters was conducted by British officers who had exclusive control of Allied intelligence and the latest *ULTRA* intercepts. Bradley also recalled that, "Monty chose this occasion to unveil a grandiose strategic plan to carry the war beyond Normandy and the Seine. It was a radical departure from the plans we had drawn up in England before D-Day and . . . it subordinated US forces to Monty's to an absurd and unacceptable degree."[509] Montgomery's new strategic plans required all Allied [including US] divisions that could be logistically supported assigned to his 21st Army Group for their drive north of the Ardennes. He would be commanding the only Allied thrust through the Pas de Calais, Antwerp, and into northern Germany via the Ruhr. This became the longest running argument of the war. At stake was the command and control of United States Army Infantry, Armor and Airborne Divisions, their transportation companies, and their engineers. It was an argument that General Omar Bradley, the odd man out, would almost always lose. Although American historians are loath to admit it, the long term strategic plan Montgomery unveiled on August 13 became the blueprint for the Allied advance into Germany. It was amended by Eisenhower a few times when the Supreme Commander came under political pressure from Washington; but it clearly followed the basic plan Montgomery had outlined on August 13. While

---

[507] Farago, 541.
[508] Bradley, *A General's Life*, 299.
[509] Bradley, *A General's Life,* 299. Italics added.

Eisenhower could never give Montgomery everything he asked for, he would eventually cut General Bradley's "secondary thrust" south of the Ardennes to bare bones.

Chester B. Hansen, Diary: "It is suggested in G-3 [Operations] that we were ordered to hold at Argentan rather than continue the drive to Falaise since our capture of that objective would infringe on the prestige of forces driving south and prevent them from securing prestige value in closing the trap. Accordingly, our forces were held at Argentan and subsequently refueled while the British were still short of their objective [and] permitted much of the strength in the pocket to escape eastward toward the Seine."[510] Again, Hansen's Diary is accurate, and represents the flavor of gossip at Bradley's headquarters.

Harry C. Butcher, Diary: "Ike had dined with General Bradley on Saturday evening and Bradley had returned the visit. In fact, Bradley was here [Ike's Hq] playing bridge as calmly and peacefully as if he had just come off the golf course on a Sunday afternoon. He stayed for dinner."[511]

George Patton, in *War As I Knew It*: "I believe that the (halt) order . . . emanated from the 21st Army Group, and was either due to [British] jealousy of the Americans or to utter ignorance of the situation or to a combination of the two. It is very regrettable that the XV Corps was ordered to halt, because it could have gone on to Falaise and made contact with the Canadians northwest of that point and definitely and positively close the escape gap." [512] Patton was right on both accounts.

F.W. Winterbotham in *The Ultra Secret*: "We knew that what was left of Eberbach's armor was virtually immobile; he was short of ammunition and fuel. It looked as if the American corps could close the gap. It was at this moment of high tension on the thirteenth that, unable to get any news from our side of the operation, I asked Stewart Menzies [Chief of the British Secret Service] what was up. He was smilingly evasive. The Air Ministry didn't appear to know anything either. *I rang Hut 3 at Bletchley, who couldn't make out what was happening at all. Everyone there had been waiting for Eberbach's report on the battle for Argentan by the Americans. Nothing came.*"[513]

---

[510] Hansen Diaries, Sunday August 13,1944.
[511] Butcher, 640.
[512] Blumenson, (Ed.), *The Patton Papers, 1940-1945,* 508, 509.
[513] Winterbotham, 155, 156. Italics added

The Allied Command structure had broken down in Normandy. Allied Ground Forces Commander, General Montgomery was clearly overwhelmed by the events, including the senseless German counterattack at Mortain and the speed of Patton's Third Army. Just how completely the Allied Command had broken down is evident in the orders Patton and Hodges received after the halt decision had been made. There were none. Bradley spent that Sunday, August 13, with Eisenhower and Montgomery. He spent the evening at Eisenhower's headquarters; he had dinner and later played bridge. There is no indication that Bradley issued any orders on August 13, other than the halt-orders to First and Third Armies. Third Army did not receive any orders the following day until very late in the afternoon. One would never suspect that Bradley's once-in-a-lifetime opportunity, his chance to destroy an entire hostile army was being frittered away. There was a picture taken of Bradley receiving a medal from Montgomery at the latter's headquarters on August 13. Bradley does not look his best.[514]

Collins' VII US Corps was sitting on or near the boundary line south of Ranes: 3rd Armored Division, 1st and 9th Infantry Divisions, with 4th Infantry Division in Corps reserve. Haislip's XV US Corps was strung out along the boundary line between Ranes, Argentan and St Leonard: 2nd French Armored and 90th U S Infantry Divisions were generally south of Argentan to Ranes; 5th US Armored and 79th US Infantry were south of a line Argentan-St. Leonard-Gace. 80th Infantry was in Corps reserve near Alencon. Additional forces were available from the vicinity of Le Mans. Patton said that Walker's XX Corps, ". . . was hitting nothing."[515] So he moved it northeast of Le Mans. XX Corps consisted of 7th Armored and 5th Infantry Divisions. The 4th Armored Division was arriving that day from Brittany, enabling Patton to form Gilbert Cook's XII Corps with 4th Armored and 35th Infantry Divisions. Counting unattached service and supply units, extra reconnaissance squadrons, artillery, and tank battalions, there must have been over two-hundred thousand Americans sitting on the open German flank.

Hodges' First US Army received their halt-order directly from Bradley at approximately 1015 hours. Patton's Third US Army received their halt-order at 1130 hours, August 13. Twenty-four hours later Third Army's Divisions were still sitting tight.

---

[514]   Hamilton, *Master*, between pages 736 and 737.
[515]   Patton, 104.

Tac HQ
21 Army Group
14 - 8 - 44

My dear Brad

It is difficult to say what enemy are inside the ring, and what have got out to the east. A good deal may have escaped.
I think your movement of 20 Corps should be N.E. towards DREUX.
Also any further stuff you can move round to LE MANS, should go N.E.
We want to head off the Germans, and stop them breaking out to the S.E.
I will get Bimbo here at 1100 hrs tomorrow and we will all meet and discuss the situation.
My landing strip is 8 miles north of VIRE at 631462. We will put out blue smoke.

Yrs. ever

B. L. Montgomery.

August 14: Limited attack by CCA 2nd Armored Division takes Domfront in First Army area at extreme south end of the Falaise Pocket. Also in First Army, 29th Infantry Division attacks toward Tinchebray.

1142 hours: At long last, Operation *Tractable*, the Canadian attack toward Falaise began south of Caen, obscured from enemy observation by a smoke screen. Bad luck continued to plague the Canadians. The Germans discovered a copy of the Canadian plan of attack in a scout car, and had ". . . redeployed with exact knowledge of the Canadian lines of advance."[516] The Canadian attack was bitterly opposed, but it was the first effort to close the gap since two American Armies were halted by Montgomery the day before. Unfortunately, it was also the only Allied effort to close the gap.

Letter, Montgomery to Bradley: One of the few times during the war, Montgomery put his instructions in writing. "My Dear Brad . . . It is difficult to say what enemy are inside the ring, and what have got out to the east. A good deal may have escaped. I think your movement of 20 Corps should be N.E. toward DREUX. Also any further stuff you can move round to LE MANS, should go N.E."[517]

Both Bradley and Patton made a great fuss over the plan to send US forces northeast toward Paris, each general insisted that the plan was his idea. But the truth is that the decision to go northeast, like the decision to halt US forces at Argentan, was Montgomery's. A factor in Montgomery's wide envelopment Plan M517 of August 6 was the decision to use airborne [and Airportee] divisions to block off the Paris-Orleans gap.[518] Those uncommitted US divisions near Le Mans allowed Montgomery to use these forces to close off the Paris-Orleans gap.[519]

Patton's Diary: "I am very happy and elated. I got all the corps moving by 2030 [hours] so that if Monty tries to be careful, it will be too late."[520] Patton didn't have to worry, the orders for him to go northeast were written by Montgomery. Three of those divisions had been camped out near Le Mans for over two days while the Battle of the Falaise Gap was in progress just fifty-five miles away. It would not look good when some historian wrote about the battle years later. Montgomery had to do something to get those Americans out of Normandy. Bradley and Patton split XV Corps by

---

[516]   Hastings, *Overlord*, 302.
[517]   Bradley, *A General's Life*, 300.
[518]   Hamilton, *Master*, 777 [map].
[519]   Hamilton, *Master*, 793 [map].
[520]   Blumenson, (Ed.), *The Patton Papers, 1940-1945*, 510.

sending 5th Armored and 79th Infantry to Dreux and leaving the 2nd French Armored, 80th and 90th Infantry in the Argentan-St Leonard-Alencon area. Walton Walker's XX Corps was sent to Chartres and Gilbert Cook's XII Corps went to Orleans.[521]

August 15: Bradley wrote: "To our astonishment it was now reported that the Germans had not yet withdrawn after all. Elements of at least five panzer divisions were at or approaching Argentan."[522] Not only had the Germans reappeared in the Falaise Pocket, they had reappeared in strength.

Patton's Diary: "Bradley came down to see me suffering from nerves. There is a rumor, which I doubt, that there are five panzer divisions at Argentan, so Bradley wants me to halt . . . I am complying with the order, and by tomorrow I can probably persuade him to let me advance . . ."[523]

The First Canadian Army attack toward Falaise was moving disappointingly slow. Their armored attack bogged down a few miles north of Falaise. 2nd Canadian Infantry lost the small town of Soulangy to strong German counterattacks.[524]

Montgomery changed the objective for the First Canadian Army's attack. He redirected the First Polish and 4th Canadian Armored Divisions to widen the jaws of their pincer by attacking toward Trun, about thirteen miles southeast of Falaise.[525]

August 16: British *ULTRA* intercept XL 6495 was released to Allied commanders at 0713 hours this date. XL 6495 was a message transmitted by the commanding general, Third Flak Corps after discussions on the evening of August 15 at German Fifth Army Headquarters: ". . . AFTER DISCUSSION AT HQ & HQ FIFTH)) ARMY AND FROM IMPRESSION GAINED ELSEWHERE SITUATION BOTH SIDES FALAISE & FALAISE APPARENTLY EXTREMELY SERIOUS. RESISTANCE OF THE TROOPS, WEAKENED TO UTMOST AS REGARDS BOTH PERSONNEL AND MATERIAL, NOT & NOT FAR FROM COLLAPSE. CONSEQUENCES INCALCULABLE."[526] The Germans were close to collapse despite the fact that there had been no attacks on their southern flank by the Americans since the evening of August 12.

---

[521] Patton, 108.
[522] Bradley, *A General's Life*, 303.
[523] Blumenson, (Ed.), *The Patton Papers, 1940-1945*, 511.
[524] Hastings, *Overlord,* 302.
[525] Hastings, *Overlord*, 302.
[526] *ULTRA* Message XL 6495

Courtney H. Hodges, Commanding, First US Army

William H. Simpson, Commanding, Ninth US Army

General Eisenhower visiting General Bradley's headquarters, they were
mum about their discussions on the evening of 12 August 1944.

Corps Commanders: Manton S. Eddy, on left, Commanding, US
XII Corps and Wade H. Haislip, Commanding, US XV Corps

George S. Patton Jr., Commanding, Third US Army

REF. CX/MSS/T277/201

XL 6495

ZZZZ

((XL 6495 £ 6495 SH 36 £ 36 SHA 80 £ 80 TG 72 £ 72

BV 99 £ 99 BVA ON CR YK ZE EF 3 £ 3 ST 80 £ 80

DL 46 £ 46 MI 90 £ 90 %

REVIEWS | FIFTEENTH B£ GOC £ GOC FLAK CORPS THREE FOR
EVENING
IMMEDIATE ATTENTI N CHARLIE IN CHARLIE COLON AFTER DISCUSSION

AT HQ £ HQ FIFTH)) ARMY AND FROM IMPRESSION GAINED

ELSEWHERE SITUATION BOTH SIDES FALAISE £ FALAISE APPARENTLY

EXTREMELY SERIOUS. REISISTANCE OF THE TROOPS, WEAKENED TO

UTMOST AS REGARDS BOTH PERSONNEL AND MATERIAL, NOT £ NOT

FAR FROM ØZX COLLAPSE. CONSEQUENCES INCALULABLE. DESPITE

REDOUBLED ALLIED AIR EFFORT, WHICH WAS INTOLERABLE FOR

THE TROOPS, FIVE HEAVY FLAK BATTERIEN HAD BEEN MADE

AVAILABLE EXCLUSIVELY FOR A/T £ A/T DEFENCE ON NORTH FRONT

AND TWO LIGHT ABTEILUNGEN FOR GROUND FIGHTING AT

ARGENTAN £ ARGENTAN. REQUESTED THAT BRINGING UP OF

AMMUNITION BE INCREASED MAXIMUM POSSIBLE

TNLB/HYD/LED   160713Z/8/44

Later the same day Montgomery decided to allow the Americans north of the boundary line at Argentan to meet the Poles at Chambois. This message may have convinced him that German resistance was nearing an end. Adolf Hitler also granted Seventh and Fifth Panzer Armies permission to leave Normandy. Documentation of the condition of the German Army in the pocket may have clinched the argument for the withdrawal from Normandy which German generals had been asking for since late July.

2nd Canadian Infantry Division entered the town of Falaise as the Germans withdrew. Hitler Jugend of the 12th SS Panzer Division fought nearly to the last man defending the school house in Falaise; only a few escaped. The town of Falaise had been reduced to rubble; it took the Canadians a full day to clear the debris and make the roads usable again. Before the invasion, Montgomery said he hoped to stage a "tank knock about on the Falaise plain on D-day." It had taken his forces D + seventy-one days to advance the twenty-four miles from their *Gold, Juno,* and *Sword* beachheads to the small Normandy town of Falaise.[527]

Elements of Patton's Third Army reach Dreux, Chateaudun, Chartres, and Orleans in one of the fastest mobile operations of the war. The distance from the *Omaha* and *Utah* beaches to Orleans via St. Lo, Avranches, and Angers is over three-hundred miles.

Eisenhower held a press conference during which he announced that Third US Army had joined the Allied Order of Battle, and that Third Army was commanded by Lieutenant General George S. Patton Jr. He also told the press that General Omar Bradley had moved up from command of First US Army to command US 12th Army Group. Command of First US Army was given to Lieutenant General Courtney H. Hodges. Eisenhower was scheduled to take command of Allied Ground Forces at this time, but declined to do so.[528]

German II SS Panzer Corps attacked US positions north and south of Argentan. The Germans hit the 90th Infantry Division hard and drove the Americans from the forest areas east of Argentan.

The Germans received permission to withdraw from the Falaise Pocket on this date. *ULTRA* decoded the message from OKW. There was still a huge hole in the Allied lines between Falaise and Argentan of sixteen miles.

---

[527]   Bradley, *A General's Life,* 303.

[528]   Butcher, 645. Also see Blumenson, (Ed.), *The Patton Papers, 1940-1945,* 512, 513.

Telephone call, Montgomery to Bradley: "Monty telephoned to suggest we try closing the gap further east at Chambois. He had already ordered Crerar to turn his Canadians southeast through Trun to Chambois. Could my forces help snap the jaws shut at Chambois?" [529] Montgomery finally allowed the Americans to move north of the inter-Army Group boundary line at Argentan, *after the Germans had been granted permission to escape the trap.*

Telephone call, Bradley to Patton: ". . . Bradley called up and directed that I [Patton] use the 2nd French, 90th and 80th Divisions to capture a town called Trun about halfway up in the gap."[530] Bradley committed a serious error. He did not give command of Patton's divisions in the Argentan sector to Leonard T. Gerow of V Corps the day before. Gerow's V Corps Headquarters had been out of the line for over a day, immediately after their 2nd Infantry Division captured Tinchebray and the 29th Infantry Division secured the heights south of Tinchebray. Bradley knew, or should have known, that Gerow's V Corps had completed their mission on August 15, and had been waiting for a reassignment since then.[531] He also knew Patton was nearly one hundred miles away heading for the Seine. Switching corps commanders between armies was Bradley's, not Patton's, responsibility. Bradley's failure to switch the command responsibility for those three divisions in a timely manner cost the Allies a full day and a half which was wasted sorting out what should have been a routine change in corps commanders.

August 17: Letter, Eisenhower to Marshall: "This is a personal and confidential report to you. Due to the extraordinary defensive measures taken by the enemy north of Falaise and which have taken so long to puncture, *it is possible that our total bag of prisoners will not be so great as I first anticipated.*" [532] Eisenhower admitted the failure of Montgomery's operations in the Falaise pocket to his boss. This information was extremely confidential at the time, and still is. Eisenhower and Bradley covered up for Montgomery on more than one occasion. They did not give the press any hint of the huge mistake Montgomery committed in Normandy. [Italics added]

---

[529] Bradley, *A General's Life*, 303.
[530] Blumenson, (Ed.), *The Patton Papers 1940-1945*, 514.
[531] Mary H. Williams, (Ed.), *Chronology 1941-1945, US Army in World War II, Special Studies*, (Washington D.C.: 1958), 15 August (1944).
[532] Chandler, (Ed.), *The Eisenhower Papers, Vol. IV*, 2071.

1445 hours, Telephone call Montgomery to Chief of Staff, First Canadian Army, "It is absolutely essential that both the Armored Divs of 2 Cdn Corps close the gap between First Cdn Army and Third US Army. 1 Polish Armored Div must thrust on past Trun to Chambois at all costs, and as quickly as possible."[533] Montgomery's verbal harassment of the Canadians and Poles served no purpose. Montgomery could have easily reinforced the Canadians with one or more British divisions then resting off the line.

Montgomery flew to Bradley's headquarters to sell him on his new plan for the Allied drive into Germany, similar to the plans he had presented to Ike and Bradley on August 13. That night, he outlined his "future plans" in a letter to Brooke: "After crossing SEINE 12 and 21 Army Groups should keep together as a solid mass of some forty divisions which would be so strong that it need fear nothing. The force should move northwards."[534]

Patton's flanks were wide open, but he was never concerned about his flanks, especially when he was moving fast. Patton's flank protection came from the 19th Tactical Air Command, commanded by General Otto P. Weyland. Patton wrote to Army Air Corps boss General H. H. Arnold to thank him, "For about two-hundred fifty miles I have seen the calling cards of the fighter-bombers, which are bullet marks in the pavement and burned tanks and trucks in the ditches . . ."[535] Patton, unlike Montgomery, developed great relationships with both his tactical air support [General Weyland's XIX TAC] and the troop carrier command flyers [C-47s].

August 18th: Chester B. Hansen, Diary: Eisenhower arrived for a conference with Bradley over future Allied strategy. "Ike feeling lighthearted and gay and he is taking active part in determining the strategy—allocating missions to Bradley and Monty . . . Believe he favors the Brad plan of driving eastward to Germany rather than diverting too much strength up over the northern route to the Lowlands and into Germany from that direction."[536]

Eisenhower had told General Patton on 4 July 1944 that he would probably have to give Montgomery one small US Army, indicating 4 to 6 US Divisions. Most US Generals believed that one Corps would be sufficient; Bradley thought that one US Corps plus Ridgeway's 18th Airborne Corps of three divisions would be enough to satisfy Montgomery.

---

[533] Hastings, *Overlord,* 303.
[534] Hamilton, *Master,* 798.
[535] Blumenson, (Ed.), *The Patton Papers 1940-1945,* 516.
[536] Hansen Diaries, 18 August 1944.

However, Eisenhower had already been convinced by Montgomery's arguments. Bradley later wrote, ". . . Ike, to my dismay wanted to give Monty a full American army . . . it would, in effect, immobilize our (US) thrust to the Saar; Patton would have neither the numerical strength nor the gasoline to carry it out."[537] This was exactly what Montgomery intended. Montgomery would devote a considerable amount of time to stopping the Americans, especially Patton. For both Montgomery and his Prime Minister, seeing that the 'British Army win through' was a very high priority.

Elements of the First Polish Armored Division were attacking toward Chambois when they were cut off and surrounded on Hill 262 by units of 2nd SS Panzer Division. One-thousand five-hundred Polish Infantry and eighty tanks managed to fight their way onto the high ground to the north on Mont-Ormel. From this dominating position, they killed large numbers of Germans trying to escape the Falaise Gap using the Chambois-Vimoutiers road.[538]

Harry C. Butcher, Diary: "A recent statement . . . (by) General Ike that Monty continues in command of all ground forces has produced, General Marshall pointed out, severe editorial reaction, which . . . is to be deplored. General Marshall states he . . . and the Secretary (Henry L. Stimson) are strongly of the opinion that the time has come for General Ike to assume and exercise direct command of the ground forces."[539]

Chester B. Hansen, Diary: "Ike furious with Wes Gallagher story indicating that Ike is now in full command of field forces, that Bradley is on parity with Monty. This great(ly) offended the latter and quick counter measures were necessary."[540] Protecting Montgomery and British political sensitivities were a priority for Eisenhower.

August 19: Letter, Eisenhower to Montgomery: ". . . you may or may not see a need for any US ground units, after the crossings of the Seine have once been secured. Initial estimates of such additional forces, should be kept to a minimum . . . because (of) . . . increased difficulties in maintenance . . . (and) because of the desirability of thrusting quickly eastward . . ."[541] Bradley's arguments apparently carried some weight with his boss.

---

[537] Bradley, *A General's Life*, 313.
[538] Hastings, *Overlord*, 304, 305. Also see Weigley, *Eisenhower's Lieutenants*, 213, 214.
[539] Butcher, 647.
[540] Hansen Diaries, 18 August 1944.
[541] Chandler, (Ed.), *The Eisenhower Papers, Vol. IV*, 2078.

1930 hours: Deployed in a skirmish line, men from G Company, 359th Infantry were clearing the last field south of Chambois. They hesitated before entering the town, the quiet was unnerving. Lieutenant Jan Karcz of the 10th Dragoons, Polish First armored Division looked into the field south of Chambois and was frightened by what he saw. A long line of infantry was coming straight at his positions. Having ordered reinforcements and artillery support, he decided to wait. What looked like German helmets from a distance turned out to be Americans. G Company Commander, Captain Laughlin W. Waters, was the first US soldier into Chambois.[542] The last gap in the Allied lines had been closed, but the Polish forces north of Chambois, near Mount Ormel were not reinforced and their line was pierced. The American line between St. Leonard and Chambois was also thinly held, reinforcements were too late to prevent the escape of thousands of Germans and some of their equipment. If closing the Allied trap took longer than expected, it was at least a bloodless venture. No friendly fire casualties were reported. Their fear of a ". . . calamitous battle between friends . . ." which caused Generals Eisenhower and Bradley so much distress on August 13th, turned out to be groundless.[543] The gap between Argentan and Falaise had been closed at Chambois, but the Poles and Americans were not strong enough to stop thousands of Germans from escaping their trap. On August 13th the Allies had 12 US divisions available to close a gap that was closed six days later by two regiments from the US 359th Infantry and the 10th Polish Dragoons of the 1st Polish Armored Division.

At a conference with his commanders: Dempsey, Bradley, Crerar, and Hodges, Montgomery learned that, "Ike wants to split the force and send half of it eastward to Nancy."[544] In other words, Eisenhower wanted to stay with the strategy that the British and Americans had agreed to prior to the invasion. Montgomery wanted to change that plan and substitute a plan which eliminated [or greatly reduced] the American thrust south of the Ardennes. Eisenhower was caught between British political interests championed by Montgomery and US political interests represented by his bosses in Washington, George Marshal and Henry L. Stimson. *Montgomery needed a strategic plan which would both disguise the inability of his 21st Army Group to conduct sustained offensive operations and at the same time protect the Second British Army as a viable military force.* Montgomery

[542] Florentin, 243.
[543] Eisenhower, 279.
[544] Hamilton, *Master*, 806.

desperately needed American divisions committed north of the Ardennes and Eisenhower would eventually provide them.

August 20: I SS Panzer Corps, 2nd and 9th SS Panzer Divisions, continued their attacks toward St Lambert and Trun in a last-ditch effort to keep escape routes open for Germans trapped in the Falaise Pocket.

Heinrich Eberbach: "During the rest of the day and throughout the night, soldiers with and without arms streamed out of the encirclement. Altogether, about fifty guns and twenty tanks might also have gotten out." Eberbach estimated the number of Germans who escaped that night at something over 2,000.[545]

Patton, Diary: ". . . one combat team of the 79th Division, XV Corps, forced a crossing [of the Seine] at Mantes."[546]

August 21: According to German General Heinrich Eberbach, "At noon on 21 Aug 44, when the arrival of soldiers from the encirclement had stopped entirely and pressure from the American and British troops . . . became so strong . . . I considered the task of the Corps (II SS Panzer Corps) fulfilled. The (German) withdraw to and over the Seine began."[547]

F.W. Winterbotham: "Only by midnight on August twentieth, was the exit from the bag finally sealed. It was some time later that Patton's bitter remarks to Bradley about Montgomery were allowed to be known, but even at the time there were some questions being asked in London as to why Patton could not try and close the gap from the south."[548] George Patton would have been very happy to answer those questions. Unfortunately, Eisenhower, Montgomery, and Bradley [and their biographers] have been successful at evading questions raised by their behavior at the Falaise Gap for over sixty years.

During the week of August 13 to August 20, Patton endured three halt-orders [August 13, August 15 and August 19]. Montgomery's 21st Army Group Headquarters had produced some of the most inept intelligence estimates ever seen on a battlefield. They failed time and again, in spite of *ULTRA,* to nail down the elusive Germans in Normandy. It had been nine

---

[545]   Eberbach, 27.
[546]   Patton, 112.
[547]   Eberbach, 28.
[548]   Winterbotham, 158.

long, agonizing days since CCA of US 5th Armored Division, ". . . moved into that portion of Argentan south of the Orne River."[549]

Eventually, the tactical incompatibility of the "short envelopment" at Argentan-Falaise and the wider "Seine envelopment" came back to haunt the Allies. The successful 'short envelopment' at Chambois-Argentan clogged the roads First US and Second British Armies were trying to use for their dash to the Seine River. It proved impossible to launch two separate, mobile operations concurrently over the same road network. As Montgomery's Chief of Staff, Sir Francis De Guingand later pointed out, ". . . it was very nearly forty-eight hours before the armies were sorted out again in their correct sectors. It was a great pity that this had to happen . . ."[550] It was closer to seventy-two hours before the British got their lines of communication sorted out, but the point is made. Confusion within the pocket allowed those Germans who had made it out of the pocket to also make it across the Seine. British military historian John Keegan estimated, ". . . at the end of five nights of ferrying, three-hundred thousand [German] soldiers and, more remarkable, twenty-five thousand vehicles had reached the north bank [of the Seine]."[551]

It was late afternoon or early evening on August 21 before the gap was closed. First Canadian Army finally made contact with elements of the Poles who had been surrounded on Mont Ormel for three long days. The last day they had come close to disaster, the Poles were short of ammunition, medicine, and food. The survivors witnessed, ". . . a climatic suicide attack of German infantry straight into Polish machine guns, in midafternoon the Canadian army at last reestablished contact and brought up supplies."[552] Montgomery had British infantry and armored divisions to spare. But they had been transferred to the relative safety of the pursuit [western] end of the Falaise Gap because there were too many German panzers at Caen.

August 23: Eisenhower and his Chief of Staff, General Bedell Smith, arrived at Conde for a meeting with Montgomery to discuss future strategy. Montgomery rudely demanded that Smith be excluded from the discussions. For whatever reasons, a compliant Eisenhower accepted the demand. General Smith waited outside Montgomery's trailer while the two senior Allied

---

[549] Cepeda, 59.
[550] De Guingand, 408.
[551] John Keegan, *The Second World War*, 410.
[552] Weigley, *Eisenhower's Lieutenants,* 214. Also see Hastings, *Overlord,* 303-305.

Commanders discussed future plans. It must have been an uncomfortable meeting for Eisenhower. Montgomery's patience was stretched to the limit, ". . . his idea of tact was to deliver a patronizing lecture on elementary strategy that a Sandhurst or West Point cadet would have found insulting."[553] Montgomery wanted to remain the Allied Ground Forces Commander. He told Eisenhower that he should remain ". . . on a very lofty perch . . . able to take a detached view of the whole intricate problem."[554] Eisenhower explained Marshall's insistence that he take command and the negative reaction in American public opinion which had been created by the current command setup. Montgomery offered to serve under Bradley, but that would have meant trouble with the British public. Eisenhower held firm on the issue of command; Marshall had left him no room to maneuver. He told Montgomery that he intended to take command of Allied ground forces on September 1.

Having denied Montgomery's request for continued ground forces command, Eisenhower was more receptive to Montgomery's requests for American troops. He gave Montgomery control of the Allied Airborne Army and the authority to effect 'operational coordination' with Hodges' First US Army. In addition, he was willing to assign Montgomery's forces a priority in supplies. Montgomery balked at Hodges' Army of nine divisions. He insisted on, ". . . an American Army of at least 12 divisions."[555] Bradley protested, "To provide Monty with three more divisions would strip Patton's army to bare bones, grind it to a halt."[556] This, of course, was exactly what Montgomery intended to happen. The only Allied troops well supplied and capable of offensive movement would have been those troops fighting north of the Ardennes, beside Montgomery's British 21st Army Group.

In the end, Montgomery got most of what he wanted. Patton and Bradley were left to debate Eisenhower's ability to stand up to Montgomery. According to George Patton, "He (Bradley) was quite worried, as he feels that Ike won't go against Monty and that the American Armies will have to turn north in whole or in part . . . Bradley was madder than I have ever seen him and wondered aloud 'what the Supreme Commander amounted to . . .'"[557]

---

[553] Ambrose, *Eisenhower,* 341.
[554] Ambrose, *Eisenhower*, 341.
[555] Bradley, *A General's Life*, 315.
[556] Bradley, *A General's Life*, 315.
[557] Blumenson, (Ed.), *The Patton Papers,* 1940-1945, 526.

From Patton's diary: "I cannot understand why Monty keeps asking for all four armies in the Calais area and then through Belgium, where tanks are practically useless now and will be wholly useless this winter."[558] Once again General Patton provided a remarkably accurate assessment of the events as they unfolded.

Since Montgomery did not get everything he asked for, he accused Eisenhower of lying to him. He later wrote: "I believe he is being pushed into his present decision by [Bedell] Smith and certain others at SHAEF. I do NOT believe that things in America are really as he says they are."[559] One wonders why Eisenhower did not show Montgomery the letter he had received from Marshall ordering him, ". . . to assume and exercise direct command of the ground forces."[560]

August 26: Patton's diary: "The airport northwest of town (Orleans) was doing a roaring business. The day before it had dispatched six hundred airplanes and was doing about the same this day. These airplanes carried gasoline and ammunition for our troops."[561]

August 29: Patton's diary: ". . . the one-hundred-forty thousand gallons of gas we were to get that day had not arrived."[562] When one commander complained that if he conducted the operation Patton ordered, his tanks would run out of gas. Patton ordered him to conduct the operation anyway, and when his tanks ran out of gas, his men were to get out and walk. Patton thought his lost supplies were ". . . due to a change of plan by the High Command, implemented. . . by General Montgomery."[563] He was right. Patton also noticed that his re-supply by air had ceased; it was Montgomery again. Bradley was upset over planning for Montgomery's airborne operations, especially the one near Tournai. Bradley later wrote, "When I saw how fast Hodges' troops were moving . . . I urged Monty to cancel the drop and return the aircraft to delivering gasoline. But Monty . . . waited until the eleventh hour before canceling. The aircraft involved were thus tied up for five or six days, denying us a total of about 5,000 tons."[564] If Eisenhower would

---

[558]   Blumenson, (Ed.), *The Patton Papers,* 1940-1945, 527.
[559]   Hamilton, *The Master,* 816.
[560]   Butcher, 647.
[561]   Patton, 119.
[562]   Patton, 119, 120.
[563]   Patton, 120.
[564]   Bradley, *A General's Life,* 320.

not stop the Americans, Montgomery would find a way. His most effective means of stopping Patton turned out to be logistics. Patton's tankers could not move without gasoline, and Montgomery was determined to increase his demands for Allied supplies until Patton's tankers ran out of gas.

August 30: Patton reached the Meuse River and just as Montgomery had planned, his tankers ran out of gas. Montgomery sent a telegram to C.I.G.S. Brooke: "I am not at all happy about this eastward thrust into the SAAR and over the RHINE. The northward thrust is now proceeding very fast and we are going to be strained administratively and will require all available resources."[565] Montgomery's newest mantra was that supplies were limited and he needed all the available supplies, while studiously ignoring the one thing, the port of Antwerp, which would have ended the Allied supply crisis in a matter of weeks.

September 1st: To soothe his bitter resentment over losing control of the American forces, General Montgomery was promoted to Field Marshal. Eisenhower took nominal command of Allied forces for political reasons; President Roosevelt demanded it. But he had no intension of taking actual command of Allied Ground Forces. Eisenhower's system of ground command would remain the same as it had been since North Africa and Sicily. At the top, Eisenhower remained the Supreme Commander and 'Chairman of the Board.' Eisenhower wrote about the new command set-up: "I carefully explained that in a theatre so vast as ours, *each army group commander would be the ground commander in chief for his particular area*; instead of one there would be three so-called commanders in chief for the ground and each would be supported by his own tactical air force."[566]

Eisenhower never desired to become one of those three 'commanders-in-chief' for ground operations. He thought the Supreme Commander should remain thoroughly Allied in outlook, while his subordinate army group commanders were free to make their own arguments for any operations within their own sector that they might choose. In this scenario, General Bradley became 'the odd man out.' Given the political nature of the Allied command arrangement, Montgomery was always free to present his arguments from the British point of view. Although he tried to represent the American point of view, General Bradley was always out-ranked

---

[565]   Hamilton, *Master*, 831.
[566]   Eisenhower, 285.

by Eisenhower's more neutral commitment to the Anglo-American alliance. In any argument over strategy between British and American interests, Bradley would usually lose. While the newly minted Field Marshal, B.L. Montgomery, emerged time and again as the big winner. As Eisenhower once explained to Bradley and Patton, 'Since Montgomery will not take orders, you had to.'

A newspaper report on Montgomery's advance into Belgium: "The British are over the Somme . . . General O'Connor's armored troops had driven 'sixty miles in forty-eight hours to seize Amiens' . . . it was clear that the British left flank was advancing as fast or faster than Patton. Amiens is ours. Last night, we had three bridges over the Somme."[567]

Patton, letter to wife, Beatrice: "The Field Marshal thing made us sick, that is Bradley and me."[568]

September 2: There was a meeting at SHAEF in Versailles with Eisenhower, Bradley, Hodges, and Patton, ". . . to discuss future operations." Aides suggested Eisenhower may have wanted to rein Patton in for stretching his supply line too far. "But Patton seized the offensive; he gleefully told Eisenhower that he had patrols on the Moselle and—stretching the truth—in Metz."[569] Eisenhower relented. He gave Patton permission to continue his offensive toward the Frankfurt gap. He also ". . . agreed to Bradley's demand that First Army stay on Patton's left, south of the Ardennes."[570] Eisenhower had now promised Hodges' First Army to both Bradley and Montgomery. The accusation that Eisenhower is guilty of agreeing with the last man he talked to is hard to deny. When Montgomery heard what Eisenhower had done, he was furious.

September 3: Visiting Manton Eddy's XII Corps, Patton ". . . was delighted to learn that he had captured one-hundred thousand gallons of aviation gasoline and so could move on—also six-hundred thousand pounds of meat."[571]

Patton reports a rumor, which he ". . . officially . . . hoped was not true, that some of our Ordinance people passed themselves off as members of the

---

[567]   Nigel Hamilton, *Monty: Final Years of the Field Marshal, 1944-1976,* (New York: McGraw-Hill, 1986), 10.

[568]   Blumenson, (Ed.), *The Patton Papers, 1940-1945,* 535.

[569]   Ambrose, *Eisenhower, Soldier, General,* 346.

[570]   Ambrose, *Eisenhower, Soldier, General,* 347.

[571]   Patton, 124.

First Army and secured quite a bit of gasoline from one of the dumps of that unit.(T)his is not war but is magnificent."[572]

Montgomery called a meeting at Amiens with Bradley and Hodges to determine future Allied operations.

Montgomery letter to CIGS Brooke: "I had a meeting today with Bradley and it is quite clear to me that the Americans are planning to make their main effort via METZ and NANCY directed on FRANKFURT and the First US Army on my flank will be depleted accordingly."[573] Any thought that the Americans would follow Allied pre-invasion plans, plans which the British had agreed to, must have been terribly distressing to Montgomery. If the Americans headed east from Paris, they would be leaving his 21st Army Group all alone north of the Ardennes. A crisis was clearly at hand. Left alone, British 21st Army Group was not strong enough to carry out the mission they had agreed to prior to the invasion. If Montgomery was going to get the American divisions committed north of the Ardennes, he was going to have to act quickly.

Montgomery's bad relations with the Canadians worsened when Commanding General Henry Crerar failed to show up for a meeting at Second British Army's tactical headquarters on September 3. General Crerar was determined to attend a parade honoring Canadian dead at Dieppe, and did so despite Montgomery's orders.[574] Crerar was suffering from dysentery and high blood pressure and would soon need to take some time off. Montgomery's disdain for Crerar, so obvious when First Canadian Army became operational in Normandy nearly matched his antagonism toward Eisenhower and the other Americans. Montgomery's written instructions to Gen. Crerar's First Canadian Army that day were, "Canadian Army will clear the costal belt and will then remain in the general area Burges-Calais until the maintenance situation allows of its employment further forward."[575] Montgomery had shut the Canadians down and given their normal supply allotment to his First British Army until it crossed the Rhine at Arnhem. Montgomery probably wished he had the same power over Patton's US Third Army; he would have shut them down just east of Paris back in mid-August.

---

[572] Patton, 125.
[573] Hamilton, *Final Years,* 18.
[574] Dickson, 331-336.
[575] Dickson, 339.

British 11th Armored Division took Antwerp 'virtually intact.' Allied intelligence estimated one-hundred-fifty thousand German soldiers trapped on the Pas de Calais. Montgomery began planning airborne operations to get his army over the Maas, Waal and Lower Rhine Rivers.

British XXX Corps Commander, General Brian Horrocks wrote: "On September 3, we still had one hundred miles of petrol per vehicle, and a further day's supply within reach, so we were not destitute."[576]

September 4: General Horrocks later wrote: "To my mind 4th September was the key date in the battle for the Rhine. Had we been able to advance that day . . . We might even have succeeded in bouncing a crossing over the Rhine."[577] Montgomery had several choices on September 4. He could hook left, clear the approaches to the port of Antwerp, the Breskens Pocket, South Beveland and Walcheren. These operations would have trapped General Gustav von Zangen's Fifteenth German Army, nearly one-hundred thousand men, by the West Schledt on the Pas de Calais and cleared the port of Antwerp for immediate use.[578] Of course, opening the port would immediately solve the Allied supply crisis, and Montgomery was using the fact that the Allies were short of supplies to further his arguments for a 'single thrust' to Berlin.

Without Antwerp operating the United States Army could not be fully deployed in Europe. Montgomery understood this and delayed opening the port of Antwerp for as long as he could. Montgomery could have hooked left and cut off the German Fifteenth Army. He would have caught them strung out in a highly vulnerable water crossing. Montgomery could have hooked right, and attempted to force a Rhine crossing near Wesel, there was little to stop him. He may have opted to go straight ahead and crossed the Rhine at Arnhem just as General Horrocks suggested; again, there was little opposition. Of course, Montgomery chose the worse possible option, which was to halt and do nothing for three days. By the time the British Army lurched forward again on September 7, German opposition had already begun to stiffen.

Letter, Eisenhower to Montgomery [and all senior Allied Commanders]: "The mission of the Northern Group of Armies [Montgomery's 21st Army Group] . . . operating northwest of the Ardennes is to secure Antwerp,

---

[576]   Sir Brian Horrocks, *A Full Life*, (London, Collins, 1960), 205.
[577]   Horrocks, 205.
[578]   Moulton, 46.

breach the sector of the Siegfried Line covering the Ruhr and then seize the Ruhr."[579] Eisenhower had the priorities right, Montgomery simply refused to follow orders.

Letter from Admiral Sir Bertram Ramsay [Allied Naval CIC] to Eisenhower and Montgomery: "It is essential if Antwerp and Rotterdam are to be opened quickly enemy must be prevented from: 1. Carrying out demolitions and blocking ports. 2. Both Antwerp and Rotterdam are highly vulnerable to mining and blocking. If the enemy succeeds in these operations the time it will take to open the ports cannot be estimated. 3. It will be necessary for costal batteries to be captured before approach channels to the river routes can be established."[580] Montgomery also ignored Admiral Ramsay's letter. By the time Montgomery's Army Group got around to Antwerp it would require a major operation to dislodge the Germans who had been given time to mine the Scheldt and prepare defensive positions along the seaward access to Antwerp. Allied efforts to open the port of Antwerp eventually cost 12,873 casualties, of which 6,367 were Canadian.[581]

Letter, Montgomery to Eisenhower: "I consider we now have reached a stage where one really powerful and full-blooded thrust toward Berlin is likely to get there and thus end the German war."[582] Montgomery then returned to his litany on the northern thrust, which he had been polishing since that uncomfortable August 13 meeting with Eisenhower and Bradley. Montgomery told Eisenhower the main thrust was within his assigned axis of advance; he had Antwerp, he had the V-weapon launching sites, he had the Ruhr and he had the short northern route to Berlin. Montgomery sensed what Patton had known for some time: the Germans were finished. If there was going to be one last battle before the final victory march into Berlin, Montgomery preferred that his British troops lead the way. These were the same highly political plans Montgomery had been proposing since August 13, masquerading as his latest effort at strategic planning. Montgomery's plans obviously favored British political interests at the expense of the naïve Americans, but Eisenhower was firmly committed to getting along with the British.

---

[579]   Chandler, (Ed.), *The Eisenhower Papers, Vol. IV*, 2116.
[580]   Letter from Admiral Sir Bertram Ramsay. See, Moulton, 37.
[581]   Moulton, 186.
[582]   Montgomery, *Memoirs*, 271, 272.

September 5: Letter, Eisenhower to Montgomery: "While agreeing with your conception of a powerful and full blooded thrust toward Berlin, I do not repeat not agree that it should be initiated at this moment to the exclusion of all other maneuver . . . While advancing we will be opening the ports of Havre and Antwerp, which are essential . . . No reallocation of our present resources would be adequate to sustain a thrust to Berlin."[583] Eisenhower was right. But Montgomery, suffering from egomania never could grasp Eisenhower's political limitations. If Eisenhower would not stop Patton for political reasons, Montgomery resolved to find a way. The method he finally chose was logistics. "The Allies do not have enough supplies for two thrusts into Germany" became the main theme of Montgomery's arguments; therefore one must be stopped. This was especially cruel, because Montgomery alone held the key to unlocking the Allies' logistical problems and Eisenhower never would summon the courage to directly confront Montgomery over the issue. The issue was Antwerp, and Montgomery would continue to ignore Antwerp for another month and a half.

September 7: Montgomery letter to Eisenhower: Montgomery again complained that he was not getting a priority in supplies. He wanted an airlift of one-thousand tons a day and he was receiving only seven-hundred and fifty tons a day. He told Eisenhower he had to cut his intake down to six-thousand tons a day, only ". . . half of what I consume and I cannot go on for long like this."[584] Montgomery had the shortest supply line of all the Allied Armies in Europe. British operations were next to the coastline. Theoretically, the 21st Army Group should have been the easiest army to resupply. Their supply line was the shortest of all Eisenhower's forces. Part of Montgomery's supply problem was that fourteen-hundred new British-built 3-ton trucks had just broken down on the road with defective pistons. Unfortunately, the spare engines to fix the problem had the same manufacturing defects that had caused the breakdowns.[585] Montgomery asked Eisenhower to come visit him, so he could explain why the Americans were now responsible for British supply problems. Eisenhower accepted despite having just reinjured his knee while pushing a small plane off the beach near his headquarters at Granville.

---

[583]   Chandler, (Ed.), *The Eisenhower Papers, Vol. IV*, 2120.
[584]   Ambrose, *Eisenhower, Soldier, General*, 347.
[585]   Bradley, *A General's Life*, 320.

Ingersoll wrote, "Despite their short supply line, the British had barely enough transport [trucks] to keep themselves in the field."[586] This problem was exacerbated by the fact the British built vehicles were notoriously unreliable.

September 10th: Meeting at Brussels airport between Montgomery, Eisenhower and Eisenhower's Deputy Supreme Commander, Air Marshal Arthur Tedder. Eisenhower's knee is still bothering him, so the meeting was held in Eisenhower's plane. ". . . (W)aving his arms, Montgomery damned (Eisenhower's) plan in extreme language, accused the Supreme Commander of double-crossing him, implied that Patton, not Eisenhower was running the war, demanded that control of the land battle be returned to him, and asserted that the double thrust would result in certain failure."[587] Eisenhower didn't say a word. Finally when Montgomery paused to take a breath, Eisenhower ". . . put his hand on Montgomery's knee and said, Steady, Monty! You can't speak to me like that. I'm your boss."[588] Montgomery apologized, but then returned to his main points.

Air Marshal Tedder later wrote, "Montgomery . . . made great play over the word 'priority' and insisted that his interpretation of the word implies absolute priority, if necessary to the exclusion of all other operations. Argument on such a basis (is) obviously futile and Eisenhower made it clear that he could not accept such an interpretation."[589] Eisenhower put it slightly differently, "Monty's suggestion is simple; give him everything, which is crazy."[590] Montgomery had apparently scaled back his Berlin ambitions. Lord Tedder wrote, ". . . the advance to Berlin was not discussed as a serious issue, nor do I think it was so intended."[591] Eisenhower, who should have insisted on the destruction of those German soldiers trapped on the Pas de Calais and an early opening of the port of Antwerp, allowed Montgomery to subvert Allied strategy in a vain attempt to force a Rhine crossing at Arnhem while denying supplies to Bradley's army group in their advance to the Rhine.

---

[586]   Ingersoll, 215.
[587]   Ambrose, *Eisenhower, Soldier, General,* 348.
[588]   Ambrose, *Eisenhower, Soldier, General,* 348.
[589]   Tedder, 591.
[590]   Ambrose, *Eisenhower, Soldier, General,* 348.
[591]   Tedder, 591.

Montgomery had devised a new plan which would finally employ those airborne divisions which SHAEF had been trying to get into combat for weeks. It was called *Operation Market-Garden* and, if successful, promised to get Montgomery's 21st Army Group over the Rhine at Arnhem, outflanking the German Siegfried Line from the north. Horrocks XXX Corps would launch the main attack from a bridgehead north of the Meuse-Escaut Canal, drive north approximately seventy miles on a single elevated highway to Eindhoven, cross three rivers and three canal bridges including the last bridge over the Lower Rhine at Arnhem.[592] The Irish Guards Armored Regiment and the 11th Armored Division would lead the attack for XXX Corps. Three-and-a-half airborne divisions would be dropped near the bridges which had to be secured for British XXX Corps. The airborne troops were also responsible for protecting XXX Corps' flanks and the one good road north to Arnhem. It was a highly ambitious, unorthodox plan.

Montgomery also expressed a concern about being able to protect his left flank with First US Army. He was authorized to effect coordination with General Hodges of First Army through General Bradley.

September 11: Signal, Montgomery to CIGS Brooke: "Second Army is in a very poor administrative condition with no reserves in the depots and it will not be possible to undertake large-scale operations involving an advance northwards to the MEUSE and the RHINE between GRAVES and ARNHEM before . . . September 23."[593] This simply was not true. Corps Commander Brian Horrocks recalled that when Montgomery ordered a halt on September 3rd his vehicles still had enough fuel to move one-hundred miles with adequate petrol stocks in the supply pipeline.[594]

September 12: Meeting between Field Marshal Montgomery and General Bedell Smith, Eisenhower's Chief of Staff: Montgomery told Smith that he needed more supplies to carry out Operation Market-Garden. He needed an additional one-thousand tons a day airlifted to the Brussels area. He also expressed concerns about his authority to effect coordination between the right flank of his Army Group and the left flank of Hodges' First US Army. Montgomery was supposed to work through Bradley to effect this coordination, but Bradley's headquarters were too far to the rear.

---

[592]   Horrocks, 207, 208 and 209.
[593]   Hamilton, *Final Years*, 57.
[594]   Horrocks, 205.

Montgomery told General Smith that if he can get the supplies he needs, *Operation Market-Garden* will go forward on September 17.

September 13: Letter, Eisenhower to Montgomery: Eisenhower addressed Montgomery's concerns one by one. First, it would not be possible to airlift one-thousand tons a day into Brussels because Montgomery would be using those planes for *Operation Market*, the airborne half of *Market-Garden*. Instead, Eisenhower grounded three US Infantry Divisions in Normandy, stole their trucks and assigned those trucks to the American Communications Zone, which transferred a like number of trucks to the British Red Lion system.[595] These trucks could deliver five-hundred tons of supplies a day to Montgomery in Brussels. Eisenhower also promised to use the airplanes on days when they were not being used by Montgomery, to deliver an additional five-hundred tons a day. This arrangement seemed to work for Montgomery. Eisenhower also promised that Hodges' First Army would be granted priority in supplies, sufficient to keep his left flank up with Montgomery. As far as co-ordination with Hodges was concerned, Eisenhower said that Montgomery could communicate directly with Hodges, as long as he sent copies of any direct communications with Hodges to Bradley.[596] Eisenhower told Montgomery that he understood that Market Garden will go on September 17. "This is very encouraging," Eisenhower wrote, "(It) will permit the earlier reassembly of United States airborne divisions which may shortly be badly needed by Bradley."[597] Ignoring Eisenhower's request, Montgomery kept the 82nd and 101st US Airborne divisions fighting as ordinary infantry in Holland well into October.

September 17: Operation Market Garden began on schedule and the initial reports were good. Airdrops for the US 101st Airborne Division near Eindhoven and 82nd Airborne Division between Grave and Nijmegen were satisfactory. British paratroopers dropping near Arnhem, however, were in trouble almost as soon as they hit the ground. The British 1st Airborne Division dropped eight miles from its objective, the bridge over the Rhine at Arnhem and was soon engaged by elements of two German panzer divisions. Given the unlucky presence of the 9th and 10th SS Panzer Divisions, which Montgomery had been warned about, and training Battalion Kraft, only

---

[595] Chandler, (Ed.), *The Eisenhower Papers, Vol. IV*, 2133.
[596] Chandler, (Ed.), *The Eisenhower Papers, Vol. IV,* 2134.
[597] Chandler, (Ed.), *The Eisenhower Papers, Vol. IV,* 2134.

Colonel John Frost's battalion managed to reach the bridge. The other battalions were heavily engaged near their assembly areas and never reached the bridge.

September 21: Letter, Montgomery to Eisenhower: "I cannot agree that our concepts are the same and I am sure you would wish me to be quite frank."[598] Montgomery was, if anything, a model of consistency. He again demanded command of all Ground Forces, he wanted operational control of First US Army and he wanted all Allied supplies diverted to his 21st Army Group. In short, he wanted the American thrust south of the Ardennes shut down. Montgomery began his demands for US troops and supplies on August 13 and never really stopped until the war was over. Worse, Montgomery's strategy was clearly politically motivated. His plans were always based on what furthered his own reputation and maintained the shaky status of the British Army in Europe.

September 22: Letter, Eisenhower to Montgomery: "No one is more anxious than I to get to the Ruhr quickly . . . It is because I am anxious to organize this final drive quickly upon the capture of the Ruhr that I insist upon the importance of Antwerp . . . I am prepared to give you everything for the capture of the approaches to Antwerp."[599] Eisenhower would continue to huff and puff over Antwerp, but it was just too much to expect Montgomery to willingly give up his main argument for halting Patton. Montgomery had been basing his arguments for the single thrust on the fact that the Allies could only support one thrust.

Eisenhower was asking him to solve the supply problem by opening Antwerp. The two men were simply talking past each other. Opening Antwerp would flood northern Europe with supplies from America, and release Patton from the constraints of Montgomery's political games. Opening Antwerp would allow the Americans to deploy all their divisions in Europe and adequately supply an American left hook through the Nancy Gap to Frankfurt and the Saar. Montgomery was resolved to prevent that for as long as he could. He continued to ignore Antwerp while protesting that his Army Group was short of supplies. Eisenhower listened to Montgomery's rants, apparently without ever questioning his motives.

---

[598] Ambrose, *Eisenhower, Soldier, General*, 351.
[599] Chandler, (Ed.), *The Eisenhower Papers, Vol. IV*, 2175.

Montgomery's military decisions were usually tainted with British politics and his disdain for foreigners. His decision to ignore Antwerp virtually reeked of politics. In the end, Montgomery was hugely successful, Antwerp did not receive it first supply ship until November 28.[600] By then, the good campaigning weather in 1944 was gone. Within a few weeks the Germans would attack in the Ardennes, giving the overstretched Americans a real bloody nose, much to Field Marshal Montgomery's great satisfaction. The German attack in the Ardennes gave Montgomery one more chance to agitate the British press into backing his demands for Eisenhower's job.

A commander's conference at Versailles was arranged by Eisenhower, ". . . to announce his plans." Eisenhower began by seeking a common agreement that the opening of Antwerp was a necessary pre-condition for any thrust into Germany. He told the group that there was a definite difference, ". . . between logistical requirements for operations to breach or outflank the West Wall (*Market-Garden*) and the requirements for a drive to Berlin."[601] Twenty-three generals, air marshals and admirals attended Eisenhower's meeting. Everyone was there except British Field Marshal Bernard Montgomery. Speaking for Montgomery was his Chief of Staff, General Francis de Guingand, who stated, ". . . the envelopment of the Ruhr from the North . . . is the main effort of the present phase of operations."[602] Eisenhower meekly agreed, although he had started the conference by insisting on the importance of Antwerp. The British again ignored the importance of Antwerp, further delaying the deployment of US divisions in the ETO. Montgomery thought the war should have been over by the Christmas in 1944. He tried to blame the Americans for extending the length of the war.[603]

Eisenhower directed Bradley to send Hodges north, ". . . in support of 21st Army Group, while limiting Third Army to local actions."[604] Hodges' First Army would take over that part of the front previously held by British VIII Corps. First Army, now with major elements north of the Ardennes, was stretched even further north, Eisenhower agreed to back Montgomery with a priority in supplies until the Ruhr was captured and gave Montgomery

---

[600]   Moulton, 184.
[601]   Ambrose, *Eisenhower, Soldier, General*, 352.
[602]   Ambrose, *Eisenhower, Soldier, General*, 353.
[603]   Dawnay Archives. From Richard Lamb, *Montgomery in Europe, 1943-1945*, (London: Buchan & Enright, 1984), 394.
[604]   Ambrose, *Eisenhower, Soldier, General*, 353.

authority to contact Hodges directly to co-ordinate their inter-Army Group boundary lines and operations.

September 23: Eisenhower, letter to Bradley: ". . . I wish you immediately to arrange to meet Field Marshal Montgomery and agree on detailed operational plans . . ."[605] Eisenhower did not give Montgomery operational control of US First Army, but he gave him everything else he wanted. "To save time . . . ," Eisenhower wrote, "the Field Marshal should communicate his desires directly to Hodges."[606] For reasons that remain a mystery today, Eisenhower was ready to back Montgomery as long as it was politically possible for him to do so. At the same time, it was not possible for Eisenhower to completely halt Patton. He could limit Patton's supplies but he could never completely restrain him.

September 24: Eisenhower letter to Montgomery: Eisenhower wrote to Montgomery about the conference he missed, ". . . we have obtained complete understandings that should hold all the way from here to . . . the capture of the Ruhr." Eisenhower would keep his promise to support Montgomery up to the Ruhr encirclement. After that, Eisenhower made no promises. To help Montgomery over the Roer River east of Liege, sixteen US divisions were eventually concentrated north of the Ardennes on Montgomery's right flank and four US divisions were spread over an eighty-mile front in the Ardennes. Patton's Third army south of the Ardennes had eight divisions in the line and two divisions in reserve. Everyone was stretched with the bulk of American forces north of the Ardennes at Montgomery's request. Eisenhower continued: ". . . *we must not blink the fact that we are getting fearfully stretched south of Aachen and may get a nasty little 'Kasserine' if the enemy chooses at any place to concentrate a bit of strength. However, I am confident that the enemy does not have the means . . .*"[607]

If there was an error in judgment because of initial German success during the Battle of the Bulge, blame for the error must be shared by both Eisenhower and Montgomery. Montgomery was the main reason the Americans were stretched in the Ardennes. Sixteen United States divisions were sent north of the Ardennes to compensate for manpower shortages within British 21st Army Group. It was similar to the Carentan, the Americans

---

[605] Chandler, (Ed.), *The Eisenhower Papers, Vol. IV*, 2183.
[606] Chandler, (Ed.), *The Eisenhower Papers, Vol. IV*, 2183.
[607] Chandler, (Ed.), *The Eisenhower Papers, Vol. IV*, 2187.

were again asked to shoulder the main burden of offensive warfare in a sector that had been reserved for His Majesty's forces. This allowed Montgomery to husband his fragile British Army. Or, as one American writer recalled, "Monty was judging the First [US] Army by the standards of the British Second Army, which had barely moved from November 7 until February 8 [1945]..."[608]

September 24 was the day Eisenhower decided to back Montgomery. Discussions about the proper Allied strategy for the advance into Germany began on a Sunday, August 13, at the height of the Battle of the Falaise Gap. Montgomery had proposed a British led single thrust north of the Ardennes. These discussions resulted in Eisenhower's agreement to give Montgomery most of what he wanted. He granted Montgomery's request to scrap the pre-invasion plan for the double thrust into Germany; and he agreed to Montgomery's plans for the major thrust north of the Ardennes. Montgomery continued to complain that he was not given 100 percent of Eisenhower's support and he was right. As Eisenhower patiently explained to him time and again, it was not politically feasible, nor was it strategically desirable, to completely shut down the American offensive south of the Ardennes.

Montgomery had asked for a US Army of twelve divisions to accompany him north of the Ardennes. By December, he had two US Armies (Hodges First and Simpson's Ninth) and sixteen US divisions on his apron strings. As a result, there were four US divisions strung out in the Ardennes sector. Bradley's secondary thrust south of the Ardennes had been reduced to only ten divisions in George Patton's Third Army. North of the Ardennes Montgomery had accumulated thirty-one divisions: fifteen (15) British/Canadian divisions to go with sixteen (16) US divisions. When Montgomery sensed a German collapse, he would have been perfectly positioned to concentrate his British Army Group for a power drive to Berlin. The Americans, to the south, would be called upon yet again to protect Montgomery's flank.

It was Eisenhower's gravest error of the war. It committed the Allies to fighting over terrain that greatly favored the German defenders during one of the worst European winters in memory. The northern German plain over which the British intended to conduct their drive to Berlin was totally unsuited to armored offensive operations. According to Ingersoll, they "... were cut by big rivers and thousands of tiny waterways and which, while wonderfully flat, were so low that the ground was rarely solid enough

---

[608]   Perret, 413.

to support heavy armored vehicle off the roads."[609] It was not surprising that British staff officers working for COSSAC on pre-invasion planning had come to exactly the opposite conclusion.[610]

Eisenhower's decision to back Montgomery gave logistical priority to the Allies' weakest ground army. It was Normandy all over again and the reasoning was exactly the same. The British were still in a manpower crisis. After Montgomery's army stalled at Caen, the Americans were forced to attack through the hedgerows and swamps of the Carentan. The names were different during the winter of 1944/45: Aachen, Schmidt, the Huertgen Forest, the Roer River Dams and the Ardennes; but the casualty lists were just as long. Eisenhower chose to ignore centuries of established military tradition: 'to cut one's losses in defeat and to reinforce success.' The result was certainly predictable, the Allied fall and winter campaign of 1944/45 was a clear disappointment. For political reasons, Eisenhower chose to reinforce the army that had failed in Normandy and now his fellow Americans would have to pay the price.

---

[609]   Ingersoll, 218.

[610]   Chandler, (Ed.), *The Eisenhower Papers, Vol. IV*, 2560, 2561.

Chapter 7

General Bernard L. Montgomery— The Early Years

> "Monty's name had come up several times before in front of the selection board; everyone always agreed that he ought to be promoted, but every other commander who had a vacancy for a major-general had always excellent reasons for finding someone else more suitable than Monty."[611] General Archibald P. Wavell discussed the appointment of B. L. Montgomery to command British 3rd Infantry Division in 1939.

Montgomery was good at tweaking the Yankee's nose and at ruffling feathers in the British Army. His reputation within the British Army was one of willful insubordination almost from the beginning of his army career. Having memorized the Field Service Regulations early on, he was able to exercise control over his superiors with an odd mixture of willpower, determination, a bullying attitude, and a wonderful ability to train young men. He was gifted with the ability to take a mountain of seemingly unrelated information, distill it down to its central features, and present these in such a way that the average soldier could remember what he had been taught. He was able to influence and control his surroundings by being 'more British and more Army' than anyone else.

Montgomery encouraged the idea that he was the supreme professional in the British Army. While other young men his age were out drinking and socializing, Montgomery stayed in his officer's quarters studying the Field Service Regulations. He worked harder than most, always doing more than was expected, and he wanted everyone within his command to adopt his own strenuous training programs. There were British officers, especially during those 'years between the wars,' who did not share Montgomery's enthusiasm for training.

---

[611] John Connell, *Wavell, Scholar and Soldier*, (New York: Harcourt, Brace, 1965), 204.

There was nothing unduly personal in Montgomery's harsh treatment of Eisenhower later in his career. Montgomery treated all his superiors the same arrogant, insubordinate way. Of course, Eisenhower had the additional liability of not being British. General Alan Brooke, his friend and mentor was one of the few superior officers Montgomery ever respected. Montgomery's irascible, hang-tough attitude with the Americans and his fervent desire to see Britain win through were major reasons the Churchill government appointed him to command Allied Ground Forces in Europe.

The biggest thorn in Eisenhower's side, from the day they first met in 1942 until the day the Germans surrendered, was a smallish British general whose defeat of Rommel at El Alamein had rung the victory bells in London. Bernard Law Montgomery was born on November 17, 1887 in a suburb near London. His father, Henry Montgomery, was to become a Bishop in the Church of England. The Bishop was usually too busy with church work to spend much time with his children.[612]

When Bernard was two, the family left England for Tasmania, where his father performed missionary work among the natives. By the time they returned to England in 1901, Bernard was thirteen.

Bernard's mother, Maud, was only sixteen when she married. She was eighteen years younger than her husband. In the first eight years of her marriage, she bore five children. Between social calls and family prayers, the children's day was tightly regulated. In Maud's house, Maud ruled. Nigel Hamilton described her as, "A girl of strong will and without great intellect."[613] Her treatment of the children was something less than enlightened, ". . . if they wasted their pocket money or infracted her rigid domestic rules they were almost invariably beaten."[614]

Of all the children, Bernard suffered the most. He became the family's "Black Sheep," engaging in a constant battle of wills with his mother.[615] As a child, he endured severe beatings. This battle of wills lasted until his mother's death in 1949. Montgomery did not attend his mother's funeral. Hamilton traces Montgomery's overbearing character to his mother: "Bernard would in turn inflict the same tyrannical discipline upon others which he found

---

[612] Nigel Hamilton, *Monty: The Making of a General, 1887-1942,* (New York: McGraw-Hill, 1981), 4 and 5.

[613] Hamilton, *Making,* 4.

[614] Hamilton, *Making,* 5.

[615] Hamilton, *Making,* 5.

stifling in his own mother. Like her, he was not intellectually gifted; like her *he had a will of steel and a fundamental inflexibility of mind.*"[616]

The young Montgomery became something of a bully. A trait he never outgrew as Lieutenant, Captain, or Field Marshal. The psychological scars inflicted by an unloving mother and his childhood beatings would never leave him. He later remarked, "My early life was a series of fierce battles from which my mother invariably emerged the victor. I never lied about my misdeeds, 'I took my punishment.'"[617]

Montgomery spent the years 1906 and 1907 at Sandhurst, where he played rugby and hockey and performed well enough academically to be promoted to Lance Corporal in only five weeks. He was held back one year for a hazing incident gone wrong which resulted in serious burns to another cadet. He passed out of Sandhurst in 1908 and joined the 1st Battalion of the Royal Warwickshire Regiment in December of that year. His Regiment was posted, ". . . on the North-West Frontier of India, at Peshawar."[618]

He began his military career with a "zest and keenness" uncommon to the average British officer. He learned the native languages, took the examination in mule transport, most importantly, studied, and *memorized the Field Service Regulations.*[619] He was soon selected to train fifty men in his battalion as scouts. On April 1, 1910, Montgomery was made a Lieutenant; he was twenty-two years old.

Military life suited the young man Bernard Montgomery had become. He would have a hard time finding another occupation which offered a more structured, regimented life style. Nor, it must be added, was he likely to find one in which the structure of that life was so carefully laid out as in the British Army 'Field Service Regulations.' Montgomery must have found great psychological relief from the anxiety created by the arbitrary discipline imposed by his mother in the highly structured life style of a British Army officer. He found the 'Field Service Regulations' far more predictable than his mother's behavior; and, having memorized the regulations, he became their master.

Montgomery took to soldiering as if he had been a soldier all his life, which, indeed, he had. Montgomery returned to England with his Regiment

---

616 Hamilton, *Making*, 5.
617 Hamilton, *Making*, 39.
618 Hamilton, *Making*, 51.
619 Hamilton, *Making*, 53.

in December 1912. The following year he bought a Ford motor car, played hockey for the Army, took up tennis, and generally enjoyed his life in the British Army.

On June 28, 1914, the Archduke Ferdinand of Austria was assassinated in Serbia. One month later, Austria declared war on Serbia and the nations of Europe began their tragic rush to war. Montgomery's Regiment was sent to defend the coast against a potential German invasion. On August 4, 1914, England went to war with Germany. Montgomery did not believe that Germany could withstand the combined attacks of the Russians, French, and British. He did not expect the war to last very long. His greatest fear was that, at the last moment, the Germans would somehow weasel out of it.

After some confusion during mobilization, Montgomery and his Regiment arrived at Boulogne, France, aboard the steamer SS Caledonia on August 23. They ran into von Kluck's First German Army in its drive south from Mons. In the confusion of retreat, attack, and counter march, Montgomery's Regiment was without proper supplies of food, ammunition, communications, or artillery. Their Corps commander ordered an attack at Le Cateau on August 26. It was a disaster. The British Army lost, ". . . eight-thousand four-hundred and eighty-three men on August 26 alone."[620]

After regrouping at Le Mans, the Royal Warwickshires were ordered forward on October 13 to participate in the first Battle of Ypres. The Germans held the high ground at the village of Meteren. Sword-drawn, Montgomery led his men forward to a trench line just short of a group of houses. He took a German prisoner by kicking the man in the lower part of his stomach, since he had no sword training. He positioned his men in the trench line they had just occupied. Montgomery then went forward to observe his defensive positions. He was shot through his chest and right lung by a sniper. He was later shot in the left knee. It was dark before the Germans vacated the village and his platoon could rescue Montgomery. By the time they got him to a dressing station, his condition was critical, but he survived. He later won the Distinguished Service Order for his actions at Meteren.[621]

Montgomery recovered in England. He was promoted to Captain in February 1915. He was later posted to the position of Brigade Major, first in the 112th Infantry Brigade, and then in the 104th. As Brigade Major,

---

[620] Hamilton, *Making*, 80.
[621] Hamilton, *Making*, 88, 89.

Montgomery handled most of the brigade's administrative and training duties. Montgomery returned to France with the 104th Infantry Brigade in January 1916.

Back in France, Montgomery spent most of his time training the 104th for trench warfare. In March, they moved up to the British line near Richebourg. The 104th was composed of men five feet to five feet three inches tall. They were nick named the "Bantams."

The French were heavily engaged with the Germans at Verdun and asked their British allies to take some of the pressure off the Verdun sector with an offensive on their section of the front. The British response became the Battle of the Somme. In a war infamous for senseless slaughter, the Somme stands out as one of the bloodiest battles ever fought. On July 1, 1916, the British lost fifty-seven thousand soldiers, nineteen thousand of them died.[622] Montgomery's 104th missed the opening battles, but was ordered to participate in the battles for Maltzhorn Farm and Trones Wood on July 20. The Brigade lost nearly one-thousand men. It was a disaster.

Brigadier-General Sandilands later wrote of the attack on Maltz Horn Ridge, "It is no exaggeration to say that the majority of officers and men of the 23rd Manchester had but little idea of what they were attacking. The attack completely failed, although the officers and men went forward with great determination."[623] On November 18, the British command abandoned the Somme offensive. Although they suffered over one million casualties, the front line had barely moved.

Nigel Hamilton believed that Montgomery learned from the mistakes made at the Somme. General Sandilands helped him understand that, ". . . officers and men must be given orders that were clear, as well as objectives they could identify and attain . . ." This, Hamilton suggests, ". . . would become the cornerstone of Bernard's later military philosophy."[624]

The following year, 1917, Field Marshal Sir Douglas Haig planned an attack on the Hindenburg Line. The battle of Arras began on April 9. It was another disaster. The British lost between 105,000 and 120,000 men during the month of April.[625] Montgomery noted American entry into the war in a letter he wrote on April 10, "I am glad America has finally declared war;

---

[622] Hamilton, *Making*, 106.
[623] Hamilton, *Making*, 111.
[624] Hamilton, *Making*, 111.
[625] Hamilton, *Making*, 119.

she ought to send us large supplies of food and money."[626] Of all the things a frontline British officer might hope for from America, somehow 'food and money' seem a bit odd.

Montgomery was promoted on July 6, 1917, to senior GSO 2, Operations, Staff, 9th Army Corps. The 9th Corps was serving under 2nd Army, Commanded by Sir Herbert Plumer. Hamilton writes that Plumer, ". . . limited his army to short, selected attacks on tactically important objectives only, using deep artillery barrages, and a leap-frogging replacement of forward troops by fresh units. The heart of Plumer's doctrine was training for specific tasks."[627] Hamilton believed that Plumer provided the young Montgomery with, ". . . (these) fundamental lessons . . . if offensives are planned on a sound tactical understanding; if the troops are well trained and have limited, realistic, and identifiable objectives; and if the full weight of modern artillery is intelligently brought to bear on a concentrated front, there is almost nothing the enemy can do except withdraw."[628] This is, almost point for point, how General Montgomery will conduct nearly all of his offensive battles during the Second World War.

Once Haig's autumn attacks had ground to a halt, he asked Plumer to assume command of the offensive. Plumer immediately ordered a three-week halt in the offensive while proper plans could be drafted and training carried out. Plumer's new plan for the autumn offensive was ". . . a sixty-page document in the unmistakable style of its young GSO 2 (Training) . . . A mind uncomplicated by subtlety and unhindered by self-consciousness transformed the complexity of command and administration to a clarity that still shocks by its absolute freshness and logical simplicity."[629]

Plumer's three autumn attacks were all successful and brought in nearly ten-thousand German prisoners. The attacks were directed on Polygon Wood, Menin Road, and Broodseinde. Eventually, Haig insisted on following up Plumer's success with an all-out attack on Passchendaele ridge, and the result was another bloodbath.

In their attacks lasting through November 11, the Canadian Corps suffered 12,403 casualties. In spite of their obvious bravery, Montgomery was not impressed with the Canadian infantry. "I was disappointed in them. At plain straightforward fighting they are magnificent, but they

---

[626] Hamilton, *Making*, 119.
[627] Hamilton, *Making*, 125.
[628] Hamilton, *Making*, 126.
[629] Hamilton, *Making*, 127.

are narrow-minded and lack soldierly instincts."[630] Soldiers, particularly officers, from Canada and later the United States never quite measured up to British standards in Montgomery's eyes.

The Russian surrender during the winter of 1917/1918 allowed the Germans to reinforce the Western Front. The first German offensive in 1918 hit the southern British front and drove the British army back nearly forty miles. The second German offensive, the Battle of the Lys, began on April 9. Ludendorff had hoped to catch the British off guard by attacking first in the south and then a few weeks later, following up with an attack in Flanders. But Ludendorff's timetable was off. He did not allow his German forces sufficient time to reinforce the Flanders assault. Haig's famous "Backs to the Wall" order of the day was issued on April 12. The British line held, but the cost was appalling. Ninth Corps alone had lost twenty-seven thousand men during the Battle of Lys. The third German offensive, the Battle of Chemin-des-Dames, was launched on May 26. Another bloodbath followed, but the Germans were spent.

Allied reinforcements from Australia, Canada, and the United States forced the Germans into a series of withdraws in July and early August. Montgomery was promoted to temporary Lt-Colonel and Chief Staff Officer (CSO-1) of the 47th (London) Division; he was serving under Major General Gorringe, his old Brigade Commander from India. On October 28, Montgomery's Division participated in the triumphal march through the city of Lille. With its Army conducting a series of strategic withdraws, the German nation was coming apart. The German Fleet at Kiel mutinied on November 7. On November 10, the Kaiser abdicated and fled to Holland, clearing the way for the German surrender.

After the war, Montgomery served in Germany and Ireland, before returning to his old Regiment, the Royal Warwickshires, in March 1925. He was posted as 'A' Company Commander. It was as a Company Commander that Montgomery would become famous, or infamous, for his training program. "As soon as the elementary principles of infantry tactics had been explained, the Company was to start practicing: use of ground and cover, field signals, fire orders, battle formations, platoon tactics, patrolling, night operations, withdrawal, attack, defense, co-operation with the air force, field engineering, support by tanks, etc."[631] Not everyone shared Montgomery's enthusiasm for this demanding new training program.

---

[630] Hamilton, *Making*, 129.
[631] Hamilton, *Making*, 182.

According to Nigel Hamilton, Montgomery's later ascent to high command had its roots in his ". . . sheer professionalism that had had no equal in the British Army since Wellington. His doctrine of command would remain largely the same, from platoon instruction to the handling of whole armies . . . (He) had a vision of what the Army should be . . . (an) Army in which every man would know his place, his duty, and what was expected of him."[632] Montgomery's army units came to resemble Maud's household, with Montgomery in complete control of the smallest detail.

Like his mother, Montgomery was a stern taskmaster, but at least he was an enlightened taskmaster. 'In Maud's house, Maud ruled.' In Montgomery's unit, there was never any doubt that he was running the show. But unlike his mother, there were rules Montgomery was required to follow; and the rules were published in the Field Service Regulations.

In July 1925, Montgomery was promoted to Major and given a three-year term of office as instructor at the Staff College in Camberley. There Montgomery met and befriended the new Director of Studies, Colonel Alan Brooke. One of their early discussions explored command problems arising when an infantry, artillery, or armored officer exercised direct command over a branch of service outside of his expertise: ". . . Brooke felt that modern cavalrymen or commanders of armored units must be trained to command infantry and other arms, as well as tanks, and vice versa, just as he, an artilleryman, had accepted that he must master infantry and armored warfare in order to merit full command."[633]

Nearly twenty years later, during the Second World War, when the same question came up, the two men were on common ground. In June 1943, Brooke wrote to Montgomery, "I am in entire agreement with you that Corps Commanders must be able to command both infantry and armored divisions. I have always supported this, and I think if you go back in your memory, you will find that I told you this was necessary at Staff College Exercises . . . It is a fundamental doctrine that I have gone for from the start, and fought against much opposition on the part of the Armored Corps."[634]

In 1925, the British were the first to address the problem of command with different branches of service. Brooke and Montgomery did not get it right in 1925, but at least they were talking about it. Amazingly, nearly twenty years later during World War II, their discussion did not seem to

---

[632]   Hamilton, *Making*, 184.
[633]   Hamilton, *Making*, 194.
[634]   Hamilton, *Making*, 194.

have advanced; despite the fact that the Germans had demonstrated that the solution was not cross-trained corps or divisional commanders, but a unified command at division level of the separate [infantry, artillery, armor, etc.] branches.

In January 1927, Montgomery was promoted to Brevet Lt-Colonel. In July of that year, he married Betty Carver, a widow with two young sons. Betty's sons remembered the Christmas trip they took with Montgomery to Switzerland that year. Betty stayed in England because she was ill. Her son John recalled, "We all three shared a room—and the beds were all in one line . . . As always, the day was planned in advance. [When] Things didn't always pan out as expected . . . we did rather pull his leg about this."[635]

Montgomery planned his vacations with the same attention to detail with which he planned a set-piece battle. He suffered extreme psychological discomfort when things did not go according to his carefully laid-out plans. Montgomery's obsession with controlling events, with punctuality, neatness, and excessive planning is apparent in all phases of his life, not just his military service. *Montgomery's mental illness may have provided some comic relief for his children on vacation; but it became deadly serious when the same illness distorted his view of the battlefield with the lives of a million soldiers hanging in the balance.*

During the summer of 1927, the War Office invited Montgomery to become Secretary of a committee to rewrite the Infantry Training Manual. Montgomery accepted this new challenge with great determination and enthusiasm. He was absolutely convinced the War Office had selected the right man for the job. Montgomery wrote, "I decided to make the book a comprehensive treatise on war for the infantry officer."[636] His initial draft of the Manual produced 'heated arguments' and 'numerous amendments' from other members of the committee. Montgomery would not accept any of the proposed changes; he considered them 'nit-picking.' It looked like a stalemate when Montgomery and the committee were unable to come to an agreement. Finally, Montgomery proposed the committee be disbanded. He would finish the Manual on his own time, incorporating the committee's amendments into his final draft.[637]

Once the War Department and the committee agreed to this, Montgomery was free to finish his work without serious interruption. "I produced the final

---

[635] Hamilton, *Making,* 210.
[636] Hamilton, *Making,* 212.
[637] Hamilton, *Making,* 213.

draft," Montgomery wrote, "omitting all the amendments the committee had put forward."[638] B. H. Liddell Hart protested one section of the Manual because Montgomery had ". . . (Left) out the passages which explain exactly how reserves could exploit weak points and be passed through holes in the enemy's line to 'expand the torrent.'"[639] Mobile warfare was an anathema to Montgomery. He dismissed mobile warfare advocates as charlatans, unschooled in the proper methods of military administration, tactics, and strategy.

In January 1931, Montgomery was given Command of the 1st Battalion, Royal Warwickshire Regiment. He and his unit were immediately shipped to Palestine. One year later, they were sent to Alexandria, Egypt. In March 1932, General Burnett-Stuart wrote the following 'Personal Report' on Montgomery, ". . . He has character, knowledge, and a quick grasp of military problems. But if he is to do himself full justice in the higher positions to which his gifts should entitle him, he must cultivate tact, tolerance, and discretion . . ."[640] Montgomery never did cultivate tact, tolerance, or discretion. In fact, as he got older, the more debilitating his mental problems became.

Montgomery and his battalion were shipped to India. After serving some months in Poona, India, as 1st Battalion Commander, he was transferred to the Staff College at Quetta, where he assumed the duties of Chief Instructor on June 29, 1934. He was now Colonel Montgomery. Within a year, the Commandant, Major General Guy Williams had written a flattering 'Confidential Report' on Montgomery, ". . . (He) has a strong personality and decided views. He is widely read and has experience both in command and on the staff in peace and in war. He demands a high standard from those under him . . . An outstanding officer whose advancement will be in the best interest of the service."[641]

The terrible memories of World War I casualties greatly influenced officers in the British Army. They were both more cautious tacticians and determined to see that their men got the proper training. Bernard Montgomery and his friend, Alan Brooke, shared this view. 'Getting it right' involved not taking chances with men's lives. The proper offensive involved careful planning and thorough training to insure that every officer and every ranker

---

[638]   Hamilton, *Making*, 213.
[639]   Hamilton, *Making*, 213.
[640]   Hamilton, *Making*, 226.
[641]   Hamilton, *Making*, 259.

knew his job. It involved the maximum use of rolling barrages of artillery at the point of the attack and it involved picking limited and achievable but strategically important objectives. Montgomery insisted upon the highest-quality staff work; this was especially true for planning offensive operations. The emphasis was on caution, firepower, and meticulous planning. This left little room for individual initiative, independent thought, or any changes to the operational plan.

Montgomery did not create the sense of caution and the devotion to meticulous planning that came to characterize the British Army; that was a legacy from the First War. He did not create it, but he thrived in the atmosphere caution had created. It was undeniable that the 'Field Service Regulations' and the highly controlled lifestyle of a career officer in the British Army suited Montgomery's mental need to control the people and events around him. As a soldier, the first thing he did was memorize the 'Field Service Regulations.' They became, over time, his emotional anchor, his badge of honor as the most professional soldier in the British Army.

It was at this stage in his career that Hamilton believes, "Bernard's tactical concept of war had now fully matured. It was not spectacular for its novel ideas, but for its unity of conception and the absolute clarity with which Bernard put over this vision."[642] Montgomery would develop into an excellent strategist but with limited tactical abilities. His greatest gift was an ability to produce a viable plan out of a complicated mass of seemingly unrelated information in a clear concise manner that was easy for the average soldier to understand.

Montgomery could clearly see what needed to be done; he could determine the correct strategy to be used against the Germans. Montgomery's problems began after the planning session was over and the tactical implementation of his strategy began. *Time and again, Montgomery's British Army proved to be tactically incapable of performing the strategic mission he asked of it.*

Montgomery's presentation of plans for Eighth Army to Brooke and Churchill in late 1942 and his presentation of the invasion plan for *OVERLORD* to the assembled allied commanders at St. Paul's in May 1944 stand out as the hallmarks of his military career.

Before his tour at the Staff College was over, Montgomery had accepted an offer from the War Office to Command the 9th Infantry Brigade at Portsmouth. On May 6, 1937, he departed India aboard the steamship *Viceroy of India*. On his way to England, he continued writing

---

[642] Hamilton, *Making,* 248.

an article, which he called "The Problem of the Encounter Battle." Montgomery's article was published in the *Royal Engineers Journal*, September 1937.[643] In the article, Montgomery wrote, "Although information may be lacking or incomplete, he (the Commander) must still make a plan and begin early to force his will on the enemy . . . If he has no plan, he will find he is being made to conform gradually to the enemy's plan."[644] Hamilton suggests, "This concentration on forward planning was the new core of Bernard's military thinking."[645] Montgomery was promoted to Brigadier General.

Montgomery was not the most popular officer in the British Army. Many officers hoped Montgomery would find employment in some other unit. General Wavell later wrote, "Monty's name had come up several times before in front of the selection board; everyone always agreed that he ought to be promoted, but every other officer who had a vacancy for a major-general always had excellent reasons for finding someone else more suitable than Monty."[646] Montgomery's insubordinate behavior and his strange, prickly nature did not endear the Brigadier to many senior officers in the British Army.

In October 1937, his wife, Betty Montgomery died from an infection caused by an insect bite. General Montgomery was deeply affected by her death. According to Montgomery's younger brother, Brian, his wife's death had a negative impact on his behavior: ". . . awkward, egocentric, sometimes vindictive, often vain . . . scarcely any close friend or colleague would not, at one time or another, find himself at extreme loggerheads with Bernard; for there could be no pretending that the psychological demon which at times motivated his behavior was an easy one to placate."[647]

Brian thought his brother was tormented by a psychological demon. Others, like B. H. Liddell Hart, thought Montgomery was a horrible bully. Some decried Montgomery's gigantic ego. Montgomery's stepson, John Carver, speculates on the relationship between Montgomery and his mother: ". . . a more interesting speculation concerns what would have happened if he and my mother had never met. I think there might have been real danger

---

[643]   Hamilton, *Making*, 263.
[644]   Hamilton, *Making, 263.*
[645]   Hamilton, *Making*, 263.
[646]   Connell, 204.
[647]   Hamilton, *Making,* 324.

that those schizoid tendencies engendered by his upbringing which were always latent might have become dominant in his personality; I mean a single-mindedness progressing to narrow-mindedness, a detachment leading to lack of human feeling and suspicion of the motives of others, and such characteristics might have developed to such an extent as to have rendered him unsuitable for high command."[648]

More than a few officers, both British and American could have told stories on the impact Montgomery's personality had on his ability to command troops in the field. As Montgomery's Chief of Staff suggests, these stories could have been quite damaging to Montgomery's military reputation. De Guingand wrote to Eisenhower in 1949, "I'm afraid Monty forgot that some of us could tell a very damaging story."[649] Many of the officers who served with Montgomery during World War II, both British and American, have remained silent out of respect for the man and his position within British society.

The real tragedy for Allied soldiers, especially for British soldiers, was that Montgomery had made quite a few enemies. Montgomery's personal relationship with British Officers did not always guarantee their cooperation. Montgomery's relationship with commanders in the Royal Air Force, the US and Canadian Armies was extremely poor. He seldom sought a solution to any disagreement and never offered a compromise. When Generals argue, cooperation between units and services is often thwarted and frontline soldiers ultimately pay the price. *Montgomery's strongest supporters cannot disagree that his ability to work with other officers of his own age and rank was severely compromised by his mental condition.*

In 1938, Montgomery was given Command of the 8th Infantry Division in Palestine. The 8th Division was one of several new units formed to control recent Arab uprisings. Montgomery was also informed that when the present Commander of the 3rd Infantry Division, Major General Denis Bernard, retired in December 1939, he would become the 'Iron' Division's new Commander. When General Bernard's retirement was stepped up to early autumn, Montgomery returned to England in July but had to take three weeks sick leave due to an illness he contracted in Palestine. After some confusion with General Bernard's retirement (he was on a fishing trip in Ireland), Montgomery was ordered to take Command of the 3rd Infantry

---

[648] Hamilton, *Making*, 278.
[649] D'Este, *Decision*, 495.

Division effective August 28, 1939.[650] At 4:45 a.m. on the morning of September 1, 1939, the Germans invaded Poland.

How the British were going to come to the aid of their Polish ally was not immediately clear. The French were dragging their feet. In Britain, there followed two days of agonized hand wringing and intense, nationwide soul-searching. In the end, twenty years of wrong-headed governmental policy came crashing to the ground. Amid cries of "Speak for England," the Chamberlain government finally sent the Germans an ultimatum to cease their war with Poland. When it expired at 11:00 a.m. on September 3, the British were at war with Germany.

In the August 1938 issue of the *Army Quarterly*, Montgomery addressed the problem of defending against an armored attack. "He acknowledged that the main enemy attack might be by armored divisions, but made it clear that, in order to succeed, such thrusts would have to be concentrated, leaving normal infantry divisions to follow up or hold flanking sectors, thus becoming vulnerable to 'encounter battle' tactics; tactics in which the choice of ground, mobility of troops, central control of artillery, trained coordination, and adequate communications were the vital factors." Montgomery believed that divisional commanders should follow a "general plan," a plan ". . . previously made known to all commanders, at every echelon."[651] Montgomery and his fellow officers in the British Army were exactly one war behind.

Montgomery sailed with the 3rd Division from South Hampton on the evening of September 29. They arrived at Cherbourg the following morning. On October 3, they received orders to take over defensive positions from the 1st Division, south of Lille. The plan directed the British and mobile French divisions to rush forward to the River Dyle in Belgium after the Germans attacked. Unfortunately, the plan had been made without considering Belgium's neutrality. "The Belgians therefore refused to allow a single allied observer even to reconnoiter the ground; whereas Gamelin, (the French Commander) bearing in mind the terrible destruction Northern France has suffered in the Great War, conversely insisted the 'encounter battle' take place in Belgium, not France."[652]

The British had declared war on Germany, but it was not a war they were prepared to fight. Nigel Hamilton wrote, "Poland was allowed to perish

---

[650]   Hamilton, *Making*, 315.
[651]   Hamilton, *Making*, 322.
[652]   Hamilton, *Making*, 330.

without a single British shot being fired to defend the very ally Britain had declared war to protect . . ."[653] While Germany was busy destroying the Polish Army, the British and French sat behind the French-Belgium border, hoping the Germans would forget their declarations of war.

In the months ahead, Montgomery planned and executed five full-scale divisional training exercises. The result of these training exercises was that Montgomery's 3rd Infantry Division became, ". . . the most highly trained mobile division in the British army."[654] One question raised by the exercises was communications. Montgomery determined that radio and telephone transmissions, ". . . could not be relied upon to function one-hundred percent efficiently in battle. Liaison officers and messengers, as of old, would also be required in modern battle."[655] British radios and other communications equipment were poorly engineered and manufactured. Montgomery was right, they were not reliable.

In January 1940, Montgomery took some time off from his unit and visited French forces serving in the Maginot Line in western France. After seeing French troops close up, it occurred to Montgomery, and his Corps Commander, Alan Brooke, that the French Army would not put up a very good fight.[656]

The German attack was scheduled for 17 January 1940 but had been postponed when a Luftwaffe officer carrying plans of the attack was shot down in allied territory. The compromised attack plans, plus bad winter weather helped to convince Hitler to postpone the attack until next spring. This gave the Germans time to rethink their offensive. They knew mobile British and French divisions were going to rush into Belgium as soon as the Germans attacked. General Erick von Manstein later produced a plan changing the axis of the main armored attack from Denmark in the north, to a flank attack behind the main enemy formations through the Ardennes to Arras and the sea.

In all of Montgomery's training exercises, he did nothing to prepare 3rd Division for an offensive operation. According to one of his staff officers, Lt-Colonel C. P. Dawnay, ". . . we did nothing in the way of training for offensive action. Although Montgomery made no predictions about the course of the battle, it followed almost exactly the way he had anticipated

---

[653] Hamilton, *Making*, 319.
[654] Hamilton, *Making*, 331.
[655] Hamilton, *Making*, 332.
[656] Hamilton, *Making*, 344.

in his exercises."[657] Absolutely convinced of the superiority of defensive positions, Montgomery apparently saw no need to waste time on an attack plan he would never use.

On May 10, 1940, the Germans invaded Belgium and Holland. Montgomery received a message from British II Corps at 0500 hours confirming the invasion. At 1100 hours, Montgomery assembled his commanding officers and put Plan D, the advance to the River Dyle into effect. The march north was, according to Hamilton, ". . . deceptively easy . . . Crowds lined the streets to watch and cheer."[658] Brooke noted in his diary that the BEF had just taken, ". . . (The) first step toward one of the greatest battles of history."[659]

The Germans soon displayed the superiority of massed tanks in an attack role. The attack was supported by infantry on motorcycles, mobile artillery, and was conducted underneath skies dominated by German fighter airplanes. The JU-87, Stuka dive-bombers provided long-range artillery support. The battle was important because of the new blitzkrieg tactics used by the Germans. It was a coordinated attack by infantry, armor, and artillery units, supported by German fighters, to which Brooke and Montgomery should have been keen observers.

In the early morning hours of May 11, advance elements of Montgomery's 3rd Division arrived at their pre-arranged sector of the Dyle River, only to find their positions already occupied by the 10th Belgium Infantry Division. British luck did not change when the Belgians mistook them for Germans and fired on them. After Montgomery corrected the mistake, he tried to convince the Belgium general to move his troops. But the Belgian refused to move saying, ". . . that he would never leave his post without orders from his King."[660] Montgomery's Corps Commander, Alan Brooke, went to see King Leopold on May 12, but could not get the orders changed. Montgomery complained bitterly about BEF Commander, Lord Gort, not standing up for British interests.

Rather than risk continuing arguments with the Belgians, Gort ordered Brooke ". . . to squeeze the 3rd Division into the left flank of I Corps."[661] Montgomery did not agree with his Commander's decision; he was

---

[657]   Hamilton, *Making,* 348.
[658]   Hamilton, *Making,* 357.
[659]   Hamilton*, Making,* 358.
[660]   Hamilton, *Making,* 359, 360.
[661]   Hamilton, *Making,* 360.

convinced that the high ground at Louvain was critical to the defense of Brussels and he was not certain that the 10th Belgium Infantry Division would fight. As Hamilton points out, "This was insubordination."[662] Brooke and Montgomery had toured the areas in question earlier that day and Brooke had given his "silent" approval to Montgomery's plan. The 3rd Infantry Division would remain where it was, forming a second line of defense behind the 10th Belgium.

On May 13, the Germans chased the retreating Belgian and French forces up to and across the Dyle. When pressure on the defensive line at Louvain began to mount, the 10th Belgium Division decided that they would not fight. Montgomery's 3rd Infantry Division immediately took over their positions.

Montgomery's 3rd Infantry held the front at Louvain against increasingly strong German pressure for three days. When Montgomery gave the order, his division conducted a perfect withdrawal. But the 4th Infantry Division, beginning their withdrawal one day later, lost all but one squadron of the 15th/19th Hussars Cavalry Regiment. According to Hamilton, "This misfortune was to have a profound effect on Bernard's attitude toward his own British armored units, reinforcing his existing prejudices about English cavalry commanders—namely that they were essentially blind Anglo-Saxon Don Quixote's whose dream was to tilt lyrically against windmills, without properly educating themselves . . ."[663]

Two days later, with their flanks again threatened, Brooke's divisions were ordered to conduct another withdrawal to the Escaut line. Montgomery used artillery to cover the movement of his brigades while the brigade anti-tank companies took their positions as rear guards.

By May 26, the British position had become dangerously exposed. Belgium infantry on their left and the French Motorized Division on their right had vanished. Loss of the Ypres—Comines Canal in the 5th Division's sector would split the center of the BEF's defensive positions. To guard against this eventuality, Brooke sent his Chief of Staff, Neil Ritchie, to Montgomery with orders to extend his forces a single battalion's width to the north. This would allow the 4th Division to move slightly to the north and help the 5th Division in its vital defensive role. Montgomery cited the large number of houses and close nature of the country in his area, he protested that it would be difficult for him to hold his present front and comply with the order.

---

[662] Hamilton, *Making*, 361.
[663] Hamilton, *Making*, 366.

This behavior was typical of Montgomery. Hamilton wrote, "Fortunately, Brooke was alive to Bernard's intractable character, and recognized that Bernard's very professionalism made it difficult for him to accept advice unless it was given either as a direct order, or in such a way that Bernard recognized the logic of what was required of him."[664] Brooke was forced to make a trip to Montgomery's headquarters and explain the delicate situation in person.

During the night of May 27, British defensive positions continued to deteriorate. Montgomery withdrew 3rd Division from the line and moved it behind the 4th, 5th and 50th Divisions to a new position at the north end of the British defensive line facing southeast about five miles from the coastline.

II Corps Commander, Alan Brooke, was recalled to Britain to begin reforming the Army for a possible German invasion. At 5:00 p.m. on the afternoon of May 30, Montgomery took command of II Corps. The I Corps Commander was Michael Barker, who was described by Montgomery as, "... an utterly useless commander, who had lost his nerve by May 30."[665] Barker was sent home on May 30 and I Corps was given to Major General Harold Alexander. Alexander had been commanding the 1st Infantry Division. He had remained calm and unruffled amid the daily chaos at Dunkirk.

Sixty-eight thousand troops were evacuated on May 31; one of them was Lord Gort, the BEF Commander. Since I Corps' defensive positions covered the port of Dunkirk, it would be the last Corps to embark. It was decided to close the port of Dunkirk to I Corps personnel until II Corps had departed. Montgomery left early on the morning of June 1, by 3:00 p.m. that afternoon he was reporting to the Chief of the Imperial General Staff at the War Office. By the evening of June 2, ". . . Alexander had managed to evacuate the entire rear guard of the BEF."[666] The British Army had done the impossible; some 250,000 British soldiers had been saved to fight another day. From the German point of view, it had taken their panzers less than three weeks to demolish the best divisions in the British and French Armies.

During the national celebration in Britain that followed Dunkirk, no one looked too closely into the cause of their dilemma. Montgomery and Brooke were among those senior British officers who were thrust into command positions because of the defeat in Belgium. They failed to grasp

---

[664]   Hamilton, *Making*, 378.
[665]   Hamilton, *Making*, 387.
[666]   Hamilton, *Making*, 393.

the significance of the new German armored formations or their deployment at the point of the attack.

While the miracle of Dunkirk had saved most of the BEF, it tended to obscure the real cause of the defeat. According to Nigel Hamilton, "The true lessons of Dunkirk foundered amid the general rejoicing; and, instead of leading to a complete rethinking of British Army Command and organization, it heralded two long years of bungling, from the debacle of Norway to the loss of Greece, Crete, the Far East, and the shores of North Africa to the very gates of Cairo."[667]

Following Dunkirk, the British Army had an excellent opportunity to reorganize itself along the lines of the highly mobile German armored units in Belgium. It was a wasted opportunity. Russell Hart wrote, ". . . the [British] army blamed poor troop performance on interwar politicians—who had left the army unprepared for overseas service—and the RAF, Royal Navy, and the French for inept support. Quick to seek scapegoats elsewhere, the army failed to evaluate its own weaknesses objectively."[668]

One of the most important lessons of World War II was the role of massed armor at the point of attack. One officer commanded all the specialized units; he was the division commander.[669] The Germans were also able to communicate with each other using radios installed in every German command vehicle. In the mid-1930s Guderian wrote, "Every modern tank has a radio receiver, and every command tank is equipped with both receiver and transmitter. Tank units are now under guaranteed command and control."[670]

The British experienced quality control problems with radios throughout the war; at times, they failed with disastrous results. In 1937, Montgomery wrote, ". . . that W/T and R/T transmission could not be relied upon to function one hundred percent efficiently in battle. Liaison officers and messengers, as of old, will be required in modern battle."[671] The British and French used runners, liaison officers, hand signals, telephones, and the

---

[667] Hamilton, *Making*, 393.

[668] Russell A. Hart, *Clash of Arms: How the Allies Won in Normandy*, (Oklahoma: University of Oklahoma Press, 2004), 104.

[669] Heinz Guderian, *Achtung-Panzer!, The Development of Armored Forces, Their Tactics and Operational Potential*, Translated by Christopher Duffy, (London: Arms and Armor Press, 1996), 178-198.

[670] Guderian, 197.

[671] Hamilton, *Making*, 332.

telegraph system to transmit orders to their units in combat. The Germans used radios.

The swift German victories in Belgium and Poland should have been a warning to British officers that a thorough reorganization of their army was long overdue. Unfortunately, neither Brooke nor Montgomery sensed that anything was wrong. "The new army that emerged in Britain after Dunkirk bore the stamp of Sir Alan Brooke, the chief of the Imperial General Staff, and Sir Brian Paget, the commander, Home Forces." Russell Hart continues, ". . . the army [did] not reconsider its employment of armor in light of its experiences in France, but the panzer myth cemented prevailing, yet misguided, armored warfare notions . . . British armored formations remained essentially massed tank forces, not balanced combined-arms teams."[672] Poor coordination between armor and infantry units in an attack role would plague the British throughout the war.

The Americans watched the events in Europe and were utterly amazed at the speed of the German advance. In 1939, the Germans required barely six weeks to defeat Poland. In 1940, it only took the Germans four weeks to shatter the British and the French Armies, which, at the time, were believed to be the best armies in the world. The Americans were so concerned by these events they organized new armored formations. US Army field exercises emphasized mobility with the armored division in an attack role. British generals had a better view of the German military buildup than the Americans, but they decided to do nothing.

The British and French had prepared to fight a defensive battle. The Germans had prepared for an offensive battle with their armored units leading an attack into the enemy's exposed flank. The British and French were magnificently prepared to fight World War I all over again, although this time in Belgium, not northern France. The Germans could not afford the luxury of re-fighting World War I; they could not afford the losses. Instead, the Germans developed what the newspapers called 'Blitzkrieg,' or 'lightning war.' The essential ingredients for 'lightning war' were mobility, firepower, air cover, communications and most importantly, a ruthless, hard-driving commander willing to take chances.[673]

Back in the 1920s during their time at the Staff College in Camberley, Brooke and Montgomery had discussed how a senior officer [a corps or divisional commander] ought to be qualified to command and coordinate

---

[672]   Hart, 106, 107.
[673]   Guderian, 183.

armor, artillery, and infantry units. The purpose seemed to have been to make the officer familiar with all three branches of the army in order to guarantee proper coordination on the battlefield. It remained for the Germans to display the combined arms teamwork that resulted when a capable, aggressive officer was given command of a fully mobilized division containing infantry, armor and artillery units.

Given Montgomery's second-hand knowledge of the Polish campaign and first-hand knowledge of the German campaign in Belgium it seems incredible to recall that neither of those armored battles caused Montgomery to rethink his understanding of modern warfare. Montgomery remained throughout the war the general who liked to isolate himself from his staff and take days, sometimes weeks to prepare a plan of attack. He became, by many accounts, the 'Master of the Set-Piece Battle.' As long as the front line in Normandy barely moved, Montgomery was in his element. As soon as the Americans broke out at St. Lo, Montgomery was very quickly in trouble. Rapid movement meant a loss of control and, as Montgomery remembered from World War I, a commander losing a tight grip on his forces is going to have high casualties.

In defense of Montgomery, it should be noted that the British were not prepared for war. In 1940 the British were short of everything. Their most serious problem was the failure to produce a battle worthy tank. When they moved, British tanks moved at the pace of walking infantry. The British had no efficient system for moving their artillery. British-built radios and telephones were also unreliable, which was at least part of the reason Montgomery insisted on using Liaison Officers to communicate with frontline units. In *The Pride and the Fall*, Correlli Barnett thoroughly documents the failure of British industry to produce sufficient numbers of "highly sophisticated" manufactured items, including radio components. Barnett wrote, "On the basis of British production costs, it was forecast in April 1943 that imports of radio components and equipment of all kinds from the United States that year would equal four-fifths of the value of Britain's own production."[674] Nearly half of the components used in making British radios in 1943 were manufactured in the United States. Given these limitations in the British manufacture of armor, artillery, and radios, the tactics Montgomery used in 1940 were the only tactics which offered a reasonable chance for success on the battlefield.

---

[674]   Barnett, *The Pride,* 170.

Montgomery's 3rd Division escaped the debacle in Belgium nearly intact with about thirteen-thousand men. It was the largest, best-organized division in the British Expeditionary Force. Montgomery was charged with writing a "Lessons Learned" from the BEF experience in Belgium, after receiving input from all the other commanders. He mentioned the speed with which the German infantry engages fixed positions, their efforts at concealment, and their highly accurate mortar fire. "What the Germans most dislike, Bernard claimed, was concentrated artillery fire—an observation which, more than any other, was to influence Bernard's approach to warfare . . ."[675] This must have been the source of those huge artillery barrages/bomber missions that preceded most of Montgomery's offensives.

By June 17, the 3rd Infantry Division was moving into the Brighton-Bognor section along the southeast coast of England. Montgomery decided to defend Britain's southern shores with a minimum of forces, while concentrating the maximum number of reserves behind the line for a counterattack when the exact location of the German landing became known. Montgomery explained his plans to Prime Minister Churchill over lunch on July 2. After Churchill seemed to agree with his deployments, Montgomery asked him why 3rd Division could not be made fully mobile and be held in the role of a mobile reserve. Headquarters for the British Home Army objected to the way Montgomery had gone outside the chain-of-command directly to the Prime Minister, but Churchill had enthusiastically adopted Montgomery's ideas. In the ensuing days, the Prime Minister badgered officers in the Home Army so often that they eventually gave in and agreed to mobilize all of Montgomery's 3rd Division.[676]

On July 19, John Dill took over as Chief of the Imperial General Staff from General Ironside, who was promoted to Field Marshal and placed on the retired list. "Sir Alan Brooke became C-in-C Homes Forces and Lt-General Auchinleck took over Brooke's post as GOC Southern Command."[677] Auchinleck's plan for defending southern England was to defeat the Germans on the beaches. He considered the possibility of creating a mobile armored reserve later, but in 1940, the British were terribly short of vehicles. Many of the Army's vehicles were left in Belgium. "The Army had lost nearly 1,200 field and heavy guns, 1,350 anti-aircraft and anti-tank guns, 6,400 anti-tank rifles, 11,000 machine guns, 75,000 motor vehicles, and

---

[675] Hamilton, *Making*, 409.
[676] Hamilton, *Making*, 412, 414.
[677] Hamilton, *Making*, 419.

almost every tank it possessed, as well as vast quantities of ammunition."[678] Division commanders were instructed, ". . . to have, in the first stage, field defenses sited well forward on the beaches . . ."[679]

On July 21, a new commander was appointed for 5th Corps. He arrived the following day and immediately halted work on the beach defenses. He cancelled Auchinleck's request for an armored mobile reserve, ". . . 5 Corps would instantly be reorganized so that it could provide its own mobile reserves."[680] Montgomery did this without consulting his superior.

Montgomery inspected the 4th Infantry Division. He found a lot of "dead wood" which needed cutting, artillery, which was "definitely below standard" and a GSO 2 who was "quite useless." Montgomery also found a host of procedural problems, such as ". . . No motor contact officers . . ."[681]

A division commander just back from the disaster at Dunkirk might simply shake his head at the "lack of a motor contact officer." But Montgomery was deadly serious. He predicted dire consequences for this division if his observations were not corrected. As Hamilton suggests, "This somewhat brazen analysis was tempered by a final note of optimism—*an increasingly characteristic Montgomery technique whereby salvation was assured if left in Bernard's willing hands* . . ."[682] Montgomery had been convinced that he was one of the few "professional soldiers" left in the British Army. It became his stoic duty to expose and eradicate incompetence, laziness, and otherwise unprofessional behavior.

Montgomery's insubordination was obvious. On August 5, Brooke wrote to Montgomery, "I know you well enough also Monty to give you a word of warning against doing wild things. You have got a name for annoying people at times with your ways, and I have found difficulties in backing you at times against this reputation . . . (I) only ask you not to let me down by doing anything silly."[683] The Montgomery/Auchinleck feud over beach defenses lasted until August 10. On that date, it was decided to ship all of Britain's armor out to Egypt, thus ending the argument in Montgomery's favor, since it was no longer possible to create the armored reserve that Auchinleck's plan required.[684]

---

678   Bryant, *Turn of the Tide,* 149.
679   Hamilton, *Making,* 419.
680   Hamilton, *Making,* 421.
681   Hamilton, *Making,* 422.
682   Hamilton, *Making,* 423.
683   Hamilton, *Making,* 433.
684   Hamilton, *Making,* 436.

Hamilton suggests that Montgomery's policy was "triumphantly vindicated," but that was not true. Their argument had been settled by strategic policy, and had nothing to do with vindicating the argument on either side. The Montgomery/Auchinleck argument over the creation of an armored reserve to back up beach defenders ultimately depended on whether one believed the Germans or British would control the sky over the invasion beaches. The German invasion was contingent on Luftwaffe control of the skies over Britain. If the Germans had won the air battles over England and gone forward with their invasion plans, it is not certain that Montgomery's armored reserves would have been able to influence the invasion battles. The argument had become ". . . (An) unfortunate quarrel that would never be resolved in their lifetime."[685] Arguments with Montgomery usually did last a lifetime; he never compromised his position and would not attempt to resolve an argument. Lord Gort's remark, "Montgomery is not quite a gentleman . . ." is only slightly off the mark.[686]

Montgomery spent the next two years training divisions in Britain. He commanded 5th Corps, then 12th Corps, and was finally given the Southeast Command. He later helped to plan Dieppe raid, but Montgomery's career was on hold until he was summoned to command Eighth Army in North Africa. Through a misunderstanding with the former Army Commander, Montgomery arrived in Cairo three days early, on August 12, 1942.[687] Within three months, Montgomery and the British Eighth Army would be making history in North Africa and Churchill would be ringing the victory bells in London.

---

[685] Hamilton, *Making*, 420.
[686] Blumenson, *Battle of the Generals*, 72.
[687] Hamilton, *Making*, 586.

Chapter 8

Montgomery Commands
British Eighth Army

"Fifteen minutes before ten o'clock on the night of October 23, 1942, 882 field and medium guns opened up at El Alamein in a barrage such as the British army had not fired since 1918 . . . The prime minister watched the progress of the battle, upon which his own fate hinged, in a mood of considerable anxiety."[688] Raymond A. Callahan on the Second Battle of El Alamein.

The year of 1942 was probably the low point of Prime Minister Winston Churchill's political career. Singapore was gone; the Prince of Wales and Repulse had been sunk. British forces in Burma were on the run. In North Africa, German General Erwin Rommel had defeated the British Eighth Army at Gazala and Mersa Matruh, chasing the British Army past the Egyptian border to El Alamein. But most importantly in the Prime Minister's mind, Tobruk had fallen. British forces in North Africa and the Far East, wrote Raymond Callahan, were ". . . sacrifices to the policy of trying to sustain an imperial position on inadequate resources."[689]

There were simply not enough British soldiers to go around. Prime Minister Churchill often tried to protect British political interests with an army that was too small to do the job he asked of it. He tended to 'look through' ongoing operations as if they were already successfully completed. He would propose new schemes with troop requirements far beyond what was available to perform the mission. He would place a successful operation in jeopardy by removing troops at a critical moment to bolster a weakness elsewhere, only to have both operations fail.

To head off criticism in the House of Commons, Churchill called for a Vote of Confidence on January 27, 1942. He won the vote handily 464 to

---

[688]   Raymond A. Callahan, *Churchill: Retreat from Empire*, (Wilmington: Scholarly Resources, 1984), 202.

[689]   Callahan, *Churchill: Retreat*, 178.

1.[690] Disaster followed disaster in the first half of 1942; a Vote of Censure was moved by Sir John Wardlaw-Milne in July of that year. Again, Churchill won handily 473 to 25.[691] As his political position in England weakened, Churchill increasingly turned to his generals to give him a victory in North Africa.

In February 1941, the British Army in North Africa was just completing one of the most brilliant offensives by any army in World War II. Under Lieutenant General R.N. O'Connor, British XIII Corps had, ". . . advanced over five-hundred miles, destroyed an Italian army of ten divisions, taken a hundred-and-thirty thousand prisoners, four-hundred tanks, one-thousand two-hundred-and-ninety guns, and two major fortresses . . ."[692]

O'Connor's operation began with a highly unorthodox plan of attack to defeat the Italian Army at Nibeiwa. His artillery would fire from the east, from British lines, with the intent of confusing the Italians rather than killing them. O'Connor's tanks and infantry, fully motorized for this operation, were to move around the Italian rear, assemble, and attack simultaneously from the west. It worked beautifully. The direction of the main attack had taken the Italians completely by surprise. Nibeiwa was an outstanding example of combining infantry with armor, of motorizing the infantry, and of using the combined arms of artillery, armor, and infantry in a well-coordinated attack. Colonel A. H. Gatehouse of 7th Armored Brigade and Major General E. Dorman-Smith assisted O'Connor in the planning stages of the operation and deserved some of the credit for the soundness and originality of a very good plan.[693]

O'Connor's corps was on the verge of a complete victory in North Africa in late January, 1941. It was poised to take Tripoli. Unfortunately, the Greek government chose this time to ask for British help in case the Germans decided to expand their operations in Bulgaria south to the Mediterranean. Prime Minister Churchill demanded that military assistance for the Greeks be made available from those troops fighting in North Africa. Churchill turned down the advice from General Kennedy of the War Office, and General John Dill, Chief of the Imperial General Staff, who warned that the British Army in North Africa was fully occupied. Further, they warned Churchill that any forces that could be withdrawn from North Africa would

---

690   Sherwood, 493, 494.
691   Sherwood, 601.
692   Correlli Barnett, *The Desert Generals,* (New York: The Viking Press, 1961), 62.
693   Barnett, *Desert Generals*, 32, 33.

be inadequate for the job in Greece. Churchill persisted. On February 12, he wrote to Wavell, General O'Connor's commander, ". . . your major effort must now be to aid Greece and/or Turkey. This rules out any serious effort against Tripoli . . ."[694] Ironically, February 12 was also the day German General Erwin Rommel arrived in Tripoli. Rommel thought that Wavell should have, ". . . continued his advance into Tripolitania [as] no resistance worthy of the name could be mounted against him."[695]

The Greek Army was no match for the Germans; it broke and ran almost on contact. The helpful British did reach their assigned defensive positions, but were forced into an immediate withdraw resulting in the loss of one fifth of their force, most of their equipment, and a few ships.[696] General Alan Brooke thought, ". . . our participation in the operations in Greece was a definite strategic blunder. Our hands were more than full at the time in the Middle East, and Greece could only result in the most dangerous disposal of force."[697] Churchill's blunder cost the British dearly. According to Barnett, ". . . the Greek episode lengthened the campaign in North Africa by two years—a campaign that sucked in the major ground efforts of the British Commonwealth, and left the Far East almost undefended against the Japanese."[698]

General O'Connor was captured by the Germans one night while he was driving in the desert. He saw no more combat in North Africa, but would escape his captors in 1943 and later returned to command British VIII Corps in northwest Europe.

Rommel drove the weakened British Army back across the desert to the Egyptian frontier, although the port of Tobruk held out. Churchill eased his conscience by blaming his Middle East Commander, Archibald Wavell for the defeats. He replaced Wavell with General Claude Auchinleck.

General Auchinleck was a soldier's general and a brilliant commander, one of the very best British Generals in World War II; but he came from the Indian Army and was not familiar with officers from the British Army. Neither of the two men he selected to command Eighth Army was up to the job. Both Lieutenant-Generals Alan Cunningham and Neil Ritchie failed as Eighth Army commanders. Corelli Barnett felt that Auchinleck allowed his

---

694   Winston S. Churchill, *The Second World War: The Grand Alliance,* (Boston: Houghton Mifflin, 1950), 64.
695   Barnett, *Desert Generals,* 62.
696   Barnett, *Desert Generals,* 59, 68.
697   Barnett, *Desert Generals,* 59.
698   Barnett, *Desert Generals,* 62.

personal feelings and loyalties to influence his decision on selecting and retaining commanders for Eighth Army.[699]

In 1941, it had been the German diversion into the Balkans and Greece, which led to the dangerous dispersal of British forces in North Africa. In early 1942, it was the Japanese attack on Pearl Harbor and their offensive rampage through Southeast Asia which led directly to a reduction in British forces sent to reinforce Auchinleck. According to Correlli Barnett, [Auchinleck lost], ". . . two divisions, four light-bomber squadrons and a consignment of anti-tank guns . . ."[700] His lost divisions were the excellent 6th and 7th Australian Infantry Divisions. Auchinleck also sent a full armored brigade group to the Far East and had to reinforce Malta with some of his remaining armor.

The weakened British Eighth Army was no match for Rommel's reinforced Africa Corps. Tobruk fell on June 21. This was an extremely bitter pill for the prime minister. He got the news while in Washington, at a meeting in the President's study when Roosevelt was handed a telegram. He read it and without saying a word, he handed the telegram to Churchill. It read, "Tobruk has surrendered, with 25,000 men taken prisoners."[701] Churchill later wrote about the fall of Tobruk, ". . . one of the heaviest blows I can recall during the war . . . it had affected the reputation of the British armies . . . I did not attempt to hide from the President the shock I had received."[702] President Roosevelt made an offer of immediate help. Churchill then asked for as many new Sherman tanks as the Americans could spare. After some discussion, the Americans agreed to ship three-hundred new Sherman tanks and one-hundred self-propelled 105-mm howitzers to the British in North Africa.[703]

Late on June 25, 1942, Auchinleck personally took command of Eighth Army. He had taken command of an Army poorly deployed just one day before the Battle of Mersa Matruh. He was much too late to influence the battle. But he did offer that, "If the battle of Mersa Matruh went badly, Eighth Army would fall back toward El Alamein."[704] In a few days, Eighth Army

---

[699]   Barnett, *Desert Generals*, 124.

[700]   Barnett, *Desert Generals,* 123.

[701]   Winston S. Churchill, *The Second World War, The Hinge of Fate*, (Boston: Houghton Mifflin, 1950), 382.

[702]   Churchill, *The Hinge*, 383.

[703]   Robert Dallek, *Franklin D. Roosevelt and American Foreign Policy, 1932-1945*, (New York: Oxford University Press, 1979), 347.

[704]   Barnett, *Desert Generals*, 175.

would be streaming back toward El Alamein a beaten force. Auchinleck's main concern was to keep the Eighth Army from being totally destroyed.

Just as Auchinleck had hoped, Rommel eventually outran his supplies and was lacking reinforcements. Rommel's Africa Corps was much smaller than the British Army he was pursuing. He had been getting by on bluff and maneuver. At El Alamein, in a series of battles from July 1 to July 17, 1942, General Auchinleck called his bluff and decisively defeated the Africa Corps.[705]

At the same time, Prime Minister Churchill was rendering a scathing criticism of General Auchinleck to the War Cabinet in London. He was terribly sensitive about the political ramifications of another military defeat in North Africa. According to C.I.G.S. Brooke, "I had an uphill task defending him (Auchinleck) and pointing out the difficulties of his present position . . . The prime minister was in one of his unpleasant moods . . . asking where the 750,000 men in the Middle East were, what they were doing, and why they were not fighting."[706] Churchill's Conservative Party had suffered a clear defeat in a by-election and the prime minister had just survived a motion of censure in Parliament.[707] Auchinleck's victory at the First Battle of El Alamein, the turning point for the British Army in North Africa, went largely unreported in London.

Winston Churchill probably decided to fire General Auchinleck before his trip to North Africa in early August 1942. The fall of Tobruk had been weighing on his conscience. As the political pressure caused by military defeats increased in London, Churchill's patience with his Commanders in the Middle East was growing short.[708] Barnett wrote, "At the end of June [1942], as Auchinleck himself had recognized, Ritchie's defeat exposed Auchinleck to dismissal. But Churchill had not dismissed him. Now Auchinleck had magnificently redeemed his errors. Thus the military case for relieving him was infinitely weaker than it had been."[709]

But Churchill was determined to fire Auchinleck. He selected Harold Alexander to replace Auchinleck as the new Commander-in-Chief of the Near East; Bernard L. Montgomery was to succeed Alexander in Command of Operation Torch. Command of British Eighth Army was given to

---

[705] Barnett, *Desert Generals*, 206, 207.
[706] Arthur Bryant, *The Turn of the Tide,* Based on the Diaries of Field Marshal Lord Alanbrooke, (New York: Doubleday, 1957), 338.
[707] Arthur Bryant, *The Turn*, 337.
[708] Barnett, *Desert Generals*, 221.
[709] Barnett, *Desert Generals*, 224.

Lieutenant General William H. E. "Strafer" Gott.[710] General Gott was on his way to his new command when his plane was shot down and he was killed. The question of who was to replace Gott at Eighth Army was answered at once. Churchill later wrote, "C.I.G.S. [Brooke] decisively recommends Montgomery for Eighth Army. Smuts and I feel this post must be filled at once."[711] Churchill then directed that Montgomery, ". . . should be sent out [from England] at once."[712]

Montgomery wasted little time is arranging his affairs in England and flying out to Egypt to accept his new command. He arrived in Cairo on August 12. He was invited to Middle East G.H.Q., where he received an interview from the outgoing CIC, General Auchinleck. The interview took place in the map room where Auchinleck, ". . . explain[ed] the general situation at Eighth Army and the plans for its future."[713] Auchinleck's plans were prepared in consultation with Major General E. Dorman-Smith after the Battle of First El Alamein. They involved setting up strong defensive positions along the coastline facing south, southwest based on the Alam el Halfa, and Ruweisat Ridges placing the British in excellent position to attack any German forces trying to bypass these defenses to the south with mobile reserves assembled specifically for that purpose.

At some point in his interview with Montgomery, Auchinleck may have mentioned contingency plans for a retreat to the Nile Delta if the next German attack was successful. Montgomery may also have become aware of these plans through the new Brigadier General Staff of Eighth Army, Francis de Guingand.[714] It had become routine for Montgomery to suggest a great change had occurred the moment he assumed command. He seized upon Auchinleck's contingency plans for a retreat in an effort to discredit the man he was replacing.

Montgomery suggested that the Eighth Army was going to retreat to the Egyptian Delta if Rommel attacked again, which was a deliberate distortion of what he had been told. The contingency plans for a retreat had been on the shelf since Auchinleck's victory over Rommel in July; but they had not been officially rescinded.

---

[710]　Churchill, *The Hinge*, 461.

[711]　Churchill, *The Hinge*, 464.

[712]　Churchill, *The Hinge*, 464.

[713]　Barnett, *Desert Generals*, 228.

[714]　R.W. Thompson, *Churchill and the Montgomery Myth*, (New York: M. Evans and Company, 1967), 82, 83.

Churchill's appointment of Montgomery to Command Eighth Army fostered a host of crude but effective attempts at re-writing history. Both Montgomery's and Churchill's supporters have a vested interest in portraying Auchinleck's dismissal as a fully justified military and political necessity. Their statements and writings have contributed, ". . . to a general belief that Auchinleck had been an 'unlucky' general who had been relieved of his command in the midst of disaster."[715] Consequently, they sought to downplay the victory Auchinleck won over Rommel in July. It was almost as if the First Battle of El Alamein had never happened.

Several historians have exposed the lies Montgomery and his followers have been repeating since 1942: Correlli Barnett in *The Desert Generals*, Philip Warner in *Auchinleck, The Lonely Soldier* and R. W. Thompson in *Churchill and the Montgomery Myth*. But the most damning indictment of Montgomery's claim came from his boss, the Commander-in-Chief of the Near East, General Alexander, who wrote, "The plan [Auchinleck's] was to hold as strongly as possible the area between the sea and the Ruweisat Ridge and to threaten from the flank any enemy advance south of the ridge from a strongly defended position in the Alam el Halfa ridge. General Montgomery, now in command of Eighth Army, accepted this plan in principle, to which I agreed."[716]

Auchinleck had been observing the German method of battle. He was beginning to understand the keys to mobile warfare in the desert. Auchinleck understood that basic changes were needed in the command structure of British divisions to enable them to conduct coordinated infantry-armor operations like the Germans. He was, in fact, implementing those changes in the desert when he was relieved of command. "Just before his dismissal, Auchinleck . . . ordered that all distinction between armor and infantry division should be abolished; and the army reorganized into 'Mobile Divisions', mainly motorized infantry but each with an armored brigade under command. Trained together, all arms commanded by common divisional commanders, these divisions would have been the mobile-mixed combinations similar to those Rommel had in his German [Army] . . ."[717] Here was the key to a modern British Army. Here was the key to a basic change in the formation of British divisions which would have broken down the old regimental prejudices harbored by so many traditionalists

---

[715] Barnett, *Desert Generals*, 224.
[716] Barnett, *Desert Generals*, 228.
[717] Barnett, *Desert Generals*, 265.

within the British Army. Naturally, Auchinleck's changes provoked bitter opposition, at least one ranking member of the British Armored Corps had to be dismissed.[718]

There can be little doubt that Auchinleck, had he remained in command, would have provided the British Army with a combined arms command system so necessary for conducting mobile operations during World War II. The military case for removing Auchinleck was terribly weak and would become even weaker as it became obvious that the man Churchill had chosen to replace him was a poor tactician and wholly unfit to conduct mobile operations. But in the realm of politics and public opinion, Churchill had discovered a winner. The new Commander of British Eighth Army would soon become Churchill's guardian angel.

Montgomery would try to fight World War II battles with World War I tactics and it cost his beloved British Eighth Army dearly. R. W. Thompson wrote, "I think it is true that Montgomery was completely formed as a soldier at the end of the First World War. He did not grow after that. He became increasingly efficient, but he did not absorb a new idea. At fifty, he was the same man he had been at thirty . . . dedicated absolutely to his profession, completely assured."[719] This is a good description of how Montgomery's mental condition stunted his mental development.

Montgomery did not readily accept any changed plans or ideas that were not his own. Officers serving under Montgomery came to understand his personal quirks and how they might overcome his initial reluctance to accept new ideas. They would try to convince Montgomery that he had thought of it first. This often involved planting a small thought in Montgomery's mind and later bringing up the topic again with the suggestion he had mentioned it a few days ago. In this way they sought to convince Montgomery that the idea was really his.[720]

On August 19, having seen the defensive plans drawn up by General Dorman-Smith and approved by Auchinleck, the new Army Commander gave a presentation of his new plans for British Eighth Army to the C. I. G. S., Alan Brooke, and Prime Minister Churchill. By all accounts, it was a masterful performance. On August 21, Churchill reported to London, ". . . a complete change of atmosphere has taken place. Alexander ordered Montgomery to prepare to take the offensive and meanwhile to hold

[718] Barnett, *Desert Generals*, 265.
[719] R.W. Thompson, *Churchill and the Montgomery Myth*, 92.
[720] Hamilton, *Making*, 828, 829.

all positions, and Montgomery issued an invigorating directive to his commanders . . . The highest alacrity and activity prevail. Positions are everywhere being strengthened, and extended forces are being sorted out and regrouped in solid units."[721]

If Churchill was impressed by Montgomery's presentation, Alan Brooke was ecstatic: "Monty's performance that evening was one of the highlights of his military career. He had only been at the head of his Command for a few days, and in that short spell he had toured the whole of his front, met all the senior Commanders, appreciated the tactical value of the various [geographical] features . . . I must confess that I was dumbfounded by the rapidity with which he had grasped the situation facing him . . . the clarity of his plans, and . . . his unbounded self-confidence . . ."[722] Montgomery had polished his abilities since creating the training manual for British IX Corps in September 1917, but the basics were the same. The so-called "Plumber principles" he had learned from General Herbert Plumer were: short, limited offensives aimed at tactically important targets, thorough, job-specific training for all personnel, massed artillery firing a creeping barrage at the point of attack, and fresh reserves to be fed into the attack to sustain momentum.[723]

Erwin Rommel, the German Commander opposing Montgomery, was terribly short of gasoline and ammunition. He also knew the British were reinforcing their Army in Egypt. Rommel wrote, ". . . if we did not act during this full moon, our last chance of an offensive would be gone forever; I gave the order for the attack to open on the night of August 30-31."[724] During the night of August 30, German sappers began working their way through British minefields south of Alam Halfa Ridge. The minefields were deeper and more extensive than the Germans had planned. They had planned to be out of the minefields by daylight into British rear areas and instead were only just into the eastern edges of the minefields.[725] They had lost the element of surprise when British artillery fire began to roll back and forth over the attacking formations.

As the Germans pressed their attack, British 7th Armored Division retreated slowly eastward and toward Alam Halfa Ridge. The Germans

---

[721]   Churchill, *The Hinge,* 520.
[722]   Bryant, *The Turn,* 388.
[723]   Hamilton, *Master,* 125, 127.
[724]   Rommel, 274, 275.
[725]   Barnett, *Desert Generals,* 247.

had intended to swing around east of Alam Halfa Ridge, but the extensive minefields and a limited fuel supply cut their attack short. They turned north instead into the mined, defensive area of 22nd Armored Brigade just west of Alam Halfa Ridge. British artillery firing from the ridge was effective against German tanks and vehicles of all types. Anti-tank and artillery fire from 2nd Armored Brigade blunted and finally stopped the German attack. That evening, the Germans retreated south into the Ragil Depression. British aircraft and artillery harassed the Germans throughout the night. Bad luck seemed to follow the German command. "General von Bismarck, of 21st Panzer Division, had been killed; Nehring, commanding the Africa Korps, was wounded."[726]

The following day the Germans came at the British again, with the same results. Well-sighted artillery fire from Alam Halfa Ridge and continual air bombardment from the RAF were decisive. The Germans were again, ". . . thrown back into the soft sand of the Ragil Depression."[727] That evening, German units began reporting that they were immobilized; they were out of gas. Rommel hesitated, unwilling to give up his last chance at victory in Egypt. The following day Rommel gave the orders for a German retreat. It took Rommel several days to refuel his divisions and get them out of the Ragil Depression into prepared defensive positions.

Several writers, including Correlli Barnett, have been critical of Montgomery for not attacking Rommel while his mobile divisions were languishing immobile in the Ragil Depression. Rommel was short of fuel, ammunition, and disorganized by defeat including the loss of two division commanders.[728] In his *Memoirs,* Montgomery says there were two reasons he did not aggressively pursue Rommel. "First, I was not too happy about the standard of training of the Army and also the equipment situation was unsatisfactory; time was needed to put these right. And secondly, I was not anxious to force Rommel to pull out and withdraw 'in being' back to the Agheila position . . . it was essential to get Rommel to stand and fight and then defeat him decisively."[729]

Montgomery's explanation would have been more credible if after training the army to his satisfaction, he was more aggressive in pursuing the enemy. That did not happen. His conduct at El Alamein set the tone

---

[726]   Barnett, *Desert Generals,* 248.

[727]   Barnett, *Desert Generals*, 249.

[728]   Barnett, *Desert Generals*, 249.

[729]   Montgomery, *Memoirs*, 110.

for Montgomery's later set-piece battles. Montgomery kept a "tight grip" on his battles, influencing command decisions down to the battalion level and sometimes below. There was little chance for individual initiative in Montgomery's Army. He barely trusted other officers, even the officers he personally selected, to get it right.

If Montgomery did not trust his officers to handle small-unit tactics, neither did he trust their ability to train the men. Hamilton wrote, "What is not generally known is that Bernard himself assumed responsibility for training in 8th Army—he had no officer on his staff to do it, nor probably could have found one. He therefore issued his own training instructions [8th Army Training Memorandum No. 1], and saw personally that all three Corps of 8th Army acted upon them."[730] Less than three days after Alam Halfa, the new training manual was available to corps and divisions within Eighth Army.

The new manual emphasized Montgomery's strict rules for battlefield operations. He advised against splitting up units piecemeal; he demanded that officers establish clear-cut goals, specific tasks for each unit, "and definite objectives."[731] Orders must be executed immediately just as they were handed down; there would be no 'bellyaching' in Montgomery's desert army. Under the sub heading "Battle operations generally," Montgomery outlined his understanding of tactics: "The whole essence of modern tactical methods is: concentration of effort, the co-operation of all arms, control, simplification, and speed of action."[732] As Rommel suggested, Montgomery knew the principles behind sound battlefield tactics; and most historians, even his critics, acknowledge that Montgomery was a gifted trainer and could distill a mountain of seemingly unrelated information into a few memorable points.

While Eighth Army was being trained and breaking in its new American equipment: [three-hundred new Sherman tanks and one-hundred self-propelled 105-mm howitzers]; Montgomery retired to his headquarters at Burg-el-Arab and began working on his plans, "To destroy the enemy forces now opposing Eighth Army."[733] His plan required one week of devoted effort and fourteen sheets of paper to publish. "The plan was called 'Lightfoot.'"[734] His new plan did not suit the armor commanders.

---

730 Hamilton, *Making*, 718.
731 Hamilton, *Making*, 720.
732 Hamilton, *Making*, 720.
733 Hamilton, *Making*, 732.
734 Hamilton, *Making*, 731.

Montgomery had another problem in Prime Minister Churchill. The prime minister's political difficulties had not gone away with the appointment of new commanders in North Africa. Indeed, they had gotten worse. "Churchill was under great strain—as he professed to his doctor later, September and October 1942 were for him the most anxious months of the entire war . . . Strafford Cripps [Leader of the House of Commons] . . . announced on September 21 that he wished to resign—in protest at the way Churchill was running the war."[735] Alam Halfa was not seen as a victory in England, but Churchill did succeed into talking Cripps out of his resignation until the results of the new British offensive in North Africa became known.[736] Churchill began asking General Alexander to conduct Eighth Army's offensive in September. Alexander put the proposition to Montgomery. Montgomery told Alexander, "Now, Alex, I wouldn't do it in September. But if I do it in October it'll be a victory."[737] When asked what to tell Churchill, Montgomery told Alexander to advise Churchill that if he attacked in September, they would probably be defeated; but if they waited until they were ready in October, Montgomery promised a victory.[738] Generals Claude Auchinleck and E. Dorman-Smith had told Churchill the same thing.

It was a subtle variation of a scheme Montgomery had been playing for years with senior officers within the British Army to gain complete control of the unit involved. Failure to heed Montgomery's advice would result in ". . . a lot of unnecessary casualties."[739] In the codeword "casualties," Montgomery had hit upon the one negative outcome all British officers instinctively hoped to avoid. When he later found himself in arguments with Canadian and United States Army officers, Montgomery changed his codeword from 'casualties' to 'politics.' By late 1944 both Canadian General H.D.G. Crerar and U.S. General Dwight Eisenhower were accused of letting national 'politics' influence their military decisions in Europe. This was an accurate charge. Of course, Montgomery, the supreme professional, would never let politics influence any of his decisions. It was just a remarkable coincidence that all of Montgomery's decisions furthered his own considerable reputation and British political interests.

---

[735]   Hamilton, *Making*, 745.
[736]   Hamilton, *Making*, 745.
[737]   Hamilton, *Making*, 744.
[738]   Hamilton, *Making*, 744, 745.
[739]   Hamilton, *Making*, 423.

Montgomery's plan to destroy Rommel's army was code named *Lightfoot*. It was published to Eighth Army exactly one week after Alam Halfa. Montgomery planned to launch two simultaneous attacks. XXX Corps would attack along Miteiriya Ridge in the north and XIII Corps would attack near Himeimat on the southern flank. The attack of XIII Corps in the south was designed to be a decoy, to draw German reserves away from the main attack in the north. Lieutenant-General Oliver Leese, XXX Corps Commander, saw a potential problem in infantry-armor cooperation: "I had been horrified at the state of ill-feeling that existed between Infantry and Armor. Neither had confidence in the other. All mutual trust seems to have been drained out in the previous battles."[740]

For the main attack in the north, the engineers and infantry of XXX Corps were to lead the attack by clearing two paths through German minefields. The path closest to the sea was aimed at Kidney Ridge and assigned to 1st Armored Division; the path further south, centered on Miteiriya Ridge was assigned to 10th Armored Division. The two armored divisions would be under X Corps Commander, Lieutenant-General Herbert Lumsden. Montgomery had assigned two corps commander's responsibility for the same constricted access corridors through the German minefields.

Montgomery asked the armor to break out of the minefields even if the infantry and engineers had not succeeded in clearing the paths through the German minefields and lead the attack on the fixed German defensive positions. General Lumsden did not agree with Montgomery's plan. Montgomery's Chief of Staff, General de Guingand, recalled what Lumsden said, ". . . there's one point I don't agree with: that tanks should be used to force their way out of minefields. Tanks must be used as cavalry: they must exploit the situation and not be kept as supporters of infantry. So I don't propose to do that."[741] Since there was little time to redraw the whole plan, Montgomery decided to make a few changes to limit the role of the Armored Corps. According to Nigel Hamilton, ". . . the attacks would go in as arranged. Only, instead of breaking out into the open beyond the minefields, the armor would simply settle itself on good ground of its own choosing and 'shield' the infantry whilst it now undertook the major role: that of methodically eating away or 'crumbling' the defending Axis troops."[742] It was hoped that the British infantry attack would provoke an attack from

---

[740] Sir Oliver Leese, unpublished memoirs. From Hamilton, *Making*, 748.
[741] Hamilton, *Making*, 752.
[742] Hamilton, *Making*, 755.

German armor, forcing them out into the open and onto the guns of X Corps tanks deployed for just this purpose. Montgomery was hoping to repeat the splendid defensive performance of his armor at Alam Halfa.[743]

At 9:40 p.m. on the evening of October 23, eight-hundred and eighty artillery pieces from Eighth Army announced a thunderous opening for the Second Battle of El Alamein.[744] Half an hour later, British infantry and engineers from XXX Corps moved forward from their positions and entered the German minefields in front of Miteiriya and Kidney Ridges. The ridges were about two miles apart. This section of the German front was manned by seven-thousand Italian infantry from the Trento Division plus five-thousand Germans from the 164th Infantry Division. The British attacking force in X and XXX Corps numbered about seventy-thousand men and six-hundred tanks. At the point of attack, the British had a numerical superiority of about six to one.[745] At this stage of the North African battles, the British enjoyed absolute air supremacy, they were able to bomb and strafe German/Italian positions at will.

British sappers were supposed to clear the minefields that night, so the following morning the armor could move through the corridors in the minefield and provide cover for the Infantry attack on the main German defensive positions. The minefields were deeper than the British had anticipated. It took far longer to clear the minefields under German fire than Montgomery had planned. None of his planned attacks reached its objective by the following morning. The infantry sappers had not been able to clear corridors for the tanks. General Lumsden's armored brigades were finding the small corridors through the minefields clogged with infantry and knocked out vehicles.

Erwin Rommel had been on sick leave in Italy and Germany when the battle began. His replacement, General George Stumme died of a heart attack the first day of the battle. Rommel left at once for the battlefield, but it took him nearly two days to reach his headquarters in Egypt. His first move was to bring 21st Panzer Division north and attack the British defensive positions at Kidney Ridge.

On the second day, some tanks assigned to the northern pincer from the 1st Armored Division did manage to get through the German minefields

---

[743]   Hamilton, *Making*, 755.

[744]   Callahan, *Churchill: Retreat*, 202. Also See Hamilton, *Making*, 774

[745]   Barnett, *Desert Generals*, 260, 261.

near Kidney Ridge.[746] But 10th Armored's main attack at Miteiriya Ridge made little progress. Montgomery ordered the armor attacks go forward as planned; he threatened to fire the Armored Corps Commander, General Lumsden and the Commander of 10th Armored Division, General A.H. Gatehouse. Lumsden tried to talk to Montgomery without success. Lumsden then agreed that Gatehouse should telephone Montgomery and try to explain the situation. General Gatehouse left his command post near the front for a telephone conversation with the new Eighth Army Commander. Gatehouse explained the difficulties encountered when trying to crest a ridge in a tank, proceed one-half mile down the front slope under the sights of enemy anti-tank guns into an unchartered minefield. Montgomery agreed to reduce the size of the armored attack from six regiments to one. The one regiment involved was ". . . the Straffordshire Yeomanry. It lost all but fifteen of its tanks and the operation ended where it had started, behind the Miteiriya Ridge."[747] Montgomery could not get the attack restarted.

In statements made after the battle, nearly all of the participants agreed with armored Generals Lumsden and Gatehouse. Bernard Freyberg questioned the ability of armor to attack a fixed position, "' . . . held in depth with 88-mm guns,' and without infantry protection, without infantry support."[748] Generals John Harding and G. P. B. Roberts shared this opinion, suggesting that Montgomery ". . . expected much more than they could possibly achieve—*much* more. I mean whenever you attack with tanks . . . you get heavy casualties . . . very heavy casualties."[749] Correlli Barnett later wrote, "In fact, the breakdown occurred because of the cumbersome two-tier organization of infantry and armor on the same narrow, mine-strewn front, and because the armor was given a role completely unsuited to it."[750] After two days fighting his tank losses were over two hundred and rising and his infantry losses were approaching six-thousand five-hundred. This was nearly two-thirds of the ten thousand casualties Montgomery had estimated for the whole operation. Montgomery decided to withdraw his armor and create a new plan. In London, Montgomery's withdraws began to look as if he had just suffered a crushing defeat.

---

[746] Barnett, *Desert Generals*, 262.

[747] Barnett, *Desert Generals*, 264.

[748] Bernard Freyberg, a letter to Sir Howard Kippenberger, see Hamilton, *Making*, 791.

[749] Hamilton, *Making*, 794. Italics in the original.

[750] Barnett, *Desert Generals*, 264.

Churchill exploded. In a meeting with C. I. G. S. Brooke, he was highly critical of Montgomery. According to Brooke's diary: "What, he asked, was my Monty doing now, allowing the battle to peter out . . . He had done nothing for the last three days, and now he was withdrawing troops from the front . . . Had we not got a single general who could even win one single battle? etc., etc."[751] Brooke came to Montgomery's defense. He tried to explain to Churchill the stages a battle goes through; Brooke thought it likely that Montgomery, after beating off Rommel's counterattacks, was simply withdrawing forces to create reserves for a new attack. Eventually Churchill calmed down. But later, in his diary, Brooke expressed his own doubts: "It had worked; confidence had been restored. I had told them what I thought Monty must be doing, and I knew him well, but there was just the possibility that I was wrong and that Monty was beat."[752]

The Germans were destroying three British tanks to every one they lost. But it was not enough. The Italian tanks were useless, and the Germans were outnumbered six or seven to one in tanks with a 75-mm gun. The British also had complete control of the air over the battlefield and this fact heightened the British advantage in armor. Worse, the Germans were terribly short of fuel and ammunition. Three days into the battle, Montgomery had lost as many tanks as the Germans had at the beginning.[753]

XXX Corps' infantry divisions gained some ground on Miteiriya Ridge on the 25th and 26th, but otherwise the British front was inactive. Montgomery spent the entire day of the 26th at his headquarters planning. The new operation Montgomery planned was another right-left combination attack, designed to keep the German defenders off balance. The right hook was to be delivered by the Australian Infantry along the coastline at the German 164th Infantry Division. The left-handed finishing blow was supposed to be delivered by the same combination of Corps [XXX Corps, Infantry and X Corps, Armor] which had gotten tangled together during the first attack. The new attack plan was codenamed Operation *Supercharge.* It was set to go on the night of October 31/ November 1, but had to be postponed for one day due to some confusion in the units that were to deliver the main blow.[754]

---

[751] Bryant, *The Turn,* 417.
[752] Bryant, *The Turn,* 419.
[753] Barnett, *Desert Generals,* 267.
[754] Barnett, *Desert Generals,* 268, 269.

The preliminary attack by the Australian infantry along the coastline got off on the night of 30/31 October and was partially successful. They had elements of the German 164th Infantry Division trapped against the ocean, but the Germans managed to escape with heavy losses. The main attack by British XXX Corps west of Miteiriya Ridge was launched early on the morning of November 2. The British were well supplied with plenty of fuel and ammunition. The Germans were running out of everything, including time. "The Axis forces heavily outnumbered at the beginning and without reinforcements or rest for seven days, had now fought almost to the limit of their strength . . . in front of the British armor of 10th Corps was Rommel and his two panzer divisions, ninety tanks against seven hundred."[755] The Germans fought with a tenacity born of desperation. Barnett suggests that, ". . . Rommel fought one of the best actions of his career in order to gain time for . . . the retreat that must soon follow."[756]

For two days, the Germans held their ground. They were tied to their positions at El Alamein by a direct order from Adolf Hitler, who demanded that Rommel stand and fight at El Alamein. Heavily outnumbered in every category, Rommel and his Panzer Army faced certain destruction by Montgomery's forces. He deployed the 90th Light Division in front of his 22 remaining tanks and awaited his fate, while 650 British tanks [7th Armored Division and X Corps] were regrouping for another assault.[757] Finally, on the evening of November 4, a message from Hitler released Rommel from his 'stand fast' order and left him free to do as he chose. Shortly thereafter, Rommel began the long retreat across the North African coastline.

A British general had finally beaten Erwin Rommel. This was cause for great celebration. It had cost Montgomery thirteen-thousand casualties and six-hundred tanks to do it; but after the Second Battle of El Alamein there could be no doubt that a British general had beaten Rommel, the 'Desert Fox.' Montgomery held a press conference the next day, proudly telling the assembled newsmen, "Gentlemen, this is complete and absolute victory."[758] Montgomery's victory was less than absolute, but for a country desperately seeking any sign of eventual victory in their long war against Germany, this was a victory worth celebrating.

---

[755] Barnett, *Desert Generals*, 269.
[756] Barnett, *Desert Generals*, 269.
[757] Barnett, *Desert Generals*, 270.
[758] Barnett, *Desert Generals*, 271.

British armored commanders [Gatehouse and Briggs] begged for a chance to get around Rommel's southern flank and block his escape, but were denied the opportunity.[759] The real tragedy, as historian R. W. Thompson suggested, was that the British should never have fought the Battle of Second El Alamein: ". . . 2nd Alamein has in it the elements of a last act in a tragedy, fore-ordained and inescapable for political reasons. Militarily, it need not have taken place at all."[760] British historian Correlli Barnett agrees, "Second Alamein was the last chance to restore British prestige, shaken after a year of defeat, with banner headlines, with the ringing of church bells . . . . The ultimate judgment of history may well be to record it as a political victory."[761] Churchill wanted an all-British victory before the Americans landed in North Africa; Montgomery's victory at Second Alamein fulfilled that wish with only days to spare.

Alexander quickly sent a telegram to the prime minister dated November 4: "After twelve days of heavy and violent fighting, the 8th Army has inflicted a severe defeat on the German and Italian forces under Rommel's command. The enemy's front has broken, and British armored formations in strength have passed through and are operating in the enemies rear areas. Such portions of the enemy's forces as can get away are in full retreat, and are being harassed by our armored and mobile forces and by our air forces . . . Fighting continues."[762]

Churchill read Alexander's telegram and wept. Montgomery's victory had saved his government. "In October 1942, Monty delivered the most important victory of the war from the prime minister's point of view, solidifying the Brooke-Monty grip on the British Army for the balance of the conflict."[763] Worldwide publicity generated by the British victory at El Alamein would carry the triumvirate of Churchill, Brooke, and Montgomery through the end of the war and further. But the Battle of Second El Alamein would prove to be a shaky foundation for such lofty reputations.

Rommel began his retreat the night of November 4. He was short of fuel. The Germans retreated west to El Daba, past Fuka, Mersa Matruh, and Tobruk. It rained during the night of November 6, soaking the desert sand and giving Montgomery an excuse for not catching Rommel's army.

759 Thompson, *Churchill and the Montgomery Myth*, 150, 151.
760 Thompson, *Churchill and the Montgomery Myth*, 106.
761 Barnett, *Desert Generals*, 256.
762 Churchill, *The Hinge*, 598, 600.
763 Callahan, *Churchill and His Generals*, 237.

Rommel stopped to deploy his army defensively at El Agheila and Buerat, forcing Montgomery to halt and draw up his administrative tail each time. Rommel's panzer divisions covered for his slower infantry formations. At Syrte, the Fifteenth Panzer and 90th Light Divisions fought a running battle with British forces that lasted for nearly four days before they fell back on Buerat. By December 29, Rommel had deployed what was left of his army in defensive positions at Buerat.[764] This brought British Eighth Army to a sudden stop.

Montgomery needed time to plan a set-piece battle, re-supply his Army, and re-group his forces for the upcoming battle. Montgomery required more than two weeks preparing for the battle; he was not ready to attack Rommel's forces until January 15. Heavy bomber attacks and a massive artillery bombardment signaled the beginning of Montgomery's offensive. The Germans were holding their front lines with only picket forces, most of Montgomery's massive bombardment fell into the desert. Rommel had already sent his infantry without transport to the rear.[765]

Montgomery's attack at Buerat was the same attack plan he had used for *Supercharge* and *Lightfoot.* The attack began with a massive aerial and artillery bombardment. This was followed by a feint attack on one flank with the main attack coming on the opposite flank. General Oliver Leese commanded the main attack on the German southern flank with 7th Armored and 2nd New Zealand Divisions. He ran into the German 15th Panzer Division which, ". . . fell slowly back on Tarhuna before Leese's attack, destroying fifty-two British tanks; the rest of Rommel's command fell back in step."[766] On January 23, Montgomery's Eighth Army captured Tripoli, nearly one-thousand four-hundred miles west of El Alamein. Montgomery was extremely pleased with himself, ". . . This has been accomplished in three months. This achievement is probably without parallel in history . . ."[767]

Back in London, two of Montgomery's supporters were hoping to come to North Africa to help him celebrate. Montgomery was pleased to provide the occasion. On February 4 the Prime Minister, his political future now secure, and the C. I. G. S., his doubts assuaged, stood with General Montgomery in Tripoli to watch the victory parade and a review of the 51st Highland Division. "There is no braver sight than that of

[764] Barnett, *Desert Generals*, 280.
[765] Barnett, *Desert Generals*, 281.
[766] Barnett, *Desert Generals*, 282.
[767] Barnett, *Desert Generals*, 282.

the Highlanders marching to the strange . . . deeply moving music of the bagpipes. It is a sound that acts like a potent drug upon the hearts and guts of men, and not surprisingly there were tears rolling down Churchill's cheeks."[768]

It is not possible today, more than sixty years after the event, to understand the depth of emotions, which must have swept over the British Isles as news of Montgomery's victory over Rommel became known. What began as very good news was hyped and hyped again due to the political nature of the event. Several unrelated yet topical circumstances worked in unison to increase the significance of the Second Battle of El Alamein. The victory was Churchill's political savior. Had Montgomery lost the battle, Churchill's government may have fallen. Churchill painted a glorious victory at El Alamein. He said that during World War I ". . . a concentration of two or three to one was required, not only in artillery but men, to pierce and break a carefully fortified line. We had nothing like this superiority at Alamein . . . the Battle of Alamein will ever make a glorious page in British military annals . . . . It may almost be said, 'Before Alamein we never had a victory. After Alamein we never had a defeat.'"[769] This simply was not true. British generals had won a host of victories in North Africa prior to Montgomery, the most recent being Auchinleck's victory in July 1942 at the First Battle of El Alamein.

There were the obvious political implications of a British victory over Germany prior to direct United States involvement in the war against Germany. For one, the prestige of the British Army was in dire need of rehabilitation after a string of disastrous defeats in 1942. The timing of Montgomery's attack began just as Alexander had hoped.[770] If Montgomery thought the battle would require ten to twelve days, then 'minus 13 of *Torch'* would guarantee a British victory. Once the Torch landings occurred, Rommel would be forced to retreat to his base in Tunisia regardless of what happened at El Alamein.[771] Rommel knew exactly what the Allied landings in Northwest Africa meant: "[November 8] . . . At about 1100 hours, this was confirmed. The Anglo-Americans had . . . landed in North-West Africa during the night . . . This spelt the end of the [German] army in Africa."[772]

---

[768]   Thompson, *Churchill and the Montgomery Myth*, 171.
[769]   Churchill, *The Hinge*, 602, 603.
[770]   Thompson, *Churchill and the Montgomery Myth*, 121.
[771]   Barnett, *Desert Generals*, 255.
[772]   Rommel, 345.

The final factor, which made the Second Battle of El Alamein such an important event, was the christening of a new national hero, the Commanding Officer of the British Eighth Army. The Montgomery legend, or more properly, 'the Montgomery Myth' begins here, after the Battle of Second Alamein. The stories coming out of North Africa stretched credibility beyond the pale; how many times could Montgomery destroy the German 90th Light Division? That didn't matter. Whatever Montgomery did or said made glorious news. R. W. Thompson wrote, ". . . it was apparent that General Montgomery enjoyed fame perhaps unique in the story of war. For one-hundred days, the headlines of the newspapers of Britain, the Dominions . . . and of the United States . . . had borne his name."[773]

Almost overnight, Montgomery became a wildly popular international celebrity. His name was on everyone's lips. "It was irresistible, and Montgomery was its indestructible hero. Every man had played his part well, including the Public Relations staff, the General's personal photographer, and the moving camera teams . . . His 'fan' mail rivaled that of a film star."[774] Montgomery's instant adulation from the press combined with his belief in his own infallibility to create a powerful public image. The power of that public image is still evident today in the manipulation of historical events both in print and on television to conform to the Montgomery legend. It is a legend that, at times, bares little resemblance to the actual event.

The general with a crippled, dysfunctional personality and an archaic understanding of how to conduct a battle had convinced the highest military authorities in Great Britain that he had become the best British general since the Duke of Wellington. There would come a time later in the war when, in the interest of Allied unity, the services of General Bernard L. Montgomery would no longer be required; but Montgomery's great popularity with the British people made it impossible for either Churchill or Eisenhower to dismiss him.[775]

After a suitable rest period for victory celebrations, re-grouping and re-supply, Montgomery's Eighth Army headed for Tunisia and the last German stronghold in North Africa. On 19 February 1943 General Harold Alexander took Command of the newly formed 18th Army Group. It consisted of General Kenneth Anderson's British First Army [from the Allied *Torch* landings] in northwest Tunisia and General Montgomery's British Eighth

---

[773] Thompson, *Churchill and the Montgomery Myth*, 170.
[774] Thompson, *Churchill and the Montgomery Myth*, 170.
[775] Hastings, *Overlord*, 243.

Army coming into Tunisia from Libya to the southeast. Montgomery hit the Mareth line with a probing attack on March 17. On March 20, the main attack went in. Four days later the Germans pulled back from the Mareth line and set-up a new defensive front on, ". . . the narrow bottleneck of the Chott position across Wadi Akarit."[776] On April 6, Montgomery committed three infantry divisions [50th and 51st British and the 4th Indian Divisions] to an attack on the Chott line. Their attack was supported by four-hundred and fifty guns.[777]

General Patton's U.S. II Corps held the German 10th Panzer Division near El Guettar. Under enormous pressure from attacks on both flanks, the German/Italian front in Tunisia finally gave way. They were running out of ammunition. By May 6, U.S. II Corps units were driving into Bizerta; British 7th Armored Division led the assault into Tunis.[778] The last Germans surrendered in Tunisia on May 13. The final tally was 275,000 soldiers; slightly over half of them were German.[779]

Rommel had left for medical treatment and to argue his case for saving the German Army in North Africa. He was not successful. 15th Panzer and the 90th Light Divisions were two of the finest formations of their type during World War II. Rommel became extremely bitter over the fate of those German soldiers who had served him so well in North Africa. The result was an enormous strategic blunder for Germany. Rommel could have probably taken Egypt with the troops Hitler belatedly sent to save Tunisia. It was too little, too late.

Erwin Rommel did not have a lot of respect for his opposing commander at Second El Alamein. He wrote, "It is . . . my belief that most senior British officers have a certain tendency to think along established lines."[780] He was clearly referring to Montgomery. Rommel said that Archibald Wavell was the only British officer, ". . . who showed a touch of genius . . ."[781] He also thought Claude Auchinleck was a very good commander, but that he left operations to his subordinates. Rommel wrote, "The principles of British command had . . . not altered; method and rigid adherence to system were still the main feature of their tactics . . . the British based their planning on

776   Thompson, *Churchill and the Montgomery Myth*, 190.
777   Thompson, *Churchill and the Montgomery Myth*, 190.
778   Thompson, *Churchill and the Montgomery Myth*, 193.
779   Ambrose, *Eisenhower, Soldier, General*, 236. Also see Thompson, *Churchill and the Montgomery Myth*, 193.
780   Rommel, 520.
781   Rommel, 520.

the principle of exact calculation, a principle which can only be followed where there is complete material superiority. They actually undertook no operations but relied simply and solely on the effect of their artillery and air force. Their command was as slow as ever in reacting."[782] It would be difficult to argue with Rommel's conclusion.

Rommel thought Montgomery was overcautious. Rommel wrote, "He risked nothing in any way doubtful and bold solutions were completely foreign to him . . . . Montgomery would never take the risk of following up boldly and overrunning us, as he could have done without any danger to himself. Indeed, such a course would have cost him fewer losses in the long run than his methodical insistence on overwhelming superiority in each tactical action, which he could only obtain at the cost of his speed."[783] U.S. General George Patton was more descriptive, "Monty is a tired little fart. War requires the taking of risks and he wouldn't take them . . ."[784] Rommel and Patton were both right. Other things being equal, the longer a unit remains under fire, the more casualties it suffers. Montgomery's slow motion, highly controlled offensives all but guaranteed high casualty rates for the units involved.

Rommel noticed the tendency of British officers to be bogged down with strategic planning. "It was indeed the general rule that the higher ranking British officers thought more in terms of strategy than tactics. As a result, the majority of their responsible officers made the error of planning operations according to what was strategically desirable rather than what was tactically attainable."[785] More to the point, Rommel wrote, "The best strategic plan is useless if it cannot be executed tactically."[786] This was precisely where Montgomery's planning usually failed. Montgomery could create a viable strategic plan; he could then explain his plan in intricate detail, making it sound like the best, most original plan ever devised. It was during the tactical execution of his plans that errors surfaced, eventually causing the plan to collapse.

The Allied campaigns in Sicily and Italy have been told in detail elsewhere and will not be repeated here. Montgomery's plan for the invasion of Sicily is important because it helps to prove a point. His plan called for

[782]   Rommel, 329.
[783]   Rommel, 360, 361.
[784]   Blumenson, (Ed.), *The Patton Papers, 1940-1945*, 608.
[785]   Rommel, 521.
[786]   Rommel, 389.

the invasion to begin with British Eighth Army landing at Syracuse and the American Seventh Army protecting its left flank by landing in the Gulf of Gela. This was a sound plan, more conservative than the plan George Patton had created, but it was strategically sound. If the German and Italian defenders on Sicily put up a stout defense of the island, the Allies would be well positioned to defend the enemy's blows with two armies side by side along the southeast coast of the island and the excellent port of Syracuse for re-supply. Montgomery's plan required the British Eighth Army to beat the island's defenders to the port of Messina, cutting off their escape from Sicily to the Italian mainland. The British Eighth Army failed in their mission. On August 17, General Patton beat Montgomery to Messina, but the Germans had already gone, by one account given on British television, 'to the last guard dog.'

As Rommel had said, "The best strategic plan is useless if it cannot be executed tactically."[787] Montgomery had a good plan, but the Army he commanded could not fulfill its mission. This gut wrenching scenario would repeat itself time and again in Northwest Europe. The Army Group Montgomery commanded repeatedly failed to close behind large German formations, which had blundered into Allied traps: in August 1944 at the Falaise Gap and along the Seine River, in September on the Pas de Calais and in December during the Battle of the Bulge. Montgomery's slow motion method of warfare had Eisenhower concerned before he got across the Straits of Messina into Italy. Eisenhower later told an interviewer, "I told General Alexander I believed we could do it in a rowboat. We sat there in Messina from 17 August until 3 September."[788] No one ever rushed Montgomery into an attack.

One symptom of *Montgomery's mental condition was a very great psychological need to be in control of his surroundings and of the people he was likely to meet.* It is impossible to understand Montgomery's odd behavior on the battlefield without factoring in his desperate psychological need to control his environment. Correlli Barnett wrote of Montgomery, ". . . though unpredictable to the point of eccentricity in his general judgment and even conduct, [he] was in war devoted to *ideals of precision, punctuality, caution and close control*; his plans were shaped and explained with the exactness

787   Rommel, 389.
788   Eisenhower Interview on Feb. 16, 1949, OCMH file at the US Army Military History Institute, from Carlo D'Este, *Eisenhower, A Soldier's Life*, (New York: Henry Holt, 2002), 449.

of a watch maker."[789] Retaining control over both people and events was essential for Montgomery's psychological well-being. In North Africa, he frequently interfered with his corps and division commanders. In northwest Europe, he would delve further down the chain of command.

Montgomery was seldom able to assess the combat effectiveness and intensions of his enemy. Barnett wrote, "A student noted that a typical scheme of Montgomery's dealt with 'our side's' plans with comprehensive exactitude and elaboration; but the 'enemy's' intentions and reactions were not imagined, either as a source of danger or opportunity."[790] Montgomery used only those details in his planning which he could control. Those factors he could not control, like the German reaction to his offensives, were usually ignored. When he had overwhelming numerical superiority, despite the high casualties his army suffered there was little danger of his losing the battle. When the odds were more even, as they were during *Goodwood* and *Market Garden,* Montgomery's forces quickly got into trouble.

---

[789] Barnett, *Desert Generals*, 236. Italics added.
[790] Barnett, *Desert Generals*, 237.

Chapter 9

General Montgomery Commands *Overlord*

"While it is evident that Winston's [Churchill's] story will in due course be disentangled, on the other hand as regards Monty the record was so skillfully adjusted at the time that I see little, if any, prospects of the truth being disentangled from the story."[791] Lord Tedder

"Thus, it became the doctrine of [Montgomery's] 21 Army Group that in combined tank and infantry attacks the tanks should lead and the infantry should follow. *Three years of experience had taught everyone, except apparently Montgomery and his lieutenants, that such tactics were ruinous.*"[792] British military historian Timothy Harrison Place.

President Roosevelt's appointment of General Eisenhower to be the Supreme Commander of *Overlord* was a signal to the British that the command arrangement which the Allies had used in the Mediterranean would be acceptable to the Americans for *Overlord*. The British were then able to select the three commanders for the land, sea and air forces. These were the commanders who would run the planning and operational phases of the invasion. The American press was slow to understand how the Allied command system was going to work in France. When Ingersoll's book *Top Secret* appeared in 1946, it attacked the Allied command structure for being too British and created much ill-feeling in England.[793]

This command arrangement would last through the subsequent build-up of Allied forces within the so-called 'lodgement area.' Based primarily on the fact that British generals had more combat experience than their

---

[791] Lord Tedder, letter to B.H. Liddell Hart, 7 March 1963, from D'Este, *Decision,* 494.

[792] Timothy Harrison Place, *Military Training in the British Army, 1940-1944, From Dunkirk to D-Day,* (London: Routledge, Taylor & Francis Group, 2008), 149. Italics added.

[793] D'Este, *Decision,* 488. Footnote.

American counterparts, the Commander of British 21st Army Group was also given overall command of US Army ground forces during the invasion and build-up phase of operations.

The British selected General Bernard L. Montgomery as Commander for the 21st Army Group. Prior to the invasion the Allies had agreed that when they had enough elbow room in the 'lodgement area' Patton's US Third Army would be deployed. At that time the number of American soldiers would begin to outnumber British soldiers in Normandy. The British had agreed to surrender Command of Allied Ground Forces to the Americans and General Eisenhower would become the new Allied Ground Forces Commander.

President Roosevelt's assessment of the command structure was purely political and did not reflect the opinion of many senior US officers who had served in the Mediterranean. Eisenhower, for one, had terribly mixed feelings about Montgomery. "He found him slow, overcautious, and selfish. He (Montgomery) 'dawdled' on the Sicilian plain and missed a golden opportunity to gain a foothold in Italy by refusing to cross the Strait of Messina."[794] Eisenhower would maintain civil relations with Montgomery through September. After that, Eisenhower saw less and less of Montgomery, by the end of the war he deliberately avoided contact with the temperamental British Field Marshal.

Roosevelt avoided European politics whenever he could. His concern for Europe was limited to the defeat of Nazi Germany and those events which threatened to become a political liability for him in the United States. President Roosevelt once told Averell Harriman, "[H]e wanted to have a lot to say about the settlement in the Pacific, but that *he considered the European questions were so impossible that he wanted to stay out of them as far as practicable*, except for the problems involving Germany."[795]

As long as the command arrangement for *Overlord* remained politically obscure behind Eisenhower's grand title of 'Supreme Commander,' United States reporters and the American public could be deluded into believing that Eisenhower was actually commanding something. Roosevelt did not usually interfere with Marshall's handling of the war and General Eisenhower was given wide latitude in occupied countries to handle civil, political and military matters. Robert Sherwood wrote, ". . . Roosevelt respected the judgment of his Chiefs of Staff, and there were not more than two occasions in the entire war when he overruled them . . . although there were various times when the

---

[794] Leonard Mosley, Marshall: *Hero for Our Times*, (New York, Hearst, 1982), 286, 287.

[795] Dallek, 503. Italics added.

Chiefs of Staff were not in complete agreement among themselves and the President . . . had to decide between one point of view and another."[796] As long as things were running smoothly, President Roosevelt saw little reason to intervene.

British Prime Minister Winston Churchill was just the opposite; as both Prime Minister and Minister of Defense he intervened constantly with British commanders in Europe, usually on a daily basis. He would also badger and bully General Eisenhower when he suspected the British viewpoint was not being given due consideration by the Americans. Three hundred years of empire building had left the British committed to running military operations and terribly fond of their own strategic plans. During World War II, unfortunately, British strategic plans often led to disappointing results.

Although the appointment of General Bernard L. Montgomery was a grave disappointment to the American Chiefs of Staff and to Eisenhower, it was not immediately perceived as a threat to the Anglo-American Alliance. Eisenhower would have preferred working with General Harold Alexander, but Alan Brooke and the British Chiefs strongly supported Montgomery.[797] The British War Cabinet knew General Alexander had worked well with the Americans; this unfortunate bit of information probably worked against him.[798]

Montgomery finally won the appointment to command *Overlord.* Montgomery did not work well with anyone. R. W. Thompson wrote, "Montgomery's invincible bloody-mindedness and his sense of infallibility may have been just what the British wanted following their changed status after Quebec and Teheran, and their grievous disappointments in the Eastern Mediterranean."[799] Given the fragile nature of any military alliance, General Montgomery was an extremely poor choice to command the Allied army.

A British War Cabinet memo dated 15 December 1943 suggested that the appointment was made, ". . . both on the merits and from the point of view of its reception by public opinion."[800] Apparently public opinion

---

[796]   Sherwood, 446. This point is disputed by Eric Larrabee in *Commander In Chief,* (New York, Simon & Schuster, 1988), 15. He cited Kent Roberts Greenfield's list of, ". . . some twenty-two major decisions made by Roosevelt 'against the advice, or over the protests, of his military advisers . . . .'"

[797]   Ronald Lewin, *Churchill as Warlord,* (New York: Stein and Day, 1982), 232.

[798]   R.W. Thompson, *The Montgomery Myth,* 251.

[799]   R.W. Thompson, *The Montgomery Myth,* 251.

[800]   Martin Gilbert, *Road to Victory, Winston S. Churchill 1941-1945,* (London: Stoddart, 1986), 606.

clinched the War Cabinet's vote for Montgomery; based strictly on military accomplishments, the case for Montgomery was very weak.

Churchill later described the War Cabinet's selection to Roosevelt, ". . . but the War Cabinet consider that the public confidence will be better sustained by the inclusion of the well known and famous name of Montgomery, and I agree with them as the operation will be to many people heart-shaking."[801] As Montgomery had done nothing in either Sicily or Italy to enhance his reputation, the glorious standing he enjoyed with the British public in early 1944 was due almost solely to his victories in North Africa.

The cocky little British general selected to lead *Overlord* was certain that the Allies had selected the right man to command their armies. He was a small man, thin, with a beaked-pointy nose and a high pitched, squeaky voice. Montgomery's political skills, which had garnered him the choice command within the British Army, would now be on center stage in the most important Anglo-American offensive of the war. Churchill and the War Office would prefer history record that Montgomery's selection was based solely on the merits. But it seems clear that Montgomery's immense popularity with the British people played a significant role in his selection to Command *Overlord's* Ground Forces.

Montgomery was a very strange personality. He tolerated no disagreement and preferred the company of young men who were lieutenants, captains or majors. "In his limited sphere he heard only those things he wished to hear. No voice would dare to question his authority in the smallest matter, and his generals were compelled to use the greatest tact in approaching him on any serious matter in which their ideas might be in conflict with his own."[802] In North Africa, three of Montgomery's staffers were convinced that his next operation [*Supercharge*] had a better chance for success if it was conducted further south, further from the coast; but Montgomery did not want to listen to their ideas. So Bill Williams, Dick McCreery and Francis de Guingand got together and hatched a plot to convince Montgomery that moving the axis of the attack away from the coast was actually his idea. Bill Williams remembered what de Guingand told McCreery, "Look I will go and talk to Monty about it again—don't you, because . . . he wouldn't do it. But if one can persuade him it's his own idea, so to speak, then I'm sure it's the right

---

[801] Prime Minister's Personal Telegram to the President, No. 514 dated 21 December 1943. See Gilbert, 606.

[802] R.W. Thompson, *Churchill and the Montgomery Myth*, 178.

thing to do."[803] Unfortunately, there was not always time in the middle of a battle to play psychological tricks on the commanding officer.

The stakes for Great Britain in 1944 were huge. The British were virtually bankrupt. Lend-lease shipments from the United States were the only thing keeping the British government solvent.[804] Montgomery would be commanding Great Britain's last great army. If the divisions coming ashore in Second British Army were destroyed, they would simply have to be written off because the British did not have the manpower reserves to rebuild them. Even if the invasion succeeded, the British would soon run out of men to cover replacements for those men who would become battlefield casualties.

The British had a poor reputation for letting their political savvy influence strategic decisions. Much of the problem was traceable to their Prime Minister, who often overestimated the ability of the force he was sending into harm's way, or underestimated the enemy, which was just as bad. "The American Chiefs of Staff believed that [Churchill] . . . had an incurable predilection for 'eccentric operations,' which had guided him in the First as well as the Second World War; he preferred operations which depended on surprise, deception and speed, in terrain . . . where there was not sufficient room for huge ground forces to be deployed."[805] Churchill's military strategy was based on the knowledge that the British Army did not have the manpower required to support infantry operations of more than ten or fifteen divisions.

The British Army was incapable of defending the Empire. Rather than make the hard decisions to determine what had to be saved for the Empire to survive and what could be temporarily sacrificed, the British tried to defend everything. This led to disaster in Greece, in the Far East and in North Africa, twice.

No one could accuse the Americans of playing politics in North Africa, Sicily or in Italy. The truth was the Americans did not want to be there. The US Army went into North Africa in 1942 simply because President Roosevelt wanted to see American boys in action against Germany in 1942. Given their limited means, the British and Americans agreed that North Africa was the one place they could engage the Germans in 1942 without courting disaster. In spite of American protests, it was a sound decision. By delaying

---

[803]   Bill Williams' interview with Nigel Hamilton, from Hamilton, *Making,* 828, 829.
[804]   Barnett, *The Pride and the Fall,* 38, 51.
[805]   Sherwood, 591.

the invasion of France until 1944, the British did their American Ally a very great favor. An invasion of Western Europe undertaken any earlier than the spring of 1944 would have·resulted in almost certain disaster.

The Americans fought for the cross-channel invasion because their strategic planners [Eisenhower, Leonard Gerow and Albert Wedemeyer] had determined that Northwestern Europe provided the best place to bring major elements of the German Army to battle and to destroy it. There was no politics involved in the decision; there was nothing in Northwestern Europe the Americans wanted. They had no treaties or alliances with any European country. Northwestern Europe, with its excellent road and communications network was simply judged the best place to engage and defeat the German Army.

The British, on the other hand, had political arrangements with nearly every nation in Europe. It was no secret that politics often influenced British military decisions; and the military event with the most political significance in 1944 was the Anglo-American invasion. Montgomery had been given command of Eighth Army in North Africa for political reasons, to quell public discontent with Churchill's military strategy. He fought a battle at Second El Alamein with limited strategic but with great political importance leading to his coronation in the press as the best British general since Wellington. He had succeeded politically far beyond everyone's reasonable expectations. Montgomery's reputation and the reputation of the Eighth Army he commanded became a lifeline for Churchill's political fortunes in Great Britain. As long as Montgomery commanded the most visible British Army in Europe, Churchill and the government controlled press could never let him lose.[806]

Montgomery was an excellent strategist but a poor tactician. He never completed the final step in becoming an infantry commander. He could never determine with certainty that this tactic was possible, but that tactic was not. He could never fix and destroy his opponent and only rarely considered his opponent's options. He had great difficulty in seeing the battlefield from his opponent's viewpoint. Since he seldom went to the front himself, he saw battles unfolding through the eyes of young liaison officers, who knew from experience what pleased their 'master' and what did not. Montgomery saw what he wanted to see and heard what he wanted to hear; most other things he managed to block out of his daily life and out of his mind.

By the time he left North Africa, it was as if Maud Montgomery, his mother, was running Eighth Army. In Maud's house, "Maud ruled; and her

---

[806] Perret, 412.

rule . . . was sometimes despotic and often blind."[807] Montgomery seldom received advice from any senior officer, with the exception of Alan Brooke; because he did not allow other officers his own age to loiter around his tactical headquarters. Nor did he tolerate any disagreement or unsolicited suggestions. Officers who spoke their minds around Montgomery were soon banished from his headquarters and from Eighth Army. Generals Herbert Lumsden and A.H. Gatehouse, the best armored commanders in the British Army, were relieved of their commands after Second El Alamein. In Maud's house Maud ruled, and her rule was absolute.

Montgomery could sort out the proper strategy, and given enough time, he was a sound planner. But Montgomery was best at developing his plan in an organized form and going over the plan sequentially, point by point, in a masterful presentation that reduced complicated operations down to a few basic points. His plan could then be easily understood by all levels of the command. Montgomery never had a problem drafting and presenting plans. It was always later, in the execution phase that his plans began to unravel. Armored commanders continued to shake their heads at the missions Montgomery assigned their units.

On 23 December 1943, while he was commanding Eighth Army in Italy, Montgomery received a note from his friend the C.I.G.S., Alan Brooke. It advised him that he had been selected to command British 21st Army Group for the invasion of northwestern France.[808] A few days later, Montgomery flew to Algiers for discussions with US General Dwight Eisenhower, who had been appointed the Supreme Commander for the invasion. Montgomery later wrote Brooke about their discussions, "Eisenhower has told me that he wants me to be his head soldier and to take complete charge of the land battle. Initially there will be only one Allied GHQ and this HQ will conduct the war."[809] They discussed the command arrangements, how they would function and how many army or army group headquarters they would need to set-up prior to the invasion.

Montgomery returned to Italy for a tearful farewell with Eighth Army officers and on December 31st he flew to Marrakesh to spend the night with Prime Minister Churchill. There Montgomery got his first look at the plans for *Overlord* created by an Anglo-American joint staff commanded by British Lieutenant-General Frederick Morgan. The first thing Montgomery noticed

---

[807] Hamilton, *Making,* 4, 5.
[808] Hamilton, *Master*, 465.
[809] Hamilton, *Master*, 475, 476.

about the plan was that the invasion force was too small and the landing area too constricted. Eisenhower had seen the same thing as had everyone else who looked at the plan. Typically, Montgomery and his supporters made a great fuss about his insistence that the invasion beachhead be enlarged, just as they had in North Africa over Auchinleck's supposed 'orders to retreat to the Delta.' Most of it was simply an exaggeration intended to enhance Montgomery's reputation.

General Morgan's problem was that he had been allocated a specific number of landing craft for the infantry and cargo airplanes to fly in the paratroopers. He had to match the size of the invasion force with the number of landing craft and airplanes he had available to accomplish the mission. The Allies later decided to postpone the invasion for one month to make an additional month's production of landing craft available for the invasion.

Montgomery did make several excellent suggestions after he had seen the invasion plans. As he explained to the prime minister, he wanted, "The initial landings . . . made on the widest possible front . . . Corps must . . . develop their operations from their own beaches. British and American areas of landing must be kept separate . . . a good port [must be] secured quickly for the British and American forces."[810] These were all excellent points. Montgomery's insistence on 'simplicity, order and precision' paid great dividends to the Allied cause both during the planning stages and in the first weeks after the invasion. The operation was vastly complex, and there were mistakes. But the overall plan was sound, almost brilliant. For this British Generals Montgomery and Morgan must share the credit. Eisenhower gave Montgomery carte blanche to run the Allied ground campaign in Normandy and Montgomery had left no doubt in anyone's mind that he was the commander.

As planning progressed, one feature near the French coastline stood out above all the others. It was the old Norman town of Caen. It was the major rail, roadway and communications center in Normandy. It was the largest city in the invasion area. The ground south and east of Caen was relatively flat, it contained several airfields which allied fighters desperately needed to reduce their flying time to the front. General Frederick Morgan wrote, "Above and beyond everything it was evident from the first moment that the objective of supreme importance was the town of Caen with its command of communications . . . With Caen, the key, firmly in our grasp the puzzle

---

[810]   Hamilton, *Master*, 488.

seemed to resolve itself with a tenable logic."[811] Montgomery agreed. He assigned Second British Army the task of capturing Caen on D-day.

Most historical problems with the war in Europe involve the feisty little British general. This is the same general who later claimed that all his battles went exactly according to plan. Montgomery separated the functions of his Tactical Headquarters and his 21st Army Group Main Headquarters. During most of the Normandy campaign his Main Headquarters remained back in England. According to Nigel Hamilton, ". . . the more Monty commanded from his Tactical Headquarters, the less constructive use he made of his Main Headquarters, which became increasingly a rear headquarters, *used for historical purposes rather than being intimately involved in the day-to-day fortunes of the battle.*"[812] When Air Marshal Tedder wrote that Montgomery 'has so skillfully adjusted the historical record,' this is probably what he was talking about.[813]

At Teheran the Americans, with considerable help from the Russians, got the British to approve *Overlord* and a second invasion in Southern France codenamed *Anvil*. The British would have preferred to continue their strategy of attacking the periphery of German occupied Europe in the Eastern Mediterranean or in Greece. British General John Kennedy wrote, "Had we had our way, I think there can be little doubt that the invasion of France would not have been done in 1944."[814] The British went along with American strategy not because they wanted to, but because they had to. British membership in the 'Big Three', their inclusion with the United States and the Soviet Union in the front rank of the world's great military powers depended on it. *Overlord and Anvil were the price Great Britain paid to remain a great power.*

The British had agreed to both invasions, but they didn't like either one. Eisenhower had muted some of the British criticism directed at *Overlord* with his subtle appointment of General Montgomery to command all Allied ground forces for the invasion. British angst eventually attached itself to the invasion of Southern France. As the number one American officer in Britain, Eisenhower found himself in the middle of bitter arguments over *Anvil*.

Montgomery had taken some time off from his *Overlord* planning to consider the *Anvil* Operation. Like most British officers he was opposed to

---

[811]   Morgan, 159.

[812]   Hamilton, *Master*, 823. Italics added.

[813]   Letter, Lord Tedder to B.H. Liddell Hart, 7 March 1963. From D'Este, *Decision*, 494.

[814]   Sir John Kennedy, *The Business of War*, Edited by Bernard Fergusson, (New York: William Morrow, 1958), 305.

Anvil. Montgomery believed that the Americans in Washington were too far removed from the battles taking place in Italy to be able to form ". . . (a) tactical picture . . . as to what is going on in Italy . . ."[815] Montgomery thought that the British, with more direct communications in the Mediterranean, had formed a better picture of the events taking place in Italy. In his diary, Montgomery wrote, "The British Chiefs of Staff in London 'get at' EISENHOWER and he is accused by Washington of being influenced by the British. So it is very necessary that we should all try and save EISENHOWER from reproaches from WASHINGTON, and save his face when he wants to come down hard on the side of what we want to do."[816] Montgomery was discussing *Anvil,* but he could have been talking about any point of Allied disagreement. Nigel Hamilton called this Eisenhower's 'piggy-in-the-middle' dilemma.

Montgomery's sense that Eisenhower could be of political use to the British was correct but he was tardy in reaching that conclusion. Winston Churchill had been using Eisenhower as a buffer between British interests and the Americans since the middle of 1942.[817]

If the Americans were stuck with Montgomery, the British were stuck with Eisenhower and they made the most of it. The care with which the British nurtured Eisenhower's position within the alliance was certainly worth the effort. Unfortunately, there were limits. The British would eventually make such an Anglophile out of the Supreme Commander that some of his decisions created negative political reactions in Washington. The British eventually discovered that they could not always protect Eisenhower from American politics.

The final presentation of Allied plans for Overlord was held at St Paul's School on May 15th. It was an august occasion. The King of England was present, as were the British Prime Minister, the British Chiefs of Staff and Field Marshal Jan Smuts from South Africa all seated in the front row. Mere ". . . generals sat behind on hard wooden benches."[818]

General Eisenhower opened the meeting and made several brief comments. He quickly turned the meeting over to his Allied Ground Forces Commander, General Montgomery. Nigel Hamilton wrote, ". . . that Montgomery, not Eisenhower, was the driving force behind the invasion."[819]

---

[815]   Hamilton, *Master,* 591.

[816]   Hamilton, *Master,* 541.

[817]   Callahan, *Churchill and His Generals,* 164. Also see Sherwood, 615.

[818]   Hamilton, *Master,* 581.

[819]   Hamilton, *Master,* 581.

That is fair. There can be little doubt General Montgomery's influence on the final Overlord plan was dominant. The clarity, the simplicity and the precision with which the invasion plan detailed the movement of men and supplies onto the Normandy beaches were all hallmarks of General Montgomery's meticulous planning process. He deserves full credit for it. The most complicated operation in the history of modern warfare was successful; and it succeeded because it was based on a sound plan. The invasion plan would be General Montgomery's major contribution to the Allied war effort.

While Montgomery was clearly the driving force behind the plans for Overlord, the strategic plan Montgomery was following originated in the US War Department's WPD [War Plans Division] section from a report prepared by then Major Albert Wedemeyer. Wedemeyer had prepared the report, called 'the Victory Program', to fulfill a 9 July 1941 Presidential request for a plan in the event the United States ever found itself at war with Germany.[820] Wedemeyer's Victory Program was the source for US strategic plans to invade northwest Europe, and was endorsed by subsequent heads of WPD Leonard Gerow and Dwight Eisenhower. It could honestly be said that Eisenhower helped to determine the strategy, while Montgomery prepared the operational plans.

Montgomery's presentation at St Paul's included a highly accurate and insightful assessment of Erwin Rommel's likely plan for a counterattack. "Rommel is an energetic and determined commander;" Montgomery told his audience, "he has made a world of difference since he took over. He is best at the spoiling attack . . . He will [try] . . . to 'Dunkirk' us . . . by using his own tanks well forward."[821] This was exactly what Rommel attempted to do.

The detail Montgomery laid out at St Paul's School for the main Allied attack was similar to the plan he had proposed for the invasion of Sicily. Both sets of plans called for a major effort from Montgomery's British divisions. Montgomery's D-day objectives for Second British Army included the town of Caen. Elsewhere he told his listeners, "We must blast our way on shore and get a good lodgement before the enemy can bring sufficient reserves up to turn us out . . . We must gain space rapidly, and peg out claims well inland."[822] Montgomery mentioned the highly critical nature of their endeavor; he said

---

[820]   Wedemeyer, 16, 17.
[821]   Hamilton, *Master*, 586.
[822]   Hamilton, *Master*, 588.

the beach invasion, ". . . will be a terrific party . . ."[823] Montgomery asked for the full and complete support from Allied naval and air forces.

Montgomery went on to explain how he thought the battle would develop. He told the audience, "Once we can get control of the main enemy lateral Grandville-Vire-Argentan-Falaise-Caen, and the area enclosed in it is firmly in our possession, then we will have the lodgement area we want and can begin to expand."[824] By all accounts Montgomery's presentation was magnificent. His absolute confidence in himself and in the plan was remarkable. One of his assistants remarked, "Monty was at his best."[825]

A lunch with South African Field Marshal Jan Smuts added to Montgomery's already substantial burden. He was already responsible for Great Britain's last great field army. Now Smuts related the depressing condition he saw evolving for post-war Europe, ". . . unless Britain took a firm hand in ensuring security and peace . . ."[826] Smuts asked Montgomery to speak out. According to Montgomery, he was asked, ". . . to speak out and say these things; he said I must give the lead in the matter . . . He said that I had made a great name, and would make a greater one still. I could say practically what I liked; my position with the public in ENGLAND was secure and they would 'swallow' whatever I said."[827] Already responsible for the last great British Army, now Smuts hung the future of Europe across Montgomery's narrow shoulders. Hamilton says that Montgomery was, ". . . flattered by Smut's attention."[828]

What else Montgomery carried away from his conversation with Field Marshal Smuts is not clear. We know that he and Alan Brooke had already convinced each other that the Americans were utterly incompetent when it came to making war. Smuts was probably suggesting that the Americans would again leave Europe, as they had done after the First World War; or that they simply did not understand European politics. Here was an added inducement, if indeed one was needed, for Montgomery and his British mentors to retain control of the Allied Armies throughout the war, regardless of those political accommodations which had been made as a sop to the Anglo-American alliance. We know from the historical record that

[823] Hamilton, *Master*, 588.
[824] Hamilton, *Master*, 588.
[825] Hamilton, *Master*, 589.
[826] Montgomery's diary of 17 May 44, See Hamilton, *Master*, 590.
[827] Montgomery's diary of 17 May 44, See Hamilton, *Master*, 590.
[828] Montgomery's diary of 17 May 44, See Hamilton, *Master*, 590.

Montgomery was largely successful in influencing Allied strategy nearly through the end of the war.

Just before the invasion, Montgomery traveled around to see every one of the British, Canadian and United States divisions which would take part in the invasion. He talked to all the officers. The response was overwhelmingly positive. Hamilton wrote, "No general in history had done as much as Monty in this respect."[829] Hamilton was right; Montgomery sold himself and he sold his plan. Allied cooperation right before the invasion was intense; most officers were studying their unit's invasion plans, intent on fulfilling their missions. They carried an almost unbearable sense of excitement produced by the certain knowledge that they would soon be participants in one of history's great events. It would require less than a month in Normandy for the Allies to exhibit signs of the animosity which would eventually compromise the alliance.

The Allied landings were scheduled for June 5, but had to be postponed one day because of the bad weather. Paratroopers were dropped during the night of June 5/6 and the infantry divisions landed the following morning. The invasion went well on all the beaches except for the 1st Infantry Division landing at Omaha Beach. Here the heavy seas caused most of the DD [dual drive] tanks to sink in the English Channel before they hit the beaches. These tanks were supposed to swim ashore to support the infantry landings.[830] The layout of the terrain, especially the high bluffs overlooking Omaha Beach gave the German defenders an enormous advantage over the attacking infantry. The unexpected presence of the excellent German 352nd Infantry Division near Omaha Beach on maneuvers added to the American's woes.[831] By the end of the day the Americans, despite heavy casualties, had scratched out a small beachhead at Omaha.

None of the Allied invasion forces managed to reach their D-day objectives. The most serious German counterattack on June 6 came in the British sector where elements of 21st Panzer Division attacked north out of Caen toward the sea past Douvres near Luc-Ser-Mer.[832] The Germans had to withdraw when British paratroopers got behind the attacking armored units.

On June 7 advance elements of 12th SS Panzer Division [Hitlerjugend] began arriving in Normandy and went into the line left of 21st Panzer and

---

[829]   Hamilton, *Master*, 596.
[830]   Bradley, *A Soldier's Story*, 268, 270.
[831]   Bradley, *A Soldier's Story*, 272, 276.
[832]   Hastings, *Overlord*, 119.

west of Caen. German I SS Panzer Corps was given command of the Caen sector with orders to repeat the attack of 21st Panzer north of Caen, but with stronger forces.[833] Montgomery's 3rd Canadian Infantry Division moved inland on June 7 and ran into the forward elements of 12th SS Panzer Division. Hastings wrote, "Throughout June 7 and 8, the Canadians and the fanatical teenagers of the SS Hitler Jugend fought some of the fiercest actions of the campaign, with heavy loss to both sides."[834] Montgomery launched three attacks at Caen; all were beaten back with heavy losses by German defenders.

The German I SS Panzer Corps finally organized a counterattack to throw the Allies back into the ocean on June 9. The attack never got started. Hans Speidel described the saturation bombing and naval gunfire which caught the I SS Panzer Corps as it was forming up for an attack. After a few local successes the attack was called off with heavy German losses in men and material.[835]

On the night of June 10/11, the Germans attempted another attack. This attack was planned by General Baron Geyr von Schweppenburg, the commanding officer of Panzer Group West. Just before the attack was set to go forward, Allied saturation bombing destroyed the headquarters of Panzer Group West, killing the Chief of Staff, the Operations Officer and several other headquarters officers. The attack had to be called off before it was launched. In less than a week the Allies had demonstrated an ability to deliver superior firepower to any point along their front, thoroughly frustrating their enemy's ability to eliminate the Allied beachhead.

None of this was lost on Erwin Rommel, Commanding German Army Group B. On June 10, Rommel wrote, "The effect of the heavy naval guns is so immense that no operation of any kind is possible in the area commanded by this rapid fire artillery, either by infantry or tanks."[836] Eventually Allied naval guns would engage German targets more than twenty miles from the coastline. Montgomery's reluctance to launch an attack in the Caen sector was based on expectations of a colossal German counterattack, an attack which never came.

German divisions continued to arrive on Montgomery's front near Caen. The German 711th Infantry Division took up defensive positions along the

---

[833] Speidel, 80.
[834] Hastings, *Overlord*, 123, 124.
[835] Speidel, 80, 81.
[836] Rommel, 477.

east flank between Caen and the coastline, 21st Panzer was on their left near Caen. 716th Infantry Division had moved into the line just west of Caen and on their left the 12th SS Hitler Jugend took up positions on June 7 and 8. Leading elements of General Fritz Bayerlein's excellent Panzer Lehr Division arrived in Normandy on June 9, the bulk of the division arrived the following day. It took up defensive positions just west of 12th SS Panzer near Tilly Sur Seulles.

Unable to crack the German center at Caen, Montgomery decided to try a left hook at Villers Bocage, where intelligence told him German resistance would be less organized. Montgomery decided to launch a left-right combination attack on his extreme flanks. On the eastern flank, he would pass the 51st Highland Infantry Division through British paratroopers holding the bridgehead east of the Orne River. The Highlanders attack made little progress.

At the extreme west end of the British line the 7th Armored Division attacked through the infantry holding defensive positions. Despite suffering few casualties, they made little progress. By the evening of June 12, they were, ". . . some six miles from the commanding hilltop town of Villers-Bocage . . ."[837] The following morning 7th Armored units bypassed weak German resistance and drove into Villers-Bocage. At about 9:00 that morning the colonel commanding the lead battalion led a reconnaissance party into nearby woods while the remainder of the 4th County of London Yeomanry dismounted and took a break by the roadside. The relaxed British tankers were soon observed by German Tiger tank commander, Michael Wittman. Without infantry support and less than adequate reconnaissance south of Villers, the British southern flank was completely exposed.

Wittman ordered his Tiger tank to move forward: "Charging down the stationary line, he slammed shell after shell into armor and trucks at almost point-blank range, finally ramming a last Cromwell ruthlessly aside . . . he destroyed three tanks of the County of London Yeomanry's HQ group . . ."[838] The day's toll on British armor was 25 tanks and 28 other armored vehicles destroyed.[839] Michael Wittman's five Tiger tanks had stopped Montgomery's left hook cold.

As the British 7th Armored Division pulled back from Villers-Bocage, American artillery shelled the town. 2nd Panzer moved into position west of Panzer Lehr. The Germans had plugged the last hole in their line opposite

---

[837]   Hastings, *Overlord*, 131.
[838]   Hastings, *Overlord*, 132.
[839]   Hastings, *Overlord*, 133.

Montgomery's forces. By June 12 it was obvious the British were having problems at Caen. Their front at Caen had moved only a few miles in any direction since D-day. The Germans still held Caen.

The Americans on the western flank had recovered from their set-backs on D-day. They had consolidated their beachheads, cleared the Foret De Cerisy in the Allied center and pushed their front line nearly 20 miles inland to the town of Caumont.

Dating from June 12/13, the battle for ground in Normandy became a brutal slugging match with high casualties for both sides. There was no more easy ground, no more weakly defended sectors. The Allies would be forced to sacrifice their men to secure the lodgement area Montgomery had asked for prior to the invasion.

The Allies could not afford to be roped off in a restricted area. They needed the ground south of Caen for their airplanes. They needed ground on both flanks to deploy the balance of their forces waiting in Great Britain and back in the United States. Allied casualty lists grew. Getting out of Normandy was going to be a long, hard, brutal fight. It was going to be more difficult for the British; they could not afford the losses.

The Germans were also desperate; they were getting few reinforcements in men and tanks. Rommel estimated that he was losing, ". . . an average of two thousand five-hundred to three-thousand [men] a day . . ."[840] The British and Americans were slowly eroding the strength of German Army Group B. Rommel and von Rundstedt met with Hitler at Soissons on June 17 to ask his permission to conduct a limited withdraw from Normandy. Rommel later explained the plan: "Infantry divisions to be put into the Orne sector. Panzer divisions . . . committed to remain west of Caen and reserve formations to be assembled on the flanks. After . . . the approach march, a limited withdraw to be made southwards, with the object of launching an armored thrust into the flank of the advancing enemy and *fighting the battle outside the range of the enemy's naval artillery* . . ."[841] Hitler refused to sanction any plans for the withdrawal.

Montgomery followed-up the attacks at Villers-Bocage with Operation *Epsom*. It was his second attempt to take Caen from the west. It would involve an attack by the newly arrived British VIII Corps, commanded by General R.N. O'Connor. O'Connor had been the hugely successful commander of British XIII Corps when he was captured in the desert in 1941. He spent

---

[840] Rommel, 486.
[841] Rommel, 479. Italics added.

the next two years as a guest of the Italians, but later escaped. British XXX Corps' 49th Infantry Division would attack on the extreme right toward Rauray. The VIII Corps would attack between Rauray and St Mauvieu with 15th Infantry Division on the left and 43rd Infantry Division on the right protecting the flanks of the 11th Armored Division in the center. The armored division's forward elements were aimed across the Odon River at Baron and on to Hill 112 to the southeast.

The initial attack on the morning of June 26 made excellent progress on a wide front; but bad luck continued to plague British offensives. As the British attack was gaining some success through Grainville and Coleville, the Germans began to mount a series of counterattacks against their exposed southern flank. General Paul Hausser's II SS Panzer Corps was arriving from the Eastern Front with the 9th and 10th SS Panzer Divisions.

On June 29 the II SS Panzer Corps launched a major counterattack on the southern British flank between Gavrus and Grainville. These attacks were skillfully repulsed by British infantry with excellent air support. General Dempsey, commanding British Second Army, was afraid that the German panzers might cut off his exposed 11th Armored Division on the east side of the Odon River, so he ordered the Division withdrawn back to the west banks of the Odon. The next day, without armored support, Hill 112 fell to the Germans and Montgomery called off Operation *Epsom*. According to Max Hastings, Epsom cost the British Second Army 4,020 men.[842]

Casualties were becoming a problem for Montgomery. General Kenneth Strong, SHAEF's Intelligence Officer, wrote about a call Eisenhower took from the Prime Minister: "I remember . . . being with Eisenhower . . . when Churchill telephoned him from London. Churchill's request was that if possible Eisenhower should avoid too many British casualties; British losses had been severe, and Britain was being assaulted by the V-weapons. Eisenhower understood the point at once, but if Britain wished to be in the van of the battle, as Montgomery had suggested, British casualties could not be avoided."[843] Strong's quote is not dated, but fits into a late June time frame. Max Hastings wrote, "By early July . . . The problem of infantry casualties, a matter of concern to the Americans, had become a crisis for the British . . . Already battalions had been broken up to fill the ranks of others in the line; now came the possibility that entire divisions might have to be

---

[842]   Hastings, *Overlord*, 141.

[843]   Sir Kenneth Strong, *Intelligence at the Top*, (New York: Doubleday, 1969), 203.

disbanded."[844] British infantry units were experiencing very high casualty rates in Normandy. This was not surprising. The British endured World War I casualty rates because they were using World War I infantry tactics.[845]

Until late July the British and American armies were approximately the same size. In late July and August additional US divisions were shipped to Europe. The number of American soldiers on the continent began to outnumber the British. As the overall British contribution to the Allied cause was being reduced, Montgomery's saw his chances for retaining overall command of Allied Ground Forces slipping away.

British casualties were just one of Montgomery's problems. The Germans still held Caen. The nasty word 'stalemate' was being whispered between Allied journalists and the name most commonly associated with the Allies' failure to gain ground was the British General in charge of Allied Ground Forces. General Smith, Eisenhower's Chief of Staff later wrote: "By June 30 the British Army had *not* captured Caen, and now Montgomery issued his first directive that showed *an intension of holding on the left and breaking through on the right.* He directed the British forces to contain the greatest possible part of the enemy forces. This was a correct evaluation, brought about by the German reaction at Caen."[846]

Martin Blumenson believed that the failure to take Caen, ". . . was the greatest single disappointment of the invasion."[847] While Montgomery's failure to take Caen did not dramatically alter Allied strategy in Normandy, it did intensify the already strained relations between Montgomery and his American Allies and between Montgomery and the airmen. It looked to the Americans like they were doing most of the fighting, while the British were sitting down at Caen. Carlo D'Este wrote, ". . . [M]any American officers . . . were unable to understand the reasons for Montgomery's actions and suspecting that U.S. forces were being used as sacrificial lambs while the British dallied around Caen."[848]

Montgomery had promised Caen to the Allied airmen on D-day or shortly thereafter. Thirty days later he still did not have Caen and showed no sense of urgency in getting it. The Commander of the British 2nd Tactical

---

[844] Hastings, *Overlord,* 221.

[845] Callahan, *Churchill and His Generals,* 140.

[846] Memorandum from General B. Smith. See Chandler (Ed.) *The Eisenhower Papers, Vol. III,* 1969. Italics in the original.

[847] Martin Blumenson, *Breakout and Pursuit,* (Washington, DC: US Department of the Army, 1963), 13, 14.

[848] D'Este, Decision, 299.

Air Force, Air-Marshal Coningham, and Air-Marshal Tedder, Eisenhower's Assistant Commander at SHAEF were both bitterly critical of Montgomery's failed offensives at Caen.

Eisenhower had criticized Montgomery's slow-motion tactics to Prime Minister Churchill. This produced an argument between Churchill and Brooke at a meeting on July 6. According to Brooke, "He [Churchill] began to abuse Monty because operations were not going faster, and apparently Eisenhower had said that he was over-cautions. I flared up and asked him if he could not trust his generals for five minutes instead of belittling them."[849] Montgomery would come under increasing pressure from both Eisenhower and Churchill to mount stronger attacks. This date also marked a month since D-day, ". . . yet objectives targeted for capture that first day [Caen] . . . was no closer to being attained. Amidst a growing tide of criticism, the time had arrived when the capture of Caen could no longer be put off despite Montgomery's plethora of problems."[850]

On July 7, Eisenhower wrote a letter to Montgomery, asking him to launch a large attack as soon as possible. He told the British general, "I am familiar with your plan for generally holding firmly with your left, attracting . . . the enemy armor, while your right pushes down the Peninsula . . . However, the advance on the right has been slow and laborious, due . . . to the nature of the country [hedgerows, swamps] . . . but [also] to the arrival on that front of reinforcements, I believe the 353rd Div . . . We have not yet attempted a major full-dress attack on the left flank supported by everything we could bring to bear."[851] Eisenhower was politely asking Montgomery to get moving. He could have added that Montgomery was not even holding German armor on his flank, Bayerlein's Panzer Lehr and 2nd SS Panzer Division had recently made their way into German defensive positions in front of the Americans, joining the newly arrived 353rd Infantry Division.[852]

One way to keep infantry casualties low was to blast the defenders with bombs before the attack began. On the night of July 7, wave after wave of heavy bombers pounded the old cathedral city of Caen with regular ordinance and time-delayed bombs, ". . . designed to clear the way for an assault by I Corps the following morning."[853] To keep from hitting

[849] Bryant, *Triumph*, 229.
[850] D'Este, *Decision*, 297.
[851] Chandler, (Ed.), *The Eisenhower Papers*, Vol. III, 1982.
[852] D'Este, *Decision*, 306.
[853] Hastings, *Overlord*, 222.

British troops on the ground, the bombers dropped their bombs behind the German front lines and directly into the city of Caen. Hastings wrote, "With hindsight, this action came to be regarded as one of the most futile air attacks of the war. Through no fault of their own, the airmen bombed well back from the forward line to avoid the risk of hitting British troops, and inflicted negligible damage upon the German defenses."[854] The British bombers did not kill many Germans, but they did destroy the ancient city of Caen.

British I Corps' infantry divisions were encouraged by the tremendous destruction wrought by their bombers the previous evening in Caen. Carlo D'Este wrote, "The mission given to Crocker's I Corps was to secure Caen and to establish bridgeheads south of the Orne while O'Connor's 8 Corps would prepare to renew the offensive against the Odon flank on short notice."[855] As the attack, codenamed *Charnwood*, went forward on the morning of July 8, the British attackers were disappointed to learn that the young men of the 12th SS Panzer Division were as determined as they had been prior to the bombing. The Germans had infiltrated partially destroyed buildings and used the rubble to conceal their positions. In other parts of Caen, building rubble blocked all movement.

The British attack ran into fierce resistance from Hitler's teenaged soldiers. The Canadians secured part of the Carpiquet Airfield; British infantry captured that part of Caen north of the Orne River, but the Germans still held the high ground. "From *Charnwood*, there was not even the compensation of having 'written down' significant German forces."[856]

Montgomery's enthusiasm for the invasion, for deep armored thrusts and for 'pegging out claims well inland' appeared to be waning. Only 30 days into the invasion, the briefing at St Paul's School seemed like a year ago. Historian Carlo D'Este observed, "The boldness that Montgomery had so confidently predicted before D-Day was impossible to generate in a strategy which lauded the defensive role his Second Army was playing on the eastern flank."[857]

Some officers in Second British Army were growing weary of their army's failure to gain ground. The limited, clumsy, half-hearted attacks

[854] Hastings, *Overlord*, 222.
[855] D'Este, *Decision*, 305.
[856] Hastings, *Overlord*, 223.
[857] D'Este, *Decision*, 297.

being carried out were bound to eventually affect morale. This was made worse by being told afterward that it was all Montgomery had intended.

Most British commanders were conscious of their country's manpower problems. Ronald Adam, British Adjutant General had come out to the battlefield during the second week of July. Adam had meetings with both Dempsey and Montgomery; he warned them that, ". . . if our *infantry* casualties continued at the recent rate it would be impossible to replace them, and we should have to 'cannibalize'—to break up some divisions in order to maintain the rest."[858] Given the nature of the close-in fighting in Normandy and the skillful German soldier, British manpower losses were not likely to decrease in the near future. Some officers began to deliberately limit their unit's offensive exposure if they judged that the attack was 'not on.'[859]

At some point during the first few weeks in July, officers in the British Second Army must have felt a sense of impending dread, a sense that something was not quite right. The British had failed repeatedly on their eastern flank near Caen. Erwin Rommel believed that, ". . . most senior British officers have a certain tendency to think along established lines."[860] C.I.G.S. Brooke thought that half the senior front line commanders in the British Army were not qualified for the jobs they held, but that it would be useless to fire them because there were no replacements available. He traced the British shortage in qualified officers to the horrible losses their officer corps suffered during World War I.[861]

Most of Eighth Army's training problems could be traced back to General Montgomery. He directed Eighth Army to produce a training manual for tank-infantry cooperation. This manual appeared in England in February 1944, after Montgomery had taken command of 21st Army Group. At that time Montgomery said, ". . . he regarded Eighth Army practice [for tank-infantry cooperation] as the new doctrinal norm for the British Army."[862] Montgomery had not changed his mind about the armor leading an attack against fixed defensive positions in spite of what Generals Lumsden and Gatehouse tried to explain to him back in November 1942. He also continued to split the command assignments of infantry and armored units.

---

[858] The Papers of Sir Basil Liddell Hart, Liddell Hart Centre for Military Archives, King's College, London. See D'Este, *Decision*, 260. Italics in the original.

[859] Hastings, *Overlord*, 137.

[860] Rommel, 520.

[861] Hastings, *Overlord*, 144.

[862] Callahan, *Churchill and His Generals*, 214.

Although he now assigned both infantry and armored divisions to a corps commander, his doctrine was unchanged in that the two commanders were given separate missions. This was a mistake, since Montgomery's training manual replaced a very good manual produced by Brigadier Harold Pyman [General Staff Officer for Training, British 21st Army Group] which had outlined operational cooperation between the two arms with infantry units, not armor, leading the attack. Given Montgomery's status within the British Army, the only officer who could have corrected him was Alan Brooke; and Alan Brooke thought Montgomery was the best British general since Wellington.[863]

British officers must have reacted to having one of Montgomery's 25 year old Liaison Officers lurking about their headquarters, taking down notes and reporting back to their boss that evening. The idea that every move they made was being watched by the 'master of the tidy set-piece battle' could not have induced many line officers to experiment tactically with their units.

Snooping liaison officers would have induced a 'by the book' behavior from junior front line officers. British historian T. H. Place wrote, ". . . a revealing sidelight on the awe in which Montgomery was held that Brigadier Clarke hastened to introduce the imported [tank] doctrine . . . even though he knew it to be misguided . . . Undoubtedly, he feared the consequences if caught in disobedience of the new C-in-C."[864] R.W. Thompson agreed. He wrote, "Montgomery's leadership not only failed to inspire, it inhibited and denied initiative."[865] Thompson traced Montgomery's leadership dilemma to ". . . his dedication since his earliest days to the 'set-piece battle,' the meticulous preparation *irrespective of the enemy to be encountered*, and his fear of flexibility and the 'expanding torrent.'"[866] Montgomery's students at the Staff College learned from bitter experience that any change from, ". . . . the strictly orthodox frontal assault would not be tolerated."[867] Brigadier Clarke was simply protecting his career within the British Army.

There was also a problem with non-trying units. Hastings wrote, ". . . following bloody losses and failures, many battalion commanders determined privately that they would husband the lives of their men when they were ordered into attack, making personal judgments about

[863] Callahan, *Churchill and His Generals*, 214, 215.
[864] T.H. Place, 151.
[865] R.W. Thompson, *Montgomery, The Field Marshal,* (New York, Charles Scribner's Sons, 1969), 294.
[866] R.W. Thompson, *Montgomery, Field Marshal*, 292. Italics in the original.
[867] R.W. Thompson, *Montgomery, Field Marshal*, 292.

the operation's value."[868] If they considered the operation very important, they would ask their men for a full effort and comply fully with the plan as handed down. If, on the other hand, they considered that the operation was not important or ill-advised, they would set limited objectives, making a token effort, so that the movement of their unit would appear to be in conformance with the original plan. According to Max Hastings, "The problem of 'non-trying' units was to become a thorn in the side of every division and corps commander . . ."[869]

By mid-July, with his D-day objective [Caen] still in German hands, Montgomery was under intense pressure to gain ground on the eastern flank. The airmen desperately needed the ground south and southeast of Caen for airfields and Montgomery still had not taken it. Worse, he did not appear to be in a hurry to get there. At SHEAF, British Air Marshal Tedder was bitterly critical of Montgomery's operations. Tedder wrote, "Asked on 8 July what I thought of the present Army plans and attacks, I could only reply: 'Company exercises.' That day I phoned Portal, who told me about his visit to Normandy on 7 July. He too was disturbed at the lack of progress by the Army. The problem was Montgomery, who could be 'neither removed nor moved' to action."[870]

Montgomery's staff had been working on a plan for a three armored division attack out of their bridgehead on the eastern bank of the Orne River. The original idea came from Montgomery's planner at Army Group Headquarters, Brigadier Charles Richardson during the first week in July. Richardson proposed a major operation rather than the one and two division attacks the British had been using in several smaller operations. The planners hoped to keep British casualties low by using tanks for the main attack.

By July 10, Dempsey was proposing a large attack with massed tanks out of the Orne River bridgehead. By July 12 these plans were sufficiently developed for Montgomery to write Eisenhower: "This operation will take place on Monday, July 17. Grateful if you will issue orders that the whole weight of the air power is to be available on that day to support my land battle . . . My whole eastern flank will burst into flames on Saturday. The operation on Monday may have far-reaching results . . ."[871] The following day Eisenhower wrote to Montgomery: "With respect to the plan, I am

[868]   Hastings, *Overlord,* 137.
[869]   Hastings, *Overlord*, 137.
[870]   Lord Tedder, 559.
[871]   Letter, Montgomery to Eisenhower dated 12 July 1944, from Forrest C. Pogue, *The Supreme Command,* (Washington: Center of Military History, United States Army, 1996), 188.

confident that it will reap a harvest from all the sowing you have been doing during the past weeks . . . O'Connor's plunge into his vitals will be decisive. I am not discounting the difficulties . . . but in this case I am viewing the prospects with the most tremendous optimism and enthusiasm. I would not be at all surprised to see you gaining a victory that will make some of the 'old classics' look like a skirmish between patrols."[872] The full weight of the Allied Air Force was made available for Montgomery's attack.

To his friend and mentor back in England, Montgomery wrote, "The Second Army is now very strong, it has in fact reached its peak . . . It will in fact get weaker as the manpower situation hits us. [Replacements] are not so well trained . . . [this] will have repercussions on what we can do . . . So I have decided that the time has come to have a real 'showdown' on the eastern flank, and to loose a corps of three armored divisions into the open country about the Caen-Falaise road."[873]

Brooke had been defending Montgomery in staff meetings with Churchill. Eisenhower was complaining to Churchill that the British were not doing their share of the fighting and that the Americans were taking most of the casualties. Eisenhower's statements were supported by SHAEF statisticians who provided Eisenhower with solid evidence to back his claims. Churchill would then ask Brooke what was 'his Monty' up to now. Brooke kept his protégé up to date on the political developments in London, going behind Eisenhower's back to communicate directly with Great Britain's senior Army officer in Normandy, just as Eisenhower was going outside the chain of command to communicate directly with General Marshall.

Montgomery was desperate for a British victory in Normandy. He needed to gain ground. He needed the rest of Caen and he needed to quell the criticism of his conduct of the battle. Hastings wrote, "By the time *Goodwood* was launched, for political and moral reasons he [Montgomery] was more seriously in need of a victory than at any time since D-Day. Yet from its inception the operation was flawed."[874] The plan was flawed primarily because it followed Montgomery's guidelines for tank-infantry cooperation. Montgomery's plan asked British armor to lead the attack without infantry protection. The major problem was that separate missions had been assigned to infantry and armor units, but that was not the only problem.

---

[872] Letter, Eisenhower to Montgomery dated 13 July 1944, from Pogue, *Supreme Command*, 188.

[873] Letter, Montgomery to Brooke, 14 July 1944, See Hastings, *Overlord*, 231.

[874] Hastings, *Overlord*, 231.

By July 15, Montgomery was having second thoughts about the upcoming operation; he and General Dempsey drove to General Richard O'Connor's VIII Corps Headquarters where Montgomery personally wrote out the directive for Operation *Goodwood*. According to General Dempsey: ". . . Montgomery said to him: 'Let's be quite clear on this'—and wrote out a personal directive for me, headed 'Notes on Second Army Operations.' It was the first time, and the last, that he gave such a written directive."[875] Carlo D'Este explained that Montgomery's last minute notes dramatically changed VIII Corps' mission, eliminating any mention of Falaise as a goal for his armored columns.[876]

In his book *Overlord*, Max Hastings tried to blame the VIII Corps Commander, General O'Connor, for the separate objectives the armor and infantry units were assigned.[877] Yet it seems clear from D'Este's account that these orders came directly from Montgomery; moreover, the idea of leading an attack with armor confirmed nicely with established 21st Army Group tank-infantry doctrine.[878] Any effort to blame General O'Connor for the *Goodwood* operation must ultimately fail.

The *Goodwood* attack was to be launched from a very restricted space within the Orne River bridgehead on the extreme right of Montgomery's front. The attack would be preceded by a massive air bombardment. It proposed that the three attacking armored divisions pivot southwest in front of Caen toward the high ground along the Bourgebus Ridge. The axis of advance would be a shallow 45 degrees across the German front. The main attack was to be delivered by the 7th, 11th and Guards Armored Divisions. Flank protection for the armored divisions would be provided by 3rd Infantry Division on the southern flank toward Troarn and by the 51st Infantry Division attacking into eastern edge of Caen. II Canadian Corps with 2nd and 3rd Canadian Infantry Divisions would launch a secondary attack through the center of Caen and along the western edge of the town across the Orne River.

At 0545 hours on July 18, 1676 heavy and 343 medium and light bombers dropped 7,700 tons of bombs on German positions on and southeast of Caen. The ground assault began at 0745 hours. There was not enough room in

---

[875]   General Miles Dempsey, *'Operation Goodwood'*, from D'Este, *Decision*, 364

[876]   D'Este, *Decision*, 364.

[877]   Hastings, *Overlord*, 233.

[878]   T.H. Place, ". . . it became the doctrine of 21 Army Group that in combined tank and infantry attacks the tanks should lead and the infantry should follow . . . .", 149. Also see T.H. Place, 151, for Montgomery's unwelcome influence on Brigadier Clarke of 34th Tank Brigade.

the restricted Orne River bridgehead to deploy all the vehicles of the three armored divisions. The 11th Armored Division went first, with the 7th and Guards Armored Divisions stacked up behind. The movement of men and vehicles was severely restricted by the Orne River bridges and the 51st Infantry Division's extensive minefield. Only narrow pathways through the minefield could be cleared for the tanks.[879] This caused further delays and created a huge traffic jam which lasted throughout the morning and well into the afternoon.

Bad luck seemed to hound British offensive efforts. There was evidence that the Germans knew the attack was coming. A British *ULTRA* intercept revealed that the commander of Luftflotte 3, ". . . signaled a forecast of a major British attack . . . 'south-eastwards from Caen about the night of 17-18.'"[880] The British had more bad luck when the tank carrying the only RAF Forward Air Controller with 11th Armored Division, ". . . was knocked out in the first two hours, with the result that close air support for the advance was lost."[881] Losing air cover during the initial attack was doubly unfortunate because the artillery could not be deployed to provide direct fire support, "Until the armor had cleared the start-line . . ."[882] The artillery deployed later and was in an excellent position to support the original advance of VII Corps' armor, but could not be readily redeployed to support the armor in its final drive toward Bourgebus Ridge.[883] The armor was delayed by the restricted crossings over Orne River Bridges and the minefield which could not be properly cleared in time without betraying the intention to attack.

The confusion and frustration which had plagued Montgomery's efforts in North Africa to get Lumsden's tanks over Miteiriya Ridge at the Second Battle of El Alamein were clearly in evidence during Operation *Goodwood*. "The only regiment of 7th Armored to approach its point of attack, after escaping the chaos around the Orne, did not reach 29th Brigade's battered squadrons until 5:00 p.m. by which time the latter had suffered 50 percent tank losses, 11th Armored losing a total of 126 tanks during the day. Guards Armored Division lost sixty tanks . . ."[884] Most of the British tanks lost to German 88mm guns were later recovered.

British armor and infantry divisions had been given different missions. It was a typical Montgomery decision. When the leading British armoured

[879]   Hastings, *Overlord*, 231.
[880]   Hastings, *Overlord*, 233.
[881]   Hastings, *Overlord*, 234.
[882]   Hastings, *Overlord*, 231.
[883]   Keegan, *Six Armies*, 204, 205.
[884]   Hastings, *Overlord*, 235.

squadrons got within range of the German 88 mm anti-tank guns near Cagny they lost tank after tank, stalling the offensive. The tanks were not able to advance without infantry protection.

After two days of heavy fighting, the battle became a slugging match with the Germans retaining possession of the high ground on the Bourgebus Ridge. Rain had made the battlefield a quagmire by the evening of the 20th. Montgomery pulled back his armored formations and replaced them on the front line with infantry. Operation *Goodwood* was over. The British lost about 400 tanks and suffered 5,537 casualties.[885]

Montgomery had gained the rest of the city of Caen. Montgomery's D-day objective was now firmly in his possession. It was D-day plus 43. British armor and Canadian infantry had pushed the German front at Caen back a total of seven miles, but they had not broken through the German defenses and the Germans retained firm possession of the high ground along Bourgebus Ridge, which they immediately reinforced.[886]

The axis of advance was too shallow to break through Germans defenses deployed five belts deep at Caen. Small groups of Germans with a few 88mm guns scattered along the southern British flank in Banneville, Emieville, and Cagny took a heavy toll on Guards Armored tanks crossing through their fields of fire.

Montgomery announced that he was well pleased with the results. He wired Brooke in London, "Operations this morning a complete success . . ."[887] He told the press that his army had broken through the German front at Caen. Fleet Street's headlines the next day reflected Montgomery's enthusiasm for the battle: "Second Army breaks through . . . British Army in full cry . . . Wide corridor through German front . . ."[888] None of it was true. When that became obvious few days later, the newspapers were scurrying to correct themselves. Montgomery's exaggerations should not have surprised experienced British journalists; he had destroyed the German 90th Light Division so many times in North Africa, it had become an inside joke.[889]

No one at SHEAF was laughing. Eisenhower was reported, ". . . blue as indigo over Monty's slowdown."[890] He wondered whether the Allies could afford to go through France at the rate of one-thousand tons of bombs per

885   Hastings, *Overlord*, 236.
886   Hastings, *Overlord*, 236.
887   Hastings, *Overlord*, 236.
888   Hastings, *Overlord*, 236.
889   R.W. Thompson, *Churchill and the Montgomery Myth*, 170
890   Butcher, 618.

mile.[891] Most other officers at SHAEF shared Eisenhower's opinion about Montgomery. British RAF officers were, if anything, more critical of Montgomery than Eisenhower. Lord Tedder wrote, "I told Eisenhower that his own people would be thinking that he had sold them to the British if he continued to support Montgomery without protest."[892] As the pressure on Eisenhower to do something about Montgomery mounted, it became the main topic of discussion at SHEAF. Butcher wrote, ". . . Ike is like a blind dog in a meat house—he can smell it, but he can't find it. How he will handle the situation [firing Montgomery] remains the principal suspended interest of the diary, at the moment."[893] The two major topics for discussion following *Goodwood* were Montgomery's future and the British manpower crisis.

The first generation of World War II military historians totally ignored the British manpower situation. They were reluctant to mention it, probably afraid they would be accused of being unfair to the British. But today there can be little doubt that the British manpower problem was on the minds of quite a few senior officers at Supreme Headquarters. Max Hastings suggests that the British manpower situation influenced important tactical decisions prior to *Goodwood*: "The forces assembled for the operation were not those judged necessary to meet the ground or the nature of the defenses, but those which the British then felt willing to expend—their tanks. The critical problem of manpower and infantry casualties thus directly influenced an important tactical decision."[894] Hastings statements must be tempered with the understanding that leading an attack with armor was also established 'armor-infantry doctrine' at 21st Army Group Headquarters.[895]

Harry Butcher was a Reserve Naval Officer. He served as Eisenhower's Naval Aide, public relations officer and bridge partner during the war. He wrote: "[His] friends at Naval Headquarters said they felt that Monty, his British Army Commander, Dempsey, the British corps commanders, and even those of the divisions are so conscious of Britain's ebbing manpower that they hesitate to commit an attack where a division may be lost. To replace the division is practically impossible. When it is lost, it's done and finished."[896]

Eisenhower was acutely aware of Montgomery's manpower problems. In his July 21 letter to Montgomery, Eisenhower specifically addresses

---

[891] Butcher, 617.
[892] Lord Tedder, 566.
[893] Butcher, 619.
[894] Hastings, *Overlord*, 238.
[895] T.H. Place, 148, 149.
[896] Butcher, 622.

this problem: "I think it is important that we are aggressive throughout the front . . . In [Bradley's] First Army, the whole front comes quickly into action . . . to support the main attack. Dempsey [British 2nd Army] should do the same. *The enemy has no immediately available reserves. We do not need to fear, at this moment, a great counter offensive.*"[897] Eisenhower goes on to suggest that by attacking on both flanks they will finish off the Germans in less time with fewer casualties.

The truth was that the Allies had little to fear from a large German counterattack after the first few days of the invasion. With Allied artillery and naval observers placed well forward in the infantry units and with Allied fighter-bombers controlling the skies over Normandy, the Germans had been unable, since the second week of June, to mass their forces for any large-scale offensive.

At the end of June Erwin Rommel explained his offensive limitations to Hitler, ". . . [We are limited] to night or bad weather operations, which cannot as a rule develop into anything more than operations with limited objective. Daylight action is, however, still possible—given sufficient A. A. defense—for a small armored combat group."[898] Awaiting the "great German offensive" was a ruse Montgomery employed to rest his tired British formations in defensive positions.

From a host of intelligence sources the Allies knew that the Germans in Normandy were tantalizingly close to collapse. Eisenhower acknowledged Montgomery's manpower problem, but then drove home a salient point: ". . . this way [by attacking] we will secure the greatest results in the quickest possible time . . . *I am convinced that in this way we will have in the long run the least number of casualties. I realize the seriousness of the reinforcement problem for Dempsey* . . . Eventually the American ground strength will necessarily be much greater than the British. But while we have equality in size we must go forward shoulder to shoulder, with honors and sacrifices equally shared." [899]

Eisenhower's argument was sound. The pressure on Eisenhower to do something, anything, to get Montgomery moving was becoming a political issue in the United States. When casualty figures up through 31 July came out, they showed that the Allies had captured 78,000 prisoners. The Americans had taken 64,000 German prisoners; the British had taken

[897]   Chandler, (Ed.), *The Eisenhower Papers, Vol. III,* 2018, 2019. Italics added.

[898]   Rommel, 485.

[899]   Chandler, (Ed), *The Eisenhower Papers, Vol. III,* 2019. Italics added.

14,000 prisoners.[900] These figures supported Eisenhower's claim that the British were not doing their share of the fighting.

Montgomery could ignore Eisenhower's letter. He could not ignore letters from the C.I.G.S. and his prime minister. Less than a week after Eisenhower's letter urged Montgomery to keep up his attacks, he got two more letters urging the same thing. Alan Brooke's letter was sent on July 27, he wrote: ". . . I feel personally quite certain that Dempsey must attack at the earliest possible moment on a large scale. We must not allow German forces to move from his front to Bradley's front or we shall give more cause than ever for criticism. I shall watch this end and keep you informed . . ."[901] Churchill's letter was sent the same day: ". . . I should like to know whether the attacks you spoke of to me . . . are going to come off. *It certainly seems very important for the British Army to strike hard and win through; otherwise there will grow comparisons between the two armies which will lead to dangerous recrimination and affect the fighting value of the Allied organization.*"[902]

Everyone was urging Montgomery to attack. It is interesting to compare their reasoning. Brooke wants Montgomery to attack because, otherwise, '(he) will give more reason than ever for criticism.' Churchill wants an attack because he does not want to create an unfavorable comparison of the British Army with their American allies. Only Eisenhower is urging Montgomery to attack because it is militarily the correct thing to do and because it would ultimately save British lives.

Clearly, the British tried to hide their manpower problems. D'Este suggests that Churchill would not have welcomed, "A full and frank admission of the plight of British manpower . . ."[903] In August the British disbanded their 59th Infantry Division in great secrecy. One day the division was there, the next day it was gone. Churchill fought against disbanding one division to make good the losses in others. He ordered Brooke and his staff in England to move heaven and earth to find other replacements for the casualties. Later in the war, Churchill wrote to Montgomery, *"I greatly fear that the dwindling of the British Army is a factor in France as it will affect our right to express our opinion upon strategic and other matters."*[904] The

---

[900]   Butcher, 632.

[901]   Bryant, *Triumph*, 245.

[902]   Churchill, *Triumph and Tragedy*, 29. Italics added.

[903]   D'Este, *Decision*, 265.

[904]   Churchill telegram to Montgomery, 12 December 1944, from D'Este, *Decision*, 265. Italics added.

British had become junior partners in the Alliance, but Churchill sought to project the image of Great Britain as a first class military power.

Operation *Goodwood* was one of the most incompetently planned and executed Allied offensive operations of the war. Nearly everything about the battle was botched from the start. Hastings writes, ". . . *Goodwood* failed because the concept, the plan, the preparations were unsound."[905]

General Dwight D. Eisenhower, the Supreme Allied Commander, visits British General Bernard L. Montgomery, Commanding, Allied Ground Forces and British 21st Army Group

---

[905]   Hastings, *Overlord*, 238.

To the man responsible for *Goodwood,* the operation was a personal disaster. Montgomery's military reputation within the Allied armies was shattered. "As a result of *Goodwood*, Montgomery's prestige within the Allied high command suffered damage from which it never recovered."[906] The general and the Army he had trained were utterly unprepared for the war they had to fight in France. Raymond Callahan wrote, "Even if Goodwood and other operations in Normandy revealed how faulty British doctrine still was, the army with which Montgomery would fight the rest of the war was now past major structural and doctrinal change."[907] The British Army had adopted Montgomery's 'set-piece' version of infantry tactics in the 1930's. He had been promoted to the most important command position within the British Army. By 1944 events had conspired to make Montgomery politically untouchable regardless of what happened in France.

British training and tactical doctrine were both a problem. Montgomery's 'fundamental inflexibility of mind' was certainly a large part of the problem. But so was Alan Brooke, who should have been seen what was happening in France. Part of the problem was a snobbishness and exclusiveness inherent in the British regimental system, which made it difficult to get cooperation from different branches of the army. D'Este wrote, "The problem of tank-infantry cooperation . . . had plagued the British army for too long for it to have been cured even by 1944."[908]

Nor was there any hint from the senior British commander that anything was amiss. Montgomery simply grinned at the press and told them everything was going according to plan. The only officers to question Montgomery's competence were from the Royal Air Force or Supreme Allied Headquarters. Incredibly, no senior British Army officer or member of the British government seriously questioned Montgomery's performance in France.

Perhaps more than any other British officers, Alan Brooke and Bernard Montgomery were responsible for the training and operational performance of the British Army in France. It was an army magnificently prepared to fight World War I battles on a World War II battlefield. The battlefield in Normandy rewarded those commanders competent at mobile operations and

---

[906] Hastings, *Overlord*, 238.
[907] Callahan, *Churchill and His Generals*, 218.
[908] D'Este, *Decision*, 291.

combined arms tactics. "All this might have mattered less if Montgomery had been correct." Raymond Callahan wrote, "Unfortunately, he was not."[909]

Montgomery's problems began back in the desert when he took command of Eighth Army from General Auchinleck. General Auchinleck had proposed eliminating the differences between armored and infantry divisions by combining elements of the two—so they had a common division commander. Up to that point amour and infantry divisions remained intact but were placed under corps commander. Montgomery scratched Auchinleck's plans to combine Eighth Army's infantry and armored units, just as he would dispose of Brigadier Pyman's training manual [on tank-infantry cooperation] when he took command of British 21st Army Group in 1944. Correlli Barnett wrote, "*His [Montgomery's] solution was in every way opposite to Auchinleck's and in every way wrong, for it carried the existing dangerous separatism still further.*"[910] Montgomery put all his armored divisions into one corps and his infantry divisions into another corps. Thus, their only common link was the Army Commander.[911]

Goodwood severely damaged Montgomery's reputation in France but did nothing to undermine his wonderful relationship with the C.I.G.S. or his prime minister. Montgomery's enormous popularity with the British people never wavered. But in Normandy, things were different. Montgomery's headlines began to wear thin. One officer on Montgomery's staff told Max Hastings, ". . . we were distinctly worried. We knew Monty put on this impenetrable act of confidence, whatever was happening. *But below Freddy de Guingand's level, it was difficult to judge whether this confidence was soundly based. My feeling was that we were getting into a bigger jam than he was prepared to admit.*"[912]

Montgomery never intimated to anyone, let alone a member of the British press that his battles were anything less than absolute victories. "The truth, which he never avowed even to Brooke, yet which seems self-evident from the course of events, was that in *Goodwood,* and throughout the rest of the campaign, Montgomery sought major ground gains for Second Army if these could be achieved at acceptable cost. He forsook them whenever casualties rose unacceptably. This occurred painfully often."[913]

While Montgomery conducted 'company exercises' at Caen, according to Air Marshal Tedder, the Americans were forced to bleed their way through the

909   Callahan, *Churchill and His Generals*, 214, 215. Also see T.H. Place, 149.
910   Barnett, *The Desert Generals*, 265. Italics added.
911   Barnett, *The Desert Generals*, 265.
912   Brigadier Richardson interview with Max Hastings, from Hastings, *Overlord*, 239. Italics added.
913   Hastings, *Overlord*, 239, 240.

hedgerows and swamps of the Carentan. It was true that the Americans would have an easier time replacing their losses than the British. Still, this did not make Montgomery's behavior any easier for the Americans to accept. "Until the very end of the war, the British demanded that they should be treated as equal partners in the alliance with the United States, and vied for a lion's share of Allied command positions. They could scarcely be surprised if the Americans showed resentment when the British flinched before heavy casualties . . ."[914]

Of course, the Americans were bitter, but they had to be careful not to let anything negative about the British get back to Eisenhower. An SOB was an SOB and that was okay. But if an SOB was also a British SOB, that remark would get you busted and if you were a field grade officer, it could get you busted and sent home. On July 7th George Patton confided to his diary: "I had lunch with Bradley, Montgomery and DeGuingand. After lunch, [we] went to the war tent. Here Montgomery went to great length explaining why the British had done nothing. Caen was their D-day objective, and they have not taken it yet."[915]

There was the rub. The British wanted the political kudos of Allied command and the headlines it produced; but they did not want to get involved in the heavy fighting, especially if it involved casualties. Discussing the delicate handling of Second British Army in Europe, Callahan wrote, *"All that could be done was to use it cautiously, husbanding its strength to maintain a credible British military contribution."*[916] *The 'credible military contribution' was, of course, a political calculation.*

If the British could maintain an Army of reasonable size in Europe, Winston Churchill, army public relations officers and the eager journalists on Fleet Street would take care of the rest. General Montgomery would probably say that a headline in tomorrow's paper is worth at least two divisions. All Montgomery had to do was hang on; his salvation was at hand.

Within a few days the rain which had turned Normandy into a quagmire, shutting down *Goodwood,* finally stopped and the skies began to clear. On 25 July 1944, over 2,400 Allied heavy, medium and fighter bombers were flying toward a rectangle along the St Lo-Periers road three and a half miles wide and one and a half miles deep.[917] General Bradley's Operation *Cobra* was just beginning. Despite the confusion caused by several loads of

---

[914]   Hastings, *Overlord,* 241.
[915]   Blumenson, (Ed.), *The Patton Papers, 1940-1945,* 479.
[916]   Callahan, *Churchill and His Generals,* 218. Italics added.
[917]   Bradley, *A General's Life,* 276, 280.

bombs dropping short, General 'Lightning Joe' Collins, Commanding US VII Corps, ordered three US Infantry Divisions, the 4th, 9th and 30th into the attack. German resistance was not coordinated; their communications and telephone lines had been severed during the bombing.

Sensing an uncoordinated German response, General Collins decided to commit his armor the following morning. Within six days elements of John Wood's 4th Armored Division had driven through Avranches and Pontaubault occupying all the bridges over the See and Selune Rivers at the base of the Brittany Peninsula. The Americans had turned the German's western flank. Montgomery's British Army was still stuck a few miles south of Caen, their D-day objective.

The lodgement area the Allies now possessed bore no resemblance to the lodgement area Montgomery had outlined at St Paul's School prior to D-day. Montgomery's pre-invasion lodgement area included Granville-Vire for the Americans and Argentan-Falaise-Caen for the British.[918] Montgomery expected his British Army to gain slightly more ground to the south than the Americans. As it turned out, the Americans at Pontaubault were 20 miles south of Granville and the British just south of Caen, were about 25 miles short of Argentan. This was not at all what Montgomery had planned.*

A few days later, British generals began congratulating each other over how magnificently Montgomery's plans had worked out. Brooke wrote to Montgomery, "I am delighted that our operations are going so successfully and conforming so closely to your plans."[919] Montgomery was very happy to be finally off the hook. On August 1 he wrote to the British War Department, "Everything is going very well. The full plan, which I have been working to all the time, is now slowly working out as planned. I hope to turn the right Corps of 12 Army Group westwards into Brittany tomorrow."[920] Montgomery's biographer, Nigel Hamilton, could barely restrain himself, "The sudden ripening of Monty's Normandy strategy had transformed the moment."[921] Indeed, it had.

*   See Map of The Normandy Battlefield on Page 27 to compare the actual position of the British Second Army on 31 July 1944 with the position Montgomery had forecast in his pre-invasion 'Lodgement Area.'

---

[918]   Hamilton, *Master*, 588.
[919]   Letter of 4.8.44 in Montgomery Papers. See Hamilton, *Master*, 770.
[920]   Hamilton, *Master*, 771.
[921]   Hamilton, *Master*, 770.

Chapter 10

General Montgomery's Bitter Pills

". . . his [Montgomery's] intrinsic loyalty to the 'home team' which made it intolerable for him to admit that failure might in part be due to a flawed instrument—his beloved British Army, and in the training and rehabilitation of which he had been so intimately involved. There was also his recognition that it had to be constantly 'binged up.'"[922] Alistair Horne with David Montgomery

The American breakout at St. Lo quelled rumors of an 'Allied stalemate in Normandy.' Temporarily at least, Montgomery was off the hook. Unfortunately, there were a host of other problems just ahead; problems which would drive General Montgomery to the point of desperation.

The front lines in Normandy had barely moved in two months. It had been possible for one commander to exercise some control over the battlefield. Through the end of July the pace of battle had been slow; it conformed nicely to the pace of combat preferred by the 'master of the set piece battle.' But on July 31, when the Americans turned the western German flank at Avranches, the pace of battle dramatically quickened. Eisenhower was seen flashing his famous smile. He told an aide, "If the intercepts are right, we are to hell and gone in Brittany and slicing 'em up in Normandy."[923]

Suddenly, Allied advances of 20, 40 and even 50 miles a day were routine. The battles of the lieutenants and captains had given way to a mobile battlefield where generals made decisions which had an instant impact on Allied strategy. Montgomery had never excelled on a mobile battlefield; the August battles would be his sternest test.

In the aftermath of Montgomery's *Goodwood* offensive, several officers tried to have him fired. The plot to fire the most popular general in the British Army was orchestrated by senior officers at SHAEF, many of them were British. One of Montgomery's most vehement critics at SHAEF was

---

[922] Alistair Horne with David Montgomery, *Monty, The Lonely Leader, 1944-1945,* (London: Macmillan, 1994), 149.

[923] Butcher, 630

Deputy Supreme Commander, Arthur Tedder of the Royal Air Force. In early July Tedder wrote, "I agreed with Coningham [Arthur, Montgomery's Tactical Air Commander] that the Army did not seem prepared to fight its own battles."[924] A few weeks later, Tedder's position had hardened and he was now ready to force a change in the British command. He wrote, "All the available evidence to me indicated a serious lack of fighting leadership in the higher direction of the British armies in Normandy."[925]

At the time, Tedder's criticism of Montgomery was effectively downplayed within the British government. He was portrayed as just another anti-Montgomery British airman. In retrospect, Lord Tedder's criticism was extremely accurate. The surprising thing is not that a British airman so completely understood the extent of Montgomery's problems in France, but that no one else in a position of authority within the British Army seemed to be aware of it.

On July 20, just after *Goodwood* closed down, Tedder talked to Eisenhower. According to Captain Butcher, ". . . Tedder phoned Ike from SHAEF Main [headquarters] and, reflecting the disappointment of the air at the slowness on the ground, said that the British Chiefs of Staff would support any recommendation that Ike might care to make with respect to Monty for not succeeding in going places with his big three-armored-division push."[926] Tedder later claimed that he was misquoted. He pointed out that he could not speak for the British Chiefs of Staff, particularly Alan Brooke, who continued to give Montgomery his firm support.[927]

Montgomery had, just barely, managed to retain his command. Only the political nature of the Allied command in Europe and Montgomery's great popularity with the British people saved him. It is now clear from the historical record that, given the opportunity, both General Eisenhower and Lord Tedder would have preferred to dismiss Montgomery in late July 1944.

Montgomery asked Eisenhower to keep visitors away from his headquarters for a few days because he was very busy. Eisenhower communicated Montgomery's request to the Prime Minister. According to Brooke's diary entry on July 19: "I found him [Churchill] in bed . . . but in an unholy rage! 'What was Monty doing dictating to him; he had every right to visit France when he wanted? Who was Monty to stop him?' At last,

---

[924]   Lord Tedder, 557.
[925]   Lord Tedder, 568.
[926]   Butcher, 617,
[927]   Lord Tedder, 563.

I discovered that Eisenhower had told him that Monty has asked not to have any visitors during the next few days, and the P.M. [thought] that Monty had aimed this restriction at him."[928]

Brooke flew to Normandy that afternoon for a long meeting with Montgomery during which he made Montgomery write a letter to Churchill inviting him to visit his headquarters any time he liked. Churchill visited Montgomery the next day, July 20. According to one of Montgomery's aides, ". . . it was 'common knowledge at Tac [headquarters] that Churchill had come to sack Monty. I mean we all knew it. He came in his blue coat with a blue cap, and in his pocket, he had the order, dismissing Monty . . . [Montgomery and the P.M. shook hands and went] . . . into the Operations caravan—and when they came out Churchill was beaming . . . . we all knew how near 'Master' had come to being sacked."[929]

Whatever Montgomery told Prime Minister Churchill apparently satisfied his concerns. Eisenhower called Churchill a few days later and asked, "What do your people think about the slowness of the situation over there?"[930] Butcher wrote that Churchill, ". . . had obviously been impressed with the strength of the military situation. The PM was supremely happy."[931] Eisenhower later asked Butcher to caution Bedell Smith, ". . . against, even hinting at 'the subject we have been discussing."[932] The subject they had been discussing was the dismissal of General Montgomery. Without Churchill's support, the plot to dismiss Montgomery was going to fail. Despite Alan Brooke's exorbitant hand wringing, it was apparent that Churchill needed Montgomery nearly as much as Montgomery needed him.

Tedder was the last officer to keep the plot against Montgomery alive. Eisenhower tried to explain to Tedder that Churchill was now happy with the situation in France. Butcher wrote in his diary, ". . . the PM was satisfied and Tedder rather uh-huhed, being not at all satisfied, and implying the PM must have sold Ike a bill of goods."[933] Without Churchill's support, Eisenhower's hands were tied. He could not proceed to build the case against Montgomery without either Churchill's or Brooke's support, and Brooke would never abandon his protégé.

---

[928] Bryant, Triumph, 234.
[929] Captain John R. Henderson, statement. From Hamilton, *Master*, 739, 740.
[930] Butcher, 623.
[931] Butcher, 623.
[932] Butcher, 623.
[933] Butcher, 624.

Montgomery was the most popular general in the British Army. Max Hastings does not see how Montgomery could have been sacked without causing an 'intolerable blow' to the British war effort.[934]

The truth would have been a powerful antidote to the Montgomery hysteria sweeping Britain, but the truth would have also created a political firestorm which could have toppled Churchill's government. Churchill had taken a look into the political abyss created by Montgomery's departure on July 20 and decided to take a step back. The prime minister had ruthlessly fired Generals Wavell and Auchinleck for less cause, but could not bring himself to fire Montgomery.

In late 1942, Churchill desperately needed a political boost, so he anointed Montgomery the heir apparent to Wellington, making him a 'household name' in Great Britain. General Montgomery had become identified with British military success and national self-esteem to a degree other generals could only envy. What was good for Bernard Law Montgomery was good for Great Britain and vice versa. Now, for good or ill, Churchill's political standing in Britain was tied to Montgomery's military performance in France. These circumstances made it very unlikely that Churchill would ever consider removing Montgomery.

On July 27, Churchill wrote Montgomery a letter warning him it was important for, ". . . the British Army to strike hard and win through . . ."[935] Otherwise, Churchill said, any comparisons between the two armies would eventually lead to 'dangerous recrimination.' As the Americans burst into the Brittany Peninsula during the first week in August, Churchill's fears were coming true. The British/Canadians were still stuck just south of Caen, and British Second Army's offensive in the Vire sector had gotten off to a slow start. Battlefield news coming from Normandy tended to be all about the Americans. By August 2, Churchill had decided to address the House of Commons on the war effort in Europe. Butcher wrote, "The PM had not reported in detail for many months and he properly wanted to emphasize the British participation to his people."[936]

Churchill wanted to mention that the officer in charge of early planning for Operation *Overlord* was British General Frederick Morgan. Butcher wrote, ". . . Ike readily consented to the PM's desire to mention General

---

[934]   Hastings, *Overlord*, 243.
[935]   Churchill, *Triumph and Tragedy*, 29.
[936]   Butcher, 632.

Morgan . . ."[937] The news had become so all-American that one British host switched off her radio, ". . . while her American officer guests were listening to the late news . . . Later she apologized . . ."[938]

The non-performance of the British Army in Normandy was having a devastating effect on British morale in England. Indeed, the Americans were dominating the news to such an extent, that even the staid, usually pro-British BBC was developing an American slant. "So much news has been made by the Americans that the BBC recently has been practically all-American."[939]

Montgomery published Plan # M515 on July 27. With the Americans gaining ground at St. Lo, Montgomery decided to transfer his British armored divisions away from the Caen sector to the extreme right of the British line northeast of Vire. This would move British tanks away from the concentration of German armor at Caen. Hamilton wrote, "The Second Army will regroup and will deliver a strong offensive on its right wing with not less than six divisions. The latest date, consistent with good weather, will be August 2"[940]

This move left the vital Caen sector in the hands of the inexperienced First Canadian Army, Commanded by General H. D. G. Crerar. General Crerar was a capable commander. He was something of a martinet, but he was also a sound tactician. He would get no help from Montgomery, and in fact, already had problems with the feisty British general.

Montgomery's battlefield instincts, however, were sound. Allied intelligence had been predicting a German collapse for weeks. If the Americans achieved a breakthrough at St. Lo, Montgomery expected the Germans to conduct a series of limited withdraws from Normandy with their armor covering the retreat of the slower infantry divisions from hills and critical road junctions. Then British Second Army would be in a good position to assist the Americans in driving the Germans out of the Vire sector and participating in the wider envelopment through Argentan-L'Aigle-Evreux and up to the Seine River.

Just after Montgomery moved the British divisions to his western flank at Vire, fighting developed south of Caen. Montgomery reported the situation to Brooke, "Very heavy fighting took place south of CAEN on 25

---

[937]   Butcher, 632.

[938]   Butcher, 627.

[939]   Butcher, 627.

[940]   Hamilton, *Master*, 753.

and 26 July and on the front of 2 Cdn DIV, *which was fighting its first battle in Normandy*, we were forced back 1000 yds in two places, i.e. at MAY and at TILLY."[941] The announcement from SHAEF indicated that the, ". . . British had sustained 'quite a serious setback.'"[942] Not true, Montgomery complained to Brooke, "I know of no 'serious setback.'"[943]

Serious or not, it made the newspaper headlines, much to Churchill's chagrin. The British/Canadian defeat south of Caen was probably the reason for Churchill's July 27 letter to Montgomery, urging him to see 'that the British Army strike hard and win through.' Montgomery continued his litany of complaints to Brooke: "It is not good for the morale of British troops in Normandy to see headlines in the British Newspapers: 'Set-back in Normandy, etc . . . ' I wonder if Grigg [Sir James, Secretary of State for War] could have lunch with some of the leading editors and get this across to them."[944] British morale in France, already shaken by the nearly all-American coverage generated by the U.S. breakout at St. Lo, was given another jolt by their defeat south of Caen. Montgomery's efforts to control the British press could be seen as an effort to maintain morale within Second British Army.

While the British and their Canadian allies were getting a bloody nose south of Caen, the Americans were enjoying more success on the other flank. This led to the very problem Churchill had warned Montgomery about, an unfortunate comparison between the British and American armies. On July 27, Brooke wrote in his diary: "The strategy of the Normandy landing is quite straightforward. But now comes the trouble; the Press chip in and we heard that the British are doing nothing and suffering no casualties whilst the Americans are bearing all the brunt of the war."[945] After looking at the casualty figures SHAEF released, it would be difficult to come to any other conclusion except the one taken by reporters. Of course, Churchill, Brooke and Montgomery did everything in their power to keep this information from reaching the public.

Montgomery's system of command and control was about to endure a severe test. By July 27, Montgomery was writing Brooke, the ". . . Americans are going great guns."[946] The war of movement had

---

[941] Hamilton, *Master*, 758. Italics in the original.
[942] Churchill, *Triumph,* 29.
[943] Hamilton, *Master*, 759.
[944] Hamilton, *Master*, 758.
[945] Bryant, *Triumph*, 243.
[946] Hamilton, *Master*, 759.

begun. Montgomery's system of command was to separate his tactical headquarters from his main headquarters. This kept him far away from the paperwork, which he hated.[947]

For reconnaissance, he would send out a squad of young men, most with the rank of major, as liaison officers. Following Montgomery's instructions, these officers would observe the units they had been instructed to visit. A typical Montgomery order to a liaison officer was: "'I want to know exactly what the form is, how far they have got, what their morale is like, have they got any problems, and so forth.' . . . And he [the LO] would go right down to the Battalion and find out from the CO [commanding officer] how things were going. And the LO would come back in the evening and brief Monty exactly where everyone was."[948] If Montgomery's LO had actually been talking to a battalion CO, he had bypassed the army commander, the corps commander, the division commander, and the regimental commander in getting down to the battalion level of command. He was reviewing information gathered on officers and units down five levels of command from his 21st Army Group.

Debriefing the liaison officers was conducted very shortly after they got back to headquarters, but they apparently still had time to clean up a bit and prepare typed notes of their activities. According to Alistair Horne, ". . . they would deliver their report orally (using typed notes) to Monty in person, standing in the map caravan—usually hunched because there was . . . headroom only for one small general. Mounted on the inside walls, the maps showed every forward position and the location of every command post in 21 Army Group."[949] Horne suggests that the LOs kept Montgomery extremely well informed, ". . . with hourly developments at the front . . ."[950] But, for reasons which are not difficult to understand, "Monty's U.S. liaison officers did not prove a great success—through no fault of their own."[951]

The presence of Montgomery's spies snooping around a subordinate's headquarters had the predictable effect. One of Montgomery's liaison officers remembered, ". . . 'this reporting over the heads of everybody else, down to seeing platoon commanders,' sometimes upset even the impeccable 'Bimbo' Dempsey, commander of Monty's British Second Army."[952] General

---

[947] Montgomery's address to his staff, 11 January 1944. From Hamilton, *Master*, 502.
[948] Horne, 132.
[949] Horne, 132.
[950] Horne, 132.
[951] Horne, 132.
[952] Horne, 132.

Dempsey had learned how to play the game. He kept his mouth shut. Other officers not familiar with Montgomery's strange behavior learned very quickly that Montgomery did not tolerate dissent within his command.

Montgomery kept himself informed about events taking place within 21st British Army Group with liaison officers because he did not trust British built radios. Montgomery had written, ". . . the W/T and R/T [wire and radio] transmission could not be relied upon to function one hundred per cent efficiently in battle. Liaison officers and messengers, as of old, would also be required in modern battle."[953] British built communications equipment was unreliable throughout the war; it broke down in critical situations. This sometimes [as in *Market Garden*] occurred with catastrophic results.

One of the lessons he had learned from the First World War was that good communications were essential to avoid the blood baths that followed so many offensives. Montgomery came to believe that if he kept tract of a unit's form, their position, their morale, etc. he could prevent disasters and keep the unit's casualties within acceptable levels. The overriding need to control casualties within the British Army combined with Montgomery's very great mental need to feel that he was in personal control of events within his command.

Montgomery did not trust his generals to get it right. Commanders within 21st British Army Group were selected more for their ability to get along with Montgomery than for their expertise as military commanders. Those who did not quickly become the Master's 'yes-men' were soon removed. Generals Lumsden and Gatewood in North Africa and O'Connor in Europe were three of Montgomery's more famous victims.

The same standard applied to officers at Montgomery's TAC headquarters. One officer remembered that Montgomery, ". . . liked holding court; he didn't want anyone too clever . . . hence Leo Russell was out . . ."[954] Nor did Montgomery tolerate the presence of senior officers at his headquarters. One of the liaison officers, Hereward Wake recalled, ". . . he never frightened one—in his relations with the LO s, young officers, he was always relaxed, lighthearted. But as soon as a senior officer came in, everything changed—he froze up. It was rather unattractive."[955] Montgomery surrounded himself with men who could be easily controlled. These men were usually young officers of lower rank, either captains or majors.

---

[953]   Hamilton, *Making*, 332.
[954]   Horne, 133.
[955]   Horne, 133, 134.

It was worse than unattractive; it was hurting the British Army. Montgomery simply did not like having senior officers around, and that same aversion apparently extended to his own headquarters staff as well.[956] For most of the battle in Normandy, 21st Army Group Main Headquarters was left behind at Southwick, England.[957] Even after Main Headquarters moved to Normandy, they were often far behind the TAC HQ. One of Montgomery's staff officers recalled: "I only saw the Chief of Staff [Major General Francis de Guingand] two or three times in the whole war!"[958] This is a damning admission. In most headquarters, particularly in the U.S. Army, the chief of staff is the commanding officer's alter ego and is seen by other headquarters officers many times each day.

Sir John Kennedy [Assistant C.I.G.S.] described Montgomery's system of command: "Monty's system of command is most impressive. He keeps his main headquarters twenty or thirty miles away and, as a rule, sees only the two chiefs, De Guingand and Graham, and them only once a day or so. They can telephone to him. This results in Monty being left in comparative peace, with plenty of time to think, and no fuss or worry about details."[959]

Montgomery had successfully isolated himself from senior officers at his own headquarters and from SHAEF. Although regularly invited to attend meetings at Eisenhower's headquarters, Montgomery found the time to attend exactly one meeting at SHAEF. "He always insisted that Eisenhower come to him."[960] Throughout the eleven months of the war in Europe, Montgomery met with Eisenhower only nine times.[961] Montgomery attempted to control the location of his meetings with Eisenhower and on at least one occasion refused to allow Eisenhower's Chief of Staff [Bedell Smith] to attend their meeting, while his own Chief of Staff [Francis de Guingand] was present.[962]

In trying to understand Montgomery's behavior, Raymond Callahan is right, it is important to see that, ". . . Montgomery was a World War I general—the heir to the techniques that had made the successes of 1918 possible."[963] But it is also important to understand that Montgomery's

---

[956]   Horne, 134, 135, 167.
[957]   Horne, 134.
[958]   Horne, 134.
[959]   Kennedy, 346.
[960]   Ambrose, *Eisenhower, Soldier, General*, 347.
[961]   Hastings, *Overlord*, 240.
[962]   Ambrose, *Eisenhower, Soldier, General*, 340, 341.
[963]   Callahan, *Churchill and His Generals*, 140.

mental condition required him to exercise control over his environment, the people he met on a daily basis, and the circumstances under which those meetings took place. If Montgomery did not trust other generals to handle their battlefield assignments, neither did he relish the thought of a chance meeting with another officer above the rank of major.

Montgomery's aversion to writing and paperwork was well known to his staff. He rarely wrote out orders and he hated paperwork. Montgomery told his staff right after taking command of the Army Group, "I will not get bogged down in details . . . . I will give orders to the next lower commanders. Nothing will be in writing either in the first place or for confirmation. *I never read any papers. Half of all papers are not read and the other half are not worth reading.*"[964] This is a damning admission from the senior Allied Ground Commander in Europe; it was particularly true for a general who had virtually isolated himself at Army Group tactical headquarters.

In early September 1944 General Eisenhower and Admiral Bertram Ramsay wrote Montgomery very important letters dealing with future Allied strategy and opening the port of Antwerp. His behavior during the months of September and October suggests that Montgomery may never have read them.

Montgomery seldom saw written criticism, unless it came in the newspapers or from Alan Brooke. He had cut himself off from his own headquarters, from Eisenhower's headquarters and from regular social contact with men of his own age and rank. He respected the opinions of Francis de Guingand and Alan Brooke, but saw these men only infrequently. Fortunately, Montgomery was not completely alone. In early July he wrote to a friend in England, ". . . I have been collecting livestock. I now have six canaries, one love bird, and two dogs."[965]

Both Brooke and Churchill had written letters to Montgomery urging him launch an attack as soon as possible. Churchill's letter was sent on July 27, Brooke's letter was sent the next day. Montgomery, sensing the urgency, wrote to Brooke on July 28, "I have ordered DEMPSEY to throw all caution overboard and to take any risks he likes and to accept any casualties and to step on the gas for VIRE."[966] This was the attack

---

[964] Notes from Staff Conference, 21st Army Group, 13 January 1944. From D'Este, *Decision*, 163. Also see Horne, 135, and Hamilton, *Master*, for Montgomery's address to the Staff College on 7 Jan. 44, 500-505. Italics added.

[965] Montgomery letter to Phyllis Reyonlds. From Horne, 163.

[966] Montgomery to Brooke, signal M69, Montgomery Papers. From Hamilton, *Master*, 768.

Montgomery had outlined in plan M515, but he moved the date of the attack forward three days to July 30.

The transfer of German armor out of the Caen sector had begun shortly after the American attack at St. Lo. By August 3d and 4th, German armor was giving both U.S. and British units a hard fight to hold the Vire hinge. Montgomery decided to launch a heavy attack from the Caen sector south toward Falaise with General Crerar's First Canadian Army. On August 4, Montgomery directed Crerar: "To break through the enemy positions to the south and south-east of CAEN, and to gain such ground in the direction of FALAISE as will cut off the enemy forces now facing Second Army . . . . The attack to be launched *as early as possible* as and in any case not later than 8 August . . ."[967] The Canadians would use the code name Operation *Totalize* for this, the first of two Canadian attacks aimed at Falaise on the eastern Allied flank south of Caen.

By August 6, Montgomery had firmed up his long standing plans for the wide envelopment to the Seine River. The plan was called M517; it proposed that all four Allied armies drive to the Seine with airborne troops blocking off the Paris-Orleans gap.

At this point, Montgomery was not sure what the Germans were going to do. If the Germans continued to strongly resist in the north, Hamilton suggests he saw, ". . . the chance for our right flank to swing round and thus cut off his escape."[968] In his directive-accompanying plan M517, Montgomery did not seem to care what the Germans in Normandy did. He wrote, "But whatever the enemy may want to do will make no difference to us. We will proceed relentlessly, and rapidly, with our own plans for his destruction."[969]

On the night of 6/7 August, the Germans counterattacked the Americans at Mortain. They hoped to crack the US 30th Infantry Division's line at Mortain and drive through to Avranches, cutting Patton's Third US Army off from its supply base. The Germans hoped to rebuild a defensive line in Normandy with its left flank anchored at Avranches. CCA of US 3rd Armored Division was joined by major elements of US 2nd Armored in sealing off the southern German flank at Barenton. On the northern flank, the German 116th Panzer Division was late in getting its advance started but then ran into Manton Eddy's 9th US Infantry Division and was stopped

---

[967] Hamilton, *Master,* 774. Italics in the original.
[968] Hamilton, *Master*, 775. Also see Montgomery, *Normandy,* 94, 95.
[969] Hamilton, *Master*, 775.

close to its start line. Leland Hobbs' 30th Infantry Division gave ground at Mortain and the Germans came to within nine miles of Avranches.[970] But when the fog lifted in mid-morning, Allied fighter-bombers swarmed over the exposed German armor columns, abruptly halting their advance.

Patton's Third Army continued to rush through the bottleneck at Avranches with Middleton's VIII Corps heading into Brittany and Haislip's XV Corps going northeast toward Le Mans. Later on August 7, Montgomery signaled the latest news to Brooke: "My L.O. has just returned from the LAVAL front and reports that the leading troops of 15 U.S. Corps have reached LOUE which is only fifteen miles from LE MANS. This is very good news . . . If only the Germans will go on attacking at Mortain for a few more days, it seems that they might not be able to get away."[971] Montgomery evidently saw the possibility of an envelopment before Bradley called him the following day.

The next day, August 8, Montgomery, in a telephone conversation with General Bradley, agreed to implement the short envelopment through Alencon-Argentan-Falaise. Hamilton suggests that Montgomery, ". . . still favored a wide envelopment that would permit Patton to shut off the Orleans escape-route and then swing north to the Seine and the Channel."[972] Hamilton supports his conclusion with a quote from Montgomery's senior staff officer, Bill Williams: "Monty was sold on the wide outflanking move—blocking the Orleans Gap with paratroops etc and switching the armor Northwards along the left bank of the Seine to form a big pocket . . . Did not change this till after Mortain began—and then only on urging of Freddie [de Guingand], Bradley and Bill [Williams]."[973] The German attack at Mortain began on the night of 6/7 August, and Bradley's phone call to Montgomery urging the short envelopment through Argentan-Falaise did not take place until mid-day August 8; Bill Williams memory was accurate. Although he may have preferred the wider, Seine envelopment, Montgomery agreed, on August 8, to conduct the shorter Argentan-Falaise envelopment.

Writing after the event, Montgomery offered a slightly different version in his book, *Normandy to the Baltic*. Concerning the situation on August 8 he wrote, "I have shown that up to this period, my plan was to make a wide enveloping movement from the southern American flank up to the Seine

970   Weigley, *Eisenhower's Lieutenants*, 198.
971   Hamilton, *Master*, 776.
972   Hamilton, *Master*, 776.
973   Notebook XIX, Wilmot Papers (15/15/62-93). From Hamilton, *Master,* 776.

about Paris, and at the same time to drive the centre and northern sectors of the Allied line straight for the river. In view of the Mortain counter stroke, I decided to attempt *concurrently* a shorter envelopment with the object of bottling up the bulk of the German forces deployed between Falaise and Mortain . . . . If we could bring off both these movements we would virtually annihilate the enemy in Normandy."[974]

Unfortunately, the two operations were not tactically compatible. If Second British and US First Armies drove hard to the Seine before US Third Army met the Canadians between Argentan and Falaise, it would be like, as Bradley suggested, ". . . squeezing the toothpaste from the bottom of the tube with no cap on."[975] They would be chasing Germans through the gap Crerar and Patton were trying to close. If, on the other hand, Patton's Third Army met Crerar's Canadians between Argentan and Falaise before the First US and Second British Armies conducted their power drive to the Seine, they would be blocking the roads these armies needed for their power drive to the Seine. This was exactly what happened between August 20 and 22. General De Guingand wrote about the confusion created after the Allies finally closed the Falaise Gap and Montgomery switched the boundary line back to Argentan: ". . . it was nearly forty-eight hours before the armies were sorted out again in their correct sectors. It was a great pity that this had to happen . . . ."[976] Montgomery had planned to use the road Argentan-Evreux for British XXX Corps' drive to the Seine.

After his telephone conversation with Bradley, Montgomery was apparently convinced that the short envelopment through Alencon-Argentan-Falaise would work. On the evening of August 8, Montgomery wrote to Brooke, "A strong force of four divisions will operate tomorrow northwards from the LE MANS area toward ALENCON . . . . I am trying to get to FALAISE and ALENCON as the first step to closing the ring behind the enemy . . ."[977] On August 9, Montgomery's enthusiasm for the short envelopment remained intact. He wrote to Brooke, "There are great possibilities in the present situation . . . If we can get to ALENCON ARGENTAN and FALAISE fairly quickly we have a good chance of closing the ring round the main German forces and I am making all plans to

---

[974] Montgomery, *Normandy*, 98, 99. *Concurrently* is italicized in the original.
[975] Bradley, *A General's Life*, 300.
[976] De Guingand, 408.
[977] Hamilton, *Master*, 778.

drop an airborne division at GACE about fifteen miles east of ARGENTAN in order to complete the block."[978]

Montgomery, Eisenhower, and Bradley were all in agreement. The short envelopment was not only worth pursuing, it offered the Allied Armies the best opportunity to destroy the Germans fighting in Normandy at little cost to themselves. There was only one potential problem, as Montgomery explained to Brooke, "'Should the Germans escape us here I shall proceed quickly with the plan outlined in M517'—the wider [Seine] envelopment."[979] Yet it was not the Germans who spoiled the party at Falaise. It was the same problem Montgomery had experienced at Caen. The British/Canadian Army under his command was simply unable to complete its mission.

The Canadian attack south of Caen, Operation *Totalize,* began during the night of 7/8 August. Spotlights reflected off the clouds were used to illuminate the night sky and tracers fired toward the German lines to indicate the direction of the main assaults. The Canadians used 'Priests,' American built self-propelled gun carriers, minus the guns, to move their infantry forward into battle. The initial attack was successful. The Canadians gained more than six miles toward Falaise. Lieutenant-General Guy Simonds [Commanding, II Canadian Corps] asked his armored units to continue their attacks through the night of August 8. "Many units simply ignored him, and withdrew to night harbors in the manner to which they were accustomed."[980]

By August 9, the Germans had recovered from the initial shock of the attack and their 88 mm anti-tank guns began to slow the Canadian tanks. On that day also, "A fierce German counter-attack by a battle-group of the 12th SS Panzer completed the chaos. The British Columbia Regiment lost almost its entire strength, 47 tanks in the day, together with 112 casualties."[981] Two days later, the Canadians, still far short of Falaise, decided to call off their attack and replaced the armor with infantry formations. The Canadians would require a new plan for another set-piece attack complete with massive air bombardments. The new Canadian attack, Operation *Tractable,* would not be ready until midday August 14.

Montgomery probably had an uneasy feeling as control of the battle slipped from his hands. The American turn north at Le Mans was a

---

[978]   Hamilton, *Master*, 779.
[979]   Hamilton, *Master*, 779.
[980]   Hastings, *Overlord*, 299.
[981]   Hastings, *Overlord*, 299.

double-edged sword. He had certainly agreed to the change in plans, in fact, he had seen the opportunity himself. The Americans had faced minimal resistance so far [through August 10], as Montgomery suggested, ". . . where hitherto protection had been afforded [the German flank] by inadequate battle groups."[982]

But what would happen if the Germans did not reinforce their southern flank in time? The Americans would be able to drive straight through to Falaise. How would that look to Churchill? He had told Montgomery it was important for, ". . . the British Army to strike hard and win through."[983] If Patton's troops took Falaise, it would create a most unfavorable comparison with his army in the press and do untold damage to his own military reputation. He simply could not let it happen.

The fast pace of events in Normandy was creating mental distress for Montgomery. "Bill [Captain Bill Culver, de Guingand's aide] amusingly reported that Monty has been showing signs of irritation lately. He had abruptly ordered a British lieutenant general to clear out of his area because 'I don't want to see your face around.'"[984]

The 'master of the set-piece battle' was losing his grip as the pace of battle quickened. Confusion and uncertainty crept into Montgomery's letters to Brooke and to Bradley. On August 9, a confident General Montgomery wrote to Brooke, "The Canadians should be able to fight their way to FALAISE . . . they will not have the easy time they fancied, but they should get there . . . The Germans will fight hard for FALAISE I think. I don't think the Americans will have any difficulty in getting to ALENCON, as there is nothing there to oppose them."[985] Montgomery was right on both counts.

By the following day, August 10, Montgomery's confidence seems to have been shaken. According to Hamilton, he had just learned that senior officers at SHAEF tried to have him fired after *Goodwood* and that some of those officers were British. Hamilton wrote, "It distressed him that British officers like Generals Gale and Morgan should have shown such little loyalty to the self-sacrificing efforts of the British forces throughout the battle, preferring to curry favor with Eisenhower and Bedell Smith by conspiring

---

982   Montgomery, *Normandy,* 101.
983   Churchill, *Triumph and Tragedy,* 29.
984   Butcher, 638.
985   Hamilton, *Master,* 780.

against the British commander in the field, and helping to polarize SHAEF and the War Office . . ."[986]

The same day, August 10, British ULTRA intelligence gave the Allies the best possible news. Hitler had ordered the Germans to plan for a renewed attack, as Montgomery wrote, ". . . between DOMFRONT and MORTAIN."[987] All the Allies had to do was close the gap behind the Germans in Normandy. The Germans were not only immobilized within the trap; they were ordered to conduct another attack at Mortain, which would drive their panzers even deeper into the Allied embrace. But then Montgomery admitted, "I do not really know what is likely to happen on that front tomorrow or in the future . . ."[988] The Allies also learned that the Germans had received permission to shorten their lines in the Mortain sector to release sufficient armored forces to eliminate the threat posed by US XV Corps at Le Mans.

On August 11, Montgomery issued plan M518. Montgomery hoped to get the Canadians to Argentan and the Americans to a line Carrouges-Sees-Mortagne.[989] He wanted to close the trap on the Germans in Normandy. He saw that the Canadians were approaching Falaise from the north and the Americans were approaching Alencon from the south.

From Montgomery's point of view, there was a huge difference in the status of the two armies. The Canadians had just called off Operation *Totalize* and would be conducting only limited operations in the Laize River valley for the next few days, in preparation for another big set-piece attack, Operation *Tractable*. The new Canadian attack was not scheduled to begin until 14 August. The Americans had just begun their attack on August 10 and in sharp battles with the German 9th Panzer and 708th German Infantry Divisions had lost 40 tanks, but the Americans were still attacking. Moreover, German defenses on their southern flank were not well organized. The German 708th Infantry had limited fighting ability and the 9th Panzer had already lost most of its Recon Battalion to the 90th U.S. Infantry in an earlier engagement. German forces were being committed piecemeal, before they had time to make a proper study of the terrain.

In Plan M518 Montgomery predicted that the Germans would react to Allied attempts to trap them in Normandy. He predicted that the Germans

---

[986]   Hamilton, *Master*, 781.

[987]   Hamilton, *Master*, 782.

[988]   Hamilton, *Master*, 782.

[989]   Hamilton, *Master*, 783. See map.

were, ". . . likely to operate in the general area DOMFRONT-ARGENTAN-ALENCON, so as to have the benefit of the difficult 'bocage' country. Their object would be to hold off the right wing of 12 Army Group . . . to facilitate the withdrawal of their forces on the FALAISE-VIRE front."[990] As Hamilton suggests, Montgomery saved his bombshell until the last. "In a final rider Monty warned, however, 'we must be ready to put into execution the full plan given in M517 [the wider Seine envelopment] should it appear likely that the enemy may escape us here.'"[991] In a telegram to Brooke that evening, Montgomery told his friend that he ordered the Americans to retain three divisions in the Le Mans sector so they would be ready to implement the wide [Seine] envelopment when it was put into action.[992]

The Allies were reading *ULTRA* messages detailing the argument between Kluge and Hitler about resumption of the German counterattack at Mortain. But Montgomery, for some curious reason, seemed to be more concerned about the possibility of a German escape from Normandy. *ULTRA* told the Allies that Hitler has ordered the Germans to return to the counterattack at Avranches after they have eliminated the threat to their southern flank posed by Haislip's XV US Corps.

As he might have expected, Montgomery's interference in the US command produced an angry response from General Bradley. The argument was addressed the next day by Bradley's aide Chester Hansen in his war diary: "There is some discussion now concerning an alleged disagreement in strategy between Brad and Monty concerning the timing for this northward movement."[993] Bradley argued in favor of the Argentan-Falaise encirclement they had agreed to on 8 August.

Montgomery was preparing his Allies for what, considering British political interests, was the worst possible set of circumstances on the southern German flank. *In Montgomery's worst case scenario, the Canadians remain bogged down north of Falaise while the Americans drive straight through to Argentan. Montgomery had probably decided that he would never allow the Americans north of Argentan.* There was a shortage of good roads northeast from Normandy into central France.[994] Montgomery was determined to retain the road axis Argentan-Evreux-Vernon for his Second Army.[995] He

---

990 Hamilton, *Master*, 784.
991 Hamilton, *Master*, 784.
992 Hamilton, *Master*, 784.
993 Hansen War Diaries, 12 Aug. 1944.
994 Montgomery, *Normandy*, 114.
995 Montgomery, *Normandy*, 107.

was equally determined to prevent George Patton and his Third Army from coming to the aid of the British and Canadian Army, whose offensive had stalled between Caen and Falaise.

With one arbitrary order Montgomery removed the protection for both of Haislip's vulnerable flanks. Ordering Bradley to withhold three divisions at Le Mans might not stop the American drive to Argentan, but it certainly would slow it down. Montgomery's orders to Bradley were issued at a time that he knew, through *ULTRA*, the Germans were preparing to attack Haislip's western flank.[996] Bradley apparently protested the order to no avail.

The following day, August 12, the speed of the American drive to Argentan was later said to have surprised Montgomery.[997] On the evening of August 11, the Americans were still short of Alencon, by the following evening 5th US Armored Division had closed to the inter-Army Group boundary line on the Orne River two miles south of Argentan. They also had a task force south of Exmes and another task force five miles south of Gace blocking the roads.

According to Max Hastings, "It seemed reasonable to assume that the Canadians, pushing south across reasonably open country, would be in Argentan before Haislip. The new boundary, the point at which XV Corps would halt its advance, was therefore set just south of Argentan."[998] That may have been a reasonable assumption but it was not what Montgomery was thinking. He wrote to Brooke on August 9, "The Germans will fight hard for Falaise . . ."[999] He was right; the 12th SS Panzer would fight nearly to the last man, only four young men were reported to have escaped from the rubble of the main school building in Falaise. The Canadians did not secure Falaise until 17 August, by which time the Americans had been sitting south of the inter-Army Group boundary at Argentan for five days.

Hastings and Hamilton can be excused for their attempt to obscure Montgomery's poor handling of Allied forces at the Falaise Gap. How could Montgomery miss the timing of the American drive to Argentan so badly? Montgomery not only erred, as Russell Weigley points out, "[He] persisted in error for days on end . . ."[1000] The short answer is that he didn't miss the timing of Patton's arrival at Argentan at all. He was following the American

---

[996]   Bradley, *A General's Life*, 298.

[997]   Hamilton, *Master*, 784.

[998]   Hastings, *Overlord*, 289.

[999]   Hamilton, *Master*, 780.

[1000]   Weigley, *Eisenhower's Lieutenants*, 216.

advance rather closely; he was kept well informed about the location of Patton's Third Army.

If Montgomery had simply been mistaken about the Canadians getting to Argentan before the Americans, as Hastings suggests, he could easily adjust his plans after the Americans arrived. Since the arrival of the Patton's XV Corps at Argentan produced no change in Montgomery's plans or his southern Army Group boundary line, it is only reasonable to assume that the appearance of Americans at Argentan was irrelevant to Montgomery's plan for the battle at the Falaise Gap. Simply put, Montgomery never entertained the possibility that Patton's Army should be allowed to move north of Argentan.

The one essential element of the agreement Montgomery and Bradley had reached on August 8 was that the Germans in Normandy should be surrounded by Patton's Army from the south and Crerar's Army from the north as soon as possible. No meeting place had been selected, but Montgomery had agreed to move his southern boundary north to just south of Argentan to accommodate the Americans. Nor was the meeting place important, the Allies could have met at Alencon, Argentan or Falaise, it simply did not matter. The timing was the critical element in the Allied plans to trap the Germans in Normandy. It was critical that the Canadians and Americans met before the combat arms of the German Fifth Panzer and Seventh Armies withdrew from Normandy.

The arrival of the Americans at Argentan did force Montgomery to make one change in his plans. He would implement the wider Seine envelopment plan [M517] a few days earlier than he had intended.

Generals Bradley and Eisenhower have been less than forthright about their experiences at the Falaise Gap. British historians tend to avoid the subject. *The truth is that on the evening of August 12 General Bradley called General Montgomery's headquarters and asked for permission to send Haislip's XV Corps north of the inter-Army Group boundary at Argentan toward Falaise. Bradley's request was denied.*

In 1947 Forrest C. Pogue interviewed Montgomery's staff officer, Brigadier E.T. [Bill] Williams. Williams said that he was in Freddie de Guingand's truck near Bayeux when Bradley's telephone call went through: "Monty said tell Bradley they ought to get back. Bradley was indignant. We were indignant on Bradley's behalf . . . Monty missed closing the sack. Bradley couldn't understand. Thought we were missing our opportunities over inter-Army rights . . . He [Montgomery] missed his chance of closing at the Seine by doing the envelopment at Falaise. Monty didn't want to do the short hook."[1001] Bradley, Francis de Guingand and Brigadier Williams argued in favor of letting the Americans move north of Argentan to close the gap, but Montgomery would not change his mind.

The political ramifications of an American thrust to Falaise for Great Britain and its top general in Europe would have been devastating. The Americans were already complaining that they were doing most of the fighting. If the Americans now drove around through Le Mans, Alencon, Argentan and up to Falaise, it would look like the Americans had come to the rescue of the Montgomery's stalled British and Canadian forces. It would give Montgomery's critics more ammunition then ever to force his relief from command and at the very least it would reduce his standing among Allied generals even lower than it had fallen after the *Goodwood* disaster.

At a briefing prior to the invasion, Montgomery had boasted about conducting a 'tank knockabout at Falaise on D-day.'[1002] Bradley later wrote, "Falaise was a long-sought British objective and, for them, a matter of immense prestige."[1003] Montgomery could not allow the Americans, especially George Patton, who had been in command of Third Army barely two weeks, to embarrass British Second Army by driving through Argentan to take Falaise. *The result would have been a disaster for Montgomery's professional reputation and a diminished political status for Great Britain within the Anglo-American Alliance.*

When Montgomery ordered the Americans to halt on the inter-Army Group boundary south of Argentan on the evening of August 12, there was only one US armored division actually near the boundary. That was Major General Lunsford Oliver's 5th Armored Division. By noon the following day 2nd French Armored Division had closed on the boundary line south of Ecouche-Argentan. In General Collins' VII Corps, Major General Maurice Rose's 3d US Armored Division had closed off Haislip's western flank at Ranes. Three US infantry divisions were immediately available to support Rose's armor: General Clarence Huebner's 1st, Raymond Barton's 4th and Manton Eddy's 9th. Two infantry divisions were supporting Haislip's armor: Ira Wyche's 79th Infantry was in support of Lunsford Oliver's 5th Armored and Raymond McLain's 90th Infantry was in support of Jacques Leclerc's

---

[1001] Dr. Forrest C. Pogue, Interviews, US Army Military History Institute, Carlisle Barracks, PA. From Carlo D'Este, *Decision*, 451, 452. Also see Rohmer, 226, 227.

[1002] Bradley, *A General's Life,* 303.

[1003] Bradley, *A General's Life*, 298.

2nd French Armored with Horace McBride's new 80th Infantry in reserve moving into defensive positions near Alencon.

Both Generals Patton of Third Army and Hodges of First Army had telephoned Bradley on the morning of August 13 to ask for permission to cross 21st Army Group's southern boundary and complete the encirclement of the German Armies in Normandy. Bradley obeyed Montgomery's instructions from the evening before and denied both requests; but ordered his operations officer to call Montgomery's headquarters again and ask for permission to cross the boundary. Following Bradley's orders, Brigadier General A. Franklin Kibler telephoned 21st Army Group Headquarters to officially request permission to cross the boundary. He talked to Francis de Guingand, Montgomery's Chief of Staff, who told him, "I am sorry, Kibler. We cannot grant the permission."[1004] Kibler's telephone call represents the last recorded American effort to move north of Argentan.

Sixty odd miles south of Argentan four additional US divisions were regrouping near Le Mans. They were waiting in Le Mans in compliance with Montgomery's August 11 orders to Bradley, instructing him to withhold three divisions at Le Mans in preparation for the wider Seine envelopment [Plan M517].[1005] These divisions were Major General Walton Walker's XX Corps with Lindsay Silvester's 7th Armored and Stafford Irwin's 5th Infantry Divisions and Major General Gilbert Cook's newly formed XII Corps with John Wood's 4th Armored [just arriving from Brittany] and Paul Baade's 35th Infantry Divisions.

By 1130 hours on August 13th, three corps in Patton's Third Army and one corps in Hodges' First Army were essentially without orders. Patton's XV Corps was halted south of Argentan; Hodges' VII Corps was halted near Ranes. Patton's XX and XII Corps were still sitting tight at Le Mans hoping for some word from Montgomery. Finally, Patton could stand the inactivity no longer. He later wrote, "On the thirteenth, it became evident that the XX Corps was hitting nothing, so we moved it northeast of Le Mans . . ."[1006] XX Corps was hitting nothing northeast of Le Mans either. With the German armies tied down in Normandy by Hitler's suicidal orders, thirteen US divisions sat helplessly on the open German flank, waiting for some sign from the British Ground Forces Commander that there was still

---

[1004] Farago, 540. Also see Weigley, *Eisenhower's Lieutenant's*, 206.
[1005] Hamilton, *Master*, 784.
[1006] Patton, 104.

a war on. They waited and they waited and they waited. August 13 became August 14 and still no word from 21st Army Group Headquarters.

By August 13, it was apparent that the German Army in Normandy was disintegrating. Montgomery chose this day, a Sunday, to hold a large staff meeting with the Americans. The meeting would include an intelligence briefing, an award ceremony for General Bradley, a luncheon, and two strategy sessions. The short term strategy discussion dealt with the events in Normandy as they were unfolding that Sunday; the long term strategy discussion involved the Allied drive into Germany

Of all the things on Montgomery's mind that Sunday, none was strategically more important than those 200,000 Americans sitting on the open German flank. Unfortunately, the Americans would have to wait. A host of problems had spawned a crisis at Montgomery's tactical headquarters. Montgomery had been looking at a pile of bitter pills on his desk for days now and he had finally come up with some solutions. He called this meeting with the Americans to see how they would react. These were delicate issues involving the British manpower crisis and command of the Allied armies in Europe. Montgomery's solutions were highly political in nature, since they clearly favored British interests at the expense of the Americans.

His first problem was British manpower. British infantry replacements failed to keep up with casualties and by August many British infantry divisions had been bled white. The British War Office had warned their generals in France to expect a shortfall in infantry replacements by September, but by mid-July it had become obvious that British infantry divisions were losing their effectiveness and would require replacements before September.

The final decision was left to General Montgomery. On August 14, a depressed Montgomery wrote to Brooke: "Regret time has now come when I must break up one infantry division. *My infantry divisions are so low in effective rifle strength that they can no—repeat NO—longer fight effectively in major operations . . . the urgency of the present battle operations forced me to delay decision . . .* Request permission to break up at once 59th Division . . . . Request matter be treated as urgent-repeat-urgent-and authority sent tomorrow."[1007] Within a few weeks, General L. O. Lyne's 59th [Straffordshire] Infantry Division disappeared from 21st Army Group's order of battle.

[1007] Montgomery cable (M-92), to War Office, PRO(CAB 106/1066). From D'Este, *Decision,* 262. Italics added.

Montgomery's second problem involved long-term Allied strategy. The Allies had decided that their advance into Germany would involve two strong thrusts. The 'main thrust' would run north through Belgium to secure the airfields and the Pas de Calais, overrunning the V-weapon sites, then north to open the port of Antwerp and finally northeast of the Ardennes to the Ruhr; it would be led by Montgomery's 21st British Army Group. The Ruhr was the one objective the German Army would have to fight to protect. The 'secondary thrust' south of the Ardennes through Verdun-Metz to the Saar and the Frankfurt Gap would be led by Bradley's 12th US Army Group.[1008]

Montgomery's problem was that if all the Americans in Bradley's 12th Army Group participated in the drive south of the Ardennes, the American thrust by virtue of their superior numbers would become the main Allied thrust. Given Montgomery's manpower problems within the British Army, without substantial reinforcement from the Americans, Montgomery saw the role for his 21st Army Group greatly reduced in status. He was determined to prevent this from happening. To maintain his role as commander of the main Allied thrust with the obvious political implications for British interests, Montgomery was going to require that those American divisions somehow be drawn north of the Ardennes on his southern flank.

Most Americans thought that the Allied Airborne Army [three airborne divisions] plus a US Corps would be sufficient to keep Montgomery happy, this would have given Montgomery 22 divisions and reduce Bradley's force to around 15 divisions.[1009] But Eisenhower had already decided to give Montgomery an American Army. On the afternoon of July 5, General Patton visited Eisenhower and recorded his feelings on how the American Army would eventually be assigned: "His current plan is for four American Armies, with one small American Army for Montgomery . . . Bradley [is] to have three large American Armies with me on the southern flank. Why an American Army has to go with Montgomery, I do not see, except to save the face of the little monkey."[1010] Patton was never fond of Montgomery.

Montgomery used his August 13 meeting with the Americans to unveil his new strategic plan which assigned most United States Army divisions to British 21st Army Group. Patton's Third Army would be given the task of

---

[1008] Pogue, *The Supreme Command*, 249-256. Also see Bradley, *A General's Life*, 299, 301.

[1009] Bradley, *A General's Life*, 313.

[1010] Blumenson, (Ed.), *The Patton Papers, 1940-1945*, 472.

clearing the Brittany ports. After Brittany, Patton would be asked to assume defensive positions east of Paris, protecting the French capital. The reminder of Bradley's Army Group would be assigned to protect Montgomery's right flank as he drove north and east from Antwerp with the southern US flank brushing the Ardennes as they passed to the north. This plan would solve Montgomery's manpower dilemma. It gave Montgomery an opportunity to concentrate his 21st Army Group for any strategic objective in his army's path. It would also obscure the participation of American generals Eisenhower and Bradley.

Montgomery's third problem involved the issue of command. The British had agreed that Eisenhower would take over command of Allied Ground Forces from General Montgomery when the Americans formed a second army [Patton's Third] in Normandy. Eisenhower had declined to take the command on August 1 as scheduled, citing communication problems at his new headquarters. Montgomery retained command of Allied Ground Forces until September 1; on that date Winston Churchill arranged for Montgomery's promotion to Field Marshal to take some of the sting out of his reduction in authority. With this promotion Montgomery outranked Eisenhower, his boss, five stars to four. The British would dispute Eisenhower's command through the end of the war.

Although the British had agreed to Montgomery's removal from Ground Forces Command prior to the invasion; it was, like their agreement to do the invasion of southern France, not an agreement they were prepared to honor. Occasionally the British reached an agreement with their Allies which did not sufficiently favor their own political interests. These agreements were treated as ongoing disputes, still open to debate and future discussion. The British seldom agreed to anything that was inimical to their own political interest.

If Montgomery could convince the Americans to give up their thrust south of the Ardennes and concentrate the great bulk of Allied divisions north of the Ardennes, it might be possible for Montgomery to retain sole command of the resulting single thrust. If, on the other hand, the Americans and French succeeded in establishing a viable thrust through southeastern France, the possibility that one general, especially a general with his headquarters north of the Ardennes, could retain control of all Allied armies was greatly reduced. This was probably why Prime Minister Churchill fought so hard to get Dragoon cancelled. Without the seaports in Southern France the Allied advance into Germany would have been forced by logistics to take a more northern route, closer to Antwerp, which eventually became the main Allied supply base.

By 18 August, Montgomery had come up with a plan that satisfied both his desperate need for American reinforcements and greatly enhanced his ability to retain control of Allied Ground Forces. On that day Montgomery wrote to Brooke, "After crossing SEINE 12 and 21 Army Groups should keep together as a solid mass of some 40 divisions which would be so strong that it need fear nothing. The force should move northwards."[1011]

British historians have tried to show that there was nothing personal or political in Montgomery's proposals to support his own drive to the north. Hamilton wrote, "To suggest . . . that Montgomery wished to strike north for political and nationalistic reasons is absurd. To his fingertips, Monty was a professional soldier . . ."[1012]

Montgomery may have been a professional soldier, but he was also a terribly persistent self-promoter. British historians ask their readers to believe that it was just a mere coincidence that all of Montgomery's plans furthered both his own reputation and British political interests. What was good for General Montgomery was obviously good for Great Britain, and Montgomery never admitted to anything that would compromise his status as the best British general since Wellington. According to Montgomery's recollection, all of his battles were glorious victories; and they all went exactly according to plan.

Bradley later wrote about their August 13 meeting: "With our [US] forces poised to close the trap at Falaise-Argentan and Monty's forces falling down on the job, Monty could not have chosen a more inappropriate time to unveil his strategic plan. Ike and I were dismayed—both at the plan and the timing . . . . [I]t subordinated U.S. forces to Monty's to an absurd and unacceptable degree."[1013] Montgomery could never understand the American's negative reaction to his plans. Empathy was one emotion Montgomery never experienced.

On the afternoon of Sunday, August 13, the survival of the German Fifth Panzer and Seventh Armies was hanging in the balance. With 200,000 Americans awaiting his instructions on the open German flank, Montgomery decided to remove the three senior Allied officers from the field of battle for an afternoon tea party, awards ceremony, intelligence briefing, and strategic planning session. Even in retrospect, the professional hubris required to call this meeting was disturbing. Any attempt to find military logic in the

---

[1011] Hamilton, *Master*, 798.
[1012] Hamilton, *Master*, 805.
[1013] Bradley, *A General's Life*, 299.

thought process that guided Montgomery's behavior that Sunday afternoon would beg the question: What about the Germans?

Montgomery used the Sunday afternoon meeting with his Allies to address every one of his problems; and in each case Montgomery opted for the political rather than the military solution. His most pressing need was to find employment for all those Americans sitting on the open German flank. Obviously, he could not allow them to come north of Argentan. If Patton's men took Falaise, it would look like the Americans were winning this war all by themselves. The political fallout from an all-American victory in Normandy might cost him the support of Churchill and Brooke and possibly his job. Sending some of Patton's people northeast at a time they were expecting [through *ULTRA*] a German attack on Haislips' XV Corps was not an ideal solution either, but it was certainly preferable to allowing Patton to move north from Argentan.

Montgomery instructed his intelligence officers to prepare an elaborate briefing for the Americans showing that too many Germans had already escaped from the Falaise Gap. He asked them for a conclusion which suggested it was time to begin implementing the wider Seine envelopment in order to trap those Germans who had already escaped from Normandy. British intelligence officers did not come right out and say that all the Germans had gotten away, but they did throw dust into the existing 'fog of battle.' As Montgomery wrote to Bradley the next day, "It is difficult to say what enemy are inside the ring, and what have gotten out to the east. *A good deal may have escaped.*"[1014]

It is not clear how much of this charade Eisenhower and Bradley believed, but Bradley followed Montgomery's instructions the following day and sent six of Patton's divisions northeast. Bradley later wrote, "The news [of the German escape from the Falaise Gap] was a shattering disappointment—one of my greatest of the war. A golden opportunity had truly been lost. I boiled inside, blaming Monty for the blunder."[1015] The news of the German escape from Falaise was, of course, a ruse, wholly concocted at British 21st Army Group Headquarters. The combat elements of those German divisions in Normandy had gone nowhere, and *ULTRA* confirmed this information. British historian Ronald Lewin wrote, ". . . whatever else Montgomery and Bradley may have lacked [at the Falaise Gap], it was not intelligence about

---

[1014] Bradley, *A General's Life*, 299, Footnote. Bradley's italics. Also see *Hamilton, Master*, 792.

[1015] Bradley, *A General's Life*, 299.

the enemy. These messages [*ULTRA*] confirm, in fact, that an explanation for the Allies' failure to cutoff the Germans completely at Falaise must be sought elsewhere."[1016] Lewin suggests, very politely, that the briefing British Intelligence presented to Bradley and Eisenhower on the afternoon of August 13 was an utter distortion of the truth; and he was right.

Based on the manipulated intelligence estimates his staff officers had produced on cue, Montgomery proceeded to sort out new missions for Bradley and Crerar. Since many of the Germans had already escaped, closing the gap between Falaise and Argentan had become less urgent. That job he gave to Crerar's First Canadian Army. The Canadians would launch their new attack around noon on August 14. Again, since many Germans had already escaped, it was now time to launch the plan Montgomery had preferred all along. This was Plan M517, the wide envelopment to the Seine. Bradley later wrote, "Primary responsibility for . . . casting the nets further northeast to entrap the fleeing Germans west of the Seine, fell on me."[1017]

Montgomery also presented his new plan to the Americans for the Allied advance into Germany. Patton's Third Army would clear the Brittany peninsula, open the ports, and then move into central France forming a defensive screen east of Paris. Hodges' First U.S. Army and any other U.S. divisions the Americans could supply would move north alongside Montgomery's right flank with the American left brushing the north edge of the Ardennes forest as they drove east. Montgomery's plan eliminated Bradley's secondary thrust south of the Ardennes; it utterly reeked of British politics.

From Montgomery's point of view, the plan had a lot to recommend it. First, it completely solved Montgomery's manpower problems. The Americans would supply all the men Montgomery needed to get his Second British Army to Berlin. Second, the plan dramatically increased the possibility that Montgomery could retain Command of all Allied Ground Forces. With the only Allied thrust north of the Ardennes in a sector assigned to him, at a minimum, Montgomery would be commanding the only Allied divisions in Europe with an offensive mission. Bradley would be left commanding only Patton's Third Army, and they would be tied down in defensive positions east of Paris.

All Montgomery had to do was to convince Eisenhower to humiliate his fellow American generals by eliminating their thrust into Germany and

---

[1016] Lewin, *ULTRA*, 342.
[1017] Bradley, *A General's Life*, 300.

by assigning their divisions to fight beside his 21st Army Group north of the Ardennes. In retrospect, Montgomery's success with Eisenhower and the British officers at SHAEF was truly remarkable. By December 1944, all that remained of Bradley's secondary thrust south of the Ardennes was Patton's Third Army. Montgomery had gotten most of what he asked for back in August.

Bradley was never given permission to move north of Argentan. Sunday, August 13th, ended the way it had begun. The German Fifth Panzer and Seventh Armies were still holding defensive positions within the Falaise Gap. The Germans were held in Normandy on Hitler's orders. The Americans were held south of Argentan on Montgomery's orders, they hadn't moved either. *Neither Hitler nor Montgomery had a clear picture of the events then unfolding in Normandy. Hitler had an excuse; he was a thousand miles away.*

From 11:30 a.m. on August 13, no Allied force under Montgomery's command was engaged in closing the trap on the Germans. The Germans just dropped from Montgomery's sight. It was almost as if 21st Army Group Headquarters had become lost in the 'fog of battle.' That same Sunday, ". . . General Crerar was told by Montgomery that he was giving Dempsey's Second British Army the task of capturing the town of Falaise but that First Canadian Army was to dominate the Falaise area . . . It was further intended that . . . Simonds [Canadian II Corps] exploit south-east and capture Trun as a matter of urgency."[1018] The Canadian attack had not been going well; they were still short of Falaise, while the Americans had been waiting at Argentan for nearly a day.

With all the political issues swirling around in his head, the general who preferred slow-motion maneuvers and set-piece battles was losing his grip. Given the emphasis on politics Churchill and Brooke insisted on, it was difficult for Montgomery to concentrate on what was militarily important in Normandy. Von Clausewitz wrote, ". . . it follows that the destruction of the enemy's forces is always the means by which the purpose of the engagement is achieved."[1019] Eisenhower tried to keep his generals focused on their enemy: "Ike keeps continually after both Montgomery and Bradley to destroy the enemy now rather than to be content with mere gains of territory,"[1020] Montgomery rarely listened to anything Eisenhower said and

---

[1018] Bellfield & Essame, *The Battle for Normandy*, p. 209. From Michael Reynolds, *Steel Inferno, I SS Panzer Corps in Normandy*, (New York: Sarpedon, 1997), 249.

[1019] Von Clausewitz, 95.

[1020] Butcher, 636.

he paid a heavy price because of it. If he had listened to Eisenhower at the Falaise Gap and less than a month later at Antwerp, Montgomery's military reputation would have been greatly enhanced.

With the *Dragoon* arguments behind him, Eisenhower was acutely aware of the British tendency to play political games with military strategy. What both Eisenhower and Bradley observed at Montgomery's headquarters that Sunday afternoon [August 13] was so unusual, so irrational the Americans must have been terribly dispirited and shaken by what they had just gone through. In a subtle understatement Bradley later wrote, "It was a distinctly uncomfortable afternoon."[1021]

On August 14, at 1142 hours the Canadian attack toward Falaise finally got underway. It was quickly in trouble. The Germans had discovered a copy of the Canadian attack plans on the body of a dead Canadian reconnaissance driver. "They redeployed with exact knowledge of the Canadian lines of advance."[1022] The commanding officer of the leading Canadian tank brigade was killed very early; this caused some confusion at the point of attack. The Canadians received more bad luck when they discovered that their usual 'yellow smoke' identifying Allied units was now being used by the RAF as 'target indicators.' According to the Canadians, Hastings wrote, ". . . the bombing disaster had a severe effect upon the morale and determination of the troops embarking upon TRACTABLE."[1023]

Air-ground coordination was always difficult within British 21st Army Group. The Canadian First Army found themselves in the unfortunate position of having to share tactical air support with the British. Dickson wrote, "Second British Army's demands kept 83 Group so busy as to effectively leave First Canadian Army without any tactical air support until HQ 84 Group could be brought to the continent."[1024] This did not happen until August 12, much too late to develop the teamwork and coordination necessary for close infantry support missions in Normandy. Everyone in Montgomery's 21st Army Group suffered because of his inability to work closely with senior RAF commanders, and this included Crerar's Canadians.

Later on the afternoon of August 14, Bradley, following Montgomery's written instructions, told Patton to send three corps northeast: Haislip's

---

[1021] Bradley, *A General's Life*, 299.
[1022] Hastings, *Overlord*, 302.
[1023] Hastings, *Overlord*, 302.
[1024] Dickson, 294.

XV Corps to Dreux, Walker's XX Corps to Chartres and Cook's XII Corps to Orleans. After he was released from Montgomery's political games in Normandy, Patton wrote, "I am very happy and elated. I got all the corps moving by 2030 so that if Monty tries to be careful, it will be too late."[1025]

By August 15, the Canadian attack was stalling. The Germans launched a strong counterattack at Soulangy. Operation Tractable had carried the Canadians to within a mile of Falaise. That evening Montgomery repeated his instructions to the Canadians to extend their axis of advance to the village of Trun, some eleven miles southeast of Falaise.

No sooner had Montgomery released Patton from Normandy than he began to have second thoughts. Patton's departure from Normandy seemed to lift the 'fog of battle' at 21st Army Group Headquarters. British intelligence had stumbled onto the obvious. Bradley wrote, "The very next day, August 15, intelligence reversed itself. To our astonishment it was now reported that the Germans had not yet withdrawn after all. Elements of at least five panzer divisions were at or approaching Argentan."[1026]

Patton recalled that General Bradley visited his headquarters that day, ". . . suffering from nerves."[1027] Bradley was not the only Allied general suffering an anxiety attack. That evening Montgomery wrote to Brooke, "The general picture in this part of the front [Third Army] is that PATTON is heading straight for Paris and is determined to get there and will probably do so."[1028] If Montgomery did not want Patton near Falaise, neither did he relish the thought of Patton's Third Army crossing the Seine and liberating Paris. The headlines created by Patton's Third United States Army liberating Paris would have caused great distress at 10 Downing Street. This was one of the reasons Eisenhower gave the liberation of Paris to Hodges' First Army.

The following day, August 16, Hitler finally gave his battered army permission to withdraw from Normandy. British *ULTRA* intelligence recorded this transmission and forwarded it to the Allied generals in France. Montgomery suddenly became alive to the fact that there were still Germans in Normandy. He could control British intelligence in the field, but he could not control *ULTRA*. The War Office controlled *ULTRA* and after the

[1025] Blumenson, (Ed.), *The Patton Papers, 1940-1945*, 510.

[1026] Bradley, *A General's Life*, 303.

[1027] Blumenson, (Ed.), *The Patton Papers, 1940-1945*, 511.

[1028] Hamilton, *Master*, 792.

war F.W. Winterbotham locked the intercepts away ". . . in the vaults of Whitehall."[1029] Both sources were beyond Montgomery's reach.

Montgomery had to react. He telephoned Bradley and asked if the Americans could help close the gap by meeting the Canadians at Chambois.[1030] Most of Patton's Army had been sent, on Montgomery's instructions, into central France to close off the Paris-Orleans gap in preparation for Montgomery's power drive to the Seine. Bradley told Montgomery he would do what he could.

Bradley ordered Patton to launch the attack that Montgomery requested, but he also told Patton that he was giving command of those divisions near Argentan to General Gerow's V Corps which had been pinched out of the action near Tinchebray. Some time was lost in the confusion when Gerow's V Corps took over from Patton's provisional staff. After getting instructions from First Army, Gerow's staff [10 officers] left in three jeeps in a heavy rain only to discover later that their one radio was out. They eventually found 90th Infantry Division Headquarters and used their facilities to set-up the planned attack.[1031] Patton had alerted the 80th Infantry Division to move into the Argentan area from its positions southwest of Alencon. 2nd French Armored Division was west of Argentan to Ecouche. General Jacques Leclerc's French tankers were ordered to hold the western flank and provide fire support for Gerow's two attacking divisions, the U.S. 80th and 90th Infantry.

The American attack began just after dark during the evening of August 17/18. The U.S. 80 Division, attacking toward Argentan, was new to combat and it showed. Their attack made some progress until they tried to cross the main Argentan-Evreux highway. Hedgerows north of the highway gave the Germans a protected field of fire. The highway was under fire from both tanks and artillery. The 80th Infantry, in their first major combat roll, hit a stone wall. "No units of the 80th Division made much progress."[1032] To the east, U.S. 90th Division had more success. By midnight on August 17/18, the 90th Division had taken both the town and the critical ridge line at le Bourg-St. Leonard.[1033] The Americans drove through St. Leonard to attack the high ground south of Chambois as German resistance stiffened.

[1029] Winterbotham, Preface, vii.

[1030] Bradley, *A General's Life*, 303. Also see Blumenson, *The Duel*, 276.

[1031] Weigley, *Eisenhower's Lieutenants*, 211.

[1032] Weigley, *Eisenhower's Lieutenants*, 212.

[1033] Weigley, *Eisenhower's Lieutenants*, 212.

On August 16, the Canadians at long last entered the town of Falaise. The town was by now just a pile of rubble and it required a full day to clear the roads. But the pivot which had been anchoring the eastern German flank since the loss of Caen had finally been broken. The following afternoon, the Canadians and Poles had fought to within a few miles of Trun. Montgomery placed an urgent telephone call to First Canadian Army Headquarters and talked to the Chief of Staff: "It is absolutely essential that both the Armored Divs of 2 Cdn Corps close the gap between First Cdn Army and Third U.S. Army. 1 Polish Armored Div must thrust on past Trun to Chambois at all costs, and as quickly as possible."[1034]

The Polish 1st Armored Division then delivered one of the bravest performances of any Allied unit fighting in Europe. Although they were new to combat and heavily outnumbered, the Poles drove through Trun and by the afternoon of August 19 had entered the town of Chambois. At 1930 hours that afternoon, Major Zgordzelski, commanding the 10th Polish Dragoons met Captain Waters, commanding G Company, 359th U.S. Infantry Regiment in Chambois.[1035] It had been seven days since U.S. 5th Armored's CCA had pulled into that part of Argentan south of the Orne but the northern and southern pincers of Allied Army Groups had finally met.

Polish bravery had gotten the 10th Dragoons into Chambois, but they were not strong enough to contain the German force they had surrounded. The German escape gap was closed but it was not sealed. "The Poles inside Chambois had lost contact with the rest of their division. The largest portion of the Polish 1st Armored, some 1,500 infantry and eighty tanks, was cut off on Mont Ormel from the rest of the Canadian 2nd Corps . . . during the night of August 19-20 . . ."[1036] The following morning, when the fog lifted, ". . . the Poles on Mont Ormel saw the whole plain west and south of them crawling with German vehicles making their way northeastward."[1037] Polish gunners took their revenge on those poor Germans coming under their sights. They killed many Germans. Soon the 2nd SS Panzer Division was joined by paratroopers and panzer grenadiers from other units in launching a series of vicious attacks into Polish positions. The Poles tightened their lines on Mont Ormel but continued to harass the retreating Germans unmercifully.

1034 Hastings, *Overlord*, 303.
1035 Florentin, 240, 243.
1036 Weigley, *Eisenhower's Lieutenants*, 213.
1037 Weigley, *Eisenhower's Lieutenants*, 213.

Through the next day and into the next night the Poles remained surrounded on Mont Ormel. They ran out of medical supplies to treat the wounded and were getting very low on ammunition. The Canadian II Corps, which should have been providing flank protection, was in a desperate battle of its own between Falaise and Trun and could not provide immediate assistance. Montgomery might have used one or two of the British divisions then inactive in the Conde-Flers sector to support the Poles, but he probably considered that they were not battle worthy.[1038]

It was not until the afternoon of August 21st that the Canadians were able to make contact with the Poles trapped on Mont Ormel and deliver much needed ammunition and medical supplies. German Army Group B reported, ". . . that from 40 to 50 percent of the encircled troops had escaped. No doubt this German estimate erred on the side of optimism."[1039] There was a great deal of confusion and chaos within the pocket on both sides. Eisenhower wrote, ". . . I was conducted through it on foot, to encounter scenes that could be described only by Dante. It was literally possible to walk for hundreds of yards at a time, stepping on nothing but dead and decaying flesh."[1040] The German escape route between Argentan, Chambois, Falaise and Vimoutiers had turned into one of the great killing fields of the war. Over ten-thousand German dead littered the battlefield.

Montgomery's failure to close the trap on the Germans between Falaise and Argentan left the Allies in possession of Normandy but also left nearly 200,000 Germans fleeing for the German border. Montgomery's confusion and the tactical mishandling of Allied forces during the battle of the Falaise Gap were clear indications that it was an error for Eisenhower to have left the British general in charge of Allied Ground Forces on August 1. Russell Weigley wrote, ". . . the fumbled closing of the Falaise gap indicated the urgency of Eisenhower's taking over as ground commander."[1041]

Montgomery's confusion was centered on the town of Falaise. Martin Blumenson wrote, "The lure of Falaise on Montgomery was strong and constant. In August he changed his instructions on who was to take it no

---

[1038] Montgomery cable (M-92), to War Office, PRO (CAB 106/1066). From D'Este, *Decision*, 262.
[1039] Weigley, *Eisenhower's Lieutenants*, 214.
[1040] Eisenhower, *Crusade*, 279.
[1041] Weigley, *Eisenhower's Lieutenants*, 216.

less than five times . . . His inconsistency on Falaise paralleled his lack of firm decision on how to trap the Germans in Normandy."[1042]

Montgomery had several things on his mind during the Battle of the Falaise Gap, as his meeting with the Americans on the afternoon of August 13 made abundantly clear. He was not intellectually gifted. He required long periods of time when he was not disturbed by events or other officers to properly arrange his thoughts and make his plans. Unfortunately, it was not possible to find long quiet periods during the period August 7 to August 21; there was simply too much going on for General Montgomery to feel comfortable with the pace of events.

Montgomery tried to plan. Blumenson wrote, ". . . they [the Allies] simply took for granted, before the event, the outcomes they desired. The result was tactical and operational carelessness and negligence, together with a misreading of what was required to vanquish the enemy." After the American breakout at St. Lo the battle became mobile, Montgomery appeared to be overwhelmed by the events. He almost seemed to lose interest.

Montgomery behaved as if all he had to do was give an order, as if in giving the order, he had accomplished what he had intended. But it is also the commander's responsibility to see that the order is carried out; and if the order was not carried out it was the commander's responsibility to set it right. Montgomery did not do that in Normandy. Weigley wrote, "But in the critical decisions about how to capitalize on Hitler's strategic blunders, Montgomery not only erred but persisted in error for days on end in his judgment of the Canadians' pace toward Argentan."[1043] Both armored divisions in First Canadian Army were new to combat; some of their difficulties could have been anticipated.

Montgomery seemed to have been paralyzed by the American's speed. To Montgomery, Patton must have seemed both a blessing and a curse. With Patton running around the southern German flank, it was never possible to create a neat, tidy order of battle for either side. This might have confused Montgomery. Blumenson wrote, "Montgomery seemed to have lost the firm grip, the master's touch . . . he had heretofore displayed, particularly in North Africa. Of the verve and arrogance formerly characteristic of him, only the arrogance was visible. He seemed tired and dispirited in Normandy. Perhaps the developments in August overwhelmed him."[1044]

[1042] Martin Blumenson, *The Battle of the Generals,* (New York: William Morrow, 1993), 217.

[1043] Weigley, *Eisenhower's Lieutenants,* 216.

[1044] Blumenson, *The Battle of the Generals,* 264.

As an Allied commander, Montgomery was an abysmal failure. He got along with neither the Americans nor the Canadians. The French absolutely refused to serve under a British commander. Such widespread mistrust of the prickly, little British general did not bode well for future Allied operations in which Montgomery played a significant role.

For a host of reasons, Montgomery's usefulness to the Allied cause came to an end in Normandy, probably within a few weeks of the invasion. Any other British general could have done as well as Montgomery did at Caen; and very few would have handled the Battle of the Falaise Gap so incompetently.

The battles in France were not conducted in a vacuum. The world was watching. Staff officers from the British War Office in London were closely watching the events in Normandy as the Allied Armies fought to close the noose on the German Seventh and Fifth Panzer Armies. Sir John Kennedy [Assistant Chief of the Imperial General Staff] described an August 17 visit he made to Montgomery's headquarters in Normandy: "I asked Monty if Patton had been out of control, because it had seemed to us that he should have turned North, and not gone to Orleans, or so far toward Paris. Monty replied that Orleans was Patton's own idea . . . [but that] He intended Patton to swing north now."[1045] Patton did originally favor the wider envelopment to the Seine, but no one who reads his diary entries for August 12 and 13 could possibly suggest that his presence at Orleans on August 17 was his own idea. Montgomery's hand written letter to General Bradley on August 14 removes any doubt on this score.

F.W. Winterbotham was another British staff officer [in *ULTRA* intelligence]; he made several interesting comments about the events in France during this period. "We knew that what was left of Eberbach's armor was virtually immobile; he was short of ammunition and fuel. It looked as if the American corps [Haislip's XV Corps] could close the gap . . . It was some time later that Patton's bitter remarks to Bradley about Montgomery were allowed to be known . . . there were some questions being asked in London as to why Patton could not try and close the gap from the south?"[1046] Clearly, Patton would have loved the opportunity to answer those questions.

Neither Sir John Kennedy nor F. W. Winterbotham was directly involved in the handling of Allied forces in Normandy. They were staff officers; they were working in London. *How did it happen that two British staff officers working in London came to understand exactly what should have happened*

[1045] Kennedy, 342.
[1046] Winterbotham, 155, 158.

in Normandy? While the General in charge of Allied Ground Forces, the best British general since Wellington, failed to grasp the significance of the U.S. XV Corps on an open German flank.

The answer is that Montgomery was fully aware of the significance of the Americans on the open German flank; but it was psychologically and politically impossible for him to allow the Americans to complete their drive to Falaise. Why?

Part of the answer lies in Montgomery's mental condition and part of it lies in his upbringing. Psychologically, Montgomery did not develop a normal personality. Historian Norman Gelb wrote, "His egocentric nature made it impossible for him to respond to the complex situation in which he found himself except by insisting that he had not been mistaken about anything . . ."[1047] Everyone, with the possible exception Winston Churchill seemed to have been aware of it. British military historians have been ignoring Montgomery's mental condition for sixty years, pretending that it did not influence his conduct on the battlefield. In retrospect, it has become very clear that Montgomery's mental condition played a significant and usually negative role in most of his battles.

Eisenhower thought Montgomery was a psychopath suffering from an inferiority complex. Montgomery's stepson, John Carver, talked about his ". . . schizoid tendencies engendered by his upbringing . . ."[1048] Montgomery's superiors often had to deal with his 'insubordination,' which led to confusion in those officers unaware of Montgomery's behavior or to nasty confrontations with an officer whose instructions had been ignored. Alan Brooke often had to keep his protégé on the rails, "[I] . . . give you a word of warning against doing wild things. You have got a name for annoying people at times with your ways . . ."[1049]

The Americans and Canadians often saw the worst side of Montgomery. After one bitter feud with Montgomery, General Crerar wrote, "Monty has been pretty trying on a couple of occasions during the last few days . . . He is very upset at the loss of operational command over the U.S. Armies, and his nomination to Field Marshal's rank has accentuated, rather than eased, *his mental disturbance.*"[1050] Eisenhower became so upset with Montgomery's

---

[1047] Norman Gelb, *Ike and Monty: Generals at War,* (New York: William Morrow, 1994), 329.

[1048] Hamilton, *Making,* 278.

[1049] Hamilton, *Making,* 433.

[1050] Letter Crerar to Stuart, 5 Sept. 1944, from Dickson, 335. Italics added.

behavior that he just quit talking to him.[1051] The British and their Allied friends were very poorly served with Bernard L. Montgomery in a command position. Yet, because of his immense popularity there was nothing anyone could do about it.

Given Montgomery's hermit-like existence, his memorization of the Field Service Regulations, "until he knew it by heart,"[1052] his planning a ski vacation with the same intricacy he would plan a set-piece battle,[1053] his insistence that all his battles went according to plan,[1054] and because of his instinctive fear of senior officers his own age and rank, it seems likely that Montgomery was suffering a personality disorder called an obsessive personality. It is also likely that Montgomery suffered from an 'Obsessive-Compulsive Disorder' or OCD.

In the book *Too Perfect*, Allan E, Mallinger, M.D. and Jeannette De Wyze list eleven personality traits associated with the disorder. "These include: a fear of making errors, a fear of making the wrong decision or choice, a strong devotion to work, a need for order or firmly established routine, frugality, a need to know and follow the rules, emotional guardedness, a tendency to be stubborn or oppositional, a heightened sensitivity to being pressured or controlled by others, an inclination to worry, ruminate, or doubt, a need to be above criticism—moral, professional, or personal, cautiousness, a chronic inner pressure to use every minute productively."[1055] Doctor Mallinger's list is, almost point by point, a mirror image of General Montgomery's troubled personality.

Montgomery's irrational behavior at the Falaise Gap was also influenced by what General Henry Crerar called, ". . . the Englishman's traditional belief in the superiority of the Englishman . . ."[1056] British political and military leaders during World War II came from the upper classes in England. Their right to lead other men was an inherited birthright, confirmed by British society through years of education and training. ". . . there is deeply ingrained in the British psyche a belief in the natural right of the British to lead. The leaders were a select group, prepared by birth and education, augmented over the generations by newly recruited talent, and imbued with the obligation to

---

[1051] Ambrose, *Eisenhower, Soldier, General*, 393.
[1052] Hamilton, *Making,* 53.
[1053] Hamilton, *Making*, 210.
[1054] Montgomery, *Normandy*, 112.
[1055] Allan E. Mallinger, M.D., and Jeanette DeWyze, *Too Perfect, When Being in Control Gets Out of Control*, (New York: Clarkson Potter, 1992), 3.
[1056] Dickson, 272.

guide the people of the world, the duty to use their gift of leadership for the benefit of all."[1057] There can be little doubt that Montgomery saw himself as one of the most 'professional' soldiers in the British Army. While he may not have seen himself as the 20th Century Duke of Wellington, he clearly wanted other people to think of him in that light.

The destruction of the German Fifth Panzer and Seventh Armies would have been a huge military prize; it represented an excellent opportunity to destroy most of the German Army in France at a minimum cost in Allied lives. It might also have ended the war. With the British economy a shambles and British manpower shortages crippling the combat effectiveness of their few infantry divisions in France, no country needed an end to the war more than the British.

Yet Montgomery was a troubled general; he had political factors to consider. He allowed British politics to influence his emotions. Montgomery's strong emotional ties to King and country melded with a strong professional animus toward the Americans in negating what should have been an obvious tactical decision. If Montgomery had destroyed the German Army in France, he would have been well on his way to winning the war with all that implied for his war weary country.

The poor performance of the British Second Army in Normandy had tied Montgomery's hands. He did not expect the Germans to be that good. No one did. But when the Americans broke the German line at St. Lo, it was the speed of the Americans he found so unnerving. Instead of turning the American's loose on the open German flank; Montgomery stopped the Americans at Argentan and then sent them northeast to close off the Paris-Orleans gap. There were simply too many bitter pills on Montgomery's desk. He could not allow the Americans, especially George Patton, to take Falaise away from his Second British Army, regardless of the cost.

From approximately the 1st of August through the end of the war, Montgomery would spend as much time planning how to slow down the Americans as he would trying to defeat the Germans. *On Sunday, August 13, both of Montgomery's new plans, his intelligence presentation suggesting the Germans had fled Normandy and his strategic plan for the Allied drive into Germany involved disrupting planned American offensives. In both cases, the plans that Montgomery designed overlooked the sounder military strategy while proposing alternate schemes that clearly favored British political interests. Given General Eisenhower's reluctance to command, it was going to be long winter for Allied soldiers.*

[1057] Blumenson, *The Battle of the Generals*, 265.

Chapter 11

What Really Happened at the
FALAISE GAP?

"For several days I really had the impression that I was reliving the situation of 1940 in reverse. Complete disarray in the enemy [German] ranks, columns surprised, etc. The picture of this attack would have been superb had it been decided to close the Argentan-Falaise Pocket. The Supreme Command was formally opposed to it. History will be the judge."[1058] Major General Jean Leclerc, in a letter to Charles DeGaulle

Prime Minister Churchill and C.I.G.S. Alan Brooke got exactly what they wanted in Normandy. In General Montgomery, they had selected a British Ground Forces commander that neither Eisenhower nor anyone else could control. Now, for better or worse, Allied armies would be subject to General Montgomery's uncertain grasp of how to conduct mobile warfare. Montgomery had never done well on a mobile battlefield; and the final battles in Normandy would provide a stern test of his abilities to think fast and adjust his tactics as battlefield conditions developed.

The plan, as Montgomery later boasted, had not changed at all from their plans prior to D-day.[1059] For planning and logistics purposes, the Allies had drawn a map of the battlefield with a series of phase lines in a giant wheel aimed at the center of France. Once the Allied front had reached Granville-Vire in the American sector and Argentan-Falaise in the British sector, they intended to turn 90 degrees from the southerly direction of attack, to an east, northeasterly direction toward Paris, the Seine and central France.

Historians often mention the planned American breakout on the western flank at St. Lo. The U.S. VII Corps did break out at St. Lo; but it was not planned. It happened because Hitler insisted his army adopt a 'no retreat'

[1058] Letter written shortly after the event by Major General Jacques Leclerc to Charles DeGaulle. From Florentin, 129. Also see H. Essame, 172.

[1059] Montgomery, *Normandy*, 112.

defense strategy in Normandy, not as the result of an Allied pre-invasion plan. The Allies had figured that the Germans would conduct a series of limited withdraws up to the Seine River where the Allies planned a pause to develop a logistical base and buildup supplies for the drive to Germany. They estimated that they would have forces on the Seine and Loire Rivers by about D + 90 or 90 days after D-day.[1060]

The original north-south inter-Army Group boundary was drawn just north of the line Domfront-Alencon. On August 3, Montgomery moved the boundary line north a few miles, just north of the line la Ferte Mace-Carrouges-Sees. Once the Americans began pouring through the towns of Avranches and Pontaubault at the base of the Brittany peninsula on July 31, plans for the giant wheel to the Seine intensified.

During the first week of August, the most significant German deployment was the movement of the Panzer divisions out of the British sector near Caen. The Allies knew German armor was pulling out, but they did not know exactly what the Germans were planning. Most Allied commanders thought the Germans were moving their armor to critical road junctions, river crossings and hills to cover the withdrawal of the slower infantry divisions from Normandy. This seemed to make the most sense, because all senior officers were agreed that the German Army had been soundly defeated in Normandy. Their only hope was to get behind the Seine without getting chopped to pieces by Allied fighter-bombers.

In spite of Bradley's statements to the contrary, the German attack at Mortain on the night of August 6/7 did not catch Allied front line troops by surprise. Thanks to a timely *ULTRA* warning the Allies had plenty of time to prepare for the Germans. But the German counter-attack at Mortain made no sense; didn't the Germans know they were a defeated army?

General Bradley looked at the map on the wall of his trailer at 12th Army Group headquarters, and must have been amazed at what he saw. If the Germans would persist at Mortain for a few days, there was a possibility the Allies could destroy the German Seventh and Fifth Panzer Armies right there in Normandy. Bradley's staff loved the plan. The following morning, August 8, he sold the plan to Eisenhower and asked Eisenhower to return to his headquarters, so they could look at a wall map and place a call to Montgomery. After Montgomery's questions about the German counter attack at Mortain had been satisfied, he readily agreed to Bradley's plan to trap the Germans

---

[1060] Eisenhower, *Crusade*, Map, 309.

in Normandy. He also agreed to move the inter-Army Group boundary line north to a few miles south of the line Briouze-Argentan-St. Leonard.[1061]

The above paragraphs outline the official [Eisenhower-Bradley] version of how the Allied generals decided to destroy the German Fifth Panzer and Seventh Armies in Normandy. British intelligence officer, Group Captain F.W. Winterbotham offers a vastly different and far more believable version of these events. In *The ULTRA Secret*, Winterbotham relates how he recorded an *ULTRA* message on, ". . . two whole sheets of my *ULTRA* paper . . ."[1062] The date was 2 August 1944. Winterbotham listed Hitler's instructions to Kluge, ". . . in considerable detail, [Kluge was] to collect together four of the armored divisions from the Caen front with sufficient supporting infantry divisions and make a decisive counter-attack to retake Avranches and thus to divide the American forces . . ."[1063]

Winterbotham recalls that he got the intercept to Churchill right away and that Eisenhower thought the message was so important that he checked on its authenticity. Satisfied that the message was authentic, according to Winterbotham, Eisenhower then directed Montgomery to close the trap on the Germans from the north while Bradley and the Americans closed the gap from the south.[1064] Winterbotham also wrote, ". . . the opportunity that had been offered to us was such that the decision to alter the entire strategy became one for Eisenhower himself, and I understand it had also to be approved by the joint Allied chiefs of staff."[1065]

Winterbotham suggests that Bradley was instructed to prepare for the German attack by preparing a ". . . defense in depth in the Avranches area . . ."[1066] Winterbotham also learned that, ". . . despite the signals from Hitler, Montgomery was still in favor of an advance on a broad front to the Seine."[1067] Although it differs significantly from the Eisenhower-Bradley version of these events, Winterbotham's account is more believable. He was not directly involved in the Allied chain-of-command in France. He had nothing to hide and was unaware of Eisenhower's private conversations with Bradley on August 12 and 13.

[1061] For a different explanation of these events see, F.W. Winterbotham, *The Ultra Secret,* 148-158 inclusive.

[1062] Winterbotham, 148.

[1063] Winterbotham, 148.

[1064] Winterbotham, 150.

[1065] Winterbotham, 150.

[1066] Winterbotham, 150.

[1067] Winterbotham, 150.

On August 8, Captain Harry Butcher made an entry in his diary: "Ike keeps continually after both Montgomery and Bradley to destroy the enemy now rather than to be content with mere gains of territory."[1068] August 8 was the day Eisenhower and Bradley agreed to conduct the short envelopment between Falaise and Argentan. Butcher's phrase, ". . . Ike keeps continually after his generals . . ." suggests that the possibility of destroying the German army in Normandy had been available for some time and was not the result of a sudden thought that popped into Bradley's head the evening before. It fits more closely with Winterbotham's account, which suggested that the Allied command had been watching the possibility of the Falaise encirclement for a few days.

Winterbotham also accurately detailed Montgomery's reluctance to conduct the short envelopment at Argentan and clearly states his preference for the wider Seine envelopment. His account is verified by Forrest Pogue's late May 1947 interview with Montgomery's intelligence officer, Brigadier E.T. Williams: "He [Montgomery] was fundamentally more interested in full envelopment [at the Seine] than this inner envelopment. He missed his chance of closing at the Seine by doing the envelopment at Falaise."[1069]

On August 9, General Eisenhower wrote to his boss in Washington: *"Under my urgent directions all possible strength in France is being turned to the destruction of the forces now facing us. I firmly believe we have a great opportunity for a victory which if fairly complete will allow us complete freedom of action in France and will have incalculable results . . . Patton, Bradley, and Montgomery are all imbued with this necessity and alive to the opportunity."*[1070] According to this letter, Eisenhower is personally involved in Allied efforts to destroy the German Army in Normandy. Eisenhower's phrase, "Under my urgent directions," suggests that Eisenhower's command presence during the final battle in Normandy was substantially greater than the interested bystander that Montgomery and Bradley described and corroborates Winterbotham's earlier statement that, "the opportunity was such that the decision to alter the entire strategy became one for Eisenhower himself."[1071]

[1068] Butcher, 636.
[1069] Pogue interview with Brigadier Williams, 30, 31 May 1947. From D'Este, *Decision*, 450.
[1070] Chandler, (Ed.), *The Eisenhower Papers, Vol. IV*, 2062. Italics added.
[1071] Winterbotham, 150.

Eisenhower continued in the same letter to General Marshall by describing how he thought the battle would develop. He wrote, *"Patton has the marching wing which will turn in rather sharply to the northeast from the general vicinity of Le Mans and just to the west thereof marching toward Alencon and Falaise . . . we have a good chance to encircle and destroy a lot of his (enemy's) forces."*[1072] Eisenhower's mention of 'Falaise' as an offensive goal for Patton's Third Army during the short envelopment is clearly prescience. This was exactly what should have happened. Again, Eisenhower's letter to Marshall seems to confirm the account of the battle provided by F.W. Winterbotham in his excellent book, *The ULTRA Secret.*[1073]

Eisenhower and Bradley both believed that Montgomery had agreed to postpone the wider Seine envelopment until the shorter envelopment had been completed. Unfortunately, Montgomery was not that flexible in his thinking. He simply did not like changing plans, especially a plan he had been working on for some time. "In view of the Mortain counter stroke," Montgomery later wrote, "I decided to attempt *concurrently* a shorter envelopment with the object of bottling up the bulk of the German forces deployed between Falaise and Mortain . . . if we could bring off both these movements we would virtually annihilate the enemy in Normandy."[1074]

It should have been pointed out to General Montgomery that the two operations he had planned were not tactically compatible. Any attempt to conduct the Falaise envelopment prior to executing the wider Seine envelopment would block the roads Montgomery planned on using for his power drive to the Seine. The power drive to the Seine by First Canadian, Second British and First US Armies was an essential feature of Montgomery's wider envelopment. It would trap the Germans against the Seine River after Allied air power had destroyed all the bridges.

George S. Patton Jr., Commanding Third Army, and Major General Wade H. Haislip, Commanding XV Corps were not aware of any disagreements at the army group level. By the evening of August 7, XV Corps had three divisions investing Le Mans: 5th Armored, 79th and 90th Infantry Divisions. The following day Le Mans fell to the Americans.

Eisenhower's exuberance was matched by General Bradley during his discussions with U.S. Secretary of the Treasury Henry Morgenthau. The same day Eisenhower wrote to George Marshall, Bradley told Secretary

---

[1072] Chandler, (Ed.), *The Eisenhower Papers, Vol. IV*, 2062. Italics added.
[1073] Winterbotham, 148-158.
[1074] Montgomery, *Normandy to the Baltic,* 99. Italics in the original.

Morgenthau, "This is an opportunity that comes to a commander not more than once in a century. We're about to destroy an entire hostile army."[1075] The American hinge at Mortain continued to hold as Patton's Third Army poured through the one good east-west road at Avranches.

In London, an interested observer was closely monitoring the events in France. Prime Minister Winston S. Churchill had been getting immediate *ULTRA* updates from F.W. Winterbotham. Winterbotham wrote that Churchill was getting copies of the German radio messages within an hour of their transmission.[1076] The German commander in France [Kluge] was in an argument with Hitler over the Mortain counterattack. Hitler insisted that the attack go forward and Kluge insisted the attack was extremely dangerous with the limited force available and that the Americans were already driving northeast around his vulnerable southern flank.

The argument was transmitted back and forth between German headquarters in East Prussia and Kluge in France by German radio messages encoded on an enigma machine, which British intelligence [*ULTRA*] was reading almost as easily as the Germans. They had obtained a copy of the machine's daily settings from a short German airdrop intended for the defenders of Brest a few weeks earlier.[1077] Winterbotham wrote, "Everybody . . . [including] the Prime Minister, was deeply involved in the Hitler-Kluge drama . . . . When I was reading these signals over the telephone to Churchill, I sensed his controlled excitement at the other end. I think we all felt that this might well be the beginning of the end of the war."[1078]

Churchill's excitement may have been tempered with the understanding that Montgomery's British Army was still stalled north of Falaise and the Americans were about to turn north at Le Mans into a vulnerable German southern flank. The Germans, Churchill knew from *ULTRA*, were terribly desperate and might be near a total collapse. Churchill may have sensed that Montgomery's British Army was getting into a jam in Normandy. Although he could not directly interfere with military affairs in France, Churchill could try to convince the senior American commander that the British were really, really upset about the invasion of southern France, thereby

---

[1075] Bradley, *A General's Life*, 296.
[1076] F.W. Winterbotham, 150.
[1077] Lewin, *ULTRA*, 340, 341.
[1078] F.W. Winterbotham, 151.

gaining Montgomery political room to maneuver in his disputes with the Americans.

On August 9, Churchill summoned Eisenhower to 10 Downing Street for another round of heated arguments over *Dragoon*. The British obviously wanted the invasion of southern France cancelled, but Churchill's timing was interesting. It had been just four days since their last arguments over *Dragoon*. The invasion of southern France was set to go forward in just six days, on August 15. Churchill blustered and bullied. He threatened and he cried. He did his best to intimidate Eisenhower. He said the Americans had become a ". . . big strong and dominating partner."[1079] He threatened ". . . to go to the King and lay down the mantle of my high office."[1080] Churchill had done his best to browbeat the American. Ambrose wrote, "Eisenhower later described the session . . . as one of the most difficult of the entire war."[1081]

Churchill gave a masterful performance. Eisenhower could do nothing to placate the prime minister's distress; he remembered that when the meeting broke up, Churchill was still crying. Churchill's performance won him an August 11 mention in Harry Butcher's diary,[1082] and a deeply personal letter from Eisenhower. On August 11, Eisenhower wrote to Churchill, "I would feel that much of my hard work . . . had been irretrievably lost if we now should lose faith in the organisms that have given higher direction to our war effort, because such lack of faith *would quickly be reflected in discord in our field commands*."[1083]

Two days later, on August 13, Eisenhower, the "big, strong, and dominating partner,' did not overrule the senior British commander in a dispute over the inter-Army Group boundary line at Argentan. Churchill had lost the *Dragoon* arguments, but he had given Montgomery a thoroughly chastised boss.

On August 9 XV Corps received two new divisions: 2nd French Armored and 80th U.S. Infantry. General Patton visited XV Corps headquarters that day, with a Bronze Star medal for General Haislip. The medal from Patton was Haislip's reward for his early capture of Le Mans.[1084] General Patton also gave Haislip oral orders, ". . . to change the Corps' direction of advance

---

[1079] Ambrose, *Eisenhower, Soldier, General*, 328.

[1080] Ambrose, *Eisenhower, Soldier, General*, 330.

[1081] Ambrose, *Eisenhower, Soldier, General*, 328.

[1082] Butcher, 639.

[1083] Chandler, (Ed.), *The Eisenhower Papers, Vol. IV*, 2065. Italics added.

[1084] Headquarters, *XV Corps United States Army, Report After Combat*, No. 17, August 9.

to the north and capture *ALENCON*."[1085] XV Corps sent its 106th Cavalry Group to the area of La Ferte Bernard with the mission of reconnaissance and protecting the Corps' eastern flank. The 80th U.S. Infantry Division, after assembling near St. Hilaire, was trucked to the vicinity of Le Mans. There, "The 80th Infantry . . . was to secure the bridgehead at *LE MANS* and to protect the left flank and rear of the Corps by holding the road centers at *SILLE-LE-GUILLAUME* and *EVRON*." [1086]

Early that morning, 5th Armored Division's Commander, Major General L.E. Oliver, received a warning order changing the direction of his attack to the north. Oliver's division knew little about the Germans between Le Mans and Alencon. They knew the Orne River was going to be an obstacle, ". . . and its lowlands twelve air miles to the north (of Le Mans)."[1087] General Oliver sent the 85th Cavalry Squadron to reconnoiter the Orne River lowlands and bridges. Later that afternoon, at 1740 hours, orders came through from XV Corps Headquarters, 5th Armored was to drive north, ". . . seize crossings over the *ORNE* River and continue north to the *CARROUGE[S]-SEES* line."[1088] These orders also contained information about the other units involved in the attack. The 5th Armored was to be followed closely by the 79th Infantry Division; one regiment of the 79th had been fully motorized so that it could keep up with the armor. Their left flank would be covered by the 2nd French Armored Division, which was then assembling in the vicinity of *VITRE*. The French Armored Division would be closely followed by the U.S. 90th Infantry Division; they also had one regiment fully motorized.

Although he had not received orders to go north until nearly 6:00 PM, Major General L. E. Oliver of 5th Armored Division decided to attack that night. Three hours later Oliver's men were heading north, two combat commands abreast. Combat Command A, Commanded by Brigadier General C.A. Regnier, was soon in a fight with elements of the German 9th Panzer and 708th Infantry Divisions for control of the five Orne River bridges near Ballon. Combat Command R, commanded by Colonel J.T. Cole, on the division's right flank, drove a few miles past Ballon to Marolles-Les-Braults and seized five more river-crossing points. Combat Command B, in division

---

[1085] Hq, *XV Corps US Army, Report,* No. 18, Aug. 9.
[1086] Hq, *XV Corps US Army, Report,* No. 18, Aug. 9.
[1087] Cepeda, 40.
[1088] Cepeda, 41.

reserve, was ordered to assemble on the eastern flank of CCR, prepared for further movement, in the vicinity of Bonne Table.[1089]

The following morning, August 10, 2nd French Armored Division caught up with the 5th Armored. "They took over the task of holding the bridges taken by CCA and also placed a column on CCA's left flank."[1090] CCA was soon fully engaged by elements of 9th Panzer Division at Marolles-Les Braults. CCR got into a fight with the same German division in the vicinity of Mamers. According to Lieutenant Colonel Cepeda's report, "It was a case of draw fire, deploy, establish a base of fire, and maneuver for the entire day . . . . Darkness and fatigue called it a day. CCA and CCR were blooded."[1091] According to General Patton's account of the day's events, ". . . 2nd French Armored and the 5th Armored had had quite a fight . . . in which they lost between them some forty tanks."[1092]

On the morning of August 11, CCA and CCR received orders to bypass resistance at Mamers and Marolles-Les-Brault and to drive toward Sees. By that evening CCR was in the vicinity of Sees. "CCA had by-passed the FORET de PERSEIGNE to the east and had crossed the SARTH River. That evening orders were received to continue on to Argentan and cut communications to the north."[1093]

By the following day, August 12, CCA and CCR succeeded in taking Sees at 1000 hours. This engagement included dispersing a battalion of Germans overtaken on the road to Sees. A column of 2nd French Armored Division vehicles had ignored XV Corps' orders and used the highway east of the *FORET de ECOUVES*, blocking trucks for several hours which had been sent to resupply and refuel 5th Armored's CCA on the main road into Sees.[1094] Just as CCA, 5th Armored left Sees heading for Argentan, ". . . they were met by the point of a column of the 116th Panzer Division that had apparently intended to enter Sees from the west and southwest. Elements of 1st [SS] and 2nd Panzer Divisions were also in the area."[1095] In a running firefight that lasted for several hours that afternoon, CCA employed massed tanks and artillery to destroy those elements of the 116th Panzer Division

---

[1089] Cepeda, 41.
[1090] Cepeda, 41, 42.
[1091] Cepeda, 42.
[1092] Patton, 103.
[1093] Cepeda, 42.
[1094] Cepeda, 42.
[1095] Cepeda, 42, 43.

blocking their way. Shattered remnants of those German formations were sent reeling back to defensive positions forming near Argentan.

That evening, CCA approached Argentan from the southeast. By 7:00 p.m., or 1900 hours, ". . . CCA was on the edge of their goal, *ARGENTAN*, just south of the *ORNE* River. Apparently, it was decided that it was not feasible to continue the attack at night because they withdrew to higher ground to the southwest overlooking the town. Patrols were successful in getting into the town during the night and they reported intense tank and infantry activity."[1096] General Oliver had sent out two task forces to cover 5th Armored's eastern flank. "Task Force Boyer dug in for the night at *EXMES*. Task Force Hamberg established a roadblock at the road junction five miles south of *GACE* by 2100 hours . . ."[1097]

At this point in their report, Lieutenant Colonel Cepeda and his fellow students at the Armored School stop to ask a question: "The question now comes to mind, why was *ARGENTAN* not taken that evening or night? CCB spent the day of August 12 in reserve in the vicinity of *FRENEAUX*."[1098] Lieutenant Colonel Cepeda makes an excellent point, why was the attack halted the evening of August 12. There are no verifiable records of a 'halt order.' CCA may have been tired and needed to rest. They may have had to perform maintenance on their tanks, since they had been leading 5th Armored's attack since the evening of August 9. But CCB was available and they were still fresh. The German defenses in Argentan on August 12 were not coordinated because German commanders were out of contact with their units. Eberbach later wrote, "No report had arrived from 116th Pz Div; whether Sees was still in our hands was not known."[1099] Later that afternoon Eberbach received a report, which indicated the 116th Panzer was meeting stiff resistance on its way to Sees. "In a subsequent report which reached headquarters in the evening," Eberbach wrote, "we learned that those advancing elements of 116 Pz Div had been destroyed by heavy artillery fire from massed enemy tanks and also that the enemy was forcing his way toward Argentan."[1100] Sees was being defended by a company of bakers. The 9th Panzer Division had been reduced to: ". . . one infantry battalion, one artillery battalion, and a half-dozen tanks."[1101] Remnants ". . . of the 708th

---

[1096] Cepeda, 43.
[1097] Cepeda, 43.
[1098] Cepeda. 43.
[1099] Eberbach, 17.
[1100] Eberbach, 17.
[1101] Eberbach, 16.

German Infantry Division and 6th Para Jg Division were on their way to barricade the area of Gace-Laigle."[1102] The German southern flank had been shattered by Haislip's XV Corps.

Despite observations of intense activity, there were few German defenders in Argentan through August 16. One local resident gave information on the Germans in Argentan to a recon party from 5th Armored: "The enemy troops still holding the town are weak . . . . Their isolation, their lack of cohesion, and lack of liaison with their artillery give us the chance of a great coup with even a handful of troops."[1103] Apparently, this information was not reliable.

The next afternoon [August 13], a detachment of sixty soldiers from the 10th Company, 3rd Tchad Foot Regiment, 2nd French Armored Division walked into Argentan by way of back paths to see, ". . . how many Jerries there are in the northern part of the town between the town hall and the Falaise road junction."[1104] The afternoon patrol reported, "Argentan seemed deserted. Two or three reconnaissance cars . . . a few not very aggressive infantrymen . . ."[1105] Other reports indicated there were German tanks in Argentan, but the French from the 3rd Tchad Foot completed their task without losing a single man.

On the night of August 12/13, German defenses in the vicinity of Argentan consisted of one anti-aircraft regiment and those remnants of 116th Panzer Division which had escaped destruction on the road to Sees earlier that day.[1106] The Germans could count no more than eighty tanks on a front of over thirty-five miles [Ecouche to L'Aigle], and many of those tanks were immobilized, they were short of fuel and ammunition. General Eberbach, the officer charged with destroying Haislips' XV Corps, spent the night moving his headquarters from Vieux Pont to Chenedouil. Eberbach later wrote, "Although the displacement was only the short distance of thirty kilometers, it required six hours to complete it."[1107] According to British Intelligence, the German defenders at Argentan were very close to collapse: "We knew that what was left of Eberbach's armor was virtually immobile; he was short of ammunition and fuel. It looked as if the American corps could

---

[1102]   Hausser, 54.

[1103]   Major Quatrecoup, *Le Pays d'Argentan, No. 63,* and conversation with author. From Florentin, 122.

[1104]   Florentin, 125.

[1105]   Florentin, 126.

[1106]   Eberbach, 18.

[1107]   Eberbach, 17.

close the gap."[1108] For four days, from the evening of August 12 through the arrival of II SS Panzer Corps on August 16, the southern German flank at Argentan-St Leonard-Gace was vulnerable to Allied attack.

Mobile elements of the 2nd Panzer and 1st SS Panzer arrived during the night of August 13/14, but their infantry did not arrive until the following day. It was not until the arrival of II SS Panzer Corps on August 16 that Eberbach considered his defensive positions fairly adequate. Almost as soon as they arrived, II SS Panzer Corps was gone, sent out of the pocket on the night of August 17 to Vimoutiers to prepare for the attack which would hold open the last German escape routes through Trun and Chambois.

On August 12, XV Corps directed the 90th Infantry Division to Alencon with orders to protect the Corps' eastern flank by occupying the high ground west and southwest of the town. The 79th Infantry was placed in Corps reserve in the vicinity of Le Mele-Sur-Sarthe, with orders to be prepared to move north, northeast, or northwest as directed.[1109]

French 2nd Armored was driving toward Argentan on Haislip's western flank. On August 12, they occupied Carrouges. General Leclerc sent one Combat Command left of the Forest of Ecouves, one down the middle and the other to the right, where they became tangled up with CCA of 5th U.S. Armored. By mid-day August 13, French 2nd Armored had made excellent progress, CCB was covering the crossroads at Castelle, and CCR was a little late after running into the remnants of 9th Panzer on their way through the center of the forest. French 2nd Armored Headquarters and General Leclerc arrived with CCA at the inter-Army Group boundary between Ecouche and Argentan ready to continue the attack.[1110] That afternoon a squad of French infantry from No. 10 Company, 3rd Tchad Foot Regiment entered Argentan on a routine reconnaissance patrol.[1111]

General Bradley said that he was concerned about Haislip's open left flank. He later wrote, "On the afternoon of August 12, as Haislip's forces closed on the 'boundary' near Argentan, Ike came to my CP to monitor Haislip's progress, and he remained through dinner."[1112] That afternoon, after getting Eisenhower's approval, Bradley ordered General Collins' VII Corps to head northeast from the Mortain sector and close off Haislips'

[1108]   Winterbotham, 155.

[1109]   Hq, *XV Corps, US Army, Report, No. 24.*, Aug. 12, 1944.

[1110]   Florentin, 119.

[1111]   Florentin, 125, 126.

[1112]   Bradley, *A General's Life*, 297, 298.

open left flank. Bradley said he believed that Collins' VII Corps contained the best divisions he had in France.

Bradley and Patton had planned to use General Walton H. Walker's XX Corps to cover Haislip's left flank.[1113] They were unable to use XX Corps because, on August 11, Montgomery ordered Bradley to withhold a Corps of at least three divisions in the Le Mans area in preparation for the wider, Seine Envelopment, to be launched at a time not yet determined.[1114]

Montgomery's orders to Bradley on August 11 produced an immediate argument from Bradley. The argument was picked up by Bradley's aide, Chester Hansen and faithfully recorded in his diary: "There is some discussion now concerning an alleged disagreement in strategy between Brad and Monty concerning the timing for this northward movement. I am told that Monty is anxious that the continued movement toward Paris in seizure of more terrain, while Brad is equally insistent that we turn north now at Lemans and trap the German army containing the hinge of the 1st Army and those elements following the 30th and 12th Corps in the 2nd British Army."[1115]

Bradley and Eisenhower later admitted to discussing Haislip's open left flank. Bradley would probably have told Eisenhower about Montgomery's orders of August 11, instructing him to withhold three U.S. divisions near Le Mans in preparation for the wider envelopment. The two generals almost certainly discussed Montgomery's change in priorities from their August 8 telephone call, when Montgomery agreed to conduct the short envelopment through Alencon-Argentan-Falaise. Given the sudden disagreement in tactics, one might have expected that Bradley or Eisenhower would pick up the telephone and talk to General Montgomery. Amazingly, neither Eisenhower nor Bradley admitted to discussing the issue with Montgomery. Indeed, Bradley states categorically that he never asked Montgomery to allow Americans to cross the inter-Army Group boundary.

The historical record says otherwise. Thanks to detailed notes from research by Dr. Forrest C. Pogue and one of Montgomery's staff officers, we actually have a first-hand account. It was given by someone who says they were there on the evening of August 12, when the telephone call went

---

[1113] Gay Diaries, Saturday, August 12, 1944, 454.

[1114] Hamilton, *Master*, 784.

[1115] Hansen Diaries, SATURDAY, 12 August 1944.

through. On May 30 and 31, 1947, Dr. Pogue interviewed Montgomery's intelligence officer, Brigadier E.T. 'Bill' Williams. These are Dr. Pogue's notes:

> "Remember (he) was in Freddie's (De Guingand) truck near Bayeux when 2nd French Armored made its swing up and crossed the road toward Falaise. *Monty said tell Bradley they ought to get back. Bradley was indignant. We were indignant on Bradley's behalf.* De Guingand said 'Monty is too tidy.' Freddie thought Bradley should have been allowed to join the Poles at Trun. Monty missed closing the sack. *Bradley couldn't understand. Thought we were missing our opportunities over inter-Army rights.* However, it should be pointed out that Monty regarded Bradley was under his command; therefore, his decision was not made on the basis of inter-Army considerations . . . Master of tidiness. He was fundamentally more interested in full envelopment than this inner envelopment. We fell between two stools. He (Montgomery) missed his chance of closing at the Seine by doing the envelopment at Falaise. Monty didn't want to do the short hook. Freddie, using my information and his own ideas, persuaded Monty into that with Bradley arguing for it from his angle. *Monty didn't want to do it but saw a chance to pull it off after he had pushed Bradley back.* In the first stage, he was looking toward a grander basis, and he thought 'Hell, those guys are excited; they are spoiling the way we are going.' Then Freddie and Bradley favor the short hook. He agrees, but it's already too late. So he misses both opportunities."[1116]

Some historians have seized upon a problem with Brigadier William's timing of the Polish advance at Trun to cast doubts on veracity of his entire interview. That is unfortunate and only confuses the issue. Montgomery's change of heart [allowing Bradley north of the inter-Army Group boundary] on August 16 occurred about the time the Allies decoded an *ULTRA* intercept giving the Germans permission to withdraw from Normandy. Brigadier William's interview with Forrest Pogue is the only firsthand account of the

---

[1116] Dr. Forrest C. Pogue, Interviews, US Army Military History Institute, Carlisle Barracks, Pa. From Carlo D'Este, *Decision*, 451, 452. And Rohmer, 226, 227. Italics added.

halt decision at the Falaise Gap in existence. Most other statements about the 'halt order' are deliberately misleading.

The evidence that Montgomery issued the 'halt order' is conclusive. Montgomery's Chief of Staff, Major General Francis De Guingand, agrees with Williams' memory: "My impressions at the time were that he (Montgomery) had been a little too optimistic about the probable progress of 21st Army Group . . . . It is just possible that *the gap might have been closed a little earlier if no restrictions had been imposed upon the 12th Army Group Commander as to the limit of his northward movement."* [1117] The only man in Normandy who could have imposed boundary restrictions on the northward movement of Bradley's 12th Army Group was General Montgomery. Bradley denies this ever happened, but de Guingand's reputation for veracity is excellent.

The Diary of Air Vice-Marshal Stephen C. Strafford is also in agreement with the memories of Brigadier Williams and Francis de Guingand. In a Diary entry from August 14, 1944, he recorded General Bradley's: ". . . general intentions. He [Bradley] stated that immediately the Germans were pinned in the area west of *ARGENTAN/FALAISE*, he wished to detach a minimum force necessary to complete the tidying up of the *BRITTANY* peninsula and the opening of the *BRITTANY* ports and then to drive East from *ALENCON* in an encircling movement against *PARIS* through the gap as early as possible. *He states that the American forces had little opposition between ALENCON and ARGENTAN and had started toward FALAISE, but had been instructed by the C-in-C, 21 Army Group to halt on the inter-army group boundary. There had been few German troops in the area when the Third Army forward elements had arrived there* and he was confident that the Third Army now held a firm front on the arc to the north of FALAISE."[1118] Bradley confirmed in Stafford's Diary what is obvious from historical research. Despite claims of stout German opposition at Argentan made later to cover up the Allies' failure to close the gap on August 12 and 13, there was in fact little German opposition in front of Patton's Third Army. According to the German commander, Heinrich Eberbach, ". . . what was left of 116 Pz Div reached the Argentan area. Together with the anti-aircraft regiment they took up a thin line on both sides of the town and held their positions . . ."

[1117] De Guingand, 407. Italics added.

[1118] From the *War Diary of Air vice Marshal Stephen C. Stafford*, Chief of Operations and Plans, AEAF, 14 August 1944. Italics added. From D'Este, *Decision*, 440, 441.

[1119] The German 116th Panzer was the same division that had already been mauled by massed U.S. tanks and artillery on the Sees-Argentan road earlier that day. After the fall of Alencon and Sees, General Eberbach had warned German Army Group B of, ". . . the necessity of an immediate and quick retreat on a large scale because otherwise a complete collapse [of the southern flank] was unavoidable."[1120]

Even staff officers at Bradley's 12th Army Group headquarters were not buying the story that Bradley issued the 'halt order.' Chester Hansen wrote, "It is suggested in G-3 [Plans, Training and Operations] that we were ordered to hold at Argentan rather than to continue the drive to Falaise since our capture of that objective would infringe on the prestige of forces [British/Canadians] driving south and prevent them from securing prestige value in closing the trap. Accordingly, our forces were held at the Argentan line and subsequently refueled while the British [were] still short of their objective permitted much of the strength in the pocket to escape eastward toward the Seine." [1121]

General George Patton saw through the ruse immediately. A few days after a telephone conversation with Bradley's Chief of Staff, Leven Allen, Patton wrote, ". . . I told him . . . it was perfectly feasible to continue the operation. Allen repeated the order [from Bradley] to halt on the line and consolidate . . . . I believe that the order . . . emanated from the 21st Army Group, and was either due to [British] jealousy of the Americans or to utter ignorance of the situation or to a combination of the two. It is very regrettable that the XV Corps was ordered to halt, because it could have gone on to Falaise and made contact with the Canadians northwest of that point and definitely and positively closed the escape gap."[1122] Patton was right, the only thing between Third Army and Falaise on the evening of August 12/13 was a regiment of anti-aircraft guns [short of ammunition], and those remnants of the 9th and 116th Panzer Divisions, which had survived massed American artillery on the road to Sees earlier that day; 9th Panzer Division's 33rd Panzer Regiment did arrive the following morning with thirty-five tanks, but their effectiveness would have been limited because of fuel and ammunition shortages.

[1119]   Eberbach, 18.
[1120]   Eberbach, 19
[1121]   Hansen Diaries, SUNDAY, 13 August 1944.
[1122]   Blumenson, (Ed.), *The Patton Papers, 1940-1945*, 508, 509.

Ralph Ingersoll wrote in *Top Secret,* "Patton's troops, who thought they had the mission of closing the gap, took Argentan in their stride and crossed the international [inter-Army Group] boundary without stopping. Montgomery, who was still nominally in charge of all ground forces, now chose to exercise his authority and ordered Patton back to his side of the international boundary line." In a note, Ingersoll adds, "Every senior officer concerned whom I have been able to talk to still feels that the failure to close the Falaise gap was the loss of the greatest single opportunity of the war."[1123] Haislip's XV Corps never took Argentan, but reconnaissance elements of CCA, 5th Armored Division did enter the town during the night of August 12, and on the afternoon of August 13, a patrol from 2nd French Armored Division spent several hours in Argentan. It would have been normal procedure for both 5th Armored Division and XV Corps to send reconnaissance patrols north of Argentan to scout the area of their impending offensive between Argentan and Falaise.

The Commanding Officer for this section of the German front was General Eberbach, who spent most of the night (12/13 August) stuck in a traffic jam trying to relocate his headquarters 30 kilometers from Vieux Pont to Chenedouil.[1124] Florentin wrote, "At Bourg-Saint-Leonard, an eyewitness observed an extraordinary sight in the afternoon [August 12th]: German vehicles of all kinds, tanks, small and large trucks, motor bicycles and carts fleeing en route for Chambois. This time it was a debacle. Some of the cars had lost their windows, others had no doors left. We saw one, carrying officers, with no front tires and another which had only three wheels."[1125] While joyful French residents watched in amusement, the once proud German Wehrmacht was disintegrating into chaos. The German defeat in Normandy had turned into a rout. Those German soldiers working in the support branches of administration, medicine and supply were fleeing from the American tanks as fast as they could.

Aside from moving Collins VII Corps east to join Haislip near Ranes and Ecouche, whatever else Bradley and Eisenhower discussed during the evening of August 12th was never made public. They certainly discussed Montgomery's refusal to allow the Americans north of the inter-Army Group boundary at Argentan. Brigadier E.T. Williams remembered that Bradley was indignant. Bradley liked to have Eisenhower by his side when he talked

---

[1123] Ingersoll, 190, 191.
[1124] Eberbach, 17.
[1125] Florentin, 110.

to Montgomery on the phone. He did not trust Montgomery. Bradley may have asked Eisenhower what he was going to do about Montgomery. General Bradley rarely showed any emotion, but this situation was different and if Bradley had found the courage to get indignant with Montgomery, he was probably not restrained in expressing himself to Eisenhower.

On the evening of August 12, Bradley was trying to decide whether to send Patton north of Montgomery's inter-Army Group boundary line. His final decision was probably still not clear in his mind. Two events were still developing which could influence his decision to send Patton north against Montgomery's wishes. First, *ULTRA* had alerted the Allies to a German attack on Haislip's vulnerable western flank. If the Germans hit Haislip hard during the night of August 12/13, Haislip and Patton might be happy to find defensive positions south of Montgomery's boundary line. The second outstanding issue was General Collins' VII Corps. How long would it take Collins' divisions to cover Haislip's left flank? If Collins ran into trouble during the night, it might be prudent to order Haislip to stop south of the inter-Army Group boundary and get ready for the German attack. If, on the other hand, Collins' VII Corps found few Germans and had little trouble closing with 2nd French Armored on Haislip's left, it might be possible to send elements of both VII Corps and XV Corps north side by side in a double envelopment. Bradley may have thought about giving VII Corps the road axis Ranes-Ecouche-Argentan-Falaise; he would then be required to move XV Corps a few miles east to St. Leonard-Trun-Fresne. This would have created a double cordon around the Germans. Eisenhower and Bradley may have agreed to delay the final decision on Montgomery's inter-Army Group boundary line until the next day, to wait and see what happened to Collins' and Haislip's corps over the night of 12/13 August.

It was unusual for a Corps under George Patton to be without orders from Army Headquarters, but that is exactly what happened during the evening on August 12th. Haislips's XV Corps had been cleared to attack up to the boundary line south of Ecouche-Argentan-St. Leonard and cut off the enemies escape routes to the east. By the evening of 12 August, XV Corps had fulfilled that mission, but nothing was forthcoming from Third Army until 2000 hours that night. Then Message No. 4 was sent to COMMANDING GENERAL, XV CORPS: "UPON CAPTURE OF ARGENTAN PUSH ON SLOWLY DIRECTION OF FALAISE ALLOWING YOUR REAR ELEMENTS TO CLOSE. ROAD: ARGENTAN-FALAISE YOUR LEFT BOUNDARY INCLUSIVE. UPON ARRIVAL FALAISE CONTINUE

TO PUSH ON SLOWLY UNTIL YOU CONTACT OUR ALLIES."[1126] The message was on a 'one-time' note pad, and was probably delivered some time that night.

Early on the morning of August 13 CCA of 5th Armored attacked just east of Argentan and suffered heavy tank losses. Apparently the attack got caught out in the open just as the morning fog lifted. CCB was supposed to attack just to the right of CCA, but the attack was called off just as it was to begin. In his 'Report After Combat' General Haislip said that he was trying to initiate the attack plan from the night before when orders came through ". . . directing the Corps to halt on the ORNE."[1127] Third Army's Gay Diaries also indicate receipt of an order from 12th Army Group that morning, ". . . to the effect that XV Corps would hold in position generally SEES-ARGENTAN-COURRAGES, prepared for movement upon Army order . . ."[1128] Lieutenant Colonel Cepeda's 'Report' from the Armored School provides the reason the temporary halt order was issued: "This order (CCB's attack order) was rescinded before the attack was launched after General Haislip . . . and General Oliver had a conference. General Haislip told General Oliver that under no conditions should the 5th Armored advance beyond the line ARGENTAN-GACE. He had been told that a large-scale bombing mission was planned to blast the area to the north of this line. General Haislip's information was apparently correct."[1129] Lt. Colonel Cepeda later recounts the heavy fighter-bomber attacks described that day near MABLOVILLE by a German prisoner of war named Fritz Bayerlein, Commander of the Panzer Lehr Division.[1130] While a series of halt orders restricted XV Corps movement to the north, there was no indication that these orders were meant to deny Third Army the authority to cross the inter-Army Group boundary.

Following Third Army's staff meeting at 0900 that Sunday morning, Major General Hugh J. Gaffey sent the following orders to Haislip at XV Corps: "Halt in the vicinity of Argentan. Assemble your command prepared for further movement to north or northeast."[1131] Haislip was ordered to prepare for movement north, toward Falaise, continuing the attack to surround the Germans in Normandy, or to attack toward the northeast, out of the Falaise

---

[1126] Gay Diaries, Message No. 4 dated 12 August 1944.
[1127] XV Corps, *Correction to Report*, No. 1, dated 18 January 1945.
[1128] Gay Diaries, Sunday, August 13, 1944.
[1129] Cepeda, 45.
[1130] Cepeda, 45.
[1131] Gay Diaries, Copy of General Gaffey's Daily Log dated 13 August 1944.

Pocket, toward the Seine. As a matter of routine, Haislip would have ordered a reconnaissance conducted of both the areas he was alerted to move his corps: both north toward Falaise and northeast toward Paris.

Sunday morning, August 13, must have been hectic at 12th Army Group Headquarters. There was a lot going on. The hand wringing over Haislip's open flank had come to naught. Eberbach simply did not have the forces to attack XV Corps' flank; the meager force available to him at Argentan was barely capable of defending itself.

Just after their staff meeting, around 1000 hours, Bradley got an excited call from General Hodges at First Army. Hodges told Bradley, ". . . General Collins called asking for more 'territory to take.' The Div was, in some places, on the very boundary itself, and General Collins felt sure that he could take Falaise and Argentan, close the gap, and 'do the job' before the British even started to move."[1132] General Hodges endorsed Collins' request and was asking Bradley officially for a change in boundaries so that VII Corps could continue the attack. ". . . but the sad news came back that First Army was to go no further than at first designated, except that a small salient around Ranes would become ours."[1133] Now General Bradley had two Army Commanders demanding the right to cross Montgomery's inter-Army Group boundary line.

Bradley was probably mad right down to the tip of his toes; he was past indignant. He did not trust his temper on the telephone with Montgomery, so he asked Brigadier Kibler to do it. Although the time of his telephone call is not provided, at some point that Sunday morning, 12th Army Group's G-3, Operations Officer, Brigadier General A. Franklin Kibler, ". . . . phoned Montgomery's headquarters trying to get permission for Patton to go beyond Argentan. He spoke with General de Guingand . . . who told him bluntly: 'I am sorry, Kibler. We cannot grant the permission.'"[1134] At sometime between ten and eleven that morning Bradley left his headquarters and drove straight to Shellburst, Eisenhower's headquarters. Bradley was seeking Eisenhower's help and advice.

Any questions Eisenhower and Bradley may have had about the viability of Patton's attack from the south had been put to rest. The Germans had failed to threaten Haislip at Argentan. Collins had found the going so easy; he thought VII Corps could take both Argentan and Falaise before the British

---

[1132] William Sylvan's Diary, Sunday, August 13th
[1133] William Sylvan's Diary, Sunday, August 13th
[1134] Farago, 540. Also see Weigley, *Eisenhower's Lieutenants*, 206.

attack even got started. Bradley was probably mad. He had serious concerns about Montgomery's halt order. These concerns are evident in Hansen's war diary, but neither Bradley nor Eisenhower chose to make their discussions on the morning of August 13 part of the historical record. The historian must very carefully infer what they discussed from what they did after their conversation.

Bradley's concerns about the 'halt order' may have poured out to Eisenhower in an emotional torrent, which would have been unusual for the normally calm, steady commander General Bradley had become. Bradley probably told Eisenhower that the halt order was wrong, it was dead wrong. It was contrary to everything they ever learned about military strategy. Patton knew it was wrong. Montgomery knew it was wrong. Everyone knew it was wrong. Future historians will roast and skewer the poor general who ends up looking responsible for it. Bradley probably asked Eisenhower to consider George Patton and the press. If American reporters ever got hold of Montgomery's chicanery, Eisenhower could kiss his precious Anglo-American Alliance good-bye. George Patton was on the telephone trying reach Bradley during Bradley's conversation with Eisenhower, but Bradley refused to talk to him. He knew that Patton was determined to continue the offensive north to Falaise.

Eisenhower might have waited until Bradley finished. He had given their problem [of Montgomery's halt order] considerable thought since their meeting the evening before. Eisenhower may have told Bradley not to worry about George Patton. Patton liked his headlines too much to risk misbehaving now. But Eisenhower probably said that he agreed with Bradley's concern about the press. If the United States press corps ever discovered that Montgomery had halted two American armies on an arbitrary inter-Army Group boundary line for reasons that defied military logic and that neither of them could understand, the Anglo-American Alliance would be shaken to its base. Eisenhower had carefully considered the uncertain aftermath and it worried him.

General Marshall had warned Eisenhower to get along with his Allies. If the American press got a hold of this thing, Montgomery might have to go and he was the only popular general the British had. Churchill would be exposed to the vagaries of British politics, he might not survive either. The Americans would have serious problems with the British public over Montgomery, even if the feisty little general somehow managed to survive the political chaos. Eisenhower may have considered it too risky to allow Montgomery's halt order to stand. He probably convinced Bradley that it would be politically expedient for them to handle Montgomery's 'halt order' within the United States chain-of-command.

Eisenhower then probably asked Bradley to issue the halt order in his own name, taking Montgomery out of the controversy. He probably told Bradley to make up any reason he liked for issuing the halt order. Eisenhower promised his full support for the halt order, and any subsequent decisions Bradley had to make in relation to it. Eisenhower may have also told Bradley that he and Marshall always considered Bradley the one officer they could count on in a crisis. Eisenhower considered that this was a crisis. Eisenhower may have reminded Bradley that it was his level bearing, his common sense and judicious behavior that played such a large role in garnering him the high position within the US command that he now enjoyed. Bradley may have cringed, but in the end he agreed to do what Eisenhower asked. He would issue the 'halt order' in his name.

At about 1120 hours that Sunday morning, while he was still at Eisenhower's headquarters, Bradley called his own headquarters and talked to his Chief of Staff, Major General Leven C. Allen. He told General Allen to call Third Army and give them a direct order to halt on the Argentan-Sees boundary line in his [Bradley's] name with the added provision that the boundary line was not to be crossed under any circumstances.[1135] At 1130 hours General Allen called Third Army Headquarters and delivered Bradley's halt order to General Gaffey, Patton's Chief of Staff.[1136]

Rather than let Montgomery wreck his own military career and possibly the Anglo-American Alliance, Eisenhower insisted that General Bradley take responsibility for an order both men knew to be a grievous tactical blunder. Eisenhower had earlier written to General Marshall about the opportunity to destroy the German Army in Normandy. He liked to lecture his subordinates about the virtues of destroying the enemy deployed on their front rather than simply gaining ground. He was right. He was also fond of quoting Carl von Clausewitz, who wrote, "It follows that the destruction of the enemy's force underlies all military action; all plans are ultimately based on it . . . . Thus it is evident that destruction of the enemy forces is always the superior, more efficient means, with which others cannot compete."[1137] Eisenhower was fully prepared to violate a fundamental strategic doctrine in order to save the Anglo-American Alliance.

[1135] Farago, 539.

[1136] Farago, 539.

[1137] Von Clausewitz, 97.

Eisenhower's decision was based on a subtle mental calculation. He had decided that the Anglo-American Alliance was worth more than the men whose lives would be forfeit to the bad tactical decision he had just made. The political alliance with Great Britain has been worth a lot. It has lasted more than 60 years and is still ongoing. On the other side of the scale, the lives of those Allied soldiers sacrificed because some 150,000 Germans escaped through the Falaise Gap to fight another day has never been calculated because of the infinite number of variables involved in such calculations.

On August 15, barely two days after Eisenhower had refused to back his own countrymen in a boundary dispute with Montgomery, he put on a freshly pressed uniform and his sternest commander's face for a press conference. Eisenhower told the assembled press corps: "One of the duties of a general is to determine the best investment of human lives. If he thinks expenditure of 10,000 lives in the current battle will save 20,000 later, it is up to him to do it."[1138] Eisenhower's aide Harry Butcher later added, "This expresses Ike's feeling about the current effort to close the bag on the Germans."[1139] Eisenhower certainly looked like the general who was prepared to take a calculated risk if it was justified. The destruction of the German Fifth Panzer and Seventh Armies in Normandy should have justified great risk; but at the critical hour Eisenhower, Churchill's 'great domineering partner,' refused to risk the alliance.

Eisenhower must have known he was going to have to deal with Montgomery sooner or later. The missed opportunity to encircle the Germans at Falaise would be followed by missed opportunities on the Pas de Calais and later in the Ardennes during the Battle of the Bulge.

When Eisenhower weighed future casualties against the survival of the Anglo-American Alliance on August 13th, he was looking at only one side of the coin. The Alliance was important to the Americans; Marshall and Roosevelt insisted on it. But what about the British, how important was the Anglo-American Alliance to Churchill, Brooke and Montgomery?

Eisenhower discovered the answer after taking command of Allied Ground Forces in March 1945. When he took Ninth Army away from Montgomery, Eisenhower may have expected the sky to fall on him. It didn't. Eisenhower was able to assign priority to Bradley's U.S.12th Army Group in their final thrust through central Germany and bring a swift end to the war. Eisenhower had always held the winning hand. He simply waited too long to play it.

[1138] Butcher, 645.
[1139] Butcher, 645.

Chapter 12

Eisenhower Takes Command: 28 March 1945

"Brad told Ike that if Monty takes control of the XIX and VII Corps of the First Army, as he wants to, he, Bradley, will ask to be relieved . . . Ike feels that we think he is selling us out but he has to, as *Monty will not take orders, so we have to.* Bradley said it was time for a showdown. I offered to resign with him, but he backed out."[1140] General George S. Patton, diary, September 15, 1944

The Allies decided to go forward with Overlord and Anvil at the Teheran Conference in late 1943. It was a bitter pill for the British. Their approval of Operation *Overlord* was the price the British had to pay to remain a dominant world power and a member of the Big Three [Soviet Union, United States and Great Britain].

Churchill and his staff were clearly disappointed, but they did not leave the conference empty handed. Franklin Roosevelt had given them a whopper of a gift; his name was Dwight D. Eisenhower. Even C.I.G.S. Alan Brooke, whose distaste for Americans is well documented, found something nice to say on the occasion of Eisenhower's appointment to command *Overlord*: "First of all, the selection of Eisenhower instead of Marshall was a good one. Eisenhower had now had a certain amount of experience as a commander and was beginning to find his feet. The combination of Eisenhower and Bedell Smith had much to be said for it. On the other hand, Marshall had never commanded anything in war except, I believe, a company in the First World War."[1141] Brooke left unsaid the major reason he was so fond of Eisenhower. Eisenhower took his role as the senior 'Allied commander' very seriously. In his desire to nurture the Anglo-American alliance, Eisenhower sided with the British most of the time to counter his position as a general in the United States Army.

[1140] Blumenson, (Ed.), *The Patton Papers, 1940-1945*, 548. Italics added.
[1141] Bryant, *Triumph*, 106.

The fact that the British preferred Eisenhower was not a well-kept secret. In the middle of strategic discussions in July 1942, Churchill twice proposed Eisenhower's name as a senior American officer acceptable to the British. He cabled Roosevelt on July 31: "It would be agreeable to us if General Marshall were designated for Supreme Command of *ROUNDUP* and that in the meantime General Eisenhower should act as his deputy here."[1142] Robert Sherwood also wrote that Churchill sought a position in *TORCH* planning for General Eisenhower, "Churchill suggested that Eisenhower should superintend the planning and organization of *TORCH* and that General Sir Harold Alexander should be in command of the task force from the British Isles . . ."[1143] The British obviously preferred Eisenhower over the other American officers they had met in 1942.

Ralph Ingersoll agreed with Sherwood about British acceptance of Eisenhower. He wrote, ". . . when Teheran came along, Eisenhower was the Empire's logical candidate—and the British popped him into the job of Supreme Commander in England. It was confidently expected by London that he would repeat his Mediterranean performance, stick to politics, and leave the management of the war in the field to those [British officers] with more experience . . ."[1144] It is doubtful that the British had as much influence with Roosevelt on Eisenhower's appointment to command *Overlord* as Ingersoll suggests. Still, there can be little doubt that Eisenhower was the American officer the British preferred.

Churchill's authority within the Alliance had been compromised by Roosevelt and Stalin. But Churchill had no intention of giving up so easily. In 1942, South African Jan Smuts reminded Churchill, "As America is now our great strategic reserve for the final blows, much of your time will have to be devoted wisely to guiding Washington in its war effort and not letting vital war direction slip out of our hands . . . Your contacts with Roosevelt are now a most valuable war asset . . ." [1145] Churchill lost this asset at Teheran.

As Prime Minister and Minister of Defense, Winston Churchill was the dominant voice in determining British strategy. Churchill tried to control the war by influencing the officers and politicians who made the strategic decisions. Ralph Ingersoll had served on Bradley's staff in Europe. He

---

[1142] Sherwood, 615.
[1143] Sherwood, 615.
[1144] Ingersoll, 78.
[1145] Churchill Papers 20/77, Telegram No. 1211, dated 7 July 1942, from Gilbert, 143, 144.

believed the British were trying to run the war for political reasons. In 1946 he wrote, "It was clear that if British generals were to run the battle—and the British saw no reason why they shouldn't—concessions would have to be made to American public opinion."[1146]

The British understood that the Americans would be soon furnishing the lion's share of men and equipment for the war effort. Churchill recognized this at Teheran when he limited the number of British divisions available for *Overlord* to sixteen.[1147] Ingersoll continued, "The most effective concession then—the concession which would give them [the British] the best press for the least price in real control—would be to give the Americans the head man and, as they say in business when they make a Chairman of the Board out of a President they don't need—kick him upstairs."[1148]

By December 1943, General Eisenhower had been 'Chairman of the Board' for the Allies in the Mediterranean for over a year. Churchill, General Alan Brooke, and other senior British officers were impressed with Eisenhower. General George S. Patton Jr. and many American officers were not. After spending a night with Eisenhower during the African campaign, Patton wrote in his diary: "Ike is acting a part . . . and is either obeying orders . . . or else the British have got him completely fooled . . . The British are running the show on the sea, on the land, and in the air. They are running it to their advantage and are playing us for suckers, not only in a military way but politically also."[1149] General Patton was not privy to the political intrigue his friend was trying to work through. Still, Patton's thoughts represented the view of many American officers who had served in North Africa and would later serve in Europe.

Eisenhower's tour of duty as Supreme Commander Allied Forces, North African Theater of Operations (AFHQ) had worked out exactly as the British hoped it would. They were extremely pleased that the same command arrangement would be carried over for the invasion of France. The fact that General Eisenhower exercised no operational control of Allied Armies did not become a political problem for Roosevelt in the Mediterranean Theater, where British troops outnumbered the Americans. It remained to be seen if the same command arrangement would work in a European Theater dominated by the Americans. General Eisenhower was to become a key

---

[1146] Ingersoll, 76.
[1147] Eubank, 259.
[1148] Ingersoll, 76.
[1149] Blumenson, (Ed.), *The Patton Papers, 1940-1945*, 222.

player in the command drama as the British struggled to retain control of the Allied armies in Europe during the fall and winter of 1944-45.

After he was appointed to command *Overlord*, Eisenhower spent a few hours with Roosevelt on the President's return trip to the United States. They flew together over the Mediterranean to Malta and then on to Sicily. Roosevelt used the opportunity to warn his new *Overlord* commander about the British: ". . . Roosevelt talked at great length to Eisenhower about the prodigious difficulties that he would confront during the next few months at his new headquarters in London, where he would be surrounded by the majesty of the British Government and the powerful personality of Winston Churchill . . ."[1150] There was little in Eisenhower's prior military training or experience that could have prepared him for the political wrangling he was about to endure in Great Britain. George Marshall was the most respected officer in the US Army, but he could not match General Eisenhower's political skills in dealing with the British.

Eisenhower's principal job would be the Supreme Allied Commander with the task of coordinating Allied efforts to plan and execute the invasion of Europe. He was also George Marshall's point man for coordinating US military strategy with the British and other Allied nations providing soldiers in Europe. He would spend countless hours arguing military strategy with Prime Minister Churchill.

Eisenhower was also the ranking US Army officer in the European Theater. He would be required to provide advice to his boss in Washington on promotions, demotions, firings, transfers, weapons procurement, logistics, VIP visits and coordinating strategy with naval and air force units not directly under his command. By the end of the war, Eisenhower was running a small city. Perret wrote, ". . . It was a huge staff: SHAEF turned into a bureaucracy employing twelve-thousand people."[1151]

Eisenhower's job had been almost entirely managerial and political since the beginning of the war. Allied strategy was determined by President Roosevelt, Prime Minister Churchill and the Combined Chiefs of Staff headquartered in Washington D.C. British complaints that Eisenhower did not know how to move 'large masses of men,' that he lacked a sense of 'strategy' or that he did not know 'infantry tactics' now sound childish, hollow and quite irrelevant. All things considered, it is hard to imagine any

---

[1150] Sherwood, 803.
[1151] Perret, 379.

other officer, either British or American, doing a better job as the Supreme Commander than General Eisenhower.

When Montgomery refused to allow the Americans to move north of the inter-Army Group boundary at Argentan on August 13, he permitted the escape of some 150,000 Germans from the Falaise Gap. Montgomery was afraid it would appear as if the Americans had won the victory in Normandy all by themselves, making his British Second Army look bad. He was mindful of Churchill's injunction to see 'that the British Army win through.'

Unfortunately, the Americans had already made his army look bad. The distance from the American beaches at Utah around through Avranches, Laval, Le Mans, to Alencon and Argentan through some of the worst 'hedgerow' country in Normandy is about 250 miles. The distance from the British beaches at Courseulles to the British/Canadian position on the evening of August 12 was barely twenty miles, or as General Bradley put it, ". . . only twelve miles in advance [south] of Caen, which was their D-day objective . . ."[1152] The complete breakdown of offensive operations within the British 21st Army Group has been carefully obscured by historians on both sides of the Atlantic.

Despite the obvious failure of the British Army on the battlefield, Montgomery and Brooke continued to undermine Eisenhower's command authority. They hoped that most of the publicity for the Allied victories in France would be given to General Montgomery and his British 21st Army Group. General Montgomery was, after all, the commanding officer for all Allied soldiers in France. As Allied Ground Forces Commander, Montgomery was responsible for the operational command and control of all Allied armies in Normandy.

Churchill kept his military advisors up until the early morning hours, sorting out strategic plans designed to favor British political interests while undermining the command authority of their American Allies. Alan Brooke wrote, ". . . Winston [Churchill] hated having to give up the position of the predominant partner . . . . He became inclined at times to put up strategic proposals which in his heart he knew were unsound, purely to spite the Americans . . . . There lay . . . in the back of his mind the desire to form a purely British theatre when the laurels would be all ours."[1153]

At least some of the misunderstanding between Eisenhower and Montgomery was Eisenhower's fault. In his excellent book, *The Supreme*

[1152] Bradley, *A General's Life*, 297.
[1153] Bryant, *Triumph*, 71.

Command, Forrest Pogue explained: ". . . while Field Marshal Montgomery was the leader of a British army group, and as such occupied the same level of authority as Generals Bradley and Devers, he was also the chief British commander in the field, in close contact with the British Chief of the Imperial General Staff and in a position to know and defend the British strategic point of view. Suggestions that he presented to the Supreme Commander might represent either ideas that the British Chiefs of Staff were expressing to the U.S. Chiefs of Staff or views of his own that would be backed by the British Chiefs in later meetings."[1154]

Generals Bradley and Devers were subordinate to Eisenhower in the United States Army chain-of-command and never directly challenged Eisenhower's authority. The odd Anglo-American system of command left General, later Field Marshal Montgomery considerable latitude for strategic argument. Montgomery was also in almost daily contact with his friend and mentor, Alan Brooke, the British C.I.G.S.

There was a further problem with the Allied command and it involved Eisenhower's personality. Ambrose explained how Eisenhower's major weakness as a commander, ". . . [Was] his eagerness to be well liked, coupled with his desire to keep everyone happy? Because of these characteristics, he would not end a meeting until at least verbal agreement had been found."[1155] As a result of his eagerness to reach an agreement with both British and American subordinates, it often appeared as if Eisenhower was guilty of agreeing with the last man he talked to.

While it was clear that Montgomery's behavior was, at times, clearly insubordinate, it would be wrong to suggest that he disobeyed a direct order from his Supreme Commander. Forrest Pogue wrote, "It is difficult to sustain the charge that Montgomery willfully disobeyed orders. It is plausible to say that he felt he was representing firmly the best interests of his country and attempting to set forth what he and his superiors in the United Kingdom considered to be the best strategy for the Allies to pursue in Europe."[1156]

Pogue is certainly correct in saying that Montgomery had a marked preference for protecting British political interests. But there should have been a limit imposed on his partisan behavior, if only to protect the lives of the men he commanded, including the Americans.

[1154] Pogue, *The Supreme Command*, 289.
[1155] Ambrose, *Eisenhower, Soldier, General*, 344.
[1156] Pogue, *The Supreme Command*, 289, 290.

Everyone knew Montgomery was a difficult subordinate. Still, it was part of Eisenhower's job to see that the lives of American soldiers were judiciously sacrificed using the best military strategy and tactics available. There were at least four occasions during the war in Europe when Eisenhower should have intervened to protect those lives, but didn't. The Battle of the Falaise Gap was one of those times.*

Eisenhower would not issue Montgomery a direct order. This caused Bradley, Tedder, Butcher and Eisenhower's other supporters at SHAEF great distress. On July 31, the day before the major command change in Normandy, Butcher wrote in his diary: ". . . although 21st Army Group [Montgomery] will retain direction for a transition period . . . he [Eisenhower] is moving to France . . . in the next few days . . . I hope the future will see Ike more definitely and prominently identified with the ground battle."[1157] Eisenhower's friends at SHAEF could not get him to issue Montgomery a clear, direct order. Eisenhower's instructions to Montgomery were more informative than directing and were always couched in vague, general language, leaving Montgomery an out if he chose to take it. He usually did.

Eisenhower would propose the broadest possible strategic agenda with Antwerp and the pre-negotiated plans for the Allied advance into Germany foremost in his mind. Since those plans had been developed prior to the invasion as a political compromise, they contained a route of advance into Germany for both the British and the Americans. There was something for everyone.

Unfortunately, the British Army was much too small to fulfill its roll in Allied pre-invasion plans. Plans, it should be pointed out, which were drawn up by a staff of mostly British officers. In Sicily, Montgomery's plans had given the British Eighth Army the primary mission of capturing Messina before the Germans fled and they had failed. In Normandy, Montgomery's plans assigned the mission of taking Caen, Falaise and Argentan to his Second British Army and they had failed a second time.

Now, as the Allies drove toward the German border, Montgomery insisted that his Army Group be assigned highest priority once again because they had Antwerp and the Ruhr in their sector. Politically, Montgomery's request made sense as a compromise typical of Eisenhower's method of command. Militarily, Montgomery's request made no sense at all; the terrain on the

---

[1157]   Butcher, 627.

*   The others: Antwerp, The Battle of the Bulge, and the Rhine River Crossings.

northern route over which Montgomery proposed to launch his main thrust was not suitable for mobile operations.[1158]

The fact that Eisenhower's weakest Army Group had been assigned the 'main thrust' mission meant that the American's 'secondary thrust' south of the Ardennes toward the Saar would have to be compromised. Whichever option the Supreme Commander selected for the drive into Germany was bound to disappoint one of the Allies. The Allies' 'main and secondary thrust' designations were clearly influenced by British politics. Eisenhower had been sent to Europe to defeat the German Army, not to occupy the Ruhr or the North German plain.

After Normandy, according to Montgomery, British infantry divisions were barely capable of sustained offensive operations.[1159] Painfully aware of these limitations, he proposed a plan that would guarantee the British some control of Allied decisions for the drive into Germany. By eliminating the American thrust south of the Ardennes and moving at least some of their divisions north to fight beside his 21st Army Group, he could disguise the manpower crisis within his Second British Army while retaining operational control of a substantial portion of the American Army. Eisenhower's refusal to take control of Allied Ground Forces on August 1, which had been agreed upon prior to the invasion, seemed to offer Montgomery some hope that he might retain control of all Allied Ground Forces as well. Montgomery's options would be improved if he could entice one or more US Armies north of the Ardennes and away from Bradley's secondary thrust south of the Ardennes.

For Montgomery and British political interests in Europe, Eisenhower's decision to support the British effort was a win-win situation. Montgomery could maintain the British Second Army in Europe by keeping it out of dangerous situations, while using the Canadians and Americans for any battle which seemed to offer high casualties and little reward. During those operations which were likely to generate front page news coverage, like the Rhine River crossings, Montgomery would assign his Second British Army the leading role.

By early September Field Marshal Montgomery and other Allied generals thought the German Army was finished. They believed that the next big battle would finish off the Germans and could become little more than a

---

[1158] Ingersoll, 218.
[1159] Hastings, *Overlord*, 239, 240. Also see Montgomery's cable to Alan Brooke dated 14 Aug. 44. From D'Este, *Decision*, 262.

victory march to Berlin.[1160] It was this understanding that led Montgomery to insist on the Market-Garden Operation over the more mundane task of opening the port of Antwerp. He ignored Eisenhower's letter of September 4 assigning Antwerp as the primary mission for his "Northern Group of Armies."[1161]

Strategically, Market-Garden was sound; it was an attempt to bypass the Siegfried Line from the north and get the British Second Army over the Rhine at Arnhem. Tactically, it was fraught with danger. Key elements of the plan did not utilize British strengths. Instead, the operation relied on speed of movement for mobile forces, communications, and infantry-armor cooperation.

Montgomery's operational control of major Allied ground forces also offered the British, and Prime Minister Churchill, the means to retain a strategic voice and some control of the Allied Armies in Europe. This was at a time when, by sheer weight of numbers, that control seemed to be slipping away to the Americans. With Montgomery in command of the largest Allied thrust, Churchill was guaranteed a strong political voice in command decisions. While this was obvious to Marshall from his vantage point as Chairman of the Combined Chiefs of Staff in Washington, it may not have been so obvious to Eisenhower in France.

Ralph Ingersoll recalled a 1943 meeting with Presidential Aide, Harry Hopkins during the month of October 1943, before the Conference at Teheran. They were discussing the upcoming Allied conference at Teheran and the appointment of the Allied Commander for *Overlord*. Ingersoll wrote, "He [Hopkins] felt that the appointment should wait until then [Teheran] . . . . He said that Churchill was the problem—that Roosevelt had decided that we were entitled, and quite able, to run our own show but that the problem was to find a general who could 'stand up to Churchill.' He pictured Churchill as very strong minded on military matters and quite able to dominate his own generals."[1162] Roosevelt's description of Winston Churchill was completely accurate. Even a cursory examination of Arthur Bryant's work, based on Field Marshal Brooke's diary, reveals the great difficulty Brooke and the other British Chiefs of Staff experienced trying to work with Prime Minister Churchill. Brooke's frustration with Churchill was detailed time and again in his diary.

[1160] Ambrose, *Eisenhower, Soldier, General,* 336, 377.
[1161] Chandler, (Ed.), *The Eisenhower Papers, Vol. IV,* 2116.
[1162] Ingersoll, 48.

By 1945, Eisenhower's bosses back in Washington were not sure he had the mental toughness to stand up to British political pressure in support of United States interests in Europe. George Marshall had told Henry L. Stimson [U.S. Secretary of War], ". . . that he had not been certain of Eisenhower's ability to stand up to the British."[1163] Secretary Stimson later wrote, "This time I also found that Marshall thought that Eisenhower had been over-conciliatory in his dealings with the British in this matter [ground commander]. I have always been afraid of this . . . . I myself have been worried lest he lose sight of . . . supporting . . . our national views where they were at variance with the British. [This was] . . . why I favored the appointment of Marshall for this European command . . ."[1164] Secretary Stimson and General Marshall were acutely aware of the problems Eisenhower was facing in Europe.

General Eisenhower was performing a delicate balancing act. He was trying to accommodate the competing political interests of two countries. This was not always possible. Two of Eisenhower's larger problems were insoluble. First, there could only be one Allied Ground Forces Commander, and the British, although they had agreed to it, never accepted Eisenhower in that role. They would continue their efforts to undermine Eisenhower's authority and attempt to install a British Ground Forces Commander between Eisenhower and his Army Group commanders.

Second, although the British Army had demonstrated an inability to sustain offensive operations at Caen in June and July 1944, they insisted, through virtually the end of the war, that Eisenhower give Montgomery's 21st Army Group and its mission north of the Ardennes the highest strategic priority. This could be done only by shrinking the size of General Bradley's American thrust south of the Ardennes.

General Bradley's 12th U.S. Army Group was the best led, best trained and best equipped attack force in the Allied arsenal. With General George Patton's Third Army providing the offensive thrust, General Bradley's Army Group offered the Allies their best chance for a quick end to the war. Time and again throughout the war in Europe, Field Marshal Montgomery intervened to thwart American offensives, just as he had at the Falaise Gap. With the Allies' best offensive weapon dogged by British politics, the war seemed to last forever.

[1163] Pogue, *Marshall: Organizer*, 509.
[1164] Henry L. Stimson Diary, 17Feb45. From Pogue, *Marshall, Organizer*, 509.

When Eisenhower complied with Montgomery's demands and moved two US Armies north of the Ardennes, the Allies soon discovered that they were fighting over ground that gave every advantage to the German defenders. This led to a disastrous fall campaign and 80,987 United States casualties during the Battle of the Bulge.[1165] It was a horrible fall campaign and the European weather was the worst in nearly 50 years.

For both British and US Armies it was fairly common for a discussion to take place between superior and subordinate officers regarding an order over which there was some disagreement. Once they reached an agreement the subordinate commander was supposed to carry out the command. According to Pogue, ". . . [Eisenhower] added to his own command problems by failing to make clear to Field Marshal Montgomery when the 'discussion' stage had ended and the 'execution' stage had begun . . . . Perhaps the Supreme Commander, accustomed to more ready compliance from his U.S. army group commanders, delayed too long in issuing positive directions to Montgomery."[1166] It would be difficult to look back over the Eisenhower-Montgomery correspondence between August 1944 and March 1945 and find Eisenhower giving any specific operational directions to Montgomery.

Stephen Ambrose, Harry Butcher, Generals W. Bedell Smith and Omar Bradley were Eisenhower's close friends and supporters; they all agonized over the 'command' issue. Smith likened Eisenhower to a football coach going up and down the line encouraging his generals.[1167] A helpful General Bradley saw Eisenhower getting more involved in command decisions during the Battle of the Falaise Gap: ". . . Ike had established and advanced SHAEF headquarters . . . near Granville and was in full-time residence. He had not yet formally taken command of the ground forces but he was ever-present. I made no major move without consulting him."[1168]

On July 31st Harry Butcher addressed the command issue in his diary: "Just how personally Ike has taken command of the ground forces is not yet clear to me. Each time I have suggested he do it, he has belligerently countered, 'Then they will have to get someone to be the Allied Commander.'"[1169] Eisenhower apparently did not think anyone should occupy the post of

---

[1165] Weigley, *Eisenhower's Lieutenants*, 574.

[1166] Pogue, *The Supreme Command*, 289.

[1167] Ambrose, *Eisenhower, Soldier, General*, 325.

[1168] Bradley, *A General's Life*, 297.

[1169] Butcher, 627

ground forces commander. In the United States Army one man in a theater is the commander. In Europe, Eisenhower was that man. Placing the three commanders of land, sea and air under the Supreme Commander for the invasion, had been a concession to the British system of command. The Allied system of command was a windfall for the British. It enabled them to give up nominal overall command while retaining operational control of all land, sea and air forces.

In fact, Eisenhower did not see the need for an Allied Ground Forces Commander. In his book, *Crusade in Europe*, Eisenhower wrote, "I carefully explained that in a theater so vast as ours each army group commander would be the ground commander in chief for his particular area; instead of one there would be three so-called commanders in chief for the ground and each would be supported by his own tactical air force."[1170] This did not stop the British from trying to insert one of their own generals between Eisenhower and his army group commanders, hoping to gain more publicity and greater strategic control of the Allied armies.[1171]

In Europe, the Allies had a commander for air and sea, but after September 1, no commander for Allied Ground Forces. This was a source of great disappointment to Field Marshal Montgomery, who believed that the job of commanding Allied Ground Forces belonged to him.

Stephen Ambrose was the most creative when it came to the question of Eisenhower and command. Ambrose wrote, "What did matter was logistics, the flow of supplies. Eisenhower allocated supplies and that was his real power. The way in which Eisenhower distributed the available supplies would determine the direction and the nature of the offensive, no matter who had the title of land commander."[1172] If supplies [logistics] were used to determine strategy, Ambrose would have a point. Strategy determines the flow of supplies; it is not the other way around. Logistics may limit but does not determine strategy. Eisenhower felt compelled to give Montgomery logistical support because of the strategic objectives and the strong endorsement of British politicians for an offensive in the British sector.

[1170] Eisenhower, *Crusade,* 285.

[1171] Peter Lyon, *Eisenhower: Portrait of the Hero,* (Boston: Little Brown and Company, 1974), 316, 317. Peter Lyon detailed five tri-weekly attempts by Montgomery to re-establish himself as Allied Ground Forces Commander. "On November 28—it was his fifth tri-weekly effort, and smack on schedule—Montgomery greeted Eisenhower at his tactical headquarters, then at Zonhoven."

[1172] Ambrose, *Eisenhower, Solider, General,* 345.

Eisenhower did not decide what strategy to follow based on the available logistic support. Strategy determines the distribution of supplies [logistics]; logistics may limit but does not determine strategy.

Because Montgomery's arguments had the strongest political support, Eisenhower was forced to follow his strategic plans for the fall campaign. Eisenhower did threaten to withhold supplies to force Montgomery's compliance in opening the strategically critical port of Antwerp. Eisenhower got the result he was looking for, but it was a command ploy he used exactly once during the entire nine month campaign in northwest Europe.

It is not possible to look back through history and sort out which event forced Eisenhower's hand on March 28. If it was something Montgomery did, there were so many examples of his insubordinate, duplicitous behavior it would be impossible to say which one was the proverbial straw. Was it Montgomery's press conference of January 7, where he took credit for the Allied victory after the Battle of the Bulge? ". . . I employed the whole available power of the British Group of Armies . . . ," Montgomery told the assembled press corps, "You have thus the picture of British troops fighting on both sides of American forces who have suffered a hard blow . . . I think possibly one of the most interesting and tricky battles I have ever handled."[1173] He left the British press with an image of British troops heavily involved in the fighting on both sides of the poor Americans who had really suffered a terrible defeat. It was mostly lies, but the British press was in full attack mode. They greedily seized upon any chance to humiliate Eisenhower and the American command.

The event which probably forced Eisenhower's hand was Montgomery's majestic Rhine crossing. The Germans had committed their armies to battle on the wrong side of the Rhine, just as Eisenhower predicted; now they had very little left to oppose the Allied crossings. Two American Armies, Hodges' First and Patton's Third, had already crossed the Rhine on a shoe string and were moving deep into Germany. Montgomery could easily have done the same thing. But the Rhine River crossing was such a huge political event, there never was much of a chance Montgomery was going to ignore one of those famous names on a map which had always impressed his prime minister. There was no strategic value in waiting for a gala public relations event, but Montgomery didn't always give priority to sound strategy when considering military operations. Montgomery's majestic Rhine

---

[1173] Ambrose, *Eisenhower, Soldier, General*, 379.

River crossing was a prime example of how British politics influenced his battlefield tactics. Yes, Montgomery got over the Rhine, but at what cost?

General William Simpson, commanding US Ninth Army under Montgomery's 21st Army Group, wanted to take the Rhine on the run. He sent plans to Montgomery for a separate Rhine crossing by his Ninth Army and was coolly turned down. The army Montgomery selected for this gala public relations event was, to no one's great surprise, the Second British Army. They had been out of the line planning the operation since November, 1944.

An opposed Rhine crossing by the Second British Army, this was a front-page news event of profound significance. The Rhine crossing at Wesel would be Montgomery's last great 'colossal crack.' It was a strange mixture of politics, large unit military maneuver, and press briefings all staged for the maximum publicity value. Churchill was there, the C.I.G.S., Alan Brooke was there. Eisenhower was there. Over one-hundred war correspondents were on hand to record the magnificent show.

One million men were to take part; two-thousand artillery pieces on a twenty-mile front produced an extravagant show of flashing lights and booming sounds.[1174] The ringmaster was at his post. There on center stage was the 'master of the set-piece battle,' Field Marshal Bernard L. Montgomery. Press adulation for his magnificent Rhine crossing and kudos from the Prime Minister and C.I.G.S. were bantered back and forth, as Montgomery strutted about the banks of the Rhine.

Churchill had pre-recorded a radio message to the British people for the BBC, touting Montgomery and his British Second Army for: ". . . the first assault crossing of the Rhine in modern history."[1175] Knowing that two American Armies, Hodges' First and Patton's Third, were already on the east bank of the Rhine and moving into Germany, did not dampen British enthusiasm. Churchill crossed the Rhine in a ". . . LCVP manned by American sailors and flying a U.S. flag. When photographs of this event appeared in British newspapers the Stars and Stripes had been inked out by Monty's censors."[1176] British censors clearly did not want any reference to American war production mucking up Montgomery's big show.

Given the size of the military display Montgomery had orchestrated, one might have expected a first rate opponent. Alan Brooke saw the ". . . the

---

[1174]　Churchill, *Triumph and Tragedy*, 411.
[1175]　Bradley, *A General's Life*, 413.
[1176]　Perret, 443.

flower of what remained of Hitler's Western Army . . ."[1177] Winston Churchill saw an even grander image, "Eighty thousand men, the advance-guard of armies a million strong, were to be hurled forward. Masses of boats and pontoons lay ready. On the far side stood the Germans, entrenched, and organized in all the strength of modern firepower."[1178]

Unfortunately, the flower of the German Army had disappeared long ago on the Eastern Front at Stalingrad, at Kursk or in North Africa. By March 1945 those German soldiers with a means of transportation were busy elsewhere, chasing after the Americans. The pitiful remnants left behind at Wesel could hardly be called the flower of anything.

Montgomery had turned down a request from General William Simpson, US Ninth Army Commander, to take the Rhine on the fly. That decision was politically motivated. He produced a plan for the Rhine crossing that left the Ninth Army Headquarters completely out of the command set-up. That decision was politically motivated. According to Ralph Ingersoll, "The British *always* mix political and military motives."[1179] Montgomery's Rhine crossing was certainly no exception.

The bridge at Wesel was built and maintained by US Army Engineers. The British Second Army requested and got access to the bridge 19 hours a day, ". . . leaving it to the U.S. Ninth Army for only five [hours]."[1180] When General Dempsey later demanded the full 24 hours a day access to the bridge, it was too much for General Simpson. The normally quiet, even-tempered American general exploded. General Simpson, ". . . put [US] tanks on the approach to the bridge and gave their crews orders to fire on any British vehicle that tried to get onto it out of turn."[1181] The British general quickly decided he did not need those extra five hours.

On March 7, First Army's 9th U.S. Armored Division stole a bridge across the Rhine at Remagen with minimal casualties. Third Armies' 5th Infantry Division crossed the Rhine at Oppenheim during the night of March 22nd, again with few casualties. Montgomery's Rhine crossing cost the Allies nearly 5,000 casualties, most of them in the British 6th and U.S. 17th Airborne Divisions. "In Operation *Varsity* [Montgomery's airborne element] . . . four-hundred and forty out of one-thousand five-hundred and

---

[1177]   Bryant, *Triumph*, 430.
[1178]   Churchill, *Triumph and Tragedy*, 411, 412.
[1179]   Ingersoll, 56. Italics in the original.
[1180]   Perret, 443.
[1181]   Perret, 443.

ninety troop carriers [airplanes] were severely damaged or destroyed and a parachutist who survived the curtains of flak would recall the horror of watching the crews of the stricken aircraft . . . wait their fate on impact."[1182] It was a horrible waste of young lives at this late stage of the war, and all for the headlines a Rhine River crossing would produce in England.

During the later stages of the war, SHAEF had become almost as anti-Montgomery as the officers at Third Army and Bradley's 12th Army Group Headquarters. One British officer at SHAEF remembered, ". . . the feeling was that if anything was to be done quickly, don't give it to Monty."[1183] Lieutenant-General Frederick Morgan felt that, ". . . Monty was the last person Ike would have chosen for the drive on Berlin-Monty would have needed at least six months to prepare."[1184]

Casualty figures for the Rhine River crossings tell a grim story. Courtney Hodges' First US Army got across the Rhine at Remagen with a first day's casualty count of thirty-one men.[1185] George Patton's Third Army got a crossing near Oppenheim, ". . . with a total loss of twenty-eight men killed and wounded."[1186] William Simpson's Ninth U.S. Army was forced to wait on Montgomery; they suffered 491 casualties crossing the Rhine south of Wessel.[1187] U.S. 17th Airborne Division lost 921 paratroopers and three-hundred and fifty air crew.[1188]

Casualties for Montgomery's Second British Army and 6th British Airborne Division are extremely difficult to find. Montgomery was trying to keep British losses low, but that did not happen during Operation *Varsity,* the airborne element of Montgomery's Rhine crossing. Richard Lamb wrote, ". . . British 6th Airborne had lost 30 percent of its personnel killed and wounded; the Airlanding Brigade, which came in gliders, had lost 70 percent of its equipment . . ."[1189] The army which needed to keep its casualty count low lost over three-thousand one-hundred men crossing the Rhine north of Wesel.[1190] Adding American losses, the total first day's casualty count for

---

[1182] Keegan, *Six Armies*, 81.

[1183] Cornelius Ryan, *The Last Battle*, (New York: Simon and Schuster, 1966), 241.

[1184] Ryan, *The Last Battle*, 241.

[1185] Eisenhower, *Crusade*, 389.

[1186] Patton, 273.

[1187] Pogue, *The Supreme Command*, 431.

[1188] Lamb, 362.

[1189] Lamb, 360-362.

[1190] Lamb, 360-362. Also see Ronald Lewin, *Montgomery, As Military Commnader,* (New York, Stein and Day, 1971), 323, and Pogue, *Supreme Command*, 431.

Montgomery's Rhine crossing came to nearly 5,000 men. U.S. First and Third Armies had gotten over the Rhine River with a total first day casualty count of 59 men. The disparity between the number of lives sacrificed at Wesel and the two earlier American Rhine crossings is striking. After Second Alamein, no one could question the willingness of British generals to sacrifice the lives of their men for political reasons. Still, the human cost of Montgomery's Rhine crossing must have shocked Eisenhower.

There can be little doubt why Eisenhower gave the last great Allied effort to General Bradley. Russell Weigley wrote, ". . . if Eisenhower . . . needed convincing evidence that his American generals and armies were swifter to seize their opportunities than Montgomery and the British, the crossings of the Rhine thoroughly confirmed the superiority of Patton, Simpson and Hodges and their American armies in bold improvisation and in designing and executing rapid advances led by armor."[1191] Nothing had changed. These were the same generals who had fought their way out of the hedgerows and swamps back in Normandy and had squeezed the Germans between Argentan and Falaise.

Eisenhower's most persistent problem had always been Montgomery. The British commander never did grasp the correct doctrine for tank-infantry cooperation in mobile warfare. *Eisenhower had wasted eight months following Montgomery's lead. Not because he agreed with Montgomery's strategy, but because Montgomery would not follow orders.*

C.I.G.S. Brooke and Prime Minister Churchill were handsomely rewarded for their faith in Montgomery's unruly behavior and his ability to disrupt the American command. Geoffrey Perret agreed, adding, "Faced with the certain prospect of failure if limited to command nothing more than the resources . . . [His Majesty] provided, Montgomery frequently became histrionic and hysterical. Yet . . . he proved a master of inter-Allied in fighting. He got much of what he wanted, without making major concessions."[1192] With the Allies crossing the Rhine, it now appeared that the German Army was near collapse.

On March 19, 1945, Eisenhower took a train to Cannes for a short vacation. He was, ". . . accompanied by Bradley, Smith, Tex Lee, and four WACs, including Kay [Summersby, his female driver]."[1193] Eisenhower was so tired that he slept for two days, getting up about mid-day for lunch and

---

[1191] Weigley, *Eisenhower's Lieutenants*, 684.

[1192] Perret, 356.

[1193] Ambrose, *Eisenhower, Soldier, General*, 389.

a few glasses of wine. During the last few days of the vacation Eisenhower spent hours discussing strategy for the final Allied thrust into Germany with General Bradley.[1194] On March 23, he flew to Wesel to watch the Rhine crossing of General William Simpson's Ninth US Army.

While he was at the Rhine River crossings, Eisenhower had a long discussion about future Allied strategy with C.I.G.S., Alan Brooke. According to Nigel Hamilton, "Brooke saw no danger in Eisenhower's new plan to surround the Ruhr from the north and by a double envelopment in the south . . ."[1195] Eisenhower also proposed increasing the size of Bradley's thrust through Frankfurt and Kassel. Brooke recorded part of their discussion in his diary: "He [Eisenhower] also wanted to know whether I agreed with his present plan of pushing in the south for Frankfurt and Kassel. I told him that, with the Germans crumbling as they are the whole situation is now altered. Evidently the Boche is cracking and what we want now is to push him relentlessly, wherever we can, until he crumbles."[1196] This conversation with Brooke confirmed Eisenhower's thoughts on future Allied strategy. The collapse of the German Army combined with Brooke's agreement to an American thrust into central Germany gave Eisenhower the political tools he needed to confront his nemesis. Now it was time to set things right and finish the war as quickly as possible.

On March 28, Eisenhower was back in his office at Reims. There were two letters on his desk. One was from his boss in Washington, General Marshall; the other was from Field Marshal Montgomery. Marshall said that given the current 'disintegration' of the German Army, Eisenhower might give some thought to meeting the Russians and how that could be accomplished without creating an unfortunate incident. He suggested a prominent line of demarcation. As for the final thrusts into Germany, Marshal suggested: ". . . Eisenhower might want to push heavy columns eastward on a broad front, on either the Nurnberg-Linz or the Karlsruhe-Munich axis."[1197]

The second letter was from Field Marshal Montgomery. Montgomery told Eisenhower that he had issued orders to his Army Commanders for operations that were only just beginning. Montgomery outlined his general plans: "I have ordered Ninth and Second Armies to move their armored

---

[1194] Ambrose, *Eisenhower, Soldier, General*, 390.
[1195] Hamilton, *Final Years*, 435.
[1196] Bryant, *Triumph*, 436.
[1197] Marshall's W 59315 (EM, Cable File). See Chandler, (Ed.), *The Eisenhower Papers, Vol. IV*, 2553.

and mobile forces forward at once and to get through to the ELBE with the utmost speed and drive. The situation looks good and events should begin to move rapidly in a few days."[1198] Montgomery gave Eisenhower his axis of advance and told him that his tactical headquarters would be moving on a line, "WESSEL-MUNSTER-WIEDENBRUCK-HERFORD-HANNOVER and thence via the Autobahn to BERLIN I hope."[1199]

Montgomery was being very kind to his commander; he usually did not keep Eisenhower so well informed of his plans. Montgomery told British General Simpson to be careful with any news Montgomery gave him: "I trust you will be careful not to send Jumbo Wilson [British Representative on the CCS in Washington] . . . any hot news you get from me. It would make things awkward for me if [General] Marshall receives from Jumbo . . . better news than he gets from Ike. Actually, you are far better informed, and in the picture, than IKE is."[1200]

This was how an operational order from Field Marshal Montgomery was given to his northern group of armies for execution. This was the system of command and control Montgomery and other British officers had used since Eisenhower first assumed the role of Supreme Commander in North Africa in late 1942.[1201] Montgomery would draw up his operational plans, hand them out to his army commanders for execution, and, if Eisenhower was lucky, he received a copy.

Eisenhower's communications to his army group commanders had always painted strategic objectives in the broadest possible strokes; he left it to his commanders to fill in the blanks. This was the American method of command; it always gave subordinate officers wide latitude in carrying out orders. American Generals Bradley and Devers usually tried to coordinate their plans with Eisenhower and his minions at SHAEF. Montgomery had usually gone his own way. George Patton wrote in his diary, ". . . Ike feels that we think he is selling us out but he has to, *as Monty will not take orders,* so we have to. Bradley said it was time for a showdown. I offered to resign with him, but he backed out."[1202]

Given Eisenhower's conversation with Alan Brooke on the banks of the Rhine, it would appear that he had made up his mind to dramatically

---

[1198] M 562 of 27.3.45, Montgomery Papers. See Hamilton, *Final Years,* 440.
[1199] M 562 of 27.3.45, Montgomery Papers. See Hamilton, *Final Years,* 440.
[1200] Letter of 28.3.45, Montgomery Papers. See Hamilton, *Final Years,* 446, 447.
[1201] Weigley, *Eisenhower's Lieutenants,* 682.
[1202] Blumenson, (Ed.), *The Patton Papers, 1940-1945,* 548. Italics added.

alter the thrust of the Allied Armies before March 28. Eisenhower may well have reached some kind of accommodation with Bradley while they were vacationing together at Cannes. At the time, he did not share his new plans with the British; which was fair, because the British had never shared any of their plans with the supreme commander. His discussions with Bradley, the cable from Marshall, and the position of the Russian Army within 35 miles of Berlin combined to give Eisenhower the opportunity to allow Bradley's often ignored [at SHAEF] 12th US Army Group a chance to lead the final thrust into central Germany. "SHAEF [and Eisenhower] in its pursuit of Allied harmony, was forever taking American troops for granted, while maintaining a solicitous attitude toward the British. Given the fragility of the British units, this was understandable. Rarely, however, was any concession made to American pride . . ."[1203] The fragile nature of the British Army and their 'by the book' commander were the main reasons they had always lagged behind, but now the time had come for a speedy end to the war.

There may have been a sinister smile on Eisenhower's face as he composed a reply to Montgomery's letter. Eisenhower wrote, "I agree in general with your plans up to the point of gaining contact with Bradley east of the Ruhr. However, as soon as you have joined hands with Bradley, *Ninth United States Army will revert to Bradley's command.* Bradley will be responsible for mopping up . . . the Ruhr and . . . will deliver his main thrust on the axis Erfurt-Leipzig-Dresden to join hands with the Russians. *The mission of your army group will be to protect Bradley's northern flank . . .*"[1204]

Montgomery must have been shocked. This had never happened. He had commanded a British Army under Eisenhower for well over two years, and he had never been asked to protect anyone's flank. Montgomery's Army Group was being asked to protect the flank of an American Army; this was simply mind-numbing. The British force under Montgomery's command had always been given the primary mission, the lion's share of men and supplies and most of the press coverage. Montgomery had dominated Allied strategic discussions since the Normandy invasion. But that was in the past. The Allied Army in Europe finally had an American Ground Forces Commander.

[1203] Perret, 433.

[1204] Eisenhower Mss., Cable FDW 18272, March 28, 1945. See Chandler, (Ed.), *The Eisenhower Papers, Vol. IV,* 2364.

The tone of Eisenhower's letter must have been disturbing to Montgomery. These were no broad strokes, there was no wiggle room, no rough outlines of what Eisenhower hoped to accomplish in the coming weeks. This was a direct order from a superior officer and there was no mistaking Eisenhower's intent. Montgomery's US Ninth Army was gone and he was being asked to protect the flanks of an army commanded by an American. Montgomery's angst must have been intensified by his belief that the German Army had finally collapsed. He had just set out on his final drive to Berlin with a victory lap through the Brandenburg Gate nearly in sight. But Montgomery needed an American Army to get there, and now Ninth Army was gone.

Montgomery howled in protest. He complained to Brooke. And Brooke complained to the British Chiefs of Staff in London who in turn complained to the CCS [Combined Chiefs of Staff] in Washington. The British did not like the fact that Eisenhower had changed his plans; they did not like the fact that he was ignoring Berlin, which the British still regarded as a huge strategic [political] prize. They were also upset that Eisenhower would communicate directly with the Soviet dictator, Joseph Stalin.[1205] Montgomery did not like the fact that he was losing the US Ninth Army. He asked Eisenhower to wait until after he had reached the Elbe to take away Simpson's Army. Churchill did not like the fact that Eisenhower's decision to take ". . . Ninth Army away from Montgomery would leave 21st Army Group too weak to carry out offensive action . . . and [relegates] His Majesty's Forces to an unexpected restricted sphere."[1206] Exactly when it became Eisenhower's responsibility to insure that the British Army in Europe retained the capacity to perform offensive operations is not clear.

Marshall addressed these British concerns in a cable to Eisenhower.[1207] Eisenhower's reply the next day became emotionally heated. He had been coddling Churchill, Brooke and Montgomery for three long, demeaning and demanding years. His patience had finally expired. Eisenhower wrote: ". . . Even cursory examination of the direction for this thrust [reveals

---

[1205] Eisenhower [taking Marshall's advice about a line of demarcation with the Russians] had asked the Allied military mission in Moscow to inform Joseph Stalin of his intension to ignore Berlin and halt his armies on the Elbe River. See Pogue, *The Supreme Command*, 441.

[1206] Churchill's #2072 dated 31 March 1945. From Chandler, (Ed.), *The Eisenhower Papers, Vol. IV*, 2563.

[1207] Marshall's W 60507, March 29, 1945, EM, Cable File. See Chandler, (Ed.), *The Eisenhower Papers, Vol. IV*, 2559.

it] should be toward the Leipzig region, [in] which area the greater part of the remaining German industrial capacity [is located]. [I am] Merely following the principle that Field Marshal Brooke has always shouted at me, I am determined to concentrate on one major thrust and all that my plan does is to place Ninth U.S. Army back under Bradley for that phase of operations . . ."[1208] Eisenhower told Marshall that Berlin is not a significant objective, and that the good ground the British have been bragging about on the north German plain simply does not exist. ". . . The so-called 'good ground' in northern Germany is not really good at this time of year . . . (it is) cut up with waterways . . . is very wet and not so favorable for rapid movement as is the higher plateau over which I am preparing to launch the main effort."[1209]

Eisenhower went on to remind Marshall about the problems they had with the British in the last eight months. He showed Marshall—point by point—where British staff work had always erred, curiously enough, on that side of the argument favoring British political interests. He reminded Marshall that the British opposed *Anvil*. The British said it would take three months for the troops landing in Southern France to fight their way up the Rhone Valley and meet the right wing of Eisenhower's forces in western France [it took twenty-seven days]. The British opposed Eisenhower's plan to destroy the German army west of the Rhine, they insisted that the route that the Americans wanted to take through the Nancy Gap to Frankfurt would involve a slow, bloody fight and just the opposite had happened. Eisenhower told Marshall that he was driven by only one idea and that was the quickest way to end the war.[1210]

Eisenhower's letter to Marshall was a strong emotional appeal. It was also supported by the facts. Through all the agony and heartache in his dealings with the British, especially Montgomery, Eisenhower had never lost Marshall's confidence. Marshall had been closely monitoring Eisenhower's problems with the British. From time to time Marshall would offer Eisenhower advice to 'take command of the U.S. contingent' or to 'make no concessions of any kind on the issue of command.' He was probably delighted that Eisenhower was finally standing up to the British.

[1208] Eisenhower, Mss., Cable File, March 30, 1945. See Chandler, (Ed.), *The Eisenhower Papers, Vol. IV*, 2560.

[1209] Eisenhower, Mss., Cable File, March 30, 1945. See Chandler, (Ed.), *The Eisenhower Papers, Vol. IV*, 2560, 2561

[1210] Chandler, (Ed.), *The Eisenhower Papers, Vol. IV*, 2561, 2562.

In strategic discussions with the British since D-day, Eisenhower had been careful to promise Montgomery that the northern [British] thrust would have Allied priority up through the Rhine River crossing and the encirclement of the Ruhr industrial complex in northern Germany. Eisenhower made no promises to Montgomery past the Ruhr encirclement.

While Berlin had been a long standing objective for Allied armies, it now appeared that the Russians would beat them to it. As Eisenhower explained to the Combined Chiefs of Staff a few days later, "Berlin as a strategic area is discounted as it is now largely destroyed . . . Moreover, it is so near to the Russian front [about thirty-five miles] that once they start moving again they will reach it in a matter of days."[1211]

Churchill still wanted Eisenhower to take Berlin. He explained to Eisenhower that if the Russians took Vienna, which now seemed likely, and Berlin they would consider that they were, "the overwhelming contributor to our common victory."[1212] Churchill said that the Russians would be difficult to deal with [politically] if they thought they had won the war by themselves.

The truth, which has been obscured by both British and American historians, was that the Russians were the overwhelming contributor to the Allied victory over Nazi Germany, and by a very wide margin. Admitting that fact would not have made the bloody, tyrannical regime of Joseph Stalin any more palatable to western governments; but it would have been the truth. The single Battle for Stalingrad cost Russia more lives than the total number of lives the British or Americans lost in all their battles during the Second World War. Regardless of what one thinks of Joseph Stalin, more than 20 million Russians died during World War II. This gave the Russians the moral high ground in political discussions with the western Allies at the end of the war. No political maneuvering, including the Allied liberation of Berlin or Prague was going to change that central fact.

The willingness of British leaders to spend the lives of their men for purely political purposes was never in doubt. Although there was no sound military reason for taking Berlin, the British persisted. Eisenhower explained his thinking to Marshall, "I am the first to admit that a war is waged in pursuit of political aims, and if the Combined Chiefs of Staff should decide

---

[1211] Eisenhower, Mss., Cable File, March 31, 1945. See Chandler, (Ed.), *The Eisenhower Papers, Vol. IV*, 2569.

[1212] Churchill Letter #2072, dated March 31, 1945. See Chandler, (Ed.), *The Eisenhower Papers, Vol. IV*, 2563.

that the Allied effort to take Berlin outweighs purely military considerations in the theater, I would cheerfully readjust my plans and my thinking so as to carry out such an operation."[1213] Bradley had estimated it would require, ". . . one-hundred thousand casualties . . ." to take Berlin.[1214] It was, Bradley said, "A pretty stiff price to pay for a prestige objective . . . As soldiers we looked naively on this British inclination to complicate the war with political foresight and non-military objectives."[1215]

The American Chiefs of Staff were completely behind Eisenhower; they strongly supported every one of his decisions. After considering the British complaint that Eisenhower should not be dealing directly with Stalin, the American Chiefs disagreed. They said, ". . . operational necessity required that the Supreme Commander, not the CCS, make modifications in his communications to Moscow."[1216]

Eisenhower had always been given support from Washington. As long as he retained Marshall's confidence, he was guaranteed support from the Combined Chiefs of Staff. In fact, the main concern for both George Marshall and Henry Stimson was that Eisenhower had been too conciliatory toward the British. They felt the tradeoffs for Eisenhower's decisions backing British interests in Europe at the expense of the Americans were not forthcoming. Marshall said he accepted Eisenhower's appointment of Montgomery to command U.S. forces during the Battle of the Bulge; but, "Afterward I came to regret it because I don't think Montgomery played at all square on the deal. He made use of it politically and through the press to Eisenhower's . . . disadvantage."[1217] Marshall and CCS support for Eisenhower left the British without recourse. Montgomery's clandestine command of Allied Ground Forces was finally over.

But the British had a good run. They managed to retain a dominant voice in Allied strategy up through the very end of the war. Eisenhower finally stopped talking to Montgomery. Talks between the two men had been fruitless since August 13 at the Falaise Gap. The Roosevelt-Churchill relationship had also come to an end. On March 28, when General Dwight D. Eisenhower finally assumed command of Allied Ground Forces in Europe, there were only forty days left in the war.

[1213] Chandler, (Ed.), *The Eisenhower Papers, Vol. IV*, 2592.
[1214] Bradley, *A Soldier's Story*, 535.
[1215] Bradley, *A Soldier's Story*, 535, 536.
[1216] Chandler, (Ed.), *The Eisenhower Papers, Vol. IV*, Note 2, 2570.
[1217] Mosley, 288.

The British had ruffled some American feathers in their angst over Eisenhower's decision to take Ninth Army away from Montgomery. It was left to Prime Minister Churchill to set things right. On April 1, Winston Churchill sent a telegram to President Roosevelt [he also sent a copy to Eisenhower]: ". . . I wish to place on record the complete confidence felt by His Majesty's Government in General Eisenhower, and our pleasure that our armies are serving under his command and our admiration of great and shining quality, character, and personality which he has proven himself to possess in all difficulties of handling an Allied command."[1218] After coddling the British for nearly three years, Eisenhower must have wondered why he had not taken command earlier.

In April, the British asked Eisenhower to capture the Czech city of Prague. They thought Eisenhower should order Patton to take it before the Russians got there. Eisenhower passed the request along to General Marshall and received this reply: "Personally and aside from all logistic, tactical, or strategic implications, I would be loath to hazard American lives for purely political purposes."[1219] Eisenhower's decision to leave Prague and Berlin to the Russians saved thousands of soldier's lives. It was, despite British protests, the correct decision. The geographical boundaries for post-war Europe had been set at Yalta. An Anglo-American occupation of Berlin or Prague at the end of the war would not have changed a thing in post-war Europe. The United States and Britain would have pulled back to their occupation zones in Western Germany, and the Russians would still have occupied Eastern Europe.

By May 7, the war was over. Eisenhower drafted the message informing the Combined Chiefs of Staff in Washington: "The Mission of this Allied Force was fulfilled at 0241 local time, May 7th, 1945, Eisenhower."[1220] Marshall's reply to Eisenhower's message was a warm appreciation of Eisenhower's wartime service: "You have commanded with outstanding success the most powerful military force that has ever been assembled . . . [You have been] selfless . . . sound and tolerant in your judgments . . . admirable in the courage and wisdom of your military decisions. You have made history . . . and you have stood for all we hope for and admire in an

---

[1218] Churchill telegram to Roosevelt, No. 2096, 1 April 1945. See Chandler, (Ed.), *The Eisenhower Papers, Vol. IV*, 2579.

[1219] Marshall to Eisenhower, W-74256, 28 Apr 45, SHAEF cbl log, From Pogue, *Supreme Command,* 468.

[1220] Pogue, *Supreme Command,* 490.

officer of the United States Army. These are my tributes and my personal thanks."[1221]

George Marshall never coddled anyone, and only rarely thanked subordinates or anyone else for a job well done. The warmth of this assessment from his boss probably had an emotional impact on Eisenhower. It may have made his decision to save the Anglo-American political alliance worth the agony it had cost. The military alliance Eisenhower fought so hard to salvage had been sacrificed to British vanity nine months earlier at the Falaise Gap.

[1221] Marshall to DDS, 5/8/45, EP. From Ambrose, *Eisenhower, Soldier, General*, 408.

Chapter 13

Conclusion: 'Caught in The British Empire Machine'

"The Americans, it is fair to say, profited far more than the British from their experience in Africa, thus confirming the axiom that education is easier than reeducation."[1222] Erwin Rommel

The Allied command structure had always combined a dash of military necessity with a few pounds of political compromise. General Eisenhower was selected because he was the American general most likely to get along with the British. President Roosevelt explained his reason for appointing Eisenhower to command *OVERLORD* to his son James, "Eisenhower is the best politician among the military men. He is a natural leader who can convince other men to follow him, and this is what we need in his position more than any other quality."[1223] Prior to the appointment, Roosevelt asked Churchill for his opinion about the selection of Eisenhower. Churchill later wrote, ". . . [Roosevelt] asked me for my opinion. I said it was for him to decide, but that we had also [in addition to Marshall] the warmest regard for General Eisenhower, and would trust our fortunes to his direction with hearty good will."[1224] Churchill must have been pleased with the selection of Eisenhower. In an unused memo about the British Eastern Mediterranean campaign, Churchill had written, ". . . Eisenhower owed me something."[1225] Churchill may have believed that he had a small hand in Eisenhower's selection.

General Eisenhower was a compromise both parties could agree upon; Montgomery was an officer the British selected on their own. They sought no compromise on their appointment of Montgomery to command Allied Ground Forces. The Americans clearly would have preferred someone

[1222] Rommel, 523.

[1223] James Roosevelt, *My Parents: A Differing View,* 176. From Eric Larrabee, *Commander in Chief,* (New York: Simon & Schuster, 1988), 438.

[1224] Winston S. Churchill, *Closing the Ring,* (Boston: Houghton Mifflin, 1951), 418.

[1225] The Churchill Papers, From Callahan, *Churchill and His Generals,* 164.

else. British historian R.W. Thompson wrote, "It is possible also that the choice of Montgomery was a symptom of British intransigence, . . . *[he] could be relied upon to argue every move with the Supreme Commander, and to maintain the course of the campaign for Europe on the lines most suitable for Britain.*"[1226] The American standard for a European command was cooperation; the British standard was manipulation.

As the Allied Ground Forces Commander the British had selected their most inflexible, most juvenile, most xenophobic, and least cooperative general. Churchill and Brooke were determined not to lose strategic control of the Allied armies in Europe. They believed that the status quo ante Churchill sought in Europe was possible only if they could dupe the Americans into backing British interests, and Montgomery seemed to offer the best hope of achieving that goal.[1227]

Unfortunately, British economic and military power had been declining since World War I. ". . . Countries that have long been Great Powers shrink from admitting that they are Great no longer."[1228] A.J.P. Taylor was certainly correct, but the reduction in British power, especially the limited reserves of the British Army, created a major problem for the Americans. General Frederick Morgan probably got it wrong. He suggested that the British lacked a, ". . . first-hand [knowledge] of the immense power and resources that the United States could throw into this battle."[1229] It would probably be more accurate to say that government officials were in a quandary deciding how the great military power of the United States Army could best serve British political interests.[1230] Raymond Callahan saw close Anglo-American relations as, ". . . critical for victory as well as for Britain's future. Indeed . . . the war was eroding British strength while it accelerated the growth of American power, such an intimate relationship enabling Britain to influence American policy might be the only way for Britain to safeguard its future position among the ranks of the major powers."[1231]

In this context, the appointment of General Montgomery to command Allied Ground Forces in France made no sense. His appointment seemed to suggest that the British were not interested in an intimate relationship with their American Allies. The ultimate decision to deny the authority

---

[1226] R.W. Thompson, *Montgomery: The Field Marshal*, 20. Italics added.
[1227] Sherwood, 837.
[1228] A.J.P. Taylor, *The Origins*, 174.
[1229] Morgan, 143.
[1230] Catherwood, 133, 136.
[1231] Callahan, *Churchill: Retreat*, 226.

of the American command and to subordinate the immense resources the United States Army to British 21st Army Group was also unfortunate.[1232] It had disastrous long-term political and economic consequences for Great Britain.

British officers had experienced problems with Bernard L. Montgomery prior to his appointment to command *OVERLORD*. Montgomery had a reputation for holding strong opinions, for insubordination and for displaying a total lack of empathy. Brooke and Churchill obviously expected that Eisenhower would experience similar problems with Montgomery.[1233] They hoped that Montgomery's intransigence would improve their chances to manipulate Allied strategy in support of British political interests. If this was their intention, they were certainly correct. Montgomery was a thorn in the side of the Americans from the moment he took command of 21st Army Group in January 1944 and announced to the world that he was now taking command the United States Army for the invasion.[1234]

Considering Franklin Roosevelt's disdain for European politics and his love of the United States Navy, it is not surprising that Roosevelt, with his eyes on the Pacific war, only rarely intervened in military affairs in Europe. Given Winston Churchill's position as both Prime Minister and Minister of Defense in Great Britain, plus his fondness for grand strategy and things military, it was not surprising that the prime minister interfered almost daily with the men trying to run the war in Europe. George Marshall told Alan Brooke that he often did not see President Roosevelt for a month or six weeks, Brooke remarked in his diary that he would be lucky if he hadn't seen Prime Minister Churchill for six hours.[1235]

Eisenhower was sent to Europe to, ". . . liberate Europe from the Germans . . . [and] undertake operations aimed at the heart of Germany and the destruction of her armed forces."[1236] He did just that; his intelligence, pleasant personality, famous smile and commitment to the alliance are beyond repute. While Eisenhower was free to concentrate solely on destroying the German Army, his British subordinate had other,

---

[1232] Pogue, *Supreme Command*, 407-416 inclusive. Also see Bradley, *A General's Life*, 402, 403.
[1233] Thompson, *Churchill and the Montgomery Myth*, 251.
[1234] Butcher, 479. Also see R.W. Thompson, *Montgomery: The Field Marshal*, 42.
[1235] Catherwood, 133.
[1236] Pogue, *Supreme Command*, 53.

more pressing matters to consider and some of these had little to do with destroying the German Army.[1237]

The senior British officer in Europe undoubtedly had the more difficult job. General Bernard L. Montgomery was responsible for recreating a status quo ante in Europe; and for reestablishing a balance of power on the continent.[1238] Churchill was particularly concerned about the old monarchies in Italy and Greece and the fate of Poland in Eastern Europe.

In agreeing to defeat the Germans first, American strategic policy fit nicely with British wishes; but in Europe the Americans would not go beyond the defeat of Nazi Germany. The Americans had little interest in seeing European countries returned to pre-war status. Nor did they have an interest in seeing the old monarchies restored in Italy or Greece; they also resisted using American soldiers to further British political interests in the Mediterranean.[1239]

The Germans and Americans gave their front line commanders great tactical flexibility; the British Army did not. When Montgomery wrote the new 1930 version of the Infantry Training Manual, it was favorably received in most circles.[1240] The new Training Manual placed an emphasis on the same vigorous staff work and intricate planning that had won Montgomery kudos for his planning during the Great War. With their new Training Manual in hand, the British Army began preparing to refight the next war with infantry tactics from 1916 and 1917.[1241] Despite the generally favorable reception given to Montgomery's Manual, there was a downside. The emphasis on caution [inherited from the First World War], which bred the reliance on meticulous planning and tight control, had left little room for individual initiative or independent thought.[1242]

[1237] Eisenhower received advice from Marshall when events in Europe became a liability for Roosevelt in Washington. An example was the command crisis in mid-August 1944 when Eisenhower refused to take command of Allied forces and US newspapers noted the all-British command structure. Marshall advised Eisenhower, ". . . to take direct command—at least of the US forces." Pogue, *Supreme Command,* 264.

[1238] Sherwood, 837.

[1239] Sherwood, 637-642.

[1240] Hamilton, *Making,* 214, 215.

[1241] Callahan, *Churchill and His Generals,* 140. Also Thompson, *Churchill and the Montgomery Myth,* 105 and T.H. Place, 170.

[1242] T.H. Place, 166, 174.

In October 1934 at the Quetta Army Staff College in India, Sir Phillip Chetwode addressed a group of British officers. He was highly critical of what he called ". . . [a] narrowness of outlook in every direction . . . It would . . . seem it is a crime . . . to be one-inch-out 'sealed pattern' and regulations . . . Am I altogether wrong in thinking of too many Englishmen to be independent in thought, to have imagination, to go outside the obvious, and to be different to others, is to be almost un-English, or even that more frightful crime, 'not sound?'"[1243] The reliance on meticulous planning and tight control was to become the Achilles heel for the British Army in Europe.

Montgomery's heavy-handed, doctrinaire approach to battle created a disaster in France. Junior officers seldom displayed an ability to adapt infantry tactics to the changing conditions on the battlefield. Hastings complained that after months of training, ". . . British tactics were shown to be not only unimaginative, but also inadequate to cope with the conditions of Normandy. Battalion and brigade commanders seemed capable of little beyond the conventional set-piece assault 'by the book.'"[1244] Montgomery had eliminated those rash, unplanned offensives, which had killed so many soldiers during the First War. Unfortunately, he had also eliminated any new and imaginative ideas his junior officers might have produced to solve their tactical problems in Normandy.

By July 1944 the Americans were getting most of the armor-infantry tactical doctrine right. One of the best German armor commanders, Erwin Rommel, wrote, "The Americans, it is fair to say, profited far more than the British from their experience in Africa, thus confirming the axiom that education is easier than reeducation."[1245] It is interesting to note that German officers thought more highly of the Americans than their British Allies.

One segment of British political intrigue during the war involved a subtle criticism of senior United States and Canadian Army generals. If the British could undermine the credibility and command authority of their Ally's senior officers, they could put forward their own officers as the best Allied commander available to perform the mission. *This was done so that British officers in command positions could control news from the front, thereby creating a public image of greater British participation in and control of the war than was actually taking place on the battlefield.*

[1243] Bond, *British Military Policy*, 68. From Callahan, *Churchill and His Generals*, 19.
[1244] Hastings, *Overlord*, 150.
[1245] Rommel, 523.

It was trifling innuendo and rumor, calculated to destroy the reputation of the generals it attacked. It involved a manipulation of the press and the British were very good at it. It was at least partially successful because of Eisenhower's injunction against the Americans criticizing anything British, especially their officers. There was no corresponding injunction against British officers criticizing U.S. or Canadian officers and they did so quite freely.

Criticism of the American command usually found its way into British newspapers. Eisenhower later wrote about the British press, "Generally speaking, the British columnists . . . try to show that my contributions in the Mediterranean were administrative accomplishments and 'friendliness in welding an allied team.' They dislike believing that I had anything particularly to do with campaigns."[1246] During the war, the American commanders proved to be far more capable at 'moving large masses of men in battle' than their British counterparts. This was especially true of Field Marshal Montgomery, who never mastered the art of mobile warfare.

Criticism of the Americans, primarily US Army officers in the British press was clearly sanctioned by the British government. This criticism was so successful that late in the war 66 percent of the British population held an unfavorable view of the Americans. ". . . Americans were actually held in lower esteem than Italians . . . . Yet nine of ten British thought well of Russia and the Russians."[1247]

It was doubtful that Churchill and Brooke intended to create the public relations monster that Montgomery became after El Alamein. Montgomery's name was closely identified with the British war effort. The combination of Brooke and Montgomery became such a dominant political force within the British Army that other officers challenged their authority only at great risk to their own careers. All other British generals receded into the background. Montgomery's boss in Africa, General Harold Alexander, ". . . was unrecognized and almost unknown."[1248]

Montgomery's organizational skills, his staff work, and his planning efforts were all first-rate. He was very careful to cover all eventualities; everything that could be foreseen was either included in his plans or in the basic arms manual; yet there was a flaw in his tactical planning. T.H. Place wrote, "The British Army excelled at planning for foreseeable eventualities.

[1246] Eisenhower diary, 2/7/44. *From* Ambrose, *Eisenhower, Soldier, General,* 299.
[1247] Lyon, 278.
[1248] R.W. Thompson, *Churchill and the Montgomery Myth,* 173.

It was the unforeseeable, or rather unpredictable, eventualities that caused the problems."[1249]

Montgomery was unable to prepare his army for the unpredictable because he had no way of controlling it. The German enemy, the unexpected and the unpredictable were never allowed to intrude into Montgomery's planning process. They were not included primarily because they could not be controlled, and things that he could not control were blocked from his mind by his 'mental disturbance.' Of course, when a subordinate tried to implement Montgomery's plan on the battlefield, he quickly discovered that the plan was tragically flawed. This happened often in Normandy. T.H. Place wrote, "It was unpredictable minor events on the ground that collectively deprived British troops of many a victory in Normandy. *Failure to prepare all ranks to function effectively when events defied the plan was the greatest flaw in the British army's training programmes between Dunkirk and D-Day.*"[1250]

The Americans and Germans both made "the unexpected and the unpredictable" part of their training program. The British didn't. Montgomery said he could not understand Clausewitz; he should have tried harder.[1251] Nineteenth century German military theorist Carl von Clausewitz described how in war even, ". . . the simplest thing is difficult."[1252] He called it "friction." Clausewitz wrote, "Friction is the only concept that more or less corresponds to the factors that distinguish real war from war on paper."[1253] Most of Montgomery's plans were impressive documents; they were strategically sound. It was during the tactical execution of those plans that things began to unravel. German Count Helmuth von Moltke wrote, "No battle plan survives contact with the enemy."[1254] Von Moltke was right; Montgomery, who suggested just the opposite, was clearly wrong.

If Montgomery could have fought his battles on paper, he may have become a military genius rivaling Napoleon. Rommel's criticism rings true, Montgomery, like most British generals, tended to, ". . . make the error of planning operations according to what was strategically desirable, rather than what was tactically attainable."[1255] According to Von Clausewitz, "Practice and

---

[1249] T.H. Place, 173.

[1250] T.H. Place, 173, 174. Italics added.

[1251] Weigley, *Eisenhower's Lieutenants*, 566.

[1252] Von Clausewitz, 119.

[1253] Von Clausewitz, 119.

[1254] Barnett, *The Desert Generals*, 138.

[1255] Rommel, 521.

experience dictate the answer: 'this is possible, that is not.'"[1256] Montgomery had trouble separating the two because his knowledge of the battlefield was incomplete. He usually underestimated the Germans. In Normandy, he totally dismissed them, [August 6], "But whatever the enemy may want to do will make no difference to us. We will proceed relentlessly . . . with our own plans for his destruction."[1257] The Germans at Caen and Arnhem did not always cooperate with Montgomery's 'forward planning.'

One cannot understand Montgomery's problems on the battlefield without first understanding the nature of his mental condition. Obsessive Compulsive Disorder [OCD] is not a physically debilitating disease; but it does influence one's behavior and thought process. *Montgomery had a strong psychological need to control people, events, and his environment. Those things he could control like "forward planning," the infantry and artillery, 21st Army Group's Tactical Headquarters, and the people he routinely worked around bore his authoritarian stamp and figured prominently in his daily life. Those things he could not control like armor, the enemy, officers of his own age and rank, criticism, a change to his "Master Plan," and the unforeseen and unexpected events on a battlefield simply never entered his thought process. Like memories of his mother Maud, he tried to place them and their unpleasant mental associations out of his mind.*

R.W. Thompson offered a good description of Montgomery's thought process: "His whole essentially tidy mind liked the 'set-piece' attack, and all went well until the breakthrough demanded exploitation. Repeatedly, his senior military friends hammered home the vital necessity for swift [armored] exploitation of the breakthrough. He accepts it, but he cannot *think* it, and he cannot do it."[1258] His friends' best opportunity to change his mind would have been to convince Montgomery that the armored exploitation was actually his idea, but that was not always possible.[1259]

Montgomery took command of 21st Army Group in January 1944. Once he got the officers he wanted at 21st Army Group, he made a good start on planning the invasion. Montgomery later found he had plenty of time on his hands. He often addressed huge, enthusiastic crowds of British citizens, "I find the army in England in very good trim. I believe that when it goes into

---

[1256] Von Clausewitz, 120.
[1257] Hamilton, *Master*, 775.
[1258] R.W. Thompson, *Churchill and the Montgomery Myth*, 90. Italics in the original.
[1259] Hamilton, *Making*, 828, 829.

battle it will prove to be the best army we have ever had."[1260] Whether or not the British Army that landed in Normandy in 1944 was their best ever is certainly debatable. But there was not the slightest doubt that General, later Field Marshal Bernard L. Montgomery exceeded all reasonable expectations in his dealings with the Americans.

Just before Montgomery's majestic Rhine River crossing in March 1945, the British government and the BBC began swamping international press organizations with news releases about Britain's most famous Field Marshal and the Second British Army. This was similar to the massive international news coverage the British generated after Montgomery's victory at the battle of Second El Alamein.

News coverage about Montgomery and the British Army reached such proportions in the United States that General Marshall decided he must warn Eisenhower to take action, ". . . as a possible antidote for an overdose of Montgomery, which is now coming into the country."[1261] Eisenhower sent his reply the next day, March 24, "I cannot quite understand why Montgomery should be getting a big play at this time in the States. It seems that even when operations carried out under his direction are of considerably less magnitude than those in other parts of the front . . . there is some influence at work that insists on giving Montgomery credit that belongs to other field commanders . . . I will continue to give my attention to this matter."[1262] US General Mark Clark would have explained it another way, *"We are caught in the British Empire machine."*[1263]

General Eisenhower and his subordinate, General Omar Bradley, chose not to tell the truth about the events at the Falaise Gap. They agreed to cover up an unpleasant decision made by the senior British officer in France, whose lapse in military etiquette was judged to be so significant that it threatened the survival of the Anglo-American alliance.

From the beginning, Bernard Montgomery was poorly qualified for his position in the Allied Army. R. W. Thompson wrote of Montgomery, "His eccentricities, the pedantry of his military dogmatism, his deliberate isolation, and his inability to enter into the problems of others rendered him

[1260] R.W. Thompson, *Montgomery: The Field Marshal*, 56.

[1261] Chandler, (Ed.), *The Eisenhower Papers, Vol. IV*, 2541.

[1262] Chandler, (Ed.), *The Eisenhower Papers, Vol. IV*, 2540, 2541

[1263] Mark Clark's diary, From Blumenson, *Mark Clark*, 232. Italics added.

peculiarly unsuitable for any cooperative role."[1264] Montgomery's failure to coordinate his strategy with the Americans surprised no one.

Allied command problems began but did not end with the Battle of the Falaise Gap. The real tragedy of the Allied failure to close the Falaise Gap was not that forty-thousand or one-hundred and fifty-thousand Germans escaped to fight another day. The real tragedy was that, due to the political nature of the Allied system of command, Ground Forces under the nominal command of General Eisenhower would remain under the dominant influence of Field Marshal Bernard L. Montgomery through the end of the war.

Eisenhower warned General Marshall that, ". . . Montgomery . . . had added weeks to the length of the Italian operation and cost the Allies thousands of lives."[1265] Eisenhower predicted that Montgomery would do the same thing in Europe. In the event, this was exactly what happened. Montgomery refused to obey orders. His strategy became, almost by default, the dominant Allied strategy through his Rhine River crossing in late March 1945. The unfortunate result of Eisenhower's inability to command Allied Ground Forces was a longer war with higher casualties.

[1264] R.W. Thompson, *Churchill and the Montgomery Myth*, 200.
[1265] Mosley, 287.

Papers, Diaries, and Special Studies

Cepeda, Emmanuel S., Lieutenant Colonel, with Majors Dailey, Hidalgo, Shedd, Anderson, Witte and Jacobson, and Captains Lippincott and Clifford, *The Fifth Armored Division in the Falaise-Argentan Sector*, Committee 2, Armored Officers Advanced Course, The Armored School, 1949-1950, Fort Knox, Kentucky, May, 1950

Chandler, Alfred D. Jr., Editor, and Stephen E. Ambrose, Associate Editor, *The Papers of Dwight David Eisenhower, The War Years, Volumes III, IV and V*, The Johns Hopkins Press, Baltimore, 1970

Eberbach, Heinrich, General of Panzer Troops, *Panzer Group Eberbach and the Falaise Encirclement*, Historical Division, Headquarters US Army, Europe, MS # A-922

Gay, Hobart R., *The Hobart R. Gay Papers*, Archives, US Army Military History Institute, Carlisle Barracks, Pa.

Hansen, Chester B. *The Chester B. Hansen Papers*, Archives, US Army Military History Institute, Carlisle Barracks, Pa.

Hausser, Paul, General of Waffen-SS, *Seventh Army in Normandy (25 Jul-20 Aug 44)*, Historical Division, Headquarters, US Army, Europe

Sylvan, William, *Major William Sylvan's Diary,* The OCMH Collection, Archives, US Army Military History Institute, Carlisle Barracks, Pa.

Williams, Mary H., *US Army in World War II, Special Studies, Chronology 1941-1945*, US Government Printing Office, Washington D.C., 1958

Bibliography

Allen, Robert S., *Lucky Forward: The History of Patton's Third US Army*, The Vanguard Press, Inc., New York, 1947

Ambrose, Steven E., *Eisenhower and Berlin, 1945, The Decision to Halt at the Elbe*, W.W. Norton & Company, Inc., New York, 1967

—*Eisenhower: Soldier, General of the Army, President Elect*, Simon and Schuster, New York, 1983

—*Band of Brothers*, Simon and Schuster, New York, 1992

—*The Victors, Eisenhower and His Boys: The Men of World War II*, Touchstone, New York, 1998

Barnett, Correlli, *The Desert Generals*, The Viking Press, New York, 1961

—Britain and Her Army, 1509-1970, William Morrow & Company, 1970

—*The Pride and the Fall, The Dream and Illusion of Britain as a Great Nation*, The Free Press, New York, 1986

Bennett, Ralph, *Ultra in the West: The Normandy Campaign 1944-1945*, Charles Scribner's Sons, New York, 1979

Blumenson, Martin, *The Duel for France*, Houghton Mifflin Company, Boston, 1963

—*The Patton Papers 1940-1945*, Houghton Mifflin Company, Boston, 1974

—*Mark Clark*, Congdon & Weed, Inc., New York, 1984

—*The Battle of the Generals: The Untold Story of the Falaise Pocket, the Campaign That Should Have Won World War II*, William Morrow and Company, Inc., New York, 1993

Bradley, Omar N., *A Soldiers Story*, Rand McNally & Company, New York, 1951

—and Clay Blair, *A General's Life*, Simon and Schuster, New York, 1983

Breuer, William B., *Death of a Nazi Army: The Falaise Pocket*, Scarborough House, United States, 1985

Bryant, Arthur, *The Turn of the Tide 1939-1943*, Based on the Diaries of Field-Marshal Lord Alanbrooke, Chief of the Imperial General Staff, Doubleday & Company, Inc., Garden City, New York, 1957

—*Triumph in the West 1943-1946*, Based on the Diaries and Autobiographical Notes of Field Marshal, The Viscount Alanbrooke, Collins, St James's Place, London, 1959

Butcher, Harry C., *My Three Years with Eisenhower*, Simon and Schuster, New York, 1946

Callahan, Raymond A., *Churchill: Retreat from Empire*, Scholarly Resources Inc., Wilmington, Delaware, 1984

—*Churchill and His Generals*, University Press of Kansas, Lawrence, Kansas, 2007

Calvocoressi, Peter, *Top Secret Ultra*, Pantheon Books, New York, 1980

Catherwood, Christopher, *Winston Churchill, the Flawed Genius of World War II*, Berkley Caliber, New York, 2009

Charmley, John, *Churchill: The End of Glory*, Harcourt Brace & Company, New York, 1993

Churchill, Winston S., *The Second World War: The Gathering Storm*, Houghton Mifflin Company, Boston, 1948

—*The Second World War: Their Finest Hour*, Houghton Mifflin Company, Boston, 1949

—*The Second World War: The Grand Alliance*, Houghton Mifflin Company, Boston, 1950

—*The Second World War: The Hinge of Fate*, Houghton Mifflin Company, Boston, 1950

—*The Second World War: Closing the Ring*, Houghton Mifflin Company, Boston, 1951

—*The Second World War: Triumph and Tragedy*, Houghton Mifflin Company, Boston, 1953

Clark, Alan, *Barbarossa: The Russian-German Conflict, 1941-1945*, Quill, New York, 1985

Clark, Mark W., *Calculated Risk*, Harper & Brothers Publishers, New York, 1950

Clarke, Peter, *The Last Thousand Days of the British Empire: Churchill, Roosevelt, and the Birth of Pax Americana*, Bloomsbury Press, New York, 2008

Clavell, James, Editor of: *The Art of War by Sun Tzu*, Delacorte Press, New York, 1983

Collier, Richard, *1940: The Avalanche*, The Dial Press/James Wade, New York, 1979

Collins, J. Lawton, *Lightning Joe: An Autobiography*, Presidio Press, Novato, California, 1994

Connell, John, *Wavell, Scholar and Soldier*, Harcourt, Brace & World, Inc., New York, 1965

Copp, Terry, *Cinderella Army, The Canadians in Northwest Europe 1944-1945*, University of Toronto Press, Toronto, Canada, 2006

D'Este, Carlo, *Decision in Normandy*, E.P. Dutton, Inc., New York, 1983

—*Patton, A Genius for War*, HarperCollins, New York, 1995

—*Eisenhower, A Soldier's Life*, Henry Holt and Company, New York, 2002

—*Warlord, The Life of Winston Churchill at War, 1874-1945*, HarperCollins Publishers, New York, NY, 2008

Dallek, Robert, *Franklin D. Roosevelt and American Foreign Policy 1932-1945*, Oxford University Press, New York, 1979

De Guingand, Sir Francis, *Operation Victory*, Hodder and Stoughton, London, 1947

Deighton, Len, *Blitzkrieg*, Alfred A. Knopf, New York, 1980

Dickson, Paul Douglas, *A Thoroughly Canadian General, A Biography of General H.D.G. Crerar*, University of Toronto Press, Toronto, 2007.

Doubler, Michael D., *Closing with the Enemy, How GIs Fought the War in Europe, 1944-1945*, University Press of Kansas, Lawrence, Kansas, 1994

Eisenhower, David, *Eisenhower at War, 1943-1945*, Vintage Books, New York, 1987

Eisenhower, Dwight D., *Crusade in Europe*, Da Capo Press, New York, 1977

Ellis, John, *Brute Force: Allied Strategy and Tactics in the Second World War*, Viking Penguin, New York, 1990

Essame, Hubert, *Patton: A Study in Command*, Charles Scribner's Sons, New York, 1974

Eubank, Keith, *Summit at Teheran, The Untold Story*, William Morrow and Company, New York, 1985.

Farago, Ladislas, *Patton: Ordeal and Triumph*, Astor-Honor, Inc., New York, 1964

Florentin, Eddy, *The Battle of the Falaise Gap*, Translated from the French by Mervyn Savill, Hawthorn Books, Inc., New York, 1967

Gavin, James M., *On to Berlin*, The Viking Press, New York, 1978

Gelb, Norman, *Ike and Monty: Generals at War*, William Morrow and Company, Inc., New York, First Edition, 1994

Gilbert, Martin, *Road to Victory, Winston S. Churchill 1941-1945*, Stoddart, Great Britain, 1986.

Glines, Carroll V. and Wendell F. Moseley, *The Legendary DC-3*, Van Nostrand Reinhold Company, New York, 1979

Goerlitz, Walter, *History of the German General Staff, 1657-1945*, Translated by Brian Battershaw, Greenwood Press, Publishers, Westport, Connecticut, 1975

Greenfield, Kent Roberts, Editor, *Command Decisions*, Department of the Army, Washington, D.C., 1960

Grigg, P.J., *Prejudice and Judgment*, Jonathan Cape, London, 1948

Guderian, Heinz, Translated by Christopher Duffy, *Achtung-Panzer: The Development of Armoured Forces, Their Tactics and Operational Potential*, Arms & Armour Press, London, 1992

Hamilton, Nigel, *Monty: The Making of a General (1887-1942)*, McGraw-Hill Book Company, New York, 1981

—*Master of the Battlefield: Monty's War Years (1942-1944),* McGraw-Hill Book Company, New York, 1983

—*Monty: The Final Years of the Field Marshal (1944-1976),* McGraw-Hill Book Company, New York, 1987

—*Monty: The Battles of Field Marshal Bernard Montgomery,* Random House, New York, 1994

Hanson, Victor Davis, *The Soul of Battle,* The Free Press, New York, 1999

Hart, B.H. Liddell, *The Other Side of the Hill,* Cassell And Company Ltd., London, 1951

—*The Memoirs of Captain Liddell Hart,* Volume Two, Cassell & Company Ltd, London, 1965 Hart, Russell A., *Clash of Arms: How the Allies Won in Normandy,* University of Oklahoma Press, Norman, 2004

Hart, Stephen Ashley, *Colossal Cracks: Montgomery's 21st Army Group in Northwest Europe, 1944-45,* Stackpole Books, Mechanicsburg, PA, 2007

Hastings, Max, *Overlord,* Simon & Schuster, Inc., New York, 1985

—*Armageddon, The Battle for Germany, 1944-1945,* Alfred A. Knopf, New York, 2004

Horne, Alistair with David Montgomery, *Monty, The Lonely Leader, 1944-1945,* HarperCollins Publishers, New York, 1994

Horrocks, Sir Brian, *A Full Life,* Collins, St James Place, London, 1960

Ingersoll, Ralph, *Top Secret,* Harcourt, Brace and Company, New York, 1946

Keegan, John, *Six Armies in Normandy,* The Viking Press, New York, 1982

—*The Second World War,* Penguin Books, New York, 1990

Kennedy, Sir John, *The Business of War,* Edited by Bernard Fergusson, William Morrow and Company, New York, 1958

Lamb, Richard, Montgomery in Europe, 1943-1945, Buchan & Enright, Publishers, London, 1984

Larrabee, Eric, *Commander in Chief, Franklin Delano Roosevelt. His Lieutenants, and Their War,* Simon & Schuster, Inc., New York, 1988

Lash, Joseph P., *Roosevelt and Churchill (1939-1941),* W.W. Norton & Company, Inc., New York, 1976

Lee, Bruce, *Marching Orders,* Crown Publishers, Inc., New York, 1995

Lewin, Ronald, *Montgomery, As Military Commander,* Stein and Day, Publishers, New York, 1971

—*Ultra Goes To War,* McGraw-Hill Book Company, New York, 1978

—*Churchill As Warlord,* Stein and Day, Publishers, New York, 1982

—*Montgomery,* Combined Publishing, Pennsylvania, 1998

Lippmann, Walter, *US Foreign Policy,* Little, Brown and Company, Boston, 1943

—*US War Aims,* Little, Brown and Company, Boston, 1944

Lucas, James & James Barker, *The Battle Of Normandy: The Falaise Gap,* Holmes & Meier Publishers, Inc., New York, 1978

Lyon, Peter, *Eisenhower, Portrait of the Hero.* Little Brown and Company, Boston, 1974.

Mallinger, Allan E., M.D., and Jeannette De Wyze, *Too Perfect, When Being in Control Gets Out of Control,* Clarkson Potter/Publishers, New York, 1992

Marshall, George C., Introduction, *Infantry in Battle,* The Infantry Journal-Incorporated, Washington, D.C., Garrett & Massie, Richmond, Virginia, 1939

Matloff, Maurice and Edwin M. Snell, *United States Army in World War II, Strategic Planning for Coalition Warfare 1941-1942,* Department of the Army, Washington, D.C., 1953

Mee, Charles L. Jr., *Meeting At Potsdam,* M. Evans & Company, Inc., New York, N.Y., 1975

—*The Marshall Plan,* Simon and Schuster, New York, 1984

Montgomery, The Viscount of Alamein, *Normandy To The Baltic,* Hutchinson & Co. Publishers, Ltd., London, 1946

Montgomery of Alamein, *The Memoirs Of Field Marshal Montgomery,* Collins, St. James's Place, London, 1958

Moorehead, Alan, *Desert War: The North African Campaign 1940-1943,* Penguin Books, New York, New York, 2001

Morgan, Sir Frederick, *Overture To Overlord,* Hodder & Stoughton Limited, London, 1950

Mosley, Leonard, *Marshall: Hero for Our Times,* Hearst Books, New York, 1982

Moulton, J.L., *Battle for Antwerp,* Ian Allan LTD, London, 1978

Patton, George S. Jr., *War As I Knew It,* Houghton Mifflin Company, Boston, 1975

Perrett, Geoffrey, *There's A War To Be Won: The United States Army In World War II,* Ballantine Books, Inc., New York, 1991

Perry, Mark, *Partners in Command, George Marshall and Dwight Eisenhower in War and Peace,* The Penguin Press, London, 2007

Persico, Joseph E., *Roosevelt's Secret War,* Random House Trade Paperbacks, New York, 2001

Place, Timothy Harrison, *Military Training in the British Army, 1940-1944: Dunkirk to D-Day,* Routledge, Taylor & Francis Group, London, 2000

Pogue, Forrest C., *The European Theater of Operations, The Supreme Command,* United States Army, Center of Military History, Washington, D.C., 1996

—*George C. Marshall: Organizer of Victory 1943-1945,* The Viking Press, New York, 1973

—*George C. Marshall, Ordeal and Hope 1939-1942,* The Viking Press, New York, 1966

—*George C. Marshall: Education of a General 1880-1939,* Macgibbon & Kee, London, 1964

Reynolds, Michael, *Steel Inferno, I SS Panzer Corps in Normandy,* Sarpedon, New York, 1997

—*Monty and Patton, Two Paths to Victory,* Spellmount, Staplehurst, 2005

Rohmer, Richard, *Patton's Gap,* Beaufort Books, Inc., New York, 1981

Rommel, Erwin, *The Rommel Papers,* Edited by B.H. Liddell Hart, Harcourt, Brace and Company, New York, 1953

Ruge, Friedrich, *Rommel in Normandy,* Translated by Ursula R. Moessner, Presidio Press, California, 1979

Ryan, Cornelius, *The Longest Day,* Simon And Schuster, New York, 1959

—*The Last Battle,* Simon and Schuster, New York, 1966

—*A Bridge Too Far,* Simon and Schuster, New York, 1974

Sainsbury, Keith, *Churchill and Roosevelt at War,* New York University Press, New York, 1994

Shachtman, Tom, *The Phony War (1939-1940),* Harper & Row, Publishers, New York, 1982

Sherwood, Robert E., *Roosevelt and Hopkins, An Intimate History,* Harper & Brothers, Publishers, New York, 1948

Showalter, Dennis, *Patton and Rommel, Men of War in the Twentieth Century,* Berkley Caliber, New York, 2005

Spears, Sir Edward L. *Assignment to Catastrophe, Volume I, Prelude to Dunkirk, July 1939-May 1940,* William Heinemann Ltd., London, 1955

Speidel, Hans, Lieutenant General, *Invasion: 1944,* Paperback Library, Inc., New York, 1968

Stacey, C.P., *The Canadian Army 1939-1945,* Edmond Cloutier, King's Printer, Ottawa, 1948

Stoler, Mark A., *Allies and Adversaries: The Joint Chiefs of Staff, The Grand Alliance, and US Strategy in World War II,* The University of North Carolina Press, Chapel Hill, 2000

—*Allies in War: Britain and America Against the Axis Powers, 1940-1945,* Hodder Education, London, 2005

Strong, Sir Kenneth, *Intelligence at the Top,* Doubleday & Company, Inc., Garden City, New York, 1969

Sullivan, John G., *Fuel to the Troops, A Memoir of the 698th Engineer Petroleum Distribution Company, 1943-1945,* Merriam Press, Vermont, 2008

Taylor, A.J.P., *The Origins Of The Second World War,* Fawcett Premier, New York, 1961

Taylor, Telford, *Munich: The Price of Peace,* Doubleday & Company, Inc., Garden City, New York, 1979

Tedder, Lord, *With Prejudice, The War Memoirs of Marshal of the Royal Air Force, Lord Tedder,* Little, Brown and Company, Boston, 1966

Thompson, R.W., *Montgomery, The Field Marshal, The Campaign in North-West Europe, 1944/45,* Charles Scribner's Sons, New York, 1969

—*Churchill and the Montgomery Myth,* M. Evans and Company, Inc., New York, 1967

Tuchman, Barbara W., *Stilwell And The American Experience In China 1911-45,* The Macmillan Company, New York, 1970

Tzu, Sun, *The Art Of War,* Edited by James Clavell, Delacorte Press, New York, 1983

Van Creveld, Martin, *Supplying War: Logistics from Wallenstein to Patton,* Cambridge University Press, Cambridge, 1977

—*Fighting Power: German and US Army Performance, 1939-1945,* Greenwood Press, Westport, Connecticut, 1982

von Clausewitz, Carl, *On War,* Edited and Translated by Michael Howard and Peter Paret, Princeton University Press, New Jersey, 1989

von Luck, Hans, *Panzer Commander: The Memoirs of Colonel Hans von Luck,* Dell Publishing, New York, 1989

von Mellenthin, F.W., *Panzer Battles,* Ballantine Books, New York, 1971

Warlimont, Walter, *Inside Hitler's Headquarters (1939-45),* Frederick A. Praeger, Publishers, New York, 1965

Warner, Philip, *Auchinleck, The Lonely Soldier,* Buchan & Enright Publishers, London, 1981

Watkins, H.B.C., and Duncan Crow, *Panzer Divisions of World War 2,* Profile Publications Ltd., Windsor, Berks, 1975

Watt, Richard M., *Bitter Glory: Poland and Its Fate 1918-1939,* Simon and Schuster, New York, 1982

Wedemeyer, Albert C., *Wedemeyer Reports,* Henry Holt & Company, New York, 1958

Weigley, Russell F., *The American Way of War, A History of United States Military Strategy and Policy,* Indiana University Press, Bloomington, 1973

—*Eisenhower's Lieutenants, The Campaign of France and Germany 1944-1945,* Indiana University Press, Bloomington, 1990

Westphal, Siegfried, *The German Army in the West,* Cassell and Company Ltd., London, 1951

Whiting, Charles, *The Field Marshal's Revenge,* Spellmount, Staplehurst, Kent, 2004

Wilmot, Chester, *The Struggle For Europe,* Greenwood Press, Publishers, Westport, Connecticut, 1972

Winterbotham, F.W., *The Ultra Secret,* Harper & Row, Publishers, New York, 1974

Zaloga, Steven J., *US Armored Divisions, The European Theater of Operations, 1944-45,* Osprey Publishing Ltd., Oxford, UK, 2004.

Appendix

US, British, Canadian and Polish Divisions in ETO by Arrival Date

United States Army Divisions:

	Date Arrived	Division	Commander
1.	6 June 1944	82nd Airborne Division	Major General Matthew B. Ridgeway
2.	6 June 1944	101st Airborne Division	Major General Maxwell D. Taylor
3.	6 June 1944	1st Infantry Division	Major General Clarence R. Huebner
4.	6 June 1944	4th Infantry Division	Major General Raymond O. Barton
5.	6 June 1944	29th Infantry Division	Major General Charles H. Gerhardt
6.	7 June 1944	2nd Infantry Division	Major General Walter M. Robertson
7.	9 June 1944	2nd Armored Division	Major General Edward H. Brooks
8.	10 June 1944	9th Infantry Division	Major General Manton S. Eddy
9.	10 June 1944	90th Infantry Division	Brigadier General Jay W. MacKelvie
10.	11 June 1944	30th Infantry Division	Major General Leland S. Hobbs
11.	14 June 1944	79th Infantry Division	Major General Ira T. Wyche
12.	18 June 1944	83rd Infantry Division	Major General Robert C. Macon
13.	24 June 1944	3rd Armored Division	Major General Leroy H. Watson
14.	4 July 1944	8th Infantry Division	Major General William C. MacMahon
15.	7 July 1944	35th Infantry Division	Major General Paul W. Baade
16.	9 July 1944	5th Infantry Division	Major General Stafford L. Irwin
17.	11 July 1944	4th Armored Division	Major General John S. Wood
18.	19 July 1944	6th Armored Division	Major General Robert W. Grow
19.	22 July 1944	28th Infantry Division	Major General Lloyd Brown
20.	24 July 1944	5th Armored Division	Major General Lunsford E. Oliver
21.	3 August 1944	80th Infantry Division	Major General Horace L. McBride
22.	14 August 1944	7th Armored Division	Major General Lindsay M. Silvester
23.	15 August 1944	3rd Infantry Division	Major General John W. O'Daniel
24.	15 August 1944	36th Infantry Division	Major General John E. Dahlquist
25.	15 August 1944	45th Infantry Division	Major General William W. Eagles
26.	7 September 1944	26th Infantry Division	Major General Willard S. Paul
27.	7 September 1944	104th Infantry Division	Major General Terry M. Allen
28.	8 September 1944	94th Infantry Division	Major General Harry J. Malony
29.	15 September 1944	44th Infantry Division	Major General Robert L. Spragins
30.	15 September 1944	95th Infantry Division	Major General Harry L. Twaddle
31.	23 September 1944	102rd Infantry Division	Major General Frank A. Keating
32.	23 September 1944	10th Armored Division	Major General W.H.H. Morris Jr.
33.	30 September 1944	9th Armored Division	Major General John W. Leonard
34.	20 October 1944	100th Infantry Division	Major General Withers A. Burress
35.	29 October 1944	14th Armored Division	Major General Vernon E. Prichard
36.	3 November 1944	99th Infantry Division	Major General Walter E. Lauer
37.	4 November 1944	84th Infantry Division	Major General Alexander R. Bolling

38.	11 November 1944	12th Armored Division	Major General R.R. Allen
39.	22 November 1944	78th Infantry Division	Major General Edwin P. Parker Jr.
40.	5 December 1944	87th Infantry Division	Major General Frank L. Culin Jr.
41.	6 December 1944	106th Infantry Division	Major General Alan W. Jones
42.	8 December 1944	63rd Infantry Division	Major General Louis E. Hibbs
43.	9 December 1944	42nd Infantry Division	Major General Harry J. Collins
44.	13 December 1944	44th Infantry Division	Major General Fay B. Prickett
45.	13 December 1944	75th Infantry Division	Major General Ray E. Porter
46.	15 December 1944	70th Infantry Division	Major General Allison J. Barnett
47.	16 December 1944	11th Armored Division	Brigadier General Charles S. Kilburn
48.	23 December 1944	17th Airborne Division	Brigadier General William M. Miley
49.	24 December 1944	66th Infantry Division	Major General Herman F. Kramer
50.	5 January 1945	8th Armored Division	Major General John M. Devine
51.	12 January 1945	76th Infantry Division	Major General William R. Schmidt
52.	21 January 1945	65th Infantry Division	Major General Stanley E. Reinhart
53.	21 January 1945	89th Infantry Division	Major General Thomas D. Finley
54.	24 January 1945	69th Infantry Division	Major General Emil F. Reinhardt
55.	29 January 1945	13th Armored Division	Major General John B. Wogan
56.	6 February 1945	71st Infantry Division	Major General Willard G. Wyman
57.	17 February 1945	16th Armored Division	Brigadier General John L. Pierce
58.	18 February 1945	20th Armored Division	Major General Orlando Ward
59.	2 March 1945	97th Infantry Division	Major General Milton B. Halsey
60.	4 March 1945	86th Infantry Division	Major General Harris M. McLasky

British, Canadian, and Polish Divisions:

1.	6 June 1944	6th British Airborne Division	Major General Richard Gale
2.	6 June 1944	3rd British Infantry Division	Major General L.G. Whistler
3.	6 June 1944	**50th British Infantry Division	Major General D.A.H. Graham
4.	6 June 1944	51st British Infantry Division	Major General D.C. Bullen-Smith
5.	6 June 1944	79th British Armored Division	Major General C.S. Hobart
6.	6 June 1944	3rd Canadian Infantry Division	Major General R.F.L. Keller
7.	8 June 1944	7th British Armored Division	Major General G.W.E.J. Erskine
8.	12 June 1944	49th British Infantry Division	Major General E.H. Barker
8.	13 June 1944	11th British Armored Division	Major General G.B. "Pip" Roberts
9.	14 June 1944	15th British Infantry Division	Major General C.M. Barber
10.	24 June 1944	43rd British Infantry Division	Major General G. Ivor Thomas
11.	27 June 1944	53rd British Infantry Division	Major General R.K. Ross
12.	27 June 1944	*59th British Infantry Division	Major General L.O. Lyne
13.	28 June 1944	British Guards Armored Division	Major General Allan Adair
14.	7 July 1944	2rd Canadian Infantry Division	Major General C. Foulkes
15.	31 July 1944	4th Canadian Armored Division	Major General G. Kitching
16.	31 July 1944	1st Polish Armored Division	Major General S. Maczek
17.	17 Sept. 1944	***1st British Airborne Division	Major General Roy Urquhart
18.	October 1944	52rd British Infantry Division	Major General Hakewill Smith
19.	March, 1945	5th British Infantry Division	Major General Richard Hull
20.	31 March 1945	5th Canadian Armored Division	Major General B.M. Hoffmeister
21.	3 April 1945	1st Canadian Infantry Division	Major General H.W. Foster

*   Disbanded for replacements August 26, 1944
**   Disbanded for replacements November 1944
*** Destroyed during *Operation Market-Garden* (September 17-25, 1944)

Index

Made in the USA
Lexington, KY
23 September 2010